VARIETIES OF
CLASSIC
SOCIAL THEORY

HENDRIK M. RUITENBEEK was born in Leyden, Holland, in 1928. He received his doctorate at the University of Leyden in 1955, and his doctoral thesis on the origins and rise of the Dutch Labor Party was published in book form in 1955. Dr. Ruitenbeek came to this country in 1955 and has taught at various colleges, the most recent being Brooklyn College where he taught sociology. He is now a practicing psychotherapist. Dr. Ruitenbeek has already published in the Dutton Paperbacks series two volumes called *Psychoanalysis and Social Science* and *Psychoanalysis and Existential Philosophy*.

VARIETIES OF CLASSIC SOCIAL THEORY

Edited, and with an Introduction by

HENDRIK M. RUITENBEEK

A Dutton  Paperback

NEW YORK
E. P. DUTTON & CO., INC.

308.2
R 85 v
61510
april 1968

ACKNOWLEDGMENTS

Grateful acknowledgment is made to the following for permission
to quote from copyright material:

Claude-Henri de Saint-Simon: *On Social Organization.* Reprinted from *Selected Writings* by Saint-Simon, edited and translated by F. M. H. Markham, Oxford, Basil Blackwell, 1952, by
permission of the publishers.

Ferdinand Tönnies: *Community and Society.* Reprinted from
Community and Society (Gemeinschaft und Gesellschaft) by Ferdi-
nand Tönnies, translated and edited by Charles P. Loomis, East
Lansing, Michigan State University Press, 1957, by permission of
the publishers. Copyright, ©, 1957, by Michigan State University
Press.

Werner Sombart: *The Sociology of Capitalism.* Reprinted from
The Quintessence of Capitalism by Werner Sombart, translated by
M. Epstein, New York, E. P. Dutton & Co., Inc., 1915, by per-
mission of the publishers.

Edward Tylor: *The Science of Culture.* Reprinted from *Primitive Culture* by Edward Tylor, London, John Murray, 1924, by
permission of the publishers.

Ernst Troeltsch: *The Sociology of Religion.* Reprinted from
The Social Teaching of the Christian Churches by Ernst Troeltsch,
New York, The Macmillan Company, 1931, by permission of the
publishers. Copyright, 1931, 1959, by The Macmillan Company.

Max Weber: *The Fundamental Concepts of Sociology.* Reprinted
from *The Theory of Social and Economic Organization* by Max
Weber, New York, Oxford University Press, 1947, by permission
of the publishers. Copyright, 1947, by Oxford University Press.

FOR

CHARLES W. CHRISTENBERRY

CONTENTS

Contents

INTRODUCTION

THE essays in this volume constitute only a sampling of classic social theory; they are not an attempt to present a systematic survey of the development of sociology as a science. The choice of material is personal and might well be challenged. Why is Sorel represented, for example, and not Pareto? Why are topics associated with the breaking of social ties more fully discussed than concepts accounting for the growth and maintenance of such ties?

Some of the reasons for my choice of representative figures may appear more clearly in the brief sketches which precede each of the selections. But since this volume has a dual purpose—that of showing the growth of sociology and illustrating the background of some current preoccupations of sociologists, such as the stress on social disorganization, its characteristics and its causes, is readily understandable. Modest though the aims of this book are, it does attempt to show something of the movement from social philosophy through social criticism to the scientific discipline which sociology has become today.

Critical philosophers like Rousseau and Herder made their contemporaries aware that they lived in a society and that the social organization which that society represented was not an accident but a historical growth. In elaborate generalizations, Auguste Comte contended that society could be understood and dealt with scientifically. We see particular varieties of society, actual and possible, described by a group of social theorists. We pass from such theorizing to a series of discussions of some basic concepts for the study of society, such as class, culture, conflict, bureaucracy, and anomie.

Thus as we read these essays, we see social philosophy becoming social theorizing and social theorizing maturing into a methodology for the systematic, even the mathematical, study of society and its phenomena. Sociology as we know it today is the outcome of this process; and in some of its more interesting contemporary expressions, sociology seems to be turning back on its track to become social theorizing once again, as certain contributions in the second volume of this anthology (*Varieties of Modern Social Theory*) illustrate.

The social philosophers presented in the opening essays of this volume may have had less technical skill and objectivity than their modern successors in the study of society, but they were no less aware of social reality and no less representative of their own *Zeitgeist*. Their work reflects the contact with preliterate societies in America and Oceania, for example, the eighteenth-century notion of happy man in a state of nature owes much to the Bougainville's reports on the South Seas and to the descriptions of pre-Columbian society by Spanish observers. More significantly, their work reflects the impact of the Enlightenment, the French Revolution, and the In-dustrial Revolution just as the work of twentieth-century sociologists reflects the impact of Freudian psychoanalysis, of the Russian Revolution, and of the continuing economic and social transformations wrought by a continuously developing technology.

The eighteenth- and nineteenth-century precursors of mod-ern sociology were still immersed in philosophy. Rousseau and Herder thought of themselves as philosophers, not social scientists. Auguste Comte and Max Weber were interested in such distinctively philosophical problems as positivism and historical determinism. Georg Simmel was primarily a philoso-pher as the titles of his principal works show. Even Emile Durkheim was strongly influenced by, and interested in, such phases of philosophy as positivism and utilitarianism.

As pioneers and as philosophers, passion for their subject did not appear unseemly to the sociologists presented here; they did not aspire to the status of "scientist" so earnestly that they felt obliged, for example, to devise a vocabulary which often seems an unintelligible jargon to all but the most persistent of non-professional readers. The eighteenth- and nineteenth-century founders of sociology could still com-municate directly with the average educated man; their insights usually passed into the intellectual community at first hand instead of through the dilution of popularizers.

Part of their ability to communicate, of course, may have been due to the small size and the high level of training of the public which these pioneers addressed; after all, the spread of mere literacy is a rather recent phenomenon. Their ability to communicate may also have come from their philo-sophical training. An important part of that *rapport* between social theorists and audience came from their social aware-ness. These pioneer students of society were sensitive to changing intellectual currents, as all good observers of society must be, and they understood the relationship between intellectual and social change. The French Revolution and the theories of human nature and social origins by which it was defended had made philosophers and political thinkers increasingly aware of the foundations upon which social institutions were based.

We are accustomed to think of our own time as a period of unprecedented and painfully rapid change. To men who lived at the end of the eighteenth century, theirs seemed an age of fearful instability. The fountains of the deep had been broken open; all truths had been challenged; all the proprieties and prescriptions had been defied. The Enlightenment had demanded that church and king show their credentials, not in tradition but in current usefulness. Men who accepted the political ideas of the Enlightenment had pressed that demand home. The French Revolution was only the most striking and the most far-reaching expression of discontent which had been long in developing and of challenges which had taken a couple of centuries to mature. The Revolution came like a storm, and like a storm it passed, but nothing that the Revolution had touched was ever again what it had been.

Social critics, such as Montesquieu, Voltaire, and Rousseau, had paved the way for the Revolution as they described and attacked abuses in the name of "the Rights of Man." The philosophers of Romanticism defended existing institutions in the name of the rights of nations. In contrast to the individualism of the Enlightenment, Herder, for example, developed the idea of *Gesellschaft* (society) as essential to the existence of men as human beings and of that society as a growth in time which could have none of its parts disturbed without evil consequences.

At the dawn of the nineteenth century, philosophic observers of the social world no longer saw it in the optimistic mood of an earlier generation. Where the prophets of the Enlightenment dwelt on the idea of progress, of the basic perfectibility of man and his ability to create a good society—if only he were free from domination by the obscurantism of churches and the power of kings and nobles—the philosophers of the nineteenth century cherished what Judith Shklar has called "the unhappy consciousness,"[1] the pessimistic melancholy of the Romantics. Although nineteenth-century social philosophers disagreed with each other, they had more in

[1] See pp. 65 ff., Judith N. Shklar, *After Utopia*, Princeton, Princeton University Press, 1957.

common with the far-ranging doubt and anguish of Kierkegaard and Nietzsche, for example, than with the acid lucidity of Voltaire, with Diderot's joy in technological advance, or
with the contemporary middle-class conviction that economic
growth was moral progress. Traditionalists like Edmund
Burke had been troubled by what men would do, and how
society would suffer, when the lower classes lost the "whole-
some prejudices" that kept them obedient to their betters in
spite of hunger and frustration. Kierkegaard probed more
deeply, analyzing the plight of the individual lost in the web
of society without the security once offered by unquestioning
acceptance of the protection offered by the institutions of
church and monarchy. Yet Kierkegaard recognized that the
old security was gone forever, never to be regained.

If the French Revolution made philosophers more aware
of social institutions, the Industrial Revolution made them
more alive to the material world of their experience. They
saw the decline of old-fashioned agriculture as a way of life;
they witnessed the growth of capital and the rise of new,
great cities. They were freshly aware of the demands of new
groups to share in political power, the assertiveness of an
economically triumphant middle class, the decline of the
landed aristocracy in many countries, and, most disturbing,
the emergence of an urban proletariat not merely as an unfortunate necessity of economic development but as a con-
tender for social influence and a possible participant in, if
not successor to, social power.

In the context of the changes brought about by the French
and Industrial Revolutions, the complex structure of European
social theory took form. Philosophers, economists, publicists,
all found themselves compelled to undertake fundamental
theoretical exploration of society and its institutions. Thus
there appear the early formulations of many of the concepts
essential to modern sociology. Hegel may be a fountainhead
of modern philosophy and social theory, but his contribution
to sociology is somewhat indirect. Marx's relation to that
discipline is more immediate. As Clinton Rossiter puts it:

"Marx looms up as one of the truly great figures in the development of Western thought. To scan the intellectual history
of the past three centuries, the centuries that produced us,
without pausing for a long look at Marx would be like staging
Julius Caesar without Caesar."[2]

[2] P. 269, Clinton Rossiter, *Marx: The View from America,* New
York, Harcourt, Brace & Co., 1960.

Where Feuerbach, Marx's contemporary rival as a social thinker, concentrated on the role of the single individual in the development of social institutions, Marx focused on the roots from which the individual sprang. Marx saw these roots in social labor, a process which had reached a climax in contemporary industralization and urbanization. Social labor created capital and wealth and in the struggle for the possession and control of that wealth, classes were born. Through that struggle, and through it alone, could man ultimately liberate himself from the need for social struggle. Thus Marx's formulation of the concept of class did much to shape modern sociologists' ideas about social adjustment and social conflict. Werner Sombart's analysis of capitalist society owes much to Marx, although Sombart did not share Marx's double role: student of society on the one hand, and social revolutionist on the other.

Unlike most of the French socialists, who were Utopian and humanitarian rather than scientific and materialist in outlook, Auguste Comte, like Marx, tried to create a science of society. But where Marx oriented his scientific approach around political and societal foci, concepts of social class and social conflict, Comte tried to apply the methods and principles of the natural sciences to the study of human society. Later, Max Weber was to turn to this approach in his effort to establish a more scientific methodology[3] for the social sciences. Although Herbert Spencer's interest in the natural sciences may have been of a different kind than Weber's, his use of evolutionary theory did rest upon Darwin's observations of biological behavior; hence, Spencer, too, may be ranked among the social theorists who attempted to base their study of society upon discoveries in the natural sciences and upon some of the methods which had led to those discoveries.

Alfred Weber, Durkheim, Simmel, and Freud are interesting not only because they are pioneers in the study of man and his socialization but because so much of their work is still relevant. Weber's studies in bureaucracy and the functioning of large-scale organization are as valid and as pertinent today as when he set them down in the 1910's. Indeed, as governmental and corporate bureaucracy becomes the modern way of life, Weber's formulations contribute increasingly to our understanding of the problems which we encounter. Also of great value are Weber's studies of older cultures, such as

[3] See his book *The Methodology of the Social Sciences*, Glencoe, The Free Press, 1949.

those of ancient Judaism which have not been outmoded by modern archeological discoveries. His description of the Protestant ethic still serves as a guide for comprehending phenomena ranging from the shaping of American character and culture to the most suitable policies for encouraging economic growth in traditional societies.

Emile Durkheim is best known for the concept of anomie and for his studies of suicide. The facts of our current "organizational society" have made contemporary sociologists particularly aware of the usefulness of anomie in understanding problems as varied as juvenile delinquency and the almost universal waning of interest in politics in the Western world.

Georg Simmel's observations on conflict are particularly pertinent to our society where social disorganization so often is expressed in violence, public and domestic. His work has aroused continuous interest during the past decade, an interest which shows the influence which his theories exert on contemporary sociology.

To students of culture and personality, as to all students of man—who is, after all, creator as well as creature of society— Sigmund Freud and his work are of major interest. His concepts have been a source of both dispute and synthesis, but just as no study of modern psychology can ignore his work, so no study of sociology can afford to pass it by.

It is difficult to assess concretely the influence of classic social theory on contemporary sociology. No discipline of a scientific character is unaffected by its past, although sociology may be particularly affected by an effort to live some of its past down. Modern sociology seeks to be objective, scientific, *Wertfrei*, liberated from preoccupation with social "values." Classic social theory, in contrast, was very much concerned with social values for, as has been pointed out, sociology as a branch of learning had its origins in the clash of values that resulted from the great surges of change which we know as the French and Industrial Revolutions. Without classic social theory, contemporary sociology would surely be a very different kind of discipline, if it existed at all. Indeed, there are some scholars who would contend that the narrower focus and more restricted language of the modern sociologist as compared to the classic theorists has depleted sociology in the process of making it more precise.

HENDRIK M. RUITENBEEK

VARIETIES OF
CLASSIC
SOCIAL THEORY

Johann Gottfried Herder
(1744–1803)

ON THE PHILOSOPHY OF HISTORY

Johann Gottfried Herder was born in the East Prussian village of Mohrungen on August 25, 1744. His father was a cantor and schoolmaster, a Pietist whose chief reading was the Bible and Johan Arnd's Four Books of True Christianity. The Herders were of Silesian origin while the mother's family was native to Mohrungen.

Young Johann grew up as the only son in a family of three children. According to Herder's own words (in a letter to his fiancée) his family was "limited in means, but not needy."

In the spring of 1762 Herder was able to enroll at the University of Königsberg. At first he enrolled as a student of medicine, which later proved to be very important to Herder since he became interested in the auxiliary sciences that were not taught in the medical curriculum. He soon abandoned the study of medicine, however, for he was unable to watch dissections. Through the influence of a school friend he shifted from medicine to theology. A stipend from the Counts of Dohma, the local aristocrats of his village, enabled him to pay his fees.

In Königsberg he was taught by Emmanuel Kant, at that time a young instructor at the University. A long standing friendship developed between Herder and Kant, but this was disrupted in later years because of the fierce attacks which Kant made on Herder's main work Ideen zur Philosophie der Geschichte der Menschheit. *This work was one of the first attempts at a philosophy of history. One will not only find here significant anthropological and sociological observations (Man's environment and his organization, Part I, Bücher I–IV), but also significant biological observations. Many concepts as developed by Herder in his* Ideen *were discussed at length with Goethe, who was a close friend of Herder's. Goethe writes as follows about his cooperation with Herder on the biological aspects of the* Ideen:

"My laborious, painful investigation was eased, even sweetened, when Herder undertook the composition of his Ideas for the Philosophy of the History of Mankind. Our daily con-

3

*versation was concerned with the earliest beginnings of the
water-earth and the organic creatures developing on it from
the earliest times. The earliest beginning and its incessant,
continual developing was constantly discussed, and our scientific possessions were daily enriched and clarified through
alternate communication and attack."*[1]

*Herder's plan for a philosophy of history was based upon
a consideration of mankind's environment in the astronomical,
physical, geological, and biological worlds. Significant also
was his break with the rationalistic Enlightenment and the
foundations which he laid for the later work of the German
romanticists.*

*His personal life was challenging. He traveled widely, in
spite of his large family which he supported by serving as a
tutor to German princes and as court preacher in several
German courts.*

*Herder knew many of his famous contemporaries personally
and established professional and personal contacts with Lessing, Kant, Goethe, Schiller, and others. He died in Weimar
in 1803.*

*One of the most recent efforts to place Herder in the history
of the development of sociology is an excellent study by
G. A. Wells, Herder and After: A study in the development
of sociology, published by Mouton & Co., The Hague, 1959.*

ON THE PHILOSOPHY OF HISTORY

Man Is Organized to Finer Instincts, and in Consequence to Freedom of Action

Men repeat, after one another, that man is void of instinct
and that this is the distinguishing character of the species;
but he has every instinct that any of the animals around him
possess; only, in conformity to his organization, he has them
softened down to a more delicate proportion.

The infant in the mother's womb seems under a necessity
of going through every state that is proper to a terrestrial
creature. He swims in water; he lies prone with open mouth;

---

[1] Quoted on p. 303 of *Herder: His Life and Thought* by Robert
T. Clark, Jr., Berkeley, University of California Press, 1955.

his jaws are large, before the lips, which are not formed till late, can cover them: no sooner does he come into the world than he gasps after air, and sucking is the first act he performs untaught. The whole process of digestion and nutrition, of hunger and thrist, proceeds instinctively, or by some still more obscure impulse. The muscular and procreative powers strive in like manner to develop themselves; and if some passion or disease deprives a man of his reason, all the animal instincts will be observable in him. Danger and necessity unfold in a man, nay, in whole nations that lead a savage life, the capacities, senses, and powers of beasts.

Man therefore is not properly deprived of instincts; but they are *repressed* in him, and made *subordinate* to the dominion of the nerves and finer senses. Without them the creature, who is still in great measure an animal, could not live.

But how are they repressed? How does nature bring them under the dominion of the nerves? Let us contemplate their progress from infancy; and this will show us what men have often so foolishly lamented as human weakness in a very different light.

The young of the human species comes into the world weaker than that of any other animal, and for an obvious reason: because it is formed to receive a figure that cannot be fashioned in the womb. The four-footed beast acquires the quadruped figure in the matrix; and though at first its head is equally disproportionate with that of man, it ultimately attains its due proportions. Such, indeed, as abound in nerves bring forth their young feeble; yet still the equilibrium of their powers is established in a few days or weeks. Man alone remains a long time weak; for his limbs are yet to be fashioned to the head, if I may be allowed the expression, which was formed disproportionately large in the womb, and so comes into the world. The other limbs, which require earthly nutriment, air, and motion for their growth, are long before they overtake it; though during the whole period of childhood and youth they are growing up to a just proportion with it, while the head does not grow equally with them. The feeble child, therefore, is an invalid, as I may say, in its superior powers, and Nature is earliest improving these, and continues incessantly to improve them. Before the child learns to walk, it learns to see, to hear, to feel, and to practice the delicate mechanism and geometry of these senses. It exercises these in the same instinctive manner as the brute, only in a nicer degree. Not by innate art and ability, for all the qualities of brutes are the consequence of gross stimuli; and if these were predominant from infancy, the man would remain a brute; being able to do everything before he learned, he would learn nothing pertaining to man. Either reason must be born with him as an instinct, which appears a contradiction in terms, or he must come into the world feeble, as he does, *that he may learn reason.*

This he learns from his infancy, being formed to it, to freedom, and to human speech, by art, as he is to his artificial mode of walking. The suckling at the mother's breast reposes on her heart; the fruit of her womb is the pupil of her embrace. His finest senses, the eye and ear, first awake, and are led forward by sound and figure: happy for him if they be fortunately led! His sense of seeing gradually unfolds itself, and attentively watches the eyes of those around, as his ear is attentive to their language, and by their help he learns to distinguish his first ideas. In the same manner his hand learns gradually to feel; and then his limbs first strive after their proper exercise. He is first a pupil of the two finest senses; for the artful instinct to be formed in him is *reason, humanity, the mode of life peculiar to man,* which no brute possesses or learns. Domesticated animals acquire some things from man, but it is as brutes; they do not become men.

Hence it appears what human reason is: a word so often misused in modern writings to imply an innate automaton, in which sense it can lead only to error. Theoretically and practically reason is nothing more than something *understood;* an acquired knowledge of the proportions and directions of the ideas and faculties, to which man is formed by his organization and mode of life. An angelic reason we know not, anymore than we are capable of having a clear preception of the internal state of a creature beneath us: the reason of man is human reason. From his infancy he compares the ideas and impressions of his finer senses, according to the delicacy and accuracy with which they perceive them, the number he receives, and the internal promptitude with which he learns to bring them together. The one whole hence arising is his thought; and the various combinations of these thoughts and perceptions to judge of what is true or false, good or bad, conducive to happiness or productive of misery, are his reason, the progressive work of the appearance of human life. This is not innate in man, but acquired; and according to the impressions he has received, the ideas he has formed, and the internal power and energy with which he has assimilated these various impressions with his mental faculties, his reason is rich or poor, sound or diseased, stunted or well grown, as is his body. If Nature deceived us by false perceptions of the senses, we must suffer ourselves to be deceived in her way; and as many men as possessed the same senses would be deceived in the same manner. If men deceive us, and we have not organs or faculties to perceive the deception, and reduce the impressions to a more accurate standard, our reason is crippled, and frequently remains so all our lives. As man must learn everything, it being his instinct and destination to learn all, even to his mode of walking, he is taught to go only by means of falls, and frequently attains truth only through the help of error; the brute, on the contrary, moves securely on his four feet, for the more strongly imprinted proportions of his senses and impulses are his guides. Man enjoys the royal prerogative of seeing far and wide with head erect; yet it must be confessed he sees much obscurely and falsely, nay often forgets his steps, and is reminded by stumbling on what a narrow basis rests the whole frame of his ideas and judgments, the offspring of his head and heart. Still he remains, conformably to his high *rational destination,* what no other creature upon earth is, a son of God, a sovereign of the world.

In order to be sensible of the preeminence of this destination, let us consider what is included in the great gifts of *reason* and *liberty,* and how much Nature hesitated, as it were, before she entrusted them to such a feeble, complicated, earthly creature as man. Brutes are but stooping slaves; though some of the nobler species carry the head erect, or at least strive after liberty with uplifted neck. Their minds, not yet ripened into reason, must be subservient to the impulses of necessity, and in this service are first remotely prepared for the proper use of the senses and appetites. Man is the first of the creation left free: he stands erect. He holds the balance of good and evil, of truth and falsehood; he can examine, and is to choose. As Nature has given him two free hands as instruments, and an inspecting eye to guide him, she has given him the power not only of placing the weights in the balance but of being, as I may say, himself a weight in the scale. He can gloss over the most delusive errors, and be voluntarily deceived; he can learn in time to love the chains with which he is unnaturally fettered, and adorn them with various flowers. As it is with deceived reason, so is it with

abused or shackled liberty: in most men it is such a proportion of powers and propensities, as habit or convenience has
established. Man seldom looks beyond these; and is capable
of becoming worse than a brute, when fettered by mean propensities and execrable habits.

Still, in right of his liberty, even when he most detestably
abuses it, is he a king. He may still choose, even though he
chooses the worst; he is obedient to his own commands, even
when he directs himself by his own will to that which is most
contemptible. Before the omniscient, who conferred on him
these powers, it is true both his liberty and reason are limited;
and they are happily limited; for he who created their sources
must have known and foreseen every channel in which they
could flow, and understand how to give them such directions,
that the stream most disorderly in its course could never
escape the reach of his hand. This, however, makes no alteration in the thing itself or in the nature of man. He is, and
remains, with regard to himself, a free creature, though all-
comprehending Goodness embraces him even in his follies,
and turns these both to his own and the general good. As the
bullet shot from the cannon's mouth cannot escape from the
atmosphere, and, when it falls, falls by one uniform law of
nature, so man, in error and in truth, in rising and in falling,
is still man; feeble indeed, but freeborn; if not yet rational,
yet capable of superior reason; if not yet formed to humanity,
yet endued with the power of attaining it. The New Zealand
cannibal and a Fénelon, a Newton and the wretched pesheray,
are all creatures of one and the same species.

It seems, indeed, as if every possible variety in the use of
these gifts were to be found upon our earth; and there is
evidently a progressive scale, from the man who borders on
the brute to the purest genius in human form. At this we
ought not to wonder, as we see the great gradation of animals
below us, and the long course Nature has been obliged to take
organically to prepare the little germinating flower of reason
and liberty in us. It appears that every thing possible to be
on our earth was actually to exist on it; and then only shall we
be able sufficiently to explain the order and wisdom of this
copious plenitude, when, advanced a step farther, we perceive
the end for which such variety was ordained to spring up in
the great garden of Nature. Here we see little more than the
laws of necessity prevail: for the whole earth was to be in-
habited, even in its remotest wildernesses; and only he who
stretched it out so far knows the reasons why he left on this

his world both pesherays and New Zealanders. The greatest contemner of the human race cannot deny that the noble plants of reason and liberty have produced beautiful fruits when warmed by the celestial beams of the sun, notwithstanding the many wild branches they have shot forth among the children of men. It would be almost incredible, did not history confirm it, to what heights human *reason* has ventured, endeavoring not merely to trace out but also to imitate the creating and sustaining Deity. In the chaos of beings which the senses point out to him, he has sought and discovered unity and intelligence, order and beauty. The most secret powers, with the internal springs of which he is unacquainted, he has observed in their external appearances, and traced motion, number, measure, life, and being, wherever he has perceived their effects, either in heaven or upon earth. All his essays, even when erroneous or visionary, are proofs of his majesty, of divine power and elevation. The Being who created all things has indeed placed a ray of his light, a stamp of his peculiar power, in our feeble frame; and low as man is, he can say to himself: "I have something in common with God; I possess faculties that the Supreme, whom I know in his works, must also possess, for he has displayed them in the things around me." Apparently *this similitude with himself* was the sum of all his works upon earth. He could produce nothing higher on this theater; but he neglected not to ascend thus high, and to carry the series of his organized beings up to this extreme point. Hence is the progress to it so uniform, through all the variety of figure that occurs.

In like manner *liberty* has produced noble fruits in man, and displayed its merits, as well in what it has rejected as in what it has pursued. That men have renounced the unsteady reins of blind appetite, and voluntarily assumed *the bonds of matrimony,* of social friendship, succor, and fidelity, in life and death; that they have given up their own wills, and chosen to be governed by laws, so as to establish and defend with their life's blood *the rule of men over men,* though it still remains far from perfection; that noble-minded mortals have sacrificed themselves for their *country,* and not only lost their lives in a tumultuous moment but, what is far more magnanimous, night and day, for months and years, have thought nothing of the uninterrupted labor of a whole life, to confer peace and happiness, at least in their opinion, on a blind, ungrateful multitude; that divine philosophers have voluntarily submitted to slander and persecution, poverty and

want, from a glorious thirst for promoting *truth, freedom,*
and *happiness* among the human species, and cherished the
idea that they had conferred on their brethren the highest
boon of which they were capable; must surely have arisen
from great human virtue, and the most powerful exertions of
that *self-government* which is inherent in us; or I know not to
what it is to be ascribed. It is true the number of those who
have thus distinguished themselves from the multitude, and
as physicians salutarily compelled them to what they would
not of themselves have chosen, has ever been but small; yet
these few have been the flower of the species, the free, immortal sons of God upon earth. The name of one such outweighs those of millions.

Man Is Organized to the Most Delicate State of Health, yet at the Same Time to the Longest Durability, and to Spread over the Earth

Man with his erect posture acquired a delicacy, warmth, and
strength that no brute can attain. In the savage state he was
in great measure covered with hair, particularly on the back;
and for the deprivation of this coat the elder Pliny has loudly
complained against Nature. The benevolent mother of all has
given man a more beautiful covering in his skin, which, with
all its delicacy, is capable of supporting the changes of season,
and the temperature of every climate, when aided by a small
portion of art, which to him is second nature.

To this art he is led not solely by naked necessity, but by
something more lovely and more appropriate to man. Whatever some philosophers may assert, modesty is natural to the
human species, and indeed something bearing an obscure
analogy to it is so to a few of the brutes; for the female ape
covers herself, and the elephant retires to some thick, un-
frequented wood to propagate his species. We know scarcely
any nation upon earth[2] so brutal that the women do not seek
some kind of veil, from the period when the passions begin
to awake; at the same time the tender sensibility of the parts
in question, and other circumstances, require a covering. Even
before man fought to protect his other limbs against the fury

[2] We are told but of two completely naked nations, and they
live in a manner like brutes: the pesherays, at the extreme point
of South America, and a savage people between Arracan and
Pegu; though I cannot implicitly credit the existence of the latter
in such a region of the world, notwithstanding it is confirmed by
one of our latest travelers: see Mackintosh's *Travels*, I, 341 (London, 1782).

of the elements, or the stings of insects, by clothes or unctions, a kind of sensual economy led him to guard the most vehement and necessary of his appetites. Among all the nobler animals the female does not offer herself, but will be sought. In this she unconsciously fulfills the purpose of Nature; and in the human species the delicate woman is the prudent guardian of charming modesty, which, in consequence of the erect posture, cannot fail to be developed at an early period.

Thus man was led to clothe himself; and no sooner had he acquired this and a few other arts, but he was capable of enduring any climate, and taking possession of every part of the earth. Few animals, scarcely any indeed except the dog, have been able to follow him into every region; and then how greatly has the form of these been changed! how much has their native constitution been altered! Man alone has but little varied, and this in no essential part. It is astonishing how uniformly he has retained his nature, when we contemplate the variations that have taken place in other migrating animals. His delicate nature is so fixed, so perfectly organized, that it stands on the highest point, and he is capable of few varieties, none of which are to be termed anomalies.

Whence comes all this? From his upright form, and from nothing else. Did we walk on all fours, like the bear and the ape, there is no doubt but the different species of the genus Man, if I may be allowed the ignoble expression, would have their more limited regions, which they would never quit. The bear-man would love his cold clime, the ape-man his warm; even as we now perceive that the more brutal a nation is, the more firmly is it enchained, body and mind, to its country and climate.

As Nature exalted man, she exalted him to rule over the earth. His upright form gave him, with a more finely organized structure, a more elaborate circulation of the blood, a more multifarious mixture of the vital fluids, and that *more intrinsic and fixed temperature of vital warmth* which alone would enable him to be an inhabitant of Siberia and of the torrid zone. Nothing but his erect, more artificial, organic structure renders him capable of bearing the two extremes of heat and cold, which no other creature upon earth can undergo and which notwithstanding alter him in a very small degree.

It must be confessed, this delicate structure and all the consequences arising from it have opened the door to a series of diseases with which no brute is acquainted and which

Moskati[3] has eloquently enumerated. The blood that carries on its circulation in a perpendicular machine, the heart pressed into an oblique position, and the bowels that perform their functions in an upright situation must be exposed to more danger of being deranged than they are in the body of a brute. The female sex in particular, it would seem, must pay dearer than we for its greater delicacy—yet the beneficence of Nature compensates and mitigates this in a thousand ways. Our health, our well-being, all our perceptions and excitements, are finer and more spiritual. No brute enjoys for a moment the health and happiness of man; no one tastes a drop of the nectarine stream that man drinks. Nay, considered merely with respect to the body, the diseases of the brute are fewer, it is true, because his corporal structure is more gross; but then they are the more obstinate, and the more constant in their effects. His cellular membrane, the coats of his nerves, his arteries, bones, and even brain are harder than ours; whence all the quadrupeds man sees around him, the elephant alone perhaps excepted, whose period of life approaches his, live a shorter time, and die a natural death, the death of indurating age, much sooner than he. Accordingly Nature has appointed man the longest life, and at the same time the healthiest and happiest, compatible with a terrestrial frame. Nothing can succor itself more easily, or in more various ways, than man's complicated nature; and it is owing to the excesses of madness and vice, of which indeed no brute is capable, that our frame is so enfeebled and deteriorated as it is in many instances. Nature has benevolently bestowed on every climate the plants that heal the diseases to which it is subject; and nothing but the confounding of all climates could have converted Europe into that sink of evils which no people living according to the dictates of Nature can experience. Still, for these self-acquired evils it has given us a self-acquired good, the only one we deserve, *physicians,* who assist Nature, when they follow her steps, and when they cannot, or dare not follow her, at least send the patient to rest according to art.

Oh, what maternal care and wisdom of the divine economy determined the stages of our lives and the duration of our existence! All living creatures here upon earth that have soon to attain perfection grow as quickly; they are early ripe,

[3] *Vom körperlichen wesentlichen Unterschiede der Thiere und Menschen* (On the Essential Bodily Difference Between Man and Brutes) (Göttingen, 1771).

and soon reach the goal of death. Man, planted upright as a tree of heaven, grows slowly. Like the elephant, he remains longest in the womb; the years of his youth are many, far more than those of any brute. Nature has spun out as long as she could the most favorable time for learning, growing, feeling the happiness of life, and enjoying it in the most innocent manner. Many animals are full grown in a few years or days; nay, even almost at the instant they are born; but they are so much the more imperfect, and die the earlier. Man must longest learn, because he has most to acquire; everything in him depends on self-taught ability, reason, and art. If his life be afterward shortened by the innumerable multitude of dangers and accidents to which he is exposed, yet he has enjoyed a long youth free from care, while with the growth of his body and mind the world grew around him, while with his slowly rising, still-extending sphere of vision the circle of his hopes enlarged, and his youthfully noble heart learned to beat more ardently in eager curiosity, in impatient enthusiasm, for everything that is great and good and beautiful. The flower of sexual appetite blooms later in a sound, unirritated man than in any other animal, for he is intended to live long, and not dissipate too early the noblest fluid of his mental and corporal powers. The insect, that soon enjoys the pleasure of love, dies speedily. All chaste monogamous animals live longer than those that do not enter into the connubial bonds. The lustful cock dies early; the constant stock dove may attain the age of fifty years. Marriage, therefore, is ordained for Nature's favorite here below; and he should spend his first years of vigor as the unopened bud, innocence itself. Hence follow long years of manly and ardent powers, in which his reason ripens; and this, as well as the prolific faculty, continues to flourish in a green old age unknown to any brute; till at length a gentle death steals on, and releases the falling dust, as well as the included spirit, from an unsuitable alliance. Thus Nature has associated with the fragile shell of the human body all the arts that a creature of this earth can attain: and, even in what shortens and enfeebles life, she has compensated the brevity of enjoyment with its acuteness, the destroying power with intensity of sensation.

MAN IS FORMED FOR HUMANITY AND RELIGION

I wish I could extend the signification of the word *humanity* so as to comprise in it everything I have thus far said on the noble conformation of man to reason and liberty, to finer senses and appetites, to the most delicate yet strong health, to the population and rule of the earth; for man has not a more dignified word for his destination than what expresses himself, in whom the image of the Creator lives imprinted as visibly as it can be here. We need only delineate his form, to develop his noblest duties.

1. All the appetites of a living being may be traced to the *support of self,* and to a *participation with others;* the organic structure of man, if a superior direction be added to it, gives to these appetites the nicest order. While a right line possesses the most stability, man has also for his protection the smallest circumference without, and the most varied velocity within. He stands on the narrowest basis, and therefore can most easily cover his limbs. His center of gravity falls between the supplest and strongest haunches that any creature upon earth can boast; and no brute displays in these parts the mobility and strength of man. His flattened, steely chest, and the position of his arms, give him the most extensive sphere of defense above, to protect his heart and guard his noblest vital parts from the head to the knee. It is no fable that men have encountered lions, and overcome them; the African, when he combines prudence and address with strength, is a match for more than one. It must be confessed, however, that man's structure is less calculated for attack than for defense; in that, he needs the assistance of art; in this, he is by nature the most powerful creature upon earth. Thus his very form teaches him to live in *peace,* not to addict himself to deeds of blood and rapine; and this constitutes the first characteristic of humanity.

2. Among the appetites that have reference to others, the desire of propagating the species is the most powerful, and this in man is subordinate to the promotion of humanity. What with four-footed beasts, even with the modest elephant, is copulation, with him, in consequence of his structure, is kissing and embracing. No brute has human lips, the delicate rim of which is the last part of the face formed in the womb; the beautiful and intelligent closing of these lips is, as it were, the last mark of the finger of love. The modest expression of ancient languages, that he knew his wife, is applicable to no brute. Ancient fables say that the two sexes at first formed a hermaphrodite, as in flowers, but were afterward separated. This and other expressive fictions were intended to convey the secret meaning of the superiority of human over brutal

love. That this desire in man is not subject to the control of seasons, as in brutes, though no accurate observations on the revolutions in the human body in this respect have yet been made, evidently shows that it is not dependent on necessity, but on the incitement of love, remains under the dominion of reason, and was designedly left to voluntary temperance, like everything pertaining to man. Thus love in man was to be *human;* and with this view Nature appointed, exclusive of his form, the later development, duration, and state of desire in both sexes; nay, she brought it under the law of a *voluntary social alliance,* and the most friendly communion between two beings, who feel themselves united in one for life.

3. As all the tender affections, except imparting and reciving love, are satisfied with participation, Nature has formed man most of all living creatures for participating in the fate of others, having framed him, as it were, out of all the rest, and organized him similarly to every part of the creation in such a degree that he can feel with each. The structure of his fibers is so fine, delicate, and elastic, his nerves are so diffused over every part of his vibrating frame, that, like an image of the all-sentient Deity, he can put himself almost in the place of every creature, and can share its feelings in the degree necessary to the creature, and which his own frame will bear without being disordered—nay, even at the hazard of disordering it. Accordingly our machine, so far as it is a growing, flourishing tree, feels even with trees; and there are men who cannot bear to see a young green tree cut down or destroyed. We regret its blighted top; we lament the withering of a favorite flower. A feeling man views not the writhing of a bruised worm with indifference; and the more perfect a creature is, the nearer its organization approaches our own, the more sympathy is excited in us by its sufferings. He must possess rigid nerves who can open a living creature and watch its convulsive movements; nothing but an insatiate thirst for fame and science can gradually deaden his organic sensibility. More delicate women cannot bear even the dissection of a dead body: they feel pain in each limb, as their eyes follow the course of the knife; and this pain is more acute in proportion to the nobleness and sensibility of the part. To see the bowels torn out excites disgust and horror; when the heart is pierced, the lungs divided, the brain cut to pieces, we feel the keen edge of the instrument in our own. We sympathize with the corpse of a dead friend, even in the grave; we feel the

cold pit, which he feels not, and shudder when we touch his bones. The common mother, who has taken all things from herself, and feels with the most intimate sympathy for all, has thus sympathetically compounded the human frame. Its vibrating fibers, its sympathizing nerves, need not the call of Reason; they run before her, they often disobediently and forcibly oppose her. Intercourse with mad people, for whom we feel, excites madness; and the sooner, the more we apprehend it.

It is singular that the ear should excite and strengthen compassion so much more powerfully than the eye. The sigh of a brute, the cry forced from him by bodily sufferance, bring about him all his fellows, who, as often has been observed, stand mournfully round the sufferer, and would willingly lend him assistance. Man, too, at the sight of suffering is more apt to be impressed with fear and tremor than with tender compassion; but no sooner does the voice of the sufferer reach him than the spell is dissolved, and he hastens to him; he is pierced to the heart. Is it that the sound converts the picture in the eye into a living being, and recalls and concenters in one point our recollection of our own and another's feelings? Or is there, as I am inclined to believe, a still deeper organic cause? Suffice it that the fact is true, and it shows that sound and language are the principal sources of man's compassion. We sympathize less with a creature that cannot sigh, as it is destitute of lungs, more imperfect, and less resembling ourselves in its organization. Some who have been born deaf and dumb have given the most horrible examples of want of compassion and sympathy with men and beasts; and instances enough may be observed among savage nations. Yet even among these the law of Nature is perceivable. Fathers who are compelled by hunger and want to sacrifice their children devote them to death in the womb, before they have beheld their eyes, before they have heard the sound of their voices; and many infanticides have confessed that nothing was so painful to them, nothing took such fast hold of their memory, as the first feeble voice, the suppliant cry of their child.

4. Beautiful is the chain by which the all-sentient Mother connects the reciprocal feeling of her children, and fashions it step by step. Where the creature is rude and insensible, so as scarcely to care for itself, it is not entrusted with the care of its offspring. The feathered inhabitants of the air hatch and bring up their young with maternal love; the stupid

ostrich, on the contrary, commits her eggs to the sand. "She forgets," says an ancient book, "that a foot may tread upon them, or a wild beast destroy them; for God has deprived her of wisdom, and imparted to her no understanding." From one and the same organic cause, whence a creature derives more brain, it also acquires more warmth, brings forth or hatches living young, gives suck, and is susceptible of parental affection. The creature that comes into the world alive is, as it were, a plexus of its mother's own nerves; the child brought up at its parent's breast is a branch of the mother plant, which she nourishes as a part of herself. On this most intimate reciprocal feeling are founded all the tender affections in the economy of the animal to which Nature could exalt its species.

In the human species maternal love is of a higher kind, a branch of the humanity of the upright form. The suckling lies beneath his mother's eye on her bosom, and drinks the softest and most delicate fluid. It is a brutal custom, and even tending to deform the body, for women to suckle their children at their backs, which in some countries they are compelled to do by necessity. Parental and domestic love soften the greatest savages; even the lioness is affectionate to her young. The first society arose in the paternal habitation, being cemented by the ties of blood, of confidence, and love. Thus to destroy the wildness of men, and habituate them to domestic intercourse, it was requisite that the infancy of the species should continue some years: Nature kept them together by tender bands that they might not separate and forget each other like the brutes, that soon arrive at maturity. The father becomes the instructor of his son, as the mother had been of her infant; and thus a new tie of humanity is formed. Here lies the ground of a necessary *human society*, without which no man could grow up and the species could not multiply. Man therefore is *born* for society: this the affection of his parents tells him; this, the years of his protracted infancy.

5. But as the sympathy of man is incapable of being universally extended, and could be but an obscure and frequently impotent conductor to him, a limited, complex being, in everything remote, his guiding Mother has subjected its numerous and lightly interwoven branches to her more unerring standard: this is the *rule of truth and justice*. Man is formed erect; and as everything in his figure is subordinate to the head, as his two eyes see only one object, his two ears hear but one sound; as Nature in his whole exterior has con-

nected symmetry with unity, and placed unity in the midst, so that what is double always refers to it, so also is the great law of justice and equiponderance the internal rule of man: *What ye would not that another should do unto you, do not to another; and do unto others what ye would they should do unto you.* This incontestible rule is written even in the breast of the savage, for when he eats the flesh of others he expects to be eaten in his turn. It is the rule of true and false, of the *idem et idem,* founded on the structure of all our senses, nay, I might say on man's erect position itself. If we saw obliquely, or the light struck us in an oblique direction, we should have no idea of a right line. If our organization were without unity, and our thoughts without judgment, our actions would fluctuate in curves devoid of rule, and human life would be destitute of reason and design. The law of truth and justice makes sincere brothers and associates; nay, when it takes place, it converts even enemies into friends. He whom I press to my bosom presses me also to his: he for whom I venture my life ventures his for me. Thus the laws of man, of nations, and of animals are founded on similarity of sentiment, unity of design among different persons, and equal truth in an alliance; for even animals that live in society obey the laws of justice; and men who avoid their ties by force or fraud are the most inhuman of all creatures, even if they be the kings and monarchs of the earth. No reason, no humanity, is conceivable without strict justice and truth.

6. The elegant and erect figure of man forms him to *decorum,* for this is the lovely friend and servant of truth and justice. Decorum of body is for it to stand as it ought, as God has fashioned it; true beauty is nothing more than the pleasing form of internal perfection and health. Consider the divine image in man disfigured by negligence and false art: the beautiful hair torn off, or clotted together in a lump; the nose and ears bored through, and stretched by a weight; the neck and the other parts of the body deformed in themselves, or by the dress that covers them. Who, even if the most capricious fashion were to judge, would discover here the decorum of the erect human frame? Just so it is with manners and actions; just so with customs, arts, and language. One and the same *humanity* pervades all these, which few nations upon earth have hit, and hundreds have disfigured by barbarism and false art. To trace this humanity is the genuine philosophy of man, which the sage called down from heaven and which

displays itself in social intercourse, as in national policy, in all the arts, as in every science.

Finally, *religion* is the highest humanity of mankind. Let no one be surprised that I thus estimate it. If the understanding be the noblest endowment of man, it is the business of the understanding to trace the connection between cause and effect, and to divine it where it is not apparent. The human understanding does this in every action, occupation, and art; for, even where it follows an established process, some understanding must previously have settled the connection between cause and effect, and thus introduced the art. But in the operations of Nature we properly see no cause in its inmost springs; we know not ourselves, we perceive not how any thing is effected in us. So in all the effects around us, everything is but a dream, a conjecture, a name; yet it is a true dream, when we frequently and constantly observe the same effect connected with the same cause. This is the progress of philosophy; and the first and last philosophy has ever been religion. Even the most savage nations have practiced it; for no people upon earth have been found entirely destitute of it, any more than of a capacity for reason and the human form, language and the connubial union, or some manners and customs proper to man. Where they saw no visible author of events, they supposed an invisible one, and inquired after the causes of things, though with a glimmering light. It is true they attended more to the phenomena than to the essence of nature, and contemplated the tremendous and transitory more than the pleasing and permanent, so that they seldom advanced so far as to refer all causes to one. Still, this first attempt was religion; and it is absurd to say that *fear* invented the gods of most people. Fear, as fear, invents nothing: it merely rouses the understanding to conjecture, and to suppose something true or false. As soon, therefore, as man learned to use his understanding on the slightest impulse, that is to say, as soon as he beheld the world in a manner different from that of a brute, he must have believed in more powerful invisible beings that benefited or injured him. These he fought to make or preserve his friends; and thus religion, true or false, right or erroneous, was introduced, the instructor of man, his comforter and guide through the dark and dangerous mazes of life.

No! Eternal Source of all life, all being, and all form, thou hast not forborn to manifest thyself to thy creatures. The prone brute obscurely feels thy power and goodness, while he exercises his faculties and appetites suitably to his organization; to him man is the visible divinity of the earth. But thou hast exalted man, so that, even without his knowing or intending it, he inquires after the causes of things, divines their connection, and thus discovers thee, thou great bond of all things, Being of beings! Thy inmost nature he knows not, for he sees not the essence of any one power; and when he would figure thee, he has erred, and must err; for thou art without figure, though the first and sole Cause of all forms. Still, this false glimmering of thee is light; and the illusive altar he has erected to thee is an unerring monument, not only of thy being, but of the power of man to know and worship thee. Thus religion, considered merely as an exercise of the understanding, is the highest humanity, the noblest blossom of the human mind.

But it is more than this: it is an exercise of the human heart, and the purest direction of its capacities and powers. If man be created free, and subject to no earthly law but what he imposes on himself, he must soon become the most savage of all creatures if he does not quickly perceive the law of God in the works of Nature, and strive as a child to imitate the perfections of his Father. Brutes are born servants in the great terrestrial family, and the slavish fear of laws and punishments is the most certain characteristic of the brute in man. The real man is free, and obeys from goodness and love; for all the laws of Nature, where he can perceive their tendency, are good; and where he perceives it not, he learns to follow them with the simplicity of a child. If thou go not willingly, say the philosophers, still thou must go: the law of Nature will not change on thy account; but the more thou discoverest its beauty, goodness, and perfection, the more will this living model form thee to the image of God in thine earthly life. True religion, therefore, is a filial service of God, an imitation of the most high and beautiful represented in the human form, with the extreme of inward satisfaction, active goodness, and love of mankind.

Hence it appears why in all religions upon earth more or less similitude of man with the Deity must have taken place, as they either exalted man to God or degraded the Father of the world to the likeness of man. We know no form superior to our own, and nothing can affect and humanize us but what we conceive and feel as men. Thus a sensual nation has exalted the human form to divine beauty; others, of more refined sentiments, have represented the perfections of the invisible being to the human eye by means of symbols. Even when the Deity has thought proper to reveal himself to us, he has spoken and acted after the manner of men, as was suitable to the spirit of the time. Nothing has so much ennobled our form and nature as religion, solely because it has led us back to our purest destination.

That the hope and belief of immortality were connected with religion, and established among men by its means, arose from the nature of the case; as they are scarcely separable from the idea of God and mankind. But how? We are children of the Eternal, whom we here learn by imitation to know and love, to the knowledge of whom everything excites us, and whom both our sufferings and enjoyments impel us to imitate. Yet since we know him so obscurely, since we imitate him so feebly and childishly—nay, even perceive the reasons why we cannot know him and imitate him otherwise in our present organization—is it possible for us to attain no other? Do our most indubitably best capacities admit of no advancement? Then, too, these our noblest faculties are so little adapted to this world; they expand themselves beyond it, since everything here is subservient to the wants of our nature. And still we feel our nobler part incessantly contending against these wants; precisely that which seems the end of man's organization finds its birthplace indeed upon the earth, but by no means its state of perfection. Has the Deity, then, broken the thread, and with all these preparations in the human frame produced at last an immature creature, deceived in the whole of his destination? All things upon earth are fragments: and shall they remain for ever and ever imperfect fragments, and the human race a group of shadows perplexing themselves with vain dreams? Here has religion knit together all the wants and hopes of mankind into *faith*, and woven an *immortal* crown for humanity.

MAN IS FORMED FOR THE HOPE OF IMMORTALITY

LET not the reader expect here any metaphysical proof of the immortality of the soul, from the simplicity of its nature, its spirituality, or the like. Natural philosophy knows nothing of this simplicity, and would rather incline to advance doubts against it, as we are acquainted with the soul only through its operations in a complicated organization, which appear to spring from a diversity of stimuli and perceptions. The most common thought is the result of innumerable single perceptions; and the ruler of our body acts upon the numerous tribe of subordinate faculties, as if she were locally present with them all.

Neither can Bonnet's philosophy, as it is called, the system of germs, be our guide here; for, in respect of the transition to a new existence, it is partly devoid of demonstration, partly inapplicable. No one has discovered in our brain a spiritual brain, the germ of a new existence; neither is the least analogy to this perceptible in its structure. The brain of the dead remains with us; and if the seed of our immortality possessed no other powers, it would lie and be consumed to dust. This system appears to me, too, to be altogether inapplicable to the subject; for we speak not here of young creatures descending from a creature of the same kind, but of a dying creature that springs up to a new state of existence. Indeed, if it were exclusively true with regard to the generation of terrestrial beings, and all our hope rested upon this, it would oppose insuperable doubts to this hope. If it be eternally fixed that the flower shall produce nothing but a flower, the brute a brute, and that every thing was mechanically framed at the beginning of creation in preformed germs, farewell enchanting hope of a superior existence! From all eternity have I lain a germ preformed for my present existence and no other; all that was destined to spring from me consists in the preformed germs of my children; and when the tree dies, all the philosophy of germs dies with it.

If we would not deceive ourselves on this important subject with fine words, we must begin deeper, take a wider sphere, and observe the general *analogy of Nature*. We cannot penetrate the inmost recesses of her powers; it would be as vain, therefore, as it is unnecessary to seek there for profound essential conclusions upon any subject. But the modes and effects of her powers lie before us; these, therefore, we can compare, and perhaps collect *hopes* from the progress of Nature here below, and its general prevailing character.

Claude Henri de Rouvroy, Comte de Saint-Simon
(1760–1825)

ON SOCIAL ORGANIZATION

Claude Henri de Rouvroy, Comte de Saint-Simon, better known to us as Henri de Saint-Simon, was born in 1760 and died in 1825. In a sense he was the child of both the Ancien Régime and of the Enlightenment.

Although Saint-Simon was a descendant of an ancient noble family and a relative of the Duc de Saint-Simon, the great biographer of Louis XIV, he was a bitter critic of royal absolutism. At the age of nineteen he went to the West Indies as a soldier; he fought with distinction with the American troops in the Battle of Yorktown. Later, in a naval defeat suffered by his fleet, Saint-Simon was wounded and imprisoned, but later released in Jamaica.

Already in his youth, Saint-Simon was deeply concerned with the need for applying reason and science to social organization and for furthering industrial development.

In his early twenties he devised plans for building canals to join the Atlantic and Pacific oceans in Nicaragua and to link Madrid with the sea. He strongly supported the idea of a Suez Canal.

Saint-Simon returned to France at twenty-three with the rank of colonel. He was very free with money and spent his fortune rapidly. However, his wealth was restored during the French Revolution (in which he took an active part) through speculation in confiscated estates, mainly church lands.

Saint-Simon enjoyed surrounding himself with the savants of his time and tried, unsuccessfully, to marry Madame de Staël. His many ideas on industrialism, scientific methods, and the application of science to social organization were stated in a stream of publications. Soon, however, he again became poverty-stricken and was dependent on the charity of friends and even that of a former servant.

A group of young students from the Ecole Polytechnique were his devoted followers. Among them were Augustin Thierry and Auguste Comte. Both served as his secretaries. At first there was a close relationship between Saint-Simon and Comte, but in 1824 a sharp break occurred between

23

them, mainly because Comte refused to support fully Saint-Simon's revolutionary socialistic philosophy. Disappointed by his lack of success in persuading others to support his proposal for social reconstruction, he attempted suicide in 1823.

In his early book, Letters from an Inhabitant of Geneva, *he stressed the use of scientific methods in order to achieve human progress. In* Reorganization of European Society, *which was published in 1814, Saint-Simon strongly advocated a confederation of Europe and the founding of parliamentary governments.* Industry, *one of his most significant studies, outlines the criteria for an industrial régime. This régime was to comprise the leaders of the industrial class, including employers as well as employees. He did not advocate social ownership of the economy. In his works one finds a perpetual concern for the interests of the poor and a strong awareness of the important role of both technology and industrialization in society.*

In 1825, the year of his death, his last work, New Christianity, *was published. In this book Saint-Simon advocated a religion founded on brotherly love and showed again his continual concern for the poor.*

Only a few of Saint-Simon's works have been translated into English. The best biography in English is that by Frank Manuel, and the best in French is Vie de Saint-Simon *by M. Leroy. There is also available an excellent study of Saint-Simon's socialistic ideas by Emile Durkheim.*[1]

ON SOCIAL ORGANIZATION

THE mechanism of social organization was inevitably very complicated so long as the majority of individuals remained in a state of ignorance and improvidence which rendered them incapable of administering their own affairs. In this state of incomplete intellectual development they were swayed by brutal passions which urged them to revolt and every kind of anarchy.

In such a situation, which was the necessary prelude to a better social order, it was necessary for the minority to be organized on military lines, to obtain a monopoly of legislation, and so to keep all power to itself, in order to hold the

[1] Emile Durkheim, *Le Socialisme,* edited by Marcel Mauss, Paris, 1928. This book has recently been translated into English.

majority in tutelage and subject the nation to strong discipline. Thus the main energies of the community have till now been directed to maintaining itself as a community, and any efforts directed to improving the moral and physical welfare of the nation have necessarily been regarded as secondary.

Today this state of affairs can and should be completely altered. The main effort should be directed to the improvement of our moral and physical welfare; only a small amount of force is now required to maintain public order, since the majority have become used to work (which eliminates disorder), and now consists of men who have recently proved that they are capable of administering property, whether in land or money.

As the minority no longer has need of force to keep the proletarian class in subordination, the course which it should adopt is as follows:

1. A policy by which the proletariat will have the strongest interest in maintaining public order.

2. A policy which aims at making the inheritance of landed property as easy as possible.

3. A policy which aims at giving the highest political importance to the workers.

Such a policy is quite simple and obvious, if one takes the trouble to judge the situation by one's own intelligence, and to shake off the yoke enforced on our minds by the political principles of our ancestors—principles which were sound and useful in their own day, but are no longer applicable to present circumstances. The mass of the population is now composed of men (apart from exceptions which occur more or less equally in every class) who are capable of administering property whether in land or in money, and therefore we can and must work directly for the improvement of the moral and physical welfare of the community.

The most direct method of improving the moral and physical welfare of the majority of the population is to give priority in state expenditure to ensuring work for all fit men, to secure their physical existence; spreading throughout the proletarian class a knowledge of positive science; ensuring for this class forms of recreation and interests which will develop their intelligence.

We must add to this the measures necessary to ensure that the national wealth is administered by men most fitted for it, and most concerned in its administration—that is to say, the most important industralists.

Thus the community, by means of these fundamental arrangements, will be organized in a way which will completely satisfy reasonable men of every class.[2]

[2] Men are not so bad as they think they are: they are more severe on themselves than they deserve. It is true that theoretically they appear to be strongly inclined to despotism, but, in actual fact, they prefer equality.

If an Englishman obtains a post in India, he goes there with enthusiasm, and in his imagination pictures the delights that despotism will procure for him. He can, if he likes, keep a harem; he will be surrounded by hundreds of servants—some to keep off the flies which might irritate him, others always ready to carry him in a palanquin. The whole population will crawl before him; he will have the power to order a beating for any Indian who does not obey his wishes with enough zeal or intelligence.

Well, this Englishman who in India wallows in the delights of despotism, hastens to return to England, as soon as he has made his fortune, to enjoy again the advantages of equality. The moment he arrives in harbor in Great Britain, he finds himself rudely hustled by the people, and yet that does not make him wish to return to the place where everybody makes way for him.

We see Russians of vast wealth leaving their country to live in western Europe, while western Europeans go to Russia only to make their fortune, and hasten to bring back to their own homes the wealth they have acquired there.

There are good reasons why rich men prefer to live in countries where equality between the members of the community is most far advanced, since these countries are at the same time those where they can most easily and fully satisfy their wants.

In any French town of some importance, a man with money can, at any hour and without previous notice, eat well at a moderate price. In Russia only the great nobles can obtain good food.

If a traveler has a breakdown of his carriage anywhere in England, he can either have his carriage repaired or buy on the spot a carriage as good as the other. In Russia a traveler whose carriage breaks down on a main road between big towns is forced to finish his journey in a peasant's cart.

Thus, in fact, the richest and most powerful men have an interest in the growth of equality, since the means of satisfying their wants increases in the same proportion as the leveling of the individuals composing the community.

It is commonly assumed that those who profit by an abuse are strongly attached to it. This is an error; what they are determined on is not to let themselves be deprived of advantages which pass into the hands of others. It was the nobles who in France initiated the suppression of the privileges which they enjoyed, and they regretted this sacrifice only when they saw, first, all the former commoners behave toward them like members of a privileged order, and then a new aristocracy growing up in which the former nobles were admitted only as inferiors.

In conclusion to this note, let me say what perhaps should have

There will no longer be a fear of insurrection, and consequently no longer a need to maintain large standing armies to suppress it; no longer a need to spend enormous sums on a police force; no longer a fear of foreign danger, for a body of thirty millions of men who are a contented community would easily repel attack, even if the whole human race combined against them.

We might add that neither princes nor peoples would be so mad as to attack a nation of thirty millions who displayed no aggressive intentions against their neighbors, and were united internally by mutual interests.

Furthermore, there would no longer be a need for a system of police-spying in a community in which the vast majority had an interest in maintaining the established order.

The men who brought about the Revolution, the men who directed it, and the men who, since 1789 and up to the present day, have guided the nation have committed a great political mistake. They have all sought to improve the governmental machine, whereas they should have subordinated it and put administration in the first place.

They should have begun by asking a question the solution of which is simple and obvious. They should have asked who, in the present state of morals and enlightenment, are the men most fitted to manage the affairs of the nation. They would have been forced to recognize the fact that the scientists, artists, and industrialists and the heads of industrial concerns are the men who possess the most eminent, varied, and most positively useful ability for the guidance of men's minds at the present time. They would have recognized the fact that the work of the scientists, artists, and industrialists is that which, in discovery and application, contributes most to national prosperity.

They would have reached the conclusion that the scientists, artists, and leaders of industrial enterprises are the men who should be entrusted with administrative power, that is to say, with the responsibility for managing the national inter-

---

been stated first, that the improvement of the lot of the masses secures the welfare of men of every class and that, to improve the lot of the masses, it is necessary not merely to transfer privilege, but to abolish it. It is necessary not merely to let abuses change hands, but to eliminate them.

ests; and that the functions of government should be limited to maintaining public order.[3]

The reformers of 1789 should have said to themselves as follows:

The kings of England have given a good example to monarchy by agreeing to give no order without the approval and signature of a minister. The magnanimity of the kings of France demands that they show still greater generosity to

[3] I propose to explain briefly how the imposition of government on top of administration produced harmful effects at the present day, when the mass of the nation consists of men who no longer require to be closely supervised, since they have shown themselves capable of administering all kinds of property. Today the proletarian class can become dangerous to public order only if the administrators of the national interests are so inept or selfish as to let them become unemployed.

It is easy to convince oneself, and others, that one has the capacity to govern, because the ability or lack of ability to govern can be proved only by experience. Any man can imagine and persuade others that he would govern well, so long as he has not governed already.

It is not the same in the case of mathematics, physics, chemistry, physiology, mechanics, poetry, painting, sculpture, architecture, farming, manufacture, commerce, and banking.

It is easy for any man to judge whether he possesses great ability in the sciences or arts; it is easy to verify whether he has attained great importance in a branch of industry. In any case, errors of this sort would not be serious, since his neighbors would soon open his eyes, if they were blinded by vanity.

It follows from what I have said that the ambition of scientists, artists, and industrialists to participate in the administration of national interests is not dangerous to the community. It is advantageous rather, since they can succeed in their ambition only through solid achievements; while the ambition which aims at a place in the government is harmful to the community, because the most incapable men may be consumed by such an ambition and, in order to satisfy it, strive to overthrow the whole social order.

One of the important effects of this ambition, which inflamed almost all Frenchmen when the government of the unfortunate Louis XVI was overturned, is very extraordinary. It was with the aim of being governed less, and less expensively, that the nation embarked on revolution. Up to the present it has achieved as a result more government, and more expensive government, than it had before the Revolution.

The industrialists produce much more than before the Revolution, but a great part of the increased production is used to pay useless military staffs and a mass of clerks who employ their time for the most part in reading newspapers and sharpening pens—a result which satisfies neither the needs nor the feelings of the producers.

their people and that they should agree to make no decision affecting the general interests of the nation without the approval of the men most fitted to judge their decisions—that is to say, without the approval of the scientists and the most eminent artists, without the approval of the most important industrialists.

The community has often been compared to a pyramid. I admit that the nation should be composed as a pyramid; I am profoundly convinced that the national pyramid should be crowned by the monarchy, but I assert that from the base of the pyramid to its summit the layers should be composed of more and more precious materials. If we consider the present pyramid, it appears that the base is made of granite, that up to a certain height the layers are composed of valuable materials, but that the upper part, supporting a magnificent diamond, is composed of nothing but plaster and gilt.

The base of the present national pyramid consists of workers in their routine occupations; the first layers above this base are the leaders of industrial enterprises, the scientists who improve the methods of manufacture and widen their application, the artists who give the stamp of good taste to all their products. The upper layers, which I assert to be composed of nothing but plaster, which is easily recognizable despite the gilding, are the courtiers, the mass of nobles whether of ancient or recent creation, the idle rich, the governing class from the prime minister to the humblest clerk. The monarchy is the magnificent diamond which crowns the pyramid.

Auguste Comte
(1798–1857)

THE SCIENCE OF SOCIETY

On January 19, 1798 Auguste Comte, considered by many sociologists to be the "father of sociology," was born in the old Roman town of Montpellier, a town famous for its university (Locke, Petrarch, and Rabelais had come to Montpellier to pursue their studies). Auguste Comte, however, attended the famous Ecole Polytechnique in Paris. He did not complete his formal schooling because he seemed to have an allergy to authority of any kind. After inciting an insurrection against the school authorities, he was expelled. Soon, however, he made the most important contact of his life by becoming secretary and friend to Saint-Simon.

He served six years as Saint-Simon's secretary and Saint-Simon undoubtedly exerted a great influence on Comte's thinking and later writings. It has even been said that Comte did little more than systematize and develop what Saint-Simon had already written. J. P. Lichtenberger makes a definite point of this in his book Development of Social Theory[1] where he writes:

"One who is familiar with Comte's system need not be told that all that remained was for him to expand and systematize the outlines laid down by de Saint-Simon, and the best critics agree that such was the primary contribution of Comte to Sociology."

Comte, however, strongly denied the influence of Saint-Simon on his writings, and it was mainly Saint-Simon's charge of plagiarism that destroyed the friendship of the two men.[2]

Comte's first important work, Positive Philosophy (Cours de philosophie positive), appeared between the years 1830 and 1842 and was mainly the result of the reading and research done by Comte during his six-year period with Saint-

---

[1] P. 243, Development of Social Theory, J. P. Lichtenberger, Appleton-Century, New York, 1936.

[2] See p. 568, Social Thought from Lore to Science, Harry Elmer Barnes and Howard Becker, D. C. Heath & Co., New York, 1938.

Simon. He also was an examiner for the Ecole Polytechnique between 1836 and 1846, but was dismissed from this position. After that Comte depended mainly on contributions from his friends for his living. Of his many friendships with women one stands out—namely, that with Clotilde de Vaux, whose friendship certainly contributed to Comte's eulogy of women, as seen especially in his Positive Polity (Système de politique positive).

Besides Saint-Simon, many others such as Concordet (he had already written of the "Law of Three Stages"), Hume (Comte called him "my principal precursor"), Blainvelle (from whom Comte derived his division between static and dynamic), Kant, Turgot (they undoubtedly gave Comte the basis for his historical determinism), Bossuet, Vico, and de Maistre have influenced Comte's writings and ideas. The last three gave Comte many of his ideas for a "New Christianity."

Among Comte's outstanding doctrines should be mentioned his classification of the hierarchy of the sciences with sociology at the top, the division of sociology itself into social statics and dynamics, the law of the three stages of universal social progress, and his view of society as a developing organism. In his approach Comte stressed the application of the scientific methods of observation, experimentation, and comparison.

Comte's works are in general an impressive encyclopedia of scientific, sociological, and philosophical data, which, on the whole, center around his principle of the "law of the three stages."

His last and most important work was his Principles of a Positive Polity (Système de politique positive) and was published in several volumes between 1851 and 1854.

THE SCIENCE OF SOCIETY

CHARACTERISTICS OF THE POSITIVE METHOD IN ITS APPLICATION TO SOCIAL PHENOMENA

IN every science, conceptions which relate to method are inseparable from those which relate to the doctrine under consideration. The method has to be so varied in its application, and so largely modified by the complexity and special

nature of the phenomena, in each case, that any general notions of method would be too indefinite for actual use. If,
therefore, we have not separated the method from the doctrine in the simpler departments of science, much less should
we think of doing so when treating of the complex phenomena
of social life, to say nothing of the great feature of this last
case—its want of positivity. In the formation of a new science,
the general spirit of it must be seized before its particular
parts can be investigated, that is, we must have some notion
of the doctrine before examining the method, and then the
method can not be estimated in any way other than by its use.
Thus I have not to offer a logical exposition of method in
social physics before proceeding to the science itself, but I
must follow the same plan here as in the case of the anterior
sciences—ascertaining its general spirit and what are the collective resources proper to it. Though these subjects may be
said to belong to the science itself, we may consider them as
belonging to the method, as they are absolutely necessary to
direct our understandings in the pursuit of this difficult study.

In the higher order of sciences—in those which are the
simplest and the most advanced—the philosophical definition
of each was almost sufficient to characterize their condition
and general resources, to which no doubt could attach. But
the case is otherwise with a recent and extremely complex
study, the very nature of which has to be settled by laborious
discussions, which are happily needless in regard to the preceding sciences. In treating of biology, we found it necessary
to dwell upon preparatory explanations which would have
secured puerile in any of the foregoing departments, because
the chief bases of a science, about which there were still so
many disputes, must be indisputably settled before it could
take rank in the positive series. It is evident that the same
process is even more needful, and must be more laborious, in
the case of the science of social development, which has
hitherto had no character of positivity at all and which some
of the ablest minds of our time sentence never to have any.
We must not be surprised, then, if, after applying here the
simplest and most radical ideas of positive philosophy, such
as would indeed appear trivial in their formal application
to the more advanced sciences, the result should appear to
many, even among the enlightened, to constitute too bold an
innovation, though the conditions may be no more than the
barest equivalent of those which are admitted in every other
case.

INFANTILE STATE OF SOCIAL SCIENCE

IF we look with a philosophical eye upon the present state of social science, we can not but recognize in it the combination of all the features of that theologico-metaphysical infancy which all the other sciences have had to pass through. The present condition of political science revives before our eyes the analogy of what astrology was to astronomy, alchemy to chemistry, and the search for the universal panacea to the system of medical studies. We may, for our present purpose, consider the theological and the metaphysical polities to-gether—the second being only a modification of the first in its relation to social science. Their attributes are the same, consisting, in regard to method, in the preponderance of imagination over observation; and, in regard to doctrine, in the exclusive investigation of absolute ideas; the result of both of which is an inevitable tendency to exercise an arbitrary and indefinite action over phenomena which are not regarded as subject to invariable natural laws. In short, the general spirit of all speculation at that stage is at once ideal in its course, absolute in its conception, and arbitrary in its application; and these are unquestionably the prevailing characteristics of social speculation at present, regarded from any point of view whatever. If we reverse all the three aspects, we shall have precisely the spirit which must actuate the formation of positive sociology and which must afterward direct its continuous development. The scientific spirit is radically distinguished from the theological and metaphysical by the steady subordination of the imagination to observation; and though the positive philosophy offers the vastest and richest field to human imagination, it restricts it to discovering and perfecting the coordination of observed facts, and the means of effecting new researches: and it is this habit of subjecting scientific conceptions to the facts whose connection has to be disclosed, which it is above all things necessary to introduce into social researches; for the observations hitherto made have been vague and ill-circumscribed, so as to afford no adequate foundation for scientific reasoning; and they are usually modified themselves at the pleasure of an imagination stimulated by the most fluctuating passions. From their complexity, and their closer connection with human passions, political speculations must be detained longer than any others in this deplorable philosophical condition, in which they are still involved, while simpler and less stimulating sciences have successively obtained emancipation; but we must remember that all other kinds of scientific conceptions have gone through the same stage, from which they have issued with the more difficulty and delay exactly in proportion to their complexity and special nature. It is, indeed, only in our own day that the more complex have issued from that condition at all, as we saw to be the case with the intellectual and moral phenomena of individual life, which are still studied in a way almost as antiscientific as political phenomena themselves. We must not, then, consider that uncertainty and vagueness in observation are proper to political subjects. It is only that the same imperfection which has had its day throughout the whole range of speculation is here more intense and protracted; and the same theory which shows how this must be the case gives us full assurance of a philosophical regeneration in this department of science analogous to that which has taken place in the rest, though by means of severer intellectual difficulty, and the embarrassment which may arise from collision with the predominant passions of men—a liability which can not but stimulate the endeavors of real thinkers.

THE RELATIVE SUPERSEDING THE ABSOLUTE

IF we contemplate the positive spirit in its relation to scientific conception, rather than the mode of procedure, we shall find that this philosophy is distinguished from the theologicometaphysical by its tendency to render relative the ideas which were at first absolute. This inevitable passage from the absolute to the relative is one of the most important philosophical results of each of the intellectual revolutions which has carried on every kind of speculation from the theological or metaphysical to the scientific state. In a scientific view, this contrast between the relative and the absolute may be regarded as the most decisive manifestation of the antipathy between the modern philosophy and the ancient. All investigation into the nature of beings, and their first and final causes, must always be absolute; whereas the study of the laws of phenomena must be relative, since it supposes a continuous progress of speculation subject to the gradual improvement of observation, without the precise reality being ever fully disclosed: so that the relative character of scientific conceptions is inseparable from the true idea of natural laws, just as the chimerical inclination for absolute knowledge accompanies every use of theological fictions and metaphysical entities. Now, it is obvious that the absolute spirit characterizes social speculation now, wherever it exists, as the different schools are all agreed in looking for an immutable political type, which makes no allowance for the regular modification of political conceptions according to the variable state of civilization. This absolute spirit, having prevailed through all social changes, and their corresponding philosophical divergences, is now so inherent in existing political science that it affords, amid all its enormous evils, the only means of restraining individual eccentricities, and excluding the influx of arbitrarily variable opinions. Thus, such philosophers as have desired to emancipate themselves from this absolutism, without having risen to the conception of a positive social philosophy, have justly incurred the reproach of representing political ideas as uncertain and even arbitrary in their nature, because they have deprived them of whatever character of consistency they had, without substituting any other. They have even cast a sort of discredit upon all philosophical enterprise in the direction of political science, which, losing its absolutism, seemed to lose its stability, and therefore its morality. A positive sociology, however, would put to flight all these natural though empirical fears; for all antecedent experience shows that in other departments of natural philosophy, scientific ideas have not become arbitrary by becoming relative, but have, on the contrary, acquired a new consistence and stability by being implicated in a system of relations which is ever extending and strengthening, and more and more restraining all serious aberration. There is therefore no fear of falling into a dangerous skepticism by destroying the absolute spirit, if it is done in the natural course of passing on toward the positive state. Here, as elsewhere, it is characteristic of the positive philosophy to destroy no means of intellectual coordination without substituting one more effectual and more extended; and it is evident that this transition from the absolute to the relative offers the only existing means of attaining to political conceptions that can gradually secure a unanimous and permanent assent.

PRESUMPTUOUS CHARACTER OF THE EXISTING POLITICAL SPIRIT

THE importance and soundness of these conditions are less conspicuous than they might be, because of the too close connection which, in social science more than any other, still exists between theory and practice, in consequence of which all speculative and abstract appreciation, however supremely important, excites only a feeble interest and inadequate attention. To show how this confusion results from the imperfection of social science, as the most complex of all, we must look at the existing political spirit in relation to its general application, and not for the moment in relation to the science itself. In this view we see that the existing political spirit is marked by its disposition to exercise an illimitable action over the corresponding phenomena, as it was once supposed possible to do in other departments of philosophy. Men were long in learning that man's power of modifying phenomena can result only from his knowledge of their natural laws; and in the infancy of each science they believed themselves able to exert an unbounded influence over the phenomena of that science. As this happened precisely at the period when they had the least power over phenomena, from ignorance of their laws, they rested their confidence on expectations of aid from supernatural agents, or mysterious forces supposed to be inherent in all that they saw. The delusion was protracted, and the growth of true science hindered in proportion, by the increasing complexity of the descending sciences, as each other of phenomena exhibited less generality than the last, and obscured the perception as to what the modifying power of man really is. Social phenomena are, of course, from their extreme complexity, the last to be freed from this pretension; but it is therefore only the more necessary to remember that the pretension existed with regard to all the rest, in their earliest stage, and to anticipate therefore that social science will, in its turn, be emancipated from the delusion. It still hangs about the class of intellectual and moral phenomena; but otherwise it is now confined to social subjects. There, amid the dawning of a sounder philosophy, we see statesmen and politicians still supposing that social phenomena can be modified at will, the human race having, in their view, no spontaneous impulsion, but being always ready to yield to any influence of the legislator, spiritual or temporal, provided he is invested with a sufficient authority. We see the theological polity, as before, more consistent than the metaphysical, explaining the monstrous disproportion between slight causes and vast effects by regarding the legislator as merely the organ of a supernatural and absolute power; and again, we see the metaphysical school following the same course, merely substituting for Providence its unintelligible entities, and especially its grand entity, Nature, which comprehends all the rest, and is evidently only an abstract deterioriation of the theological principle. Going further than the theological school in its disdain of the subjection of effects to causes, it escapes from difficulty by attributing observed events to chance, and sometimes, when that method is too obviously absurd, exaggerating ridiculously the influence of the individual mind upon the course of human affairs. The result is the same in both cases. It represents the social action of man to be indefinite and arbitrary, as was once thought in regard to biological, chemical, physical, and even astronomical phenomena, in the earlier stages of their respective sciences. It is easy to see that true political science would be unacceptable, because it must impose limits on political action, by dissipating for ever the pretension of governing at will this class of phenomena, and withdrawing them from human or superhuman caprice. In close connection with the tendency to absolute conceptions, we must recognize in this delusion the chief intellectual cause of the social disturbance which now exists; for the human race finds itself delivered over, without logical protection, to the ill-regulated experimentation of the various political schools, each one of which strives to set up, for all future time, its own immutable type of government. We have seen what are the chaotic results of such a strife: and we shall find that there is no chance of order and agreement but in subjecting social phenomena, like all others, to invariable natural laws, which shall, as a whole, prescribe for each period, with entire certainty, the limits and character of political action—in other words, introducing into the study of social phenomena the same positive spirit which has regenerated every other branch of human speculation. Such a procedure is the true scientific basis of human dignity, as the chief tendencies of man's nature thus acquire a solemn character of authority which must be always respected by rational legislation; whereas the existing belief in the indefinite power of political combinations, which seems at first to exalt the importance of man, issues in attributing to him a sort of social automatism passively directed by some supremacy of either Providence or the human ruler. I have said enough to show that the central difficulty in the task of regenerating political science is to rectify such an error of conception at a time when our prevailing intellectual habits render it difficult to seize social conceptions in any other than their practical

aspect, and when their scientific, and yet more, their logical
relations are obscured by the prepossessions of the general
mind.

PREVISION OF SOCIAL PHENOMENA

THE last of the preliminary considerations that we have to
review is that of the scientific prevision of phenomena, which,
as the test of true science, includes all the rest. We have to
contemplate social phenomena as susceptible of prevision, like
all other classes, within the limits of exactness compatible
with their higher complexity. Comprehending the three characteristics of political science which we have been examining,
prevision of social phenomena supposes, first, that we have
abandoned the region of metaphysical idealities, to assume
the ground of observed realities by a systematic subordination
of imagination to observation; second, that political conceptions have ceased to be absolute, and have become relative to
the variable state of civilization, so that theories, following
the natural course of facts, may admit of our foreseeing them;
and, third, that permanent political action is limited by determinate laws, since, if social events were always exposed to
disturbance by the accidental intervention of the legislator,
human or divine, no scientific prevision of them would be
possible. Thus, we may concentrate the conditions of the
spirit of positive social philosophy on this one great attribute
of scientific prevision. This concentration is all the more apt
for the purpose of our inquiry, because there is no other view
in which the new social philosophy is so clearly distinguished
from the old. Events ordered by a supernatural will may leave
room for a supposition of revelation; but the very thought of
prevision in that case is sacrilegious; and the case is essentially the same when the direction of events is assigned to
metaphysical entities, except that it leaves the chance of
revelation, the existence of which chance shows that the metaphysical conception is a mere modification of the theological.
The old conceptions may evidently be applied to explain
opposite facts equally well; and they can never afford the
slightest indication of those which are yet future. And, if it
be objected that, at all times, a great number of secondary
political facts have been considered susceptible of prevision,
this proves only that the old philosophy has never been strictly
universal, but has always been tempered by an admixture of

feeble and imperfect positivism, without more or less of which society could not have held on its course. This admixture has, however, been hitherto insufficient to allow anything worthy the name of prevision—anything more than a sort of popular forecast of some secondary and partial matters—never rising above an uncertain and rough empiricism, which might be of some provisional use but could not in any degree supply the need of a true political philosophy.

Having now ascertained the fundamental position of the problems of political philosophy, and thus obtained guidance as to the scientific aim to be attained, the next step is to exhibit the general spirit of social physics, whose conditions we have been deciding.

SPIRIT OF SOCIAL SCIENCE

THE philosophical principle of the science being that social phenomena are subject to natural laws, admitting of rational prevision, we have to ascertain what is the precise subject and what the peculiar character of those laws. The distinction between the statical and dynamical conditions of the subject must be extended to social science; and I shall treat of the conditions of social existence as, in biology, I treated of organization under the head of anatomy; and then of the laws of social movement, as in biology of those of life, under the head of physiology. This division, necessary for exploratory purposes, must not be stretched beyond that use: and, as we saw in biology, that the distinction becomes weaker with the advance of science, so shall we see that when the science of social physics is fully constituted, this division will remain for analytical purposes, but not as a real separation of the science into two parts. The distinction is not between two classes of facts, but between two aspects of a theory. It corresponds with the double conception of order and progress; for order consists (in a positive sense) in a permanent harmony among the conditions of social existence; and progress consists in social development; and the conditions in the one case, and the laws of movement in the other, constitute the statics and dynamics of social physics. And here we find again the constant relation between the science and the art—the theory and the practice. A science which proposes a positive study of the laws of order and of progress cannot be charged with speculative rashness by practical men of any intelligence, since it offers the only rational basis for the practical means of satisfying the needs of society, as to order and progress; and the correspondence in this case will be found to be analogous to that which we have seen to exist between biological science and the arts which relate to it—the medical art especially. One view of the deepest interest in this connection is that the ideas of order and progress which are in perpetual conflict in existing society, occasioning infinite disturbance, are thus reconciled, and made necessary to each other, becoming as truly inseparable as the ideas of organization and life in the individual being. The further we go in the study of the conditions of human society, the more clearly will the organizing and progressive spirit of the positive philosophy become manifest.

STATICAL STUDY

THE statical study of sociology consists in the investigation of the laws of action and reaction of the different parts of the social system—apart, for the occasion, from the fundamental movement which is always gradually modifying them. In this view, sociological prevision, founded upon the exact general knowledge of those relations, acts by judging by each other the various statical indications of each mode of social existence, in conformity with direct observation—just as is done daily in the case of anatomy. This view condemns the existing philosophical practice of contemplating social elements separately, as if they had an independent existence; and it leads us to regard them as in mutual relation, and forming a whole which compels us to treat them in combination. By this method, not only are we furnished with the only possible basis for the study of social movement; we are also put in possession of an important aid to direct observation, since many social elements which cannot be investigated by immediate observation may be estimated by their scientific relation to others already known. When we have a scientific knowledge of the interior relation of the parts of any science or art; and again, of the relations of the sciences to each other; and again, of the relations of arts to their respective sciences, the observation of certain portions of the scheme enables us to pronounce on the state of other portions, with a true philosophical security. The case is the same when, instead of studying the collective social phenomena of a single nation, we include in the study those of contemporary nations, whose reciprocal influence cannot be disputed, though it is much reduced in modern times, and, as in the instance of western Europe and eastern Asia, apparently almost effaced.

SOCIAL ORGANIZATION

THE only essential case in which this fundamental relation is misconceived or neglected is that which is the most important of all—involving, as it does, social organization, properly so called. The theory of social organization is still conceived of as absolute and isolated, independent altogether of the general analysis of the corresponding civilization, of which it can, in fact, constitute only one of the principal elements. This vice is chargeable in an almost equal degree upon the most opposite political schools, which agree in abstract discussions of political systems, without thinking of the coexisting state of civilization, and usually conclude with making their immutable political type coincide with an infantile state of human development. If we ascend to the philosophical source of this error, we shall find it, I think, in the great theological dogma of the Fall of Man. This fundamental dogma, which reappears, in one form or another, in all religions, and which is supported in its intellectual influence by the natural propensity of men to admire the past, tends, directly and necessarily, to make the continuous deterioration of society coincide with the extension of civilization. We have noticed before how, when it passes from the theological into the metaphysical state, this dogma takes the form of the celebrated hypothesis of a chimerical state of nature, superior to the social state, and the more remote, the farther we advance in civilization. We cannot fail to perceive the extreme seriousness, in a political as well as a philosophical sense, of an error so completely incorporated with existing doctrines, and so deeply influencing, in an unconscious way, our collective social speculations—the more disastrously, perhaps, for not being expressly maintained as a general principle. If it were so presented, it must immediately give way before sound philosophical discussion; for it is in direct contradiction to many ideas in political philosophy which, without having attained any scientific consistency, are obtaining some intellectual ascendancy, through the natural course of events or the expansion of the general mind.

POLITICAL AND SOCIAL CONCURRENCE

FOR instance, all enlightened political writers acknowledge more or less mutual relation between political institutions; and this is the first direct step toward the rational conception of the agreement of the special system of institutions with the total system of civilization. We now see the best thinkers admitting a constant mutual connection between the political and the civil power: which means, in scientific language, that preponderating social forces always end in assuming the direction of society. Such partial advances toward a right view—such fortunate feeling after the right path, must not, however, induce us to relax in our requirements of a true philosophical conception of that general social agreement which can alone constitute organization. Desultory indications, more literary than scientific, can never supply the place of a strict philosophical doctrine, as we may see from the fact that, from Aristotle downward (and even from an earlier period), the greater number of philosophers have constantly reproduced the famous aphorism of the necessary subordination of laws to manners, without this germ of sound philosophy having had any effect on the general habit of regarding institutions as independent of the coexisting state of civilization—however strange it may seem that such a contradiction should live through twenty centuries. This is, however, the natural course with intellectual principles and philosophical opinions, as well as with social manners and political institutions. When once they have obtained possession of men's minds, they live on, notwithstanding their admitted impotence and inconvenience, giving occasion to more and more serious inconsistencies, till the expansion of human reason originates new principles, of equivalent generality and superior rationality. We must not therefore take for more than their worth the desultory attempts that we see made in the right direction, but must insist on the principle which lies at the heart of every scheme of social organization—the necessary participation of the collective political regime in the universal consensus of the social body.

The scientific principle of the relation between the political and the social condition is simply this—that there must always be a spontaneous harmony between the whole and the parts of the social system, the elements of which must inevitably be, sooner or later, combined in a mode entirely conformable to their nature. It is evident that not only must political institutions and social manners on the one hand, and manners and ideas on the other, be always mutually connected; but, further, that this consolidated whole must be always connected, by its nature, with the corresponding state of the integral development of humanity, considered in all its aspects, of intellectual, moral, and physical activity: and the only object of any political system whatever, temporal or spiritual, is to regulate the spontaneous expansion so as best to direct it toward its determinate end. Even during revolutionary periods, when the harmony appears furthest from being duly realized, it still exists; for without it there would be a total dissolution of the social organism. During those exceptional seasons, the political regime is still, in the long run, in conformity with the corresponding state of civilization, as the disturbances which are manifest in the one proceed from equivalent derangements in the other. It is observable that when the popular theory attributes to the legislator the permanent power of infringing the harmony we are speaking of, it supposes him to be armed with a sufficient authority. But every social power, whether called authority or anything else, is constituted by a corresponding assent, spontaneous or deliberate, explicit or implicit, of various individual wills, resolved from certain preparatory convictions, to concur in a common action, of which this power is first the organ and then the regulator. Thus, authority is derived from concurrence, and not concurrence from authority (setting aside the necessary reaction), so that no great power can arise otherwise than from the strongly prevalent disposition of the society in which it exists; and when there is no strong preponderance, such powers as exist are weak accordingly; and the more extensive the society, the more irresistible is the correspondence. On the other hand, there is no denying the influence which, by a neecssary reaction, the political system, as a whole, exercises over the general system of civilization and which is so often exhibited in the action, fortunate or disastrous, of institutions, measures, or purely political events, even upon the course of the sciences and arts, in all ages of society, and especially the earliest. We need not dwell on this, for no one denies it. The common error, indeed, is to exaggerate it, so as to place the reaction before the primary action. It is evident, considering their scientific relation to each other, that both concur in creating that fundamental agreement of the social organism which I propose to set forth in a brief manner, as the philosophical principle of statical sociology.

We shall have to advert repeatedly to the subject of the general correspondence between the political regime and the contemporary state of civilization, in connection with the question of the necessary limits of political action, and in the chapter which I must devote to social statics; but I did not think fit to wait for these explanations before pointing out that the political system ought always to be regarded as relative. The relative point of view, substituted for the absolute tendency of the ordinary theories, certainly constitutes the chief scientific character of the positive philosophy in its political application. If, on the one hand, the conception of this connection between government and civilization presents all ideas of political good or evil as necessarily relative and variable (which is quite another thing than being arbitrary), on the other hand, it provides a rational basis for a positive theory of the spontaneous order of human society, already vaguely perceived, in regard to some minor relations, by that part of the metaphysical polity which we call political economy; for, if the value of any political system can consist in nothing but its harmony with the corresponding social state, it follows that in the natural course of events, and in the absence of intervention, such a harmony must necessarily be established.

INTERCONNECTION OF THE SOCIAL ORGANIZATION

THERE are two principal considerations which induce me to insist on this elementary idea of the radical consensus proper to the social organism: first, the extreme philosophical importance of this master thought of social statics, which must, from its nature, constitute the rational basis of any new political philosophy; and, second, in an accessory way, that dynamical considerations of sociology must prevail throughout the rest of this work, as being at present more interesting, and therefore better understood; and it is, on that account, the more necessary to characterize now the general spirit of social statics, which will henceforth be treated only in an indirect and implicit way. As all artificial and voluntary order is simply a prolongation of the natural and involuntary order to which all human society tends, every rational political institution must rest upon an exact preparatory analysis of corresponding spontaneous tendencies, which alone can furnish a sufficiently solid basis. In brief, it is our business to contemplate order, that we may perfect it; and not to create it, which would be impossible. In a scientific view, this master thought of universal social interconnection becomes the consequence and complement of a fundamental idea established, in our view of biology, as eminently proper to the study of living bodies. Not that this idea of interconnection is peculiar to that study: it is necessarily common to all phenomena; but amidst immense differences in intensity and variety, and therefore in philosophical importance. It is, in fact, true that wherever there is any system whatever, a certain interconnection must exist. The purely mechanical phenomena of astronomy offer the first suggestion of it; for the perturbations of one planet may sensibly affect another, through a modified gravitation. But the relation becomes closer and more marked in proportion to the complexity and diminished generality of the phenomena, and thus it is in organic systems that we must look for the fullest mutual connection. Hitherto, it had been merely an accessory idea; but then it becomes the basis of positive conceptions; and as it becomes more marked, the more compound are the organisms, and the more complex the phenomena in question—the animal interconnection being more complete than the vegetable, and the human more than the brute, the nervous system being the chief seat of the biological interconnection. The idea must therefore be scientifically preponderant in social physics, even more than in biology, where it is so decisively recognized by the best order of students. But the existing political philosophy supposes the absence of any such interconnection among the aspects of society; and it is this which has rendered it necessary for me now to establish the point—leaving the illustration of it to a future portion of the volume. Its consideration is, in fact, as indispensable in assigning its encyclopedic rank to social science as we before saw it to be in instituting social physics as a science at all.

It follows from this attribute that there can be no scientific study of society, either in its conditions or its movements, if it is separated into portions and its divisions are studied apart. I have already remarked upon this, in regard to what is called political economy. Materials may be furnished by the observation of different departments; and such observation may be necessary for that object; but it can not be called science. The methodical division of studies which takes place in the simple inorganic sciences is thoroughly irrational in the recent and complex science of society, and can produce no results. The day may come when some sort of subdivision may be practicable and desirable; but it is impossible for us now to anticipate what the principle of distribution may be; for the principle itself must arise from the development of the science; and that development can take place no otherwise than by our formation of the science as a whole. The complete body will indicate for itself, at the right season, the particular points which need investigation; and then will be the time for such special study as may be required. By any other method of proceeding, we shall find ourselves encumbered only with special discussions, badly instituted, worse pursued, and accomplishing no purpose other than that of impeding the formation of real science. It is no easy matter to study social phenomena in the only right way—viewing each element in the light of the whole system. It is no easy matter to exercise such vigilance as that no one of the number of contemporary aspects shall be lost sight of. But it is the right and the only way; and we may perceive in it a clear suggestion that this lofty study should be reserved for the highest order of scientific minds, better prepared than others, by wise educational discipline, for sustained speculative efforts, aided by a habitual subordination of the passions to the reason. There is no need to draw out any lengthened comparison between this state of things as it should be and that which is. And no existing degree of social disturbance can surprise us when we consider how intellectual anarchy is at the bottom of such disturbance, and see how anarchical our intellectual condition appears in the presence of the principle I have laid down.

ORDER OF STATICAL STUDY

BEFORE we go on to the subject of social dynamics, I shall just remark that the prominent interconnection we have been considering prescribes a procedure in organic studies different from that which suits inorganic. The metaphysicians announce as an aphorism that we should always, in every kind of study, proceed from the simple to the compound: whereas it appears most rational to suppose that we should follow that or the reverse method, as may best suit our subject. There can be no absolute merit in the method enjoined, apart from its suitableness. The rule should rather be (and there probably was a time when the two rules were one) that we must proceed from the more known to the less. Now, in the inorganic sciences, the elements are much better known to us than to the whole which they constitute: so that in that case we must proceed from the simple to the compound. But the reverse method is necessary in the study of man and of society; man and society as a whole being better known to us, and more accessible subjects of study, than the parts which constitute them. In exploring the universe, it is as a whole that it is inaccessible to us; whereas in investigating man or society our difficulty is in penetrating the details. We have seen, in our survey of biology, that the general idea of animal nature is more distinct to our minds than the simpler notion of vegetable nature; and that man is the biological unity; the idea of man being at once the most compound, and the starting point of speculation in regard to vital existence. Thus, if we compare the two halves of natural philosophy, we shall find that in the one case it is the last degree of composition, and in the other the last degree of simplicity, that is beyond the scope of our research. As for the rest, it may obviate some danger of idle discussions to say that the positive philosophy, subordinating all fancies to reality, excludes logical controversies about the absolute value of this or that method, apart from its scientific application. The only ground of preference being the superior adaptation of any means to the proposed end, this philosophy may, without any inconsistency, change its order of proceeding when the one first tried is found to be inferior to its converse—a discovery of which there is no fear in regard to the question we have now been examining.

DYNAMICAL STUDY

PASSING on from statical to dynamical sociology, we shall contemplate the philosophical conception which should govern our study of the movement of society. Part of this subject is already dispatched, from the explanations made in connection with statics having simplified the chief difficulties of the case. And social dynamics will be so prominent throughout the rest of this work, that I may reduce within very small compass what I have to say now under that head.

Though the statical view of society is the basis of sociology, the dynamical view is not only the more interesting of the two but the more marked in its philosophical character from its being more distinguished from biology by the master thought of continuous progress, or rather, of the gradual development of humanity. If I were writing a methodical treatise

on political philosophy, it would be necessary to offer a preliminary analysis of the individual impulses which make up
the progressive force of the human race, by referring them
to that instinct which results from the concurrence of all our
natural tendencies and which urges man to develop the whole
of his life, physical, moral, and intellectual, as far as his
circumstances allow. But this view is admitted by all enlightened philosophers; so that I may proceed at once to
consider the continuous succession of human development,
regarded in the whole race, as if humanity were one. For
clearness, we may take advantage of Condorcet's device of
supposing a single nation to which we may refer all the consecutive social modifications actually witnessed among distinct
peoples. This rational fiction is nearer the reality than we are
accustomed to suppose; for, in a political view, the true successors of such or such a people are certainly those who,
taking up and carrying out their primitive endeavors, have
prolonged their social progress, whatever may be the soil
which they inhabit, or even the race from which they spring.
In brief, it is political continuity which regulates sociological
succession, though the having a common country must usually
affect this continuity in a high degree. As a scientific artifice
merely, however, I shall employ this hypothesis, and on the
ground of its manifest utility.

SOCIAL CONTINUITY

THE true general spirit of social dynamics then consists in
conceiving of each of these consecutive social states as the
necessary result of the preceding, and the indispensable
mover of the following, according to the axiom of Leibniz—
The present is big with the future. In this view, the object of
science is to discover the laws which govern this continuity,
and the aggregate of which determines the course of human
development. In short, social dynamics studies the laws of
succession, while social statics inquires into those of coexistence; so that the use of the first is to furnish the true theory
of progress to political practice, while the second performs
the same service in regard to order; and this suitability to the
needs of modern society is a strong confirmation of the philosophical character of such a combination.

PRODUCE BY NATURAL LAWS

IF the existence of sociological laws has been established in
the more difficult and uncertain case of the statical condition,

we may assume that they will not be questioned in the dynamical province. In all times and places, the ordinary course of even our brief individual life has disclosed certain remarkable modifications which have occurred, in various ways, in the social state; and all the most ancient representations of human life bear unconscious and most interesting testimony to this, apart from all systematic estimate of the fact. Now, it is the slow, continuous accumulation of these successive changes which gradually constitutes the social movement, whose steps are ordinarily marked by generations, as the most appreciable elementary variations are wrought by the constant renewal of adults. At a time when the average rapidity of this progression seems to all eyes to be remarkably accelerated, the reality of the movement can not be disputed, even by those who most abhor it. The only question is about the constant subjection of these great dynamical phenomena to invariable natural laws, a proposition about which there is no question to anyone who takes his stand on positive philosophy. It is easy, however, to establish, from any point of view, that the successive modifications of society have always taken place in a determinate order, the rational explanation of which is already possible in so many cases that we may confidently hope to recognize it ultimately in all the rest. So remarkable is the steadiness of this order, moreover, that it exhibits an exact parallelism of development among distinct and independent populations, as we shall see when we come to the historical portion of this volume. Since, then, the existence of the social movement is unquestionable on the one hand, and on the other the succession of social states is never arbitrary, we cannot but regard this continuous phenomenon as subject to natural laws as positive as those which govern all other phenomena, though more complex. There is in fact no intellectual alternative; and thus it is evident that it is on the ground of social science that the great conflict must soon terminate which has gone on for three centuries between the positive and the theologico-metaphysical spirit. Banished forever from all other classes of speculation, in principle at least, the old philosophies now prevail in social science alone; and it is from this domain that they have to be excluded, by the conception of the social movement being subject to invariable natural laws, instead of to any will whatever.

Though the fundamental laws of social interconnection are especially verified in this condition of movement, and though there is a necessary unity in this phenomenon, it may be use-

fully applied, for preparatory purposes, to the separate elementary aspects of human existence, physical, moral, intellectual and, finally, political—their mutual relation being kept in
view. Now, in whichever of these ways we regard, as a
whole, the movement of humanity, from the earliest periods
till now, we shall find that the various steps are connected
in a determinate order; as we shall hereafter see, when we
investigate the laws of this succession. I need refer here only
to the intellectual evolution, which is the most distinct and
unquestionable of all, as it has been the least impeded and
most advanced of any, and has therefore been usually taken
for guidance. The chief part of this evolution, and that which
has most influenced the general progression, is no doubt the
development of the scientific spirit, from the primitive labors
of such philosophers as Thales and Pythagoras to those of
men like Lagrange and Bichat. Now, no enlightened man can
doubt that, in this long succession of efforts and discoveries,
the human mind has pursued a determinate course, the exact
preparatory knowledge of which might have allowed a cultivated reason to foresee the progress proper to each period.
Though the historical considerations cited in previous pages
were only incidental, anyone may recognize in them numerous
and indisputable examples of this neecssary succession, more
complex perhaps, but not more arbitrary than any natural
law, whether in regard to the development of each separate
science, or to the mutual influence of the different branches
of natural philosophy. In accordance with the principles laid
down at the beginning of this work, we have already seen, in
various signal instances, that the chief progress of each
period, and even generation, was a necessary result of the
immediately preceding state; so that the men of genius, to
whom such progression has been too exclusively attributed,
are essentially only the proper organs of a predetermined
movement which would, in their absence, have found other
issues. We find a verification of this in history, which shows
that various eminent men were ready to make the same great
discovery at the same time, while the discovery required only
one organ. All the parts of the human evolution admit of
analogous observations, as we shall presently see, though they
are more complex and less obvious that that which I have just
cited. The natural progression of the arts of life is abundantly
evident; and in our direct study of social dynamics we shall
find an explanation of the apparent exception of the fine arts,
which will be found to oppose no contradiction to the general

course of human progression. As to that part of the movement which appears at present to be at least reducible to natural laws, the political movement (still supposed to be governed by wills of adequate power), it is as clear as in any other case that political systems have exhibited a historical succession, according to a traceable filiation, in a determinate order, which I am prepared to show to be even more inevitable than that of the different states of human intelligence.

The interconnection which we have examined and established in a statical view may aid us in developing the conception of the existence of positive laws in social dynamics. Unless the movement was determined by those laws, it would occasion the entire destruction of the social system. Now, that interconnection simplifies and strengthens the preparatory indications of dynamic order; for, when it has once been shown in any relation, we are authorized to extend it to all others; and this unites all the partial proofs that we can successively obtain of the reality of this scientific conception. In the choice and the application of these verifications, we must remember that the laws of social dynamics are most recognizable when they relate to the largest societies, in which secondary disturbances have the smallest effect. Again, these fundamental laws become the more irresistible, and therefore the more appreciable, in proportion to the advancement of the civilization upon which they operate, because the social movement becomes more distinct and certain with every conquest over accidental influences. As for the philosophical coordination of these preparatory evidences, the combination of which is important to science, it is clear that the social evolution must be more inevitably subject to natural laws, the more compound are the phenomena, and the less perceptible, therefore, the irregularities which arise from individual influences. This shows how inconsistent it is, for instance, to suppose the scientific movement to be subject to positive laws, while the political movement is regarded as arbitrary; for the latter, being more composite, must overrule individual disturbances, and be therefore more evidently predetermined than the former, in which individual genius must have more power. Any paradoxical appearance which this statement may exhibit will disappear in the course of further examination.

If I confined myself strictly to a scientific view, I might satisfy myself with proving the fact of social progression, without taking any notice of the question of human perfectibility. But so much time and effort are wasted in groundless speculation on that interesting question, argued as it is on the supposition that political events are arbitrarily determined, that it may be as well to notice it in passing; and the more, because it may serve as a natural transition to the estimate of the limits of political action.

NOTION OF HUMAN PERFECTIBILITY

WE have nothing to do here with the metaphysical controversy about the absolute happiness of man at different stages of civilization. As the happiness of every man depends on the harmony between the development of his various faculties and the entire system of the circumstances which govern his life; and as, on the other hand, this equilibrium always establishes itself spontaneously to a certain extent, it is impossible to compare in a positive way, either by sentiment or reasoning, the individual welfare which belongs to social situations that can never be brought into direct comparison; and therefore the question of the happiness of different animal organisms, or of their two sexes, is merely impracticable and unintelligible. The only question, therefore, is of the effect of the social evolution, which is so undeniable that there is no reasoning with anyone who does not admit it as the basis of the inquiry. The only ground of discussion is whether development and improvement—the theoretical and the practical aspect—are one; whether the development is necessarily accompanied by a corresponding amelioration, or progress, properly so called. To me it appears that the amelioration is as unquestionable as the development from which it proceeds, provided we regard it as subject, like the development itself, to limits, general and special, which science will be found to prescribe. The chimerical notion of unlimited perfectibility is thus at once excluded. Taking the human race as a whole, and not any one people, it appears that human development brings after it, in two ways, an ever-growing amelioration, first, in the radical condition of man, which no one disputes; and next, in his corresponding faculties, which is a view much less attended to. There is no need to dwell upon the improvement in the conditions of human existence, both by the increasing action of man on his environment through the advancement of the sciences and arts, and by the constant amelioration of his customs and manners; and again, by the gradual improvement in social organization. We shall presently see that in the Middle Ages, which are charged with political retrogression, the progress was more political than any other. One fact is enough to silence sophistical declamation on this subject; the continuous increase of population all over the globe, as a consequence of civilization, while the wants of individuals are, as a whole, better satisfied at the same time. The tendency to improvement must be highly spontaneous and irresistible to have persevered notwithstanding the enormous faults—political faults especially—which have at all times absorbed or neutralized the greater part of our social forces. Even throughout the revolutionary period, in spite of the marked discordance between the political system and the general state of civilization, the improvement has proceeded not only in physical and intellectual, but also in moral, respects, though the transient disorganization could not but disturb the natural evolution. As for the other aspect of the question, the gradual and slow improvement of human nature, within narrow limits, it seems to me impossible to reject altogether the principle proposed (with great exaggeration, however) by Lamarck, of the necessary influence of a homogeneous and continuous exercise in producing, in every animal organism, and especially in man, an organic improvement, susceptible of being established in the race, after a sufficient persistence. If we take the best-marked case—that of intellectual development, it seems to be unquestionable that there is a superior aptitude for mental combinations, independent of all culture, among highly civilized people; or, what comes to the same thing, an inferior aptitude among nations that are less advanced—the average intellect of the members of those societies being taken for observation. The intellectual faculties are, it is true, more modified than the others by the social evolution; but then they have the smallest relative effect in the individual human constitution, so that we are authorized to infer from their amelioration a proportionate improvement in aptitudes that are more marked and equally exercised. In regard to morals, particularly, I think it indisputable that the gradual development of humanity favors a growing preponderance of the noblest tendencies of our nature—as I hope to prove further on. The lower instincts continue to manifest themselves in modified action, but their less sustained and more repressed exercise must tend to debilitate them by degrees; and their increasing regulation certainly brings them into involuntary concurrence in the maintenance of a good social economy; and especially in the case of the least marked organisms, which constitute a vast majority. These two aspects of social evolution, then—the *development* which brings after it the *improvement*—we may consider to be admitted as facts.

Adhering to our relative, in opposition to the absolute, view, we must conclude the social state, regarded as a whole, to have been as perfect, in each period, as the coexisting condition of humanity and of its environment would allow. Without this view, history would be incomprehensible; and the relative view is as indispensable in regard to progress as, in considering social statics, we saw it to be in regard to order. If, in a statical view, the various social elements can not but maintain a spontaneous harmony, which is the first principle of order, neither can any of them help being as advanced, at any period, as the whole system of influences permits. In either case, the harmony and the movement are the result of invariable natural laws which produce all phenomena whatever, and are more obscure in social science merely on account of the greater complexity of the phenomena concerned.

LIMITS OF POLITICAL ACTION

AND now occurs, as the last aspect of social dynamics, the question of the general limits of political action. No enlightened man can be blind to the necessary existence of such limits, which can be ignored only on the old theological supposition of the legislator being merely the organ of a direct and continuous Providence, which admits of no limits. We need not stop to confute that hypothesis, which has no existence but in virtue of ancient habits of thought. In any case, human action is very limited, in spite of all aids from concurrence and ingenious methods; and it is difficult to perceive why social action should be exempt from this restriction, which is an inevitable consequence of the existence of natural laws. Through all the self-assertions of human pride, every statesman of experience knows well the reality of the bounds prescribed to political action by the aggregate of social influences, to which he must attribute the failure of the greater number of the projects which he had secretly cherished; and perhaps the conviction is most thorough, while most carefully hidden, in the mind of the most powerful of statesmen, because his inability to struggle against natural laws must be decisive in proportion to his implication with them. Seeing that social science would be impossible in the absence of this principle, we need not dwell further upon it, but may proceed to ascertain the fitness of the new political philosophy to determine, with all the precision that the subject admits, what is the nature of their limits, general or special, permanent or temporary.

Two questions are concerned here: first, in what way the course of human development may be affected by the aggregate of causes of variation which may be applied to it; and next, what share the voluntary and calculated action of our political combinations may have among these modifying influences. The first question is by far the most important, both because it is a general principle, which the second is not, and because it is fully accessible, which, again, the second is not.

SOCIAL PHENOMENA MODIFIED

WE must observe, in the first place, that social phenomena may, from their complexity, be more easily modified than any others, according to the law which was established to that effect on preceding pages. Thus, the limits of variation are wider in regard to sociological than any other laws. If, then, human intervention holds the same proportionate rank among modifying influences as it is natural at first to suppose, its influence must be more considerable in the first case than in the other, all appearances to the contrary notwithstanding. This is the first scientific foundation of all rational hopes of a systematic reformation of humanity; and on this ground illusions of this sort certainly appear more excusable than on any other subject. But though modifications, from all causes, are greater in the case of political than of simpler phenomena, still they can never be more than modifications: that is, they will always be in subjection to those fundamental laws, whether statical or dynamical, which regulate the harmony of the social elements, and the filiation of their successive variations. There is no disturbing influence, exterior or human, which can make incompatible elements coexist in the political system, nor change in any way the natural laws of the development of humanity. The inevitable gradual preponderance of continuous influences, however imperceptible their power may be at first, is now admitted with regard to all natural phenomena; and it must be applied to social phenomena, whenever the same method of philosophizing is extended to them. What, then, are the modifications of which the social organism and social life are susceptible, if nothing can alter the laws either of harmony or of succession? The answer is that modifications act upon the intensity and secondary operation of phenomena, but without affecting their nature or their filiation. To suppose that they could would be to exalt the disturbing above the fundamental cause, and would destroy the whole economy of laws. In the political system this principle of positive philosophy shows that, in a statical view, any possible variations can affect only the intensity of the different tendencies belonging to each social situation, without in any way hindering or producing, or, in a word, changing the nature of, those tendencies; and in the same way, in a dynamical view, the progress of the race must be considered susceptible of modification only with regard to its speed, and without any reversal in the order of development, or any interval of any importance being overleaped. These variations are analogous to those of the animal organism, with the one difference that in sociology they are more complex; and, as we saw that the limits of variation remain to be established in biology, it is not to be expected that sociology should be more advanced. But all we want here is to obtain a notion of the general spirit of the law, in regard both to social statics and dynamics; and looking at it from both points of view, it seems to me impossible to question its truth. In the intellectual order of phenomena, for instance, there is no accidental influence, nor any individual superiority, which can transfer to one period the discoveries reserved for a subsequent age, in the natural course of the human mind; nor can there be the reverse case of postponement. The history of the sciences settles the question of the close dependence of even the most eminent individual genius on the contemporary state of the human mind; and this is above all remarkable in regard to the improvement of methods of investigation, either in the way of reasoning or experiment. The same thing happens in regard to the arts; and especially in whatever depends on mechanical means in substitution for human action. And there is not, in reality, any more room for doubt in the case of moral development, the character of which is certainly determined, in each period, by the corresponding state of the social evolution, whatever may be the modifications caused by education or individual organization. Each of the leading modes of social existence determines for itself a certain system of morals and manners, the common aspect of which is easily recognized in all individuals, in the midst of their characteristic differences;

for instance, there is a state of human life in which the best individual natures contract a habit of ferocity, from which very inferior natures easily emancipate themselves, in a better state of society. The case is the same, in a political point of view, as our historical analysis will hereafter show. And in fact, if we were to review all the facts and reflections which establish the existence of the limits of variation, whose principle I have just laid down, we should find ourselves reproducing in succession all the proofs of the subjection of social phenomena to invariable laws; because the principle is neither more nor less than a strict application of the philosophical conception.

ORDER OF MODIFYING INFLUENCES

WE cannot enlarge upon the second head: that is the classification of modifying influences according to their respective importance. If such a classification is not yet established in biology, it would be premature indeed to attempt it in social science. Thus, if the three chief causes of social variation appear to me to result from, first, race; second, climate; third, political action in its whole scientific extent, it would answer none of our present purposes to inquire here whether this or some other is the real order of their importance. The political influences are the only ones really open to our intervention; and to that head general attention must be directed, though with great care to avoid the conclusion that that class of influences must be the most important because it is the most immediately interesting to us. It is owing to such an illusion as this that observers who believe themselves emancipated from old prejudices cannot obtain sociological knowledge, because they enormously exaggerate the power of political action. Because political operations, temporal or spiritual, can have no social efficacy but inasfar as they are in accordance with the corresponding tendencies of the human mind, they are supposed to have produced what is in reality occasioned by a spontaneous evolution, which is less conspicuous, and easily overlooked. Such a mistake proceeds in neglect of numerous and marked cases in history, in which the most prodigious political authority has left no lasting traces of its well-sustained development, because it moved in a contrary direction to modern civilization; as in the instances of Julian, of Philip II, of Napoleon Bonaparte, and so on. The inverse cases, unhappily too few, are still more decisive: those cases in which political action, sustained by an equally powerful authority, has nevertheless failed in the pursuit of ameliorations that were premature, though in accordance with the social movement of the time. Intellectual history, as well as political, furnishes examples of this kind in abundance. It has been sensibly remarked by Fergusson, that even the action of one nation upon another, whether by conquest or otherwise, though the most intense of all social forces, can effect merely such modifications as are in accordance with its existing tendencies; so that, in fact, the action merely accelerates or extends a development which would have taken place without it. In politics, as in science, *opportuneness* is always the main condition of all great and durable influence, whatever may be the personal value of the superior man to whom the multitude attribute social action of which he is merely the fortunate organ. The power of the individual over the race is subject to these general limits, even when the effects, for good or for evil, are as easy as possible to produce. In revolutionary times, for instance, those who are proud of having aroused anarchical passions in their contemporaries do not see that their miserable triumph is due to a spontaneous disposition, determined by the aggregate of the corresponding social state, which has produced a provisional and partial relaxation of the general harmony. As for the rest, it being ascertained that there are limits of variation among social phenomena, and modifications dependent on systematic political action, and as the scientific principle which is to describe such modifications is now known, the influence and scope of that principle must be determined in each case by the direct development of social science, applied to the appreciation of the corresponding state of circumstances. It is by such estimates, empirically attempted, that men of genius have been guided in all great and profound action upon humanity in any way whatever; and it is only thus that they have been able to rectify, in a rough way, the illusory suggestions of the irrational doctrines in which they were educated. Everywhere, as I have so often said, foresight is the true source of action.

The inaccurate intellectual habits which as yet prevail in political philosophy may induce an apprehension that, according to such considerations as those just presented, the new science of social physics may reduce us to mere observation of human events, excluding all continuous intervention. It is, however, certain that, while dissipating all ambitious illusions about the indefinite action of man on civilization, the principle of rational limits to political action establishes, in the most exact and unquestionable manner, the true point of contact between social theory and practice. It is by this principle only that political art can assume a systematic character, by its release from arbitrary principles mingled with empirical notions. It is thus only that political art can pass upward as medical art has done, the two cases being strongly analogous. As political intervention can have no efficacy unless it rests on corresponding tendencies of the political organism or life, so as to aid its spontaneous development, it is absolutely necessary to understand the natural laws of harmony and succession which determine, in every period, and under every social aspect, what the human evolution is prepared to produce, pointing out, at the same time, the chief obstacles which may be got rid of. It would be exaggerating the scope of such an art to suppose it capable of obviating, in all cases, the violent disturbances which are occasioned by impediments to the natural evolution. In the highly complex social organism, maladies and crises are necessarily even more inevitable than in the individual organism. But, though science is powerless for the moment amid wild disorder and extravagance, it may palliate and abridge the crises, by understanding their character and foreseeing their issue, and by more or less intervention, where any is possible. Here, as in other cases, and more than in other cases, the office of science is, not to govern, but to modify phenomena; and to do this, it is necessary to understand their laws.

Thus, then, we see what is the function of social science. Without extolling or condemning political facts, science regards them as subjects of observation: it contemplates each phenomenon in its harmony with coexisting phenomena, and in its connection with the foregoing and the following state of human development; it endeavors to discover, from both points of view, the general relations which connected all social phenomena; and each of them is *explained*, in the scientific sense of the word, when it has been connected with the whole of the existing situation, and the whole of the preceding movement. Favoring the social sentiment in the highest degree, this science fulfills the famous suggestion of Pascal, by representing the whole human race, past, present, and future, as constituting a vast and eternal social unit, whose different organs, individual and national, concur, in their various modes and degrees, in the evolution of humanity. Leading us on, like every other science, with as much exactness as the extreme complexity of its phenomena allows, to a systematic prevision of the events which must result from either a given situation or a given aggregate of antecedents, political science enlightens political art, not only in regard to the tendencies which should be aided, but as to the chief means that should be employed, so as to avoid all useless or ephemeral and therefore dangerous action; in short, all waste of any kind of social force.

MEANS OF INVESTIGATION

THIS examination of the general spirit of political philosophy has been much more difficult than the same process in regard to any established science. The next step, now that this is accomplished, is to examine, according to my usual method, the means of investigation proper to social science. In virtue of a law before recognized, we may expect to find in sociology a more varied and developed system of resources than in any other, in proportion to the complexity of the phenomena, while yet, this extension of means does not compensate for the increased imperfection arising from the intricacy. The extension of the means is also more difficult to verify than in any prior case, from the novelty of the subject; and I can scarcely hope that such a sketch as I must present here will command such confidence as will arise when a complete survey of the science shall have confirmed what I now offer.

As social physics assumes a place in the hierarchy of sciences after all the rest and therefore dependent on them, its means of investigation must be of two kinds: those which are peculiar to itself, and which may be called direct, and those which arise from the connection of sociology with the other sciences; and these last, though indirect, are as indispensable as the first. I shall review, first, the direct resources of the science. Here, as in all the other cases, there are three methods of proceeding—by observation, experiment, and comparison.

OBSERVATION

VERY imperfect and even vicious notions prevail at present as to what observation can be and can effect in social science. The chaotic state of doctrine of the last century has extended to method; and amid our intellectual disorganization, difficulties have been magnified; precautionary methods, experimental and rational, have been broken up; and even the possibility of obtaining social knowledge by observation has been dogmatically denied; but if the sophisms put forth on this subject were true, they would destroy the certainty, not only of social science but of all the simpler and more perfect ones that have gone before. The ground of doubt assigned is the uncertainty of human testimony; but all the sciences, up to the most simple, require proofs of testimony; that is, in the elaboration of the most positive theories, we have to admit observations which could not be directly made, nor even repeated, by those who use them, and the reality of which rests only on the faithful testimony of the original investigators, there being nothing in this to prevent the use of such proofs, in concurrence with immediate observations. In astronomy, such a method is obviously necessary; it is equally, though less obviously, necessary even in mathematics; and of course much more evidently in the case of the more complex sciences. How could any science emerge from the nascent state—how could there be any organization of intellectual labor, even if research were restricted to the utmost, if everyone rejected all observations but his own? The stoutest advocates of historical skepticism do not go so far as to advocate this. It is only in the case of social phenomena that the paradox is proposed; and it is made use of there because it is one of the weapons of the philosophical arsenal which the revolutionary metaphysical doctrine constructed for the intellectual overthrow of the ancient political system. The next great hindrance to the use of observation is the empiricism which is introduced into it by those who, in the name of impartiality, would interdict the use of any theory whatever. No logical dogma could be more thoroughly irreconcilable with the spirit of the positive philosophy, or with its special character in regard to the study of social phenomena, than this. No real observation of any kind of phenomena is possible, except inasfar as it is first directed, and finally interpreted, by some theory: and it was this logical need which, in the infancy of human reason, occasioned the rise of theological philosophy, as we shall see in the course of our historical survey. The positive philosophy does not dissolve this obligation, but, on the contrary, extends and fulfills it more and more, the further the relations of phenomena are multiplied and perfected by it. Hence it is clear that, scientifically speaking, all isolated, empirical observation is idle, and even radically uncertain; that science can use only those observations which are connected, at least hypothetically, with some law; that it is such a connection which makes the chief difference between scientific and popular observation, embracing the same facts but contemplating them from different points of view; and that observations empirically conducted can at most supply provisional materials, which must usually undergo an ulterior revision. The rational method of observation becomes more necessary in proportion to the complexity of the phenomena, amid which the observer would not know what he ought to look at in the facts before his eyes, but for the guidance of a preparatory theory; and thus it is that by the connection of foregoing facts we learn to see the facts that follow. This is undisputed with regard to astronomical, physical, and chemical research, and in every branch of biological study, in which good observation of its highly complex phenomena is still very rare, precisely because its positive theories are very imperfect. Carrying on the analogy, it is evident that in the corresponding divisions, statical and dynamical, of social science, there is more need than anywhere else of theories which shall scientifically connect the facts that are happening with those that have happened; and the more we reflect, the more distinctly we shall see that in proportion as known facts are mutually connected we shall be better able, not only to estimate, but to perceive, those which are yet unexplored. I am not blind to the vast difficulty which this requisition imposes on the institution of positive sociology—obliging us to create at once, so to speak, observations and laws, on account of their indispensable connection, placing us in a sort of vicious circle from which we can issue only by employing in the first instance materials which are badly elaborated and doctrines which are ill-conceived. How I may succeed in a task so difficult and delicate, we shall see at its close; but, however that may be, it is clear that it is the absence of any positive theory which at present renders social observations so vague and incoherent. There can never be any lack of facts; for in this case even more than in others, it is the commonest sort of facts that are most important, whatever the collectors of secret anecdotes may think; but, though we are steeped to the lips in them, we can make no use of them, nor even be aware of them, for want of speculative guidance in examining them. The statical observation of a crowd of phenomena cannot take place without some notion, however elementary, of the laws of social interconnection; and dynami-

cal facts could have no fixed direction if they were not attached, at least by a provisional hypothesis, to the laws of
social development. The positive philosophy is very far from
discouraging historical or any other erudition; but the precious
night watchings, now so lost in the laborious acquisition of a
conscientious but barren learning, may be made available by
it for the constitution of true social science, and the increased
honor of the earnest minds that are devoted to it. The new
philosophy will supply fresh and nobler subjects, unhoped-for
insight, a loftier aim, and therefore a higher scientific dignity.
It will discard none but aimless labors, without principle and
without character; as in physics, there is no room for compi-
lations of empirical observations; and at the same time,
philosophy will render justice to the zeal of students of a
past generation, who, destitute of the favorable guidance
which we, of this day, enjoy, followed up their laborious
historical researches with an instinctive perseverance, and in
spite of the superficial disdain of the philosophers of the time.
No doubt the same danger attends research here as elsewhere: the danger that, from the continuous use of scientific
theories, the observer may sometimes pervert facts, by erroneously supposing them to verify some ill-grounded speculative prejudices of his own. But we have the same guard here
as elsewhere—in the further extension of the science; and the
case would not be improved by a recurrence to empirical
methods, which would be merely leaving theories that may be
misapplied but can always be rectified, for imaginary notions
which cannot be substantiated at all. Our feeble reason may
often fail in the application of positive theories; but at least
they transfer us from the domain of imagination to that of
reality, and expose us infinitely less than any other kind of
doctrine to the danger of seeing in facts that which is not.

It is now clear that social science requires, more than any
other, the subordination of observation to the statical and
dynamical laws of phenomena. No social fact can have any
scientific meaning till it is connected with some other social
fact; without which connection it remains a mere anecdote,
involving no rational utility. This condition so far increases the
immediate difficulty that good observers will be rare at first,
though more abundant than ever as the science expands; and
here we meet with another confirmation of what I said at the
outset of this volume—that the formation of social theories
should be confided only to the best-organized minds, prepared
by the most rational training. Explored by such minds, accord-

ing to rational views of coexistence and succession, social phenomena no doubt admit of much more varied and extensive means of investigation than phenomena of less complexity. In this view, it is not only the immediate inspection or direct description of events that affords useful means of positive exploration; but the consideration of apparently insignificant customs, the appreciation of various kinds of monuments, the analysis and comparison of languages, and a multitude of other resources. In short, a mind suitably trained becomes able by exercise to convert almost all impressions from the events of life into sociological indications, when once the connection of all indications with the leading ideas of the science is understood. This is a facility afforded by the mutual relation of the various aspects of society, which may partly compensate for the difficulty caused by that mutual connection: if it renders observation more difficult, it affords more means for its prosecution.

EXPERIMENT

It might be supposed beforehand that the second method of investigation, experiment, must be wholly inapplicable in social science; but we shall find that the science is not entirely deprived of this resource, though it must be one of inferior value. We must remember (what was before explained) that there are two kinds of experimentation—the direct and the indirect, and that it is not necessary to the philosophical character of this method that the circumstances of the phenomenon in question should be, as is vulgarly supposed in the learned world, artificially instituted. Whether the case be natural or factitious, experimentation takes place whenever the regular course of the phenomenon is interfered with in any determinate manner. The spontaneous nature of the alteration has no effect on the scientific value of the case, if the elements are known. It is in this sense that experimentation is possible in sociology. If direct experimentation had become too difficult amidst the complexities of biology, it may well be considered impossible in social science. Any artificial disturbance of any social element must affect all the rest, according to the laws both of coexistence and succession; and the experiment would therefore, if it could be instituted at all, be deprived of all scientific value, through the impossibility of isolating either the conditions or the results of the phenomenon. But we saw, in our survey of biology, that pathological cases are the true scientific equivalent of pure experimentation, and why. The same reasons apply, with even more force, to sociological researches. In them, pathological analysis consists in the examination of cases, unhappily too common, in which the natural laws, either of harmony or of succession, are disturbed by any causes, special or general, accidental or transient; as in revolutionary times especially, and above all, in our own. These disturbances are, in the social body, exactly analogous to diseases in the individual organism: and I have no doubt whatever that the analogy will be more evident (allowance being made for the unequal complexity of the organisms), the deeper the investigation goes. In both cases it is, as I said once before, a noble use to make of our reason, to disclose the real laws of our nature, individual or social, by the analysis of its sufferings. But if the method is imperfectly instituted in regard to biological questions, much more faulty must it be in regard to the phenomena of social science, for want even of the rational conceptions to which they are to be referred. We see the most disastrous political experiments forever renewed, with only some insignificant and irrational modifications, though their first operation should have fully satisfied us of the uselessness and danger of the expedients proposed. Without forgetting how much is ascribable to the influence of human passions, we must remember that the deficiency of an authoritative rational analysis is one of the main causes of the barrenness imputed to social experiments, the course of which would become much more instructive if it were better observed. The great natural laws exist and act in all conditions of the organism, for, as we saw in the case of biology, it is an error to suppose that they are violated or suspended in the case of disease; and we are therefore justified in drawing our conclusions, with due caution, from the scientific analysis of disturbance to the positive theory of normal existence. This is the nature and character of the indirect experimentation which discloses the real economy of the social body in a more marked manner than simple observation could do. It is applicable to all orders of sociological research, whether relating to existence or to movement, and regarded under any aspect whatever, physical, intellectual, moral, or political; and to all degrees of the social evolution, from which, unhappily, disturbances have never been absent. As for its present extension, no one can venture to offer any statement of it, because it has never been duly applied in any investigation in political philosophy, and it can become customary only by the institution of the new science which I am endeavoring to establish. But I could not omit this notice of it as one of the means of investigation proper to social science.

COMPARISON

As for the third of those methods, comparison, the reader must bear in mind the explanations offered in our survey of biological philosophy, of the reasons why the comparative method must prevail in all studies of which the living organism is the subject; and the more remarkably, in proportion to the rank of the organism. The same considerations apply in the present case, in a more conspicuous degree; and I may leave it to the reader to make the application, merely pointing out the chief differences which distinguish the use of the comparative method in sociological inquiries.

COMPARISON WITH INFERIOR ANIMALS

It is a very irrational disdain which makes us object to all comparison between human society and the social state of the lower animals. This unphilosophical pride arose out of the protracted influence of the theologico-metaphysical philosophy; and it will be corrected by the positive philosophy, when we better understand and can estimate the social state of the higher orders of mammifers, for instance. We have seen how important is the study of individual life, in regard to intellectual and moral phenomena—of which social phenomena are the natural result and complement. There was once the same blindness to the importance of the procedure in this case as now in the other; and as it has given way in the one case, so it will in the other. The chief defect in the kind of sociological comparison that we want is that it is limited to statical considerations; whereas the dynamical are, at the present time, the preponderant and direct subject of science. The restriction results from the social state of animals being, though not so stationary as we are apt to suppose, yet susceptible only of extremely small variations, in no way comparable to the continued progression of humanity in its feeblest days. But there is no doubt of the scientific utility of such a comparison, in the statical province, where it characterizes the elementary laws of social interconnection, by exhibiting their action in the most imperfect state of society, so as even to suggest useful inductions in regard to human society. There cannot be a stronger evidence of the natural character of the chief social relations, which some people fancy that they can transform at pleasure. Such sophists will cease to regard the great ties of the human family as factitious and arbitrary when they find them existing, with the same essential characteristics, among the animals, and more conspicuously, the nearer the organisms approach to the human type. In brief, in all that part of sociology which is almost one with intellectual and moral biology, or with the natural history of man; in all that relates to the first germs of the social relations, and the first institutions which were founded by the unity of the family or the tribe, there is not only great scientific advantage, but real philosophical necessity for employing the rational comparison of human with other animal societies. Perhaps it might even be desirable not to confine the comparison to societies which present a character of voluntary cooperation, in analogy to the human. They must always rank first in importance; but the scientific spirit, extending the process to its final logical term, might find some advantage in examining those strange associations, proper to the inferior animals, in which an involuntary cooperation results from an indissoluble organic union, either by simple adhesion or real continuity. If the science gained nothing by this extension, the method would. And there is nothing that can compare with such a habitual scientific comparison for the great service of casting out the absolute spirit which is the chief vice of political philosophy. It appears to me, moreover, that in a practical view the insolent pride which induces some ranks of society to suppose themselves as, in a manner, of another species than the rest of mankind is in close affinity with the irrational disdain that repudiates all comparison between human and other animal nature. However all this may be, these considerations apply only to a methodical and special treatment of social philosophy. Here, where I can offer only the first conception of the science, in which dynamical considerations must prevail, it is evident that I can make little use of the kind of comparison; and this makes it all the more necessary to point it out, lest its omission occasion such scientific inconveniences as I have just indicated. The commonest logical procedures are generally so characterized by their very application that nothing more of a preliminary nature is needed than the simplest examination of their fundamental properties.

COMPARISON OF COEXISTING STATES OF SOCIETY

To indicate the order of importance of the forms of society which are to be studied by the Comparative Method, I begin with the chief method, which consists in a comparison of the different coexisting states of human society on the various parts of the earth's surface—those states being completely independent of one another. By this method, the different stages of evolution may all be observed at once. Though the progression is single and uniform, in regard to the whole race, some very considerable and very various populations have, from causes which are little understood, attained extremely unequal degrees of development, so that the former states of the most civilized nations are now to be seen, amid some partial differences, among contemporary populations inhabiting different parts of the globe. In its relation to observation, this kind of comparison offers the advantage of being applicable both to statical and dynamical inquiries, verifying the laws of both, and even furnishing occasionally valuable direct inductions in regard to both. In the second place, it exhibits all possible degrees of social evolution to our immediate observation. From the wretched inhabitants of Tierra del Fuego to the most advanced nations of western Europe, there is no social grade which is not extant in some points of the globe, and usually in localities which are clearly apart. In the historical part of this work, we shall find that some interesting secondary phases of social development, of which the history of civilization leaves no perceptible traces, can be known only by this comparative method of study; and these are not, as might be supposed, the lowest degrees of evolution, which everyone admits can be investigated in no other way. And between the great historical aspects, there are numerous intermediate states which must be observed thus, if at all. This second part of the comparative method verifies the indications afforded by historical analysis, and fills up the gaps it leaves; and nothing can be more rational than the method, as it rests upon the established principle that the development of the human mind is uniform in the midst of all diversities of climate, and even of race, such diversities having no effect upon anything more than the rate of progress. But we must beware of the scientific dangers attending the process of comparison by this method. For instance, it can give us no idea of the order of succession, as it presents all the states of development as coexisting: so that, if the order of development were not established by other methods, this one would infallibly mislead us. And again, if we were not misled as to the order, there is nothing in this method which discloses the filiation of the different systems of society; a matter in which the most distinguished philosophers have been mistaken in various ways and degrees. Again, there is the danger of mistaking modifications for primary phases; as when social differences have been ascribed to the political influence of climate, instead of that inequality of evolution which is the real cause. Sometimes, but more rarely, the mistake is the other way. Indeed, there is nothing in the matter than can show which of two cases presents the diversity that is observed. We are in danger of the same mistake in regard to races; for, as the sociological comparison is instituted between peoples of different races, we are liable to confound the effects of race and of the social period. Again, climate comes in to offer a third source of interpretation of comparative phenomena, sometimes agreeing with, and sometimes contradicting the two others, thus multiplying the chances of error, and rendering the analysis which looked so promising almost impracticable. Here, again, we see the indispensable necessity of keeping in view the positive conception of human development as a whole. By this alone can we be preserved from such errors as I have referred to, and enriched by any genuine results of analysis. We see how absurd in theory and dangerous in practice are the notions and declamations of the empirical school, and of the enemies of all social speculation; for it is precisely in proportion to their elevation and generality that the ideas of positive social philosophy become real and effective—all illusion and uselessness belonging to conceptions which are too narrow and too special, in the departments either of science or of reasoning. But it is a consequence from these last considerations that this first sketch of sociological science, with the means of investigation that belong to it, rests immediately upon the primary use of a new method of observation, which is so appropriate to the nature of the phenomena as to be exempt from the dangers inherent in the others. This last portion of the Comparative Method is the Historical Method, properly so called; and it is the only basis on which the system of political logic can rest.

COMPARISON OF CONSECUTIVE STATES

THE historical comparison of the consecutive states of humanity is not only the chief scientific device of the new political philosophy. Its rational development constitutes the sub-stratum of the science, in whatever is essential to it. It is this which distinguishes it thoroughly from biological science, as we shall presently see. The positive principle of this separation results from the necessary influence of human generations upon the generations that follow, accumulating continuously till it constitutes the preponderating consideration in the direct study of social development. As long as this preponderance is not directly recognized, the positive study of humanity must appear a simple prolongation of the natural history of man: but this scientific character, suitable enough to the earlier generations, disappears in the course of the social evolution, and assumes at length a wholly new aspect, proper to sociological science, in which historical considerations are of immediate importance. And this preponderant use of the historical method gives its philosophical character to sociology in a logical as well as a scientific sense. By the creation of this new department of the Comparative Method, sociology confers a benefit on the whole of natural philosophy; because the positive method is thus completed and perfected, in a manner which, for scientific importance, is almost beyond our estimate. What we can now comprehend is that the His-torical Method verifies and applies, in the largest way, that chief quality of sociological science—its proceeding from the whole to the parts. Without this permanent condition of social study, all historical labor would degenerate into being a mere compilation of provisional materials. As it is in their development, especially, that the various social elements are interconnected and inseparable, it is clear that any partial filiation must be essentially untrue. Where, for instance, is the use of any exclusive history of any one science or art, un-less meaning is given to it by first connecting it with the study of human progress generally? It is the same in every direction, and especially with regard to political history, as it is called; as if any history could be other than political, more or less! The prevailing tendency to specialty in study would reduce history to a mere accumulation of unconnected delinea-tions, in which all idea of the true filiation of events would be lost amid the mass of confused descriptions. If the historical comparisons of the different periods of civilization are to have any scientific character, they must be referred to the general social evolution: and it is only thus that we can obtain the guiding ideas by which the special studies themselves must be directed.

In a practical view, it is evident that the preponderance of the Historical Method tends to develop the social sentiment, by giving us an immediate interest in even the earliest experiences of our race, through the influence that they exercised over the evolution of our own civilization. As Condorcet observed, no enlightened man can think of the battles of Marathon and Salamis without perceiving the importance of their consequences to the race at large. This kind of feeling should, when we are treating of science, be carefully distinguished from the sympathetic interest which is awakened by all delineations of human life—in fiction as well as in history. The sentiment I refer to is deeper, because in some sort personal; and more reflective, because it results from scientific conviction. It cannot be excited by popular history, in a descriptive form; but only by positive history, regarded as a true science, and exhibiting the events of human experience in coordinated series which manifest their own graduated connection. This new form of the social sentiment must at first be the privilege of the choice few; but it will be extended, somewhat weakened in force, to the whole of society, in proportion as the general results of social physics become sufficiently popular. It will fulfill the most obvious and elementary idea of the habitual connection between individuals and contemporary nations, by showing that the successive generations of men concur in a final end, which requires the determinate participation of each and all. This rational disposition to regard men of all times as fellow workers is as yet visible in the case of only the most advanced sciences. By the philosophical preponderance of the Historical Method, it will be extended to all the aspects of human life, so as to sustain, in a reflective temper, that respect for our ancestors which is indispensable to a sound state of society, and so deeply disturbed at present by the metaphysical philosophy.

As for the course to be pursued by this method—it appears to me that its spirit consists in the rational use of social series, that is, in a successive estimate of the different states of humanity which shall show the growth of each disposition, physical, intellectual, moral, or political, combined with the decline of the opposite disposition, whence we may obtain a scientific prevision of the final ascendency of the one and extinction of the other—care being taken to frame our conclusions according to the laws of human development. A considerable accuracy of prevision may thus be obtained, for any determinate period, and with any particular view; as historical analysis will indicate the direction of modifications, even in the most disturbed times. And it is worth noticing that the prevision will be nearest the truth in proportion as the phenomena in question are more important and more general; because then continuous causes are predominant in the social movement, and disturbances have less power. From these first general aspects, the same rational certainty may extend to secondary and special aspects, through their statical relations with the first; and thus we may obtain conclusions sufficiently accurate for the application of principles.

If we desire to familiarize ourselves with this Historical Method, we must employ it first upon the past, by endeavoring to deduce every well-known historical situation from the whole series of its antecedents. In every science we must have learned to predict the past, so to speak, before we can predict the future; because the first use of the observed relations among fulfilled facts is to teach us by the anterior succession what the future succession will be. No examination of facts can explain our existing state to us if we have not ascertained, by historical study, the value of the elements at work; and thus it is in vain that statesmen insist on the necessity of political observation, while they look no further than the present or a very recent past. The present is, by itself, purely, misleading, because it is impossible to avoid confounding principal with secondary facts, exalting conspicuous transient manifestations over fundamental tendencies, which are generally very quiet; and above all, supposing these powers, institutions, and doctrines, to be in the ascendant, which are, in fact, in their decline. It is clear that the only adequate corrective of all this is a philosophical understanding of the past; that the comparison cannot be decisive unless it embraces the whole of the past; and that the sooner we stop, in travelling up the vista of time, the more serious will be the mistakes we fall into. Before our very eyes, we see statesmen going no farther back than the last century, to obtain an explanation of the confusion in which we are living; the most abstract of politicians may take in the preceding century, but the philosophers themselves hardly venture beyond the sixteenth; so that those who are striving to find the issue of the revolutionary period have actually no conception of it as a whole, though that whole is itself only a transient phase of the general social movement.

The most perfect methods may, however, be rendered deceptive by misuse: and this we must bear in mind. We have seen that mathematical analysis itself may betray us into substituting signs for ideas, and that it conceals inanity of conception under an imposing verbiage. The difficulty in the case of the Historical Method in sociology is in applying it, on account of the extreme complexity of the materials we have to deal with. But for this, the method would be entirely safe. The chief danger is of our supposing a continuous decrease to indicate a final extinction, or the reverse; as in mathematics it is a common sophism to confound continuous variations, more or less, with unlimited variations. To take a strange and very marked example: if we consider that part of social development which relates to human food, we cannot but observe that men take less food as they advance in civilization. If we compare savage with more civilized peoples, in the Homeric poems or in the narratives of travelers, or compare country with town life, or any generation with the one that went before, we shall find this curious result—the sociological law of which we shall examine hereafter. The laws of individual human nature aid in the result by making intellectual and moral action more preponderant as man becomes more civilized. The fact is thus established, both by the experimental and the logical way. Yet nobody supposes that men will ultimately cease to eat. In this case, the absurdity saves us from a false conclusion; but in other cases, the complexity disguises much error in the experiment and the reasoning. In the above instance, we must resort to the laws of our nature for that verification which, taken all together, they afford to our sociological analysis. As the social phenomenon, taken as a whole, is simply a development of humanity, without any real creation of faculties, all social manifestations must be to be found, if only in their germ, in the primitive type which biology constructed by anticipation for sociology. Thus every law of social succession disclosed by the Historical Method must be unquestionably connected, directly or indirectly, with the positive theory of human nature; and all inductions which cannot stand this test will prove to be illusory, through some sort of insufficiency in the observations on which they are founded. The main scientific strength of sociological demonstrations must ever lie in the accordance between the conclusions of historical analysis and the preparatory conceptions of the biological theory. And thus we find, look where we will, a confirmation of that chief intellectual character of the new science—the philosophical preponderance of the spirit of the whole over the spirit of detail.

COMPARISON OF A FOURTH METHOD

THIS method ranks, in sociological science, with that of
zoological comparison in the study of individual life; and we
shall see, as we proceed, that the succession of social states
exactly corresponds, in a scientific sense, with the gradation
of organisms in biology; and the social series, once clearly
established, must be as real and as useful as the animal
series. When the method has been used long enough to disclose its properties, I am disposed to think that it will be regarded as so very marked a modification of positive research
as to deserve a separate place; so that, in addition to observation, properly so called, experiment, and comparison, we shall
have the Historical Method, as a fourth and final mode of
the art of observing. It will be derived, according to the usual
course, from the mode which immediately precedes it, and it
will be applied to the analysis of the most complex
phenomena.

I must be allowed to point out that the new political
philosophy, sanctioning the old leadings of popular reason,
restores to history all its scientific rights as a basis of wise
social speculation, after the metaphysical philosophy had
striven to induce us to discard all large consideration of the
past. In the foregoing departments of natural philosophy, we
have seen that the positive spirit, instead of being disturbing
in its tendencies, is remarkable for confirming, in the essential
parts of every science, the inestimable intuitions of popular
good sense; of which indeed science is merely a systematic
prolongation, and which a barren metaphysical philosophy
alone could despise. In this case, so far from restricting the
influence which human reason has ever attributed to history
in political combinations, the new social philosophy increases
it, radically and eminently. It asks from history something
more than counsel and instruction to perfect conceptions
which are derived from another source: it seeks its own
general direction, through the whole system of historical
conclusions. . . .

Karl Marx
(1818–1883)

AN ANALYSIS OF CLASS

Karl Marx was born in the little Rhenish town of Trier in the Rhineland. Although his parents were Jewish by birth, the whole family was converted to Christianity when Marx was six years old. As a result, Marx grew up without any consciousness of himself as a Jew. Marx studied at the universities of Bonn and Berlin, and it was especially at Berlin that he became influenced by the thoughts of the young Hegelians. His main fields of study were philology, theology, and law. In 1841 he received his doctorate from the University of Jena for a dissertation on the philosophies of Democritus and Epicurus. Immediately after, in 1842, Marx became the editor of the Reinische Zeitung. After his paper was suppressed in 1843 he moved with his wife, whom he had married in the same year, to Paris.

In Paris he met Friedrich Engels who became a lifelong friend. Engels not only helped Marx financially, but also was instrumental in shaping and developing Marx's ideas. In a few years Marx was exiled to Brussels and there joined the Communist League. It was there that Marx wrote his famous Communist Manifesto. Both Marx and Engels were involved in the revolution of 1848, at which time Marx edited the Neue Rheinische Zeitung. He finally settled down in London and devoted himself to writing and research. He wrote Das Kapital and various other works in London, and for a long time he was the European correspondent for the then socialistic New York Tribune.

The impact of Marxist philosophy on the political and social thinking of the Western world in the nineteenth and twentieth centuries has been very great. His influence on contemporary social science is unquestionable, and his theories of class are still a significant part of contemporary sociological theory. American social scientists such as Veblen, Beard, Ward, and Sumner all were influenced by Marx's ideas. Lewis S. Feuer has written:

"The faith of these Americans in the ordinary man, in the

underlying population, was also the messianic socialist one; their faith in science as the method of liberation and their belief in the primacy of the economic factor in human history were as powerful as Marx's."[1]

Marx undoubtedly emphasized the economic significance of class structure, as one can easily detect in his Communist Manifesto, *the first part of which is included here under the title of* An Analysis of Class, *but I agree with Sydney Hook that Marx used the term class in various senses, not only in terms of the rôle a group plays in the production of goods, but also in the forming of patterns of culture and traditions.*[2]

AN ANALYSIS OF CLASS

A SPECTER is haunting Europe—the specter of Communism. All the powers of old Europe have entered into a holy alliance to exorcise this specter: pope and tsar, Metternich and Guizot, French Radicals and German police spies.

Where is the party in opposition that has not been decried as Communistic by its opponents in power? Where is the opposition that has not hurled back the branding reproach of Communism against the more advanced opposition parties, as well as against its reactionary adversaries?

Two things result from this fact:

1. Communism is already acknowledged by all European powers to be itself a power.

2. It is high time that Communists should openly, in the face of the whole world, publish their views, their aims, their tendencies, and meet this nursery tale of the specter of Communism with a manifesto of the party itself.

To this end, Communists of various nationalities have assembled in London, and sketched the following manifesto, to be published in the English, French, German, Italian, Flemish, and Danish languages.

[1] P. x, Lewis Feuer, *Marx and Engels,* New York, Doubleday Anchor Books, 1959.

[2] P. 39, Sydney Hook, *Marx and the Marxists,* New York, Anvil Books, 1955.

I. BOURGEOISIE AND PROLETARIAT[3]

THE history of all hitherto existing society[4] is the history of class struggles.

Freeman and slave, patrician and plebeian, lord and serf, guildmaster[5] and journeyman, in a word, oppressor and oppressed stood in constant opposition to one another, carried on an uninterrupted, now hidden, now open fight, a fight that each time ended either in a revolutionary reconstitution of society at large or in the common ruin of the contending classes.

In the earlier epochs of history, we find almost everywhere a complicated arrangement of society into various orders, a manifold gradation of social rank. In ancient Rome we have patricians, knights, plebeians, slaves; in the Middle Ages, feudal lords, vassals, guildmasters, journeymen, apprentices, serfs; in almost all of these classes, again, subordinate gradations.

The modern bourgeois society that has sprouted from the

---

[3] By bourgeoisie is meant the class of modern capitalists, owners of the means of social production and employers of wage labor. By proletariat, the class of modern wage laborers who, having no means of production of their own, are reduced to selling their labor power in order to live. [*Note by Engels to the English edition of 1888.*]

[4] That is, all *written* history. In 1847 the prehistory of society, the social organization existing previous to recorded history, was all but unknown. Since then August von Haxthausen (1792-1866) discovered common ownership of land in Russia, Georg Ludwig von Maurer proved it to be the social foundation from which all Teutonic races started in history; and, by and by, village communities were found to be, or to have been, the primitive form of society everywhere from India to Ireland. The inner organization of this primitive Communistic society was laid bare, in its typical form, by Lewis Henry Morgan's (1818-1881) crowning discovery of the true nature of the *gens* and its relation to the *tribe*. With the dissolution of these primeval communities, society begins to be differentiated into separate and finally antagonistic classes. I have attempted to retrace this process of dissolution in *Der Ursprung der Familie, des Privateigenthums und des Staats (The Origin of the Family, Private Property and the State)*, second edition, Stuttgart, 1886. [*Note by Engels to the English edition of 1888.*]

[5] Guildmaster, that is, a full member of a guild, a master within, not a head of a guild. [*Note by Engels to the English edition of 1888.*]

ruins of feudal society has not done away with class antagonisms. It has but established new classes, new conditions of
oppression, new forms of struggle in place of the old ones.

Our epoch, the epoch of the bourgeoisie, possesses, however, this distinctive feature: It has simplified the class antagonisms. Society as a whole is more and more splitting up
into two great hostile camps, into two great classes directly
facing each other—bourgeoisie and proletariat.

From the serfs of the Middle Ages sprang the chartered
burghers of the earliest towns. From these burgesses the first
elements of the bourgeoisie were developed.

The discovery of America, the rounding of the Cape,
opened up fresh ground for the rising bourgeoisie. The East-
Indian and Chinese markets, the colonization of America,
trade with the colonies, the increase in the means of exchange
and in commodities generally, gave to commerce, to navigation, to industry, an impulse never before known, and thereby,
to the revolutionary element in the tottering feudal society, a
rapid development.

The feudal system of industry, in which industrial production was monopolized by closed guilds, now no longer sufficed
for the growing wants of the new markets. The manufacturing
system took its place. The guildmasters were pushed aside by
the manufacturing middle class; division of labor between the
different corporate guilds vanished in the face of division of
labor in each single workshop.

In the meantime the markets kept ever growing, the demand ever rising. Even manufacture no longer sufficed. Thereupon, steam and machinery revolutionized industrial production. The place of manufacture was taken by the giant,
modern industry, the place of the industrial middle class by
industrial millionaires, the leaders of whole industrial armies,
the modern bourgeois.

Modern industry has established the world market, for
which the discovery of America paved the way. This market
has given an immense development to commerce, to navigation, to communication by land. This development has, in its
turn, reacted on the extension of industry; and in proportion
as industry, commerce, navigation, railways extended, in the
same proportion the bourgeoisie developed, increased its
capital, and pushed into the background every class handed
down from the Middle Ages.

We see, therefore, how the modern bourgeoisie is itself the

product of a long course of development, of a series of revolutions in the modes of production and of exchange.

Each step in the development of the bourgeoisie was accompanied by a corresponding political advance of that class. An oppressed class under the sway of the feudal nobility, an armed and self-governing association in the medieval commune;[6] here independent urban republic (as in Italy and Germany), there taxable "third estate" of the monarchy (as in France); afterward, in the period of manufacture proper, serving either the semifeudal or the absolute monarchy as a counterpoise against the nobility, and, in fact, cornerstone of the great monarchies in general—the bourgeoisie has at last, since the establishment of modern industry and of the world market, conquered for itself, in the modern representative state, exclusive political sway. The executive of the modern state is but a committee for managing the common affairs of the whole bourgeoisie.

The bourgeoisie, historically, has played a most revolutionary part.

The bourgeoisie, wherever it has got the upper hand, has put an end to all feudal, patriarchal, idyllic relations. It has pitilessly torn asunder the motely feudal ties that bound man to his "natural superiors," and has left no other nexus between man and man than naked self-interest, than callous "cash payment." It has drowned the most heavenly ecstasies of religious fervor, of chivalrous enthusiasm, of philistine sentimentalism, in the icy water of egotistical calculation. It has resolved personal worth into exchange value, and in place of the numberless indefeasible chartered freedoms, has set up that single, unconscionable freedom—Free Trade. In one word, for exploitation, veiled by religious and political illusions, it has substituted naked, shameless, direct, brutal exploitation.

6 "Commune" was the name taken, in France, by the nascent towns even before they had conquered from their feudal lords and masters local self-government and political rights of the "Third Estate." Generally speaking, for the economical development of the bourgeoisie, England is here taken as the typical country; for its political development, France. [*Note by Engels to the English edition of 1888.*]

This was the name given their urban communities by the townsmen of Italy and France, after they had purchased or wrested their initial rights of self-government from their feudal lords. [*Note by Engels to the German edition of 1890.*]

The bourgeoisie has stripped of its halo every occupation hitherto honored and looked up to with reverent awe. It has converted the physician, the lawyer, the priest, the poet, the man of science, into its paid wage laborers.

The bourgeoisie has torn away from the family its sentimental veil, and has reduced the family relation to a mere money relation.

The bourgeoisie has disclosed how it came to pass that the brutal display of vigor in the Middle Ages, which reactionaries so much admire, found its fitting complement in the most slothful indolence. It has been the first to show what man's activity can bring about. It has accomplished wonders far surpassing Egyptian pyramids, Roman aqueducts, and Gothic cathedrals; it has conducted expeditions that put in the shade all former exoduses of nations and crusades.

The bourgeoisie cannot exist without constantly revolutionizing the instruments of production, and thereby the relations of production, and with them the whole relations of society. Conservation of the old modes of production in unaltered form, was, on the contrary, the first condition of existence for all earlier industrial classes. Constant revolutionizing of production, uninterrupted disturbance of all social conditions, everlasting uncertainty and agitation distinguish the bourgeois epoch from all earlier ones. All fixed, fast-frozen relations, with their train of ancient and venerable prejudices and opinions, are swept away; all new-formed ones become antiquated before they can ossify. All that is solid melts into air, all that is holy is profaned, and man is at last compelled to face with sober senses his real conditions of life and his relations with his kind.

The need of a constantly expanding market for its products chases the bourgeoisie over the whole surface of the globe. It must nestle everywhere, settle everywhere, establish connections everywhere.

The bourgeoisie has through its exploitation of the world market given a cosmopolitan character to production and consumption in every country. To the great chagrin of reactionaries, it has drawn from under the feet of industry the national ground on which it stood. All old-established national industries have been destroyed or are being destroyed. They are dislodged by new industries, whose introduction becomes a life-and-death question for all civilized nations, by industries that no longer work up indigenous raw material, but raw material drawn from the remotest zones; industries whose products are consumed, not only at home but in every quarter of the globe. In place of the old wants, satisfied by the production of the country, we find new wants, requiring for their satisfaction the products of distant lands and climes. In place of the old local and national seclusion and self-sufficiency, we have intercourse in every direction, universal interdependence of nations. And as in material, so also in intellectual production. The intellectual creations of individual nations become common property. National one-sidedness and narrow-mindedness become more and more impossible, and from the numerous national and local literatures there arises a world literature.

The bourgeoisie, by the rapid improvement of all instruments of production, by the immensely facilitated means of communication, draws all, even the most barbarian, nations into civilization. The cheap prices of its commodities are the heavy artillery with which it batters down all Chinese walls, with which it forces the barbarians' intensely obstinate hatred of foreigners to capitulate. It compels all nations, on pain of extinction, to adopt the bourgeois mode of production; it compels them to introduce what it calls civilization into their midst, that is, to become bourgeois themselves. In one word, it creates a world after its own image.

The bourgeoisie has subjected the country to the rule of the towns. It has created enormous cities, has greatly increased the urban population as compared with the rural, and has thus rescued a considerable part of the population from the idiocy of rural life. Just as it has made the country dependent on the towns, so it has made barbarian and semibarbarian countries dependent on the civilized ones, nations of peasants on nations of bourgeois, the East on the West.

The bourgeoisie keeps more and more doing away with the scattered state of the population, of the means of production, and of property. It has agglomerated population, centralized means of production, and has concentrated property in a few hands. The necessary consequence of this was political centralization. Independent, or but loosely connected provinces, with separate interests, laws, governments, and systems of taxation, became lumped together into one nation, with one government, one code of laws, one national class interest, one frontier and one customs tariff.

The bourgeoisie, during its rule of scarce one hundred years, has created more massive and more colossal productive forces than have all preceding generations together. Subjection of nature's forces to man, machinery, application of chemistry to industry and agriculture, steam navigation, railways, electric telegraphs, clearing of whole continents for cultivation, canalization of rivers, whole populations conjured out of the ground—what earlier century had even a presentiment that such productive forces slumbered in the lap of social labor?

We see then: the means of production and of exchange, on whose foundation the bourgeoisie built itself up, were generated in feudal society. At a certain stage in the development of these means of production and of exchange, the conditions under which feudal society produced and exchanged, the feudal organization of agriculture and manufacturing industry, in one word, the feudal relations of property became no longer compatible with the already developed productive forces; they became so many fetters. They had to be burst asunder; they were burst asunder.

Into their place stepped free competition, accompanied by a social and political constitution adapted to it, and by the economic and political sway of the bourgeois class.

A similar movement is going on before our own eyes. Modern bourgeois society with its relations of production, of exchange and of property, a society that has conjured up such gigantic means of production and of exchange, is like the sorcerer who is no longer able to control the powers of the nether world whom he has called up by his spells. For many a decade past the history of industry and commerce is but the history of the revolt of modern productive forces against modern conditions of production, against the property relations that are the conditions for the existence of the bourgeoisie and of its rule. It is enough to mention the commercial crises that by their periodical return put the existence of the entire bourgeois society on its trial, each time more threateningly. In these crises a great part not only of the existing products but also of the previously created productive forces are periodically destroyed. In these crises there breaks out an epidemic that, in all earlier epochs, would have seemed an absurdity—the epidemic of overproduction. Society suddenly finds itself put back into a state of momentary barbarism; it appears as if a famine, a universal war of devastation had cut off the supply of every means of subsistence; industry and commerce seem to be destroyed. And why? Because there is too much civilization, too much means of subsistence, too much industry, too much commerce. The productive forces at the disposal of society no longer tend to further the development of the conditions of bourgeois property; on the contrary, they have become too powerful for these conditions, by which they are fettered, and so soon as they overcome these fetters, they bring disorder into the whole of bourgeois society, endanger the existence of bourgeois property. The conditions of bourgeois society are too narrow to comprise the wealth created by them. And how does the bourgeoisie get over these crises? On the one hand, by enforced destruction of a mass of productive forces; on the other, by the conquest of new markets, and by the more thorough exploitation of the old ones. That is to say, by paving the way for more extensive and more destructive crises, and by diminishing the means whereby crises are prevented.

The weapons with which the bourgeoisie felled feudalism to the ground are now turned against the bourgeoisie itself.

But not only has the bourgeoisie forged the weapons that bring death to itself; it has also called into existence the men who are to wield those weapons—the modern working class—the proletarians.

In proportion as the bourgeoisie, that is, capital, is developed, in the same proportion is the proletariat, the modern working class, developed—a class of laborers who live only so long as they find work, and who find work only so long as their labor increases capital. These laborers, who must sell themselves piecemeal, are a commodity, like every other article of commerce, and are consequently exposed to all the vicissitudes of competition, to all the fluctuations of the market.

Owing to the extensive use of machinery and to division of labor, the work of the proletarians has lost all individual character and, consequently, all charm for the workman. He becomes an appendage of the machine, and it is only the most simple, most monotonous, and most easily acquired knack that is required of him. Hence, the cost of production of a workman is restricted, almost entirely, to the means of subsistence that he requires for his maintenance, and for the propagation of his race. But the price of a commodity, and therefore also of labor, is equal to its cost of production. In proportion, therefore, as the repulsiveness of the work increases, the wage decreases. Nay more, in proportion as the use of machinery and division of labor increases, in the same proportion the burden of toil also increases, whether by prolongation of the working hours, by increase of the work exacted in a given time, or by increased speed of the machinery, and so on.

Modern industry has converted the little workshop of the patriarchal master into the great factory of the industrial capitalist. Masses of laborers, crowded into the factory, are organized like soldiers. As privates of the industrial army they are placed under the command of a perfect hierarchy of officers and sergeants. Not only are they slaves of the bourgeois class, and of the bourgeois state; they are daily and hourly enslaved by the machine, by the overlooker, and, above all, by the individual bourgeois manufacturer himself. The more openly this despotism proclaims gain to be its end and aim, the more petty, the more hateful, and the more embittering it is.

The less the skill and exertion of strength implied in manual labor, in other words, the more modern industry becomes developed, the more is the labor of men superseded by that of women. Differences of age and sex have no longer any distinctive social validity for the working class. All are instruments of labor, more or less expensive to use, according to their age and sex.

No sooner is the exploitation of the laborer by the manufacturer so far at an end that he receives his wages in cash, than he is set upon by the other portions of the bourgeoisie, the landlord, the shopkeeper, the pawnbroker, and so on.

The lower strata of the middle class—the small tradespeople, shopkeepers, and retired tradesmen generally, the handicraftsmen and peasants—all these sink gradually into the proletariat, partly because their diminutive capital does not suffice for the scale on which modern industry is carried on, and is swamped in the competition with the large capitalists, partly because their specialized skill is rendered worthless by new methods of production. Thus the proletariat is recruited from all classes of the population.

The proletariat goes through various stages of development. With its birth begins its struggle with the bourgeoisie. At first the contest is carried on by the individual laborers, then by the work people of a factory, then by the operatives of one trade, in one locality, against the individual bourgeois who directly exploits them. They direct their attacks not against the bourgeois conditions of production, but against the instruments of production themselves; they destroy imported wares that compete with their labor, they smash machinery to pieces, they set factories ablaze, they seek to restore by force the vanished status of the workman of the Middle Ages.

At this stage the laborers still form an incoherent mass scattered over the whole country, and broken up by their mutual competition. If anywhere they unite to form more compact bodies, this is not yet the consequence of their own active union but of the union of the bourgeoisie, which class, in order to attain its own political ends, is compelled to set the whole proletariat in motion, and is moreover yet, for a time, able to do so. At this stage, therefore, the proletarians do not fight their enemies, but the enemies of their enemies, the remnants of absolute monarchy, the landowners, the nonindustrial bourgeois, the petty bourgeoisie. Thus the whole historical movement is concentrated in the hands of the bourgeoisie; every victory so obtained is a victory for the bourgeoisie.

But with the development of industry the proletariat not only increases in number; it becomes concentrated in greater masses, its strength grows, and it feels that strength more. The various interests and conditions of life within the ranks of the proletariat are more and more equalized in proportion as machinery obliterates all distinctions of labor, and nearly everywhere reduces wages to the same low level. The growing competition among the bourgeois, and the resulting commercial crises, make the wages of the workers ever more fluctuating. The unceasing improvement of machinery, ever more rapidly developing, makes their livelihood more and more precarious; the collisions between individual workmen and individual bourgeois take more and more the character of collisions between two classes. Thereupon the workers begin to form combinations (trade unions) against the bourgeois; they club together in order to keep up the rate of wages; they found permanent associations in order to make provisions beforehand for these occasional revolts. Here and there the contest breaks out into riots.

Now and then the workers are victorious, but only for a time. The real fruit of their battles lies, not in the immediate result, but in the ever-expanding union of the workers. This union is helped on by the improved means of communication that are created by modern industry and that place the workers of different localities in contact with one another. It was just this contact that was needed to centralize the numerous local struggles, all of the same character, into one national struggle between classes. But every class struggle is a political struggle. And that union, to attain which the burghers of the Middle Ages, with their miserable highways, required centuries, the modern proletarians, thanks to railways, achieve in a few years.

This organization of the proletarians into a class, and consequently into a political party, is continually being upset again by the competition between the workers themselves. But it ever rises up again, stronger, firmer, mightier. It compels legislative recognition of particular interests of the workers, by taking advantage of the divisions among the bourgeoisie itself. Thus the ten-hours' bill in England was carried.

Altogether, collisions between the classes of the old society further in many ways the course of development of the proletariat. The bourgeoisie finds itself involved in a constant battle, at first with the aristocracy, later on, with those portions of the bourgeoisie itself whose interests have become antagonistic to the progress of industry, at all times with the bourgeoisie of foreign countries. In all these battles it sees itself compelled to appeal to the proletariat, to ask for its help, and thus to drag it into the political arena. The bourgeoisie itself, therefore, supplies the proletariat with its own elements of political and general education; in other words, it furnishes the proletariat with weapons for fighting the bourgeoisie.

Further, as we have already seen, entire sections of the ruling classes are, by the advance of industry, precipitated into the proletariat, or are at least threatened in their conditions of existence. These also supply the proletariat with fresh elements of enlightenment and progress.

Finally, in times when the class struggle nears the decisive hour, the process of dissolution going on within the ruling class, in fact within the whole range of old society, assumes such a violent, glaring character, that a small section of the ruling class cuts itself adrift, and joins the revolutionary class, the class that holds the future in its hands. Just as, therefore, at an earlier period, a section of the nobility went over to the bourgeoisie, so now a portion of the bourgeoisie goes over to the proletariat, and in particular, a portion of the bourgeois ideologists, who have raised themselves to the level of comprehending theoretically the historical movement as a whole.

Of all the classes that stand face to face with the bourgeoisie today, the proletariat alone is a really revolutionary class. The other classes decay and finally disappear in the face of modern industry; the proletariat is its special and essential product. The lower middle class, the small manufacturer, the shopkeeper, the artisan, the peasant, all these fight against the bourgeoisie, to save from extinction their existence as fractions of the middle class. They are therefore not revolutionary, but conservative. Nay more, they are reactionary, for they try to roll back the wheel of history. If by chance they are revolutionary, they are so only in view of their impending transfer into the proletariat; they thus defend not their present, but their future interests; they desert their own standpoint to place themselves at that of the proletariat.

The "dangerous class," the social scum, that passively rotting mass thrown off by the lowest layers of old society, may, here and there, be swept into the movement by a proletarian revolution; its conditions of life, however, prepare it far more for the part of a bribed tool of reactionary intrigue.

In the conditions of the proletariat, those of old society at large are already virtually swamped. The proletarian is without property; his relation to his wife and children has no longer anything in common with the bourgeois family relations: modern industrial labor, modern subjection to capital, the same in England as in France, in America as in Germany, has stripped him of every trace of national character. Law, morality, religion, are to him so many bourgeois prejudices behind which lurk in ambush just as many bourgeois interests.

All the preceding classes that got the upper hand sought to fortify their already acquired status by subjecting society at large to their conditions of appropriation. The proletarians cannot become masters of the productive forces of society except by abolishing their own previous mode of appropriation, and thereby also every other previous mode of appropriation. They have nothing of their own to secure and to fortify: their mission is to destroy all previous securities for, and insurances of, individual property.

All previous historical movements were movements of minorities, or in the interest of minorities. The proletarian movement is the self-conscious, independent movement of the immense majority, in the interest of the immense majority.

The proletariat, the lowest stratum of our present society, cannot stir, cannot raise itself up, without the whole superincumbent strata of official society being sprung into the air.

Though not in substance, yet in form, the struggle of the proletariat with the bourgeoisie is at first a national struggle. The proletariat of each country must, of course, first of all settle matters with its own bourgeoisie.

In depicting the most general phases of the development of the proletariat, we traced the more or less veiled civil war, raging within existing society, up to the point where that war breaks out into open revolution and where the violent overthrow of the bourgeoisie lays the foundation for the ways of the proletariat.

Hitherto, every form of society has been based, as we have already seen, on the antagonism of oppressing and oppressed classes. But in order to oppress a class, certain conditions must be assured to it under which it can, at least, continue its slavish existence. The serf, in the period of serfdom, raised himself to membership in the commune, just as the petty bourgeois, under the yoke of feudal absolutism, managed to develop into a bourgeoisie. The modern laborer, on the contrary, instead of rising with the progress of industry, sinks deeper and deeper below the conditions of existence of his own class. He becomes a pauper, and pauperism develops more rapidly than population and wealth. And here it becomes evident that the bourgeoisie is unfit any longer to be the ruling class in society and to impose its conditions of existence upon society as an overriding law. It is unfit to rule because it is incompetent to assure an existence to its slave within his slavery, because it cannot help letting him sink into such a state that it has to feed him, instead of being fed by him. Society can no longer live under this bourgeoisie; in other words, its existence is no longer compatible with society.

The essential condition for the existence and for the sway of the bourgeois class is the formation and augmentation of capital; the condition for capital is wage labor. Wage labor rests exclusively on competition between the laborers. The advance of industry, whose involuntary promoter is the bourgeoisie, replaces the isolation of the laborers, because of competition, by their revolutionary combination, because of association. The development of modern industry, therefore, cuts from under its feet the very foundation on which the bourgeoisie produces and appropriates products. What the bourgeoisie therefore produces, above all, are its own gravediggers. Its fall and the victory of the proletariat are equally inevitable.

II. Proletarians and Communists

In what relation do the Communists stand to the proletarians as a whole?

The Communists do not form a separate party opposed to other working-class parties.

They have no interests separate and apart from those of the proletariat as a whole.

They do not set up any sectarian principles of their own by which to shape and mold the proletarian movement.

The Communists are distinguished from the other working-class parties by this only: (1) In the national struggles of the proletarians of the different countries, they point out and bring to the front the common interests of the entire proletariat, independently of all nationality. (2) In the various stages of development which the struggle of the working class against the bourgeoisie has to pass through, they always and everywhere represent the interests of the movement as a whole.

The Communists, therefore, are on the one hand, practically, the most advanced and resolute section of the working-class parties of every country, that section which pushes forward all others; on the other hand, theoretically, they have over the great mass of the proletariat the advantage of clearly understanding the line of march, the conditions, and the ultimate general results of the proletarian movement.

The immediate aim of the Communists is the same as that of all the other proletarian parties: formation of the proletariat into a class, overthrow of the bourgeois supremacy, conquest of political power by the proletariat.

The theoretical conclusions of the Communists are in no way based on ideas or principles that have been invented, or discovered, by this or that would-be universal reformer.

They merely express, in general terms, actual relations springing from an existing class struggle, from a historical movement going on under our very eyes. The abolition of existing property relations is not at all a distinctive feature of Communism.

All property relations in the past have continually been subject to historical change consequent upon the change in historical conditions.

The French Revolution, for example, abolished feudal property in favor of bourgeois property.

The distinguishing feature of Communism is not the abolition of property generally, but the abolition of bourgeois property. But modern bourgeois private property is the final and most complete expression of the system of producing and appropriating products that is based on class antagonisms, on the exploitation of the many by the few.

In this sense, the theory of the Communists may be summed up in the single phrase: Abolition of private property.

We Communists have been reproached with the desire of abolishing the right of personally acquiring property as the fruit of a man's own labor, which property is alleged to be the groundwork of all personal freedom, activity, and independence.

Hard-won, self-acquired, self-earned property! Do you mean the property of the petty artisan and of the small peasant, a form of property that preceded the bourgeois form? There is no need to abolish that: the development of industry has to a great extent already destroyed it, and is still destroying it daily.

Or do you mean modern bourgeois private property?

But does wage labor create any property for the laborer? Not a bit. It creates capital, that is, that kind of property which exploits wage labor and which cannot increase except upon condition of begetting a new supply of wage labor for fresh exploitation. Property, in its present form, is based on the antagonism of capital and wage labor. Let us examine both sides of this antagonism.

To be a capitalist is to have not only a purely personal, but a social, *status* in production. Capital is a collective product, and only by the united action of many members, nay, in the last resort, only by the united action of all members of society, can it be set in motion.

Capital is therefore not a personal, it is a social power.

When, therefore, capital is converted into common property, into the property of all members of society, personal property is not thereby transformed into social property. It is only the social character of the property that is changed. It loses its class character.

Let us now take wage labor.

The average price of wage labor is the minimum wage, that is, that quantum of the means of subsistence which is absolutely requisite to keep the laborer in bare existence as a laborer. What, therefore, the wage laborer appropriates by means of his labor merely suffices to prolong and reproduce a bare existence. We by no means intend to abolish this personal appropriation of the products of labor, an appropriation that is made for the maintenance and reproduction of human life and that leaves no surplus wherewith to command the labor of others. All that we want to do away with is the miserable character of this appropriation, under which the laborer lives merely to increase capital, and is allowed to live only insofar as the interest of the ruling class requires it.

In bourgeois society, living labor is but a means to increase accumulated labor. In Communist society, accumulated labor is but a means to widen, to enrich, to promote the existence of the laborer.

In bourgeois society, therefore, the past dominates the present; in Communist society the present dominates the past. In bourgeois society capital is independent and has individuality, while the living person is dependent and has no individuality.

And the abolition of this state of things is called by the bourgeois, abolition of individuality and freedom! And rightly so. The abolition of bourgeois individuality, bourgeois independence, and bourgeois freedom is undoubtedly aimed at.

By freedom is meant, under the present bourgeois conditions of production, free trade, free selling and buying.

But if selling and buying disappear, free selling and buying disappear also. This talk about free selling and buying, and all the other "brave words" of our bourgeoisie about freedom in general, have a meaning, if any, only in contrast with restricted selling and buying, with the fettered traders of the Middle Ages, but have no meaning when opposed to the Communist abolition of buying and selling, of the bourgeois conditions of production, and of the bourgeoisie itself.

You are horrified at our intending to do away with private property. But in your existing society, private property is already done away with for nine-tenths of the population; its existence for the few is solely due to its nonexistence in the hands of those nine-tenths. You reproach us, therefore, with intending to do away with a form of property the necessary condition for whose existence is the nonexistence of any property for the immense majority of society.

In one word, you reproach us with intending to do away with your property. Precisely so; that is just what we intend.

From the moment when labor can no longer be converted

into capital, money, or rent, into a social power capable of being monopolized, that is, from the moment when individual property can no longer be transformed into bourgeois property, into capital, from that moment, you say, individuality vanishes.

You must, therefore, confess that by "individual" you mean no other person than the bourgeois, than the middle-class owner of property. This person must, indeed, be swept out of the way, and made impossible.

Communism deprives no man of the power to appropriate the products of society; all that it does is to deprive him of the power to subjugate the labor of others by means of such appropriation.

It has been objected that upon the abolition of private property all work will cease, and universal laziness will overtake us.

According to this, bourgeois society ought long ago to have gone to the dogs through sheer idleness; for those of its members who work acquire nothing, and those who acquire anything do not work. The whole of this objection is but another expression of the tautology: There can no longer be any wage labor when there is no longer any capital.

All objections urged against the Communistic mode of producing and appropriating material products have, in the same way, been urged against the Communistic modes of producing and appropriating intellectual products. Just as to the bourgeois, the disappearance of class property is the disappearance of production itself, so the disappearance of class culture is to him identical with the disappearance of all culture.

That culture, the loss of which he laments, is, for the enormous majority, a mere training to act as a machine.

But don't wrangle with us so long as you apply, to our intended abolition of bourgeois property, the standard of your bourgeois notions of freedom, culture, law, and so on. Your very ideas are but the outgrowth of the conditions of your bourgeois production and bourgeois property, just as your jurisprudence is but the will of your class made into a law for all, a will whose essential character and direction are determined by the economical conditions of existence of your class.

The selfish misconception that induces you to transform into eternal laws of nature and of reason the social forms springing from your present mode of production and form of property—historical relations that rise and disappear in the progress of production—this misconception you share with every ruling class that has preceded you. What you see clearly in the case of ancient property, what you admit in the case of feudal property, you are of course forbidden to admit in the case of your own bourgeois form of property.

Abolition of the family! Even the most radical flare up at this infamous proposal of the Communists.

On what foundation is the present family, the bourgeois family, based? On capital, on private gain. In its completely developed form this family exists only among the bourgeoisie. But this state of things finds its complement in the practical absence of the family among the proletarians, and in public prostitution.

The bourgeois family will vanish as a matter of course when its complement vanishes, and both will vanish with the vanishing of capital.

Do you charge us with wanting to stop the exploitation of children by their parents? To this crime we plead guilty.

But, you will say, we destroy the most hallowed of relations when we replace home education by social.

And your education! Is not that also social, and determined by the social conditions under which you educate, by the intervention direct or indirect, of society, by means of schools, and so on? The Communists have not invented the intervention of society in education; they do but seek to alter the character of that intervention, and to rescue education from the influence of the ruling class.

The bourgeois claptrap about the family and education, about the hallowed correlation of parent and child, becomes all the more disgusting, the more, by the action of modern industry, all family ties among the proletarians are torn asunder, and their children transformed into simple articles of commerce and instruments of labor.

But you Communists would introduce community of women, screams the whole bourgeoisie in chorus.

The bourgeois sees in his wife a mere instrument of production. He hears that the instruments of production are to be exploited in common, and, naturally, can come to no other conclusion than that the lot of being common to all will likewise fall to the women.

He has not even a suspicion that the real point aimed at is to do away with the status of women as mere instruments of production.

For the rest, nothing is more ridiculous than the virtuous indignation of our bourgeois at the community of women which, they pretend, is to be openly and officially established by the Communists. The Communists have no need to introduce community of women; it has existed almost from time immemorial.

Our bourgeois, not content with having the wives and daughters of their proletarians at their disposal, not to speak of common prostitutes, take the greatest pleasure in seducing each other's wives.

Bourgeois marriage is in reality a system of wives in common, and thus, at the most, what the Communists might possibly be reproached with is that they desire to introduce, in substitution for a hypocritically concealed, an openly legalized community of women. For the rest, it is self-evident that the abolition of the present system of production must bring with it the abolition of the community of women springing from that system, that is, of prostitution both public and private.

The Communists are further reproached with desiring to abolish countries and nationality.

The workingmen have no country. We cannot take from them what they have not got. Since the proletariat must first of all acquire political supremacy, must rise to be the leading class of the nation, must constitute itself *the* nation, it is, so far, itself national, though not in the bourgeois sense of the word.

National differences and antagonisms between peoples are daily more and more vanishing, owing to the development of the bourgeoisie, to freedom of commerce, to the world market, to uniformity in the mode of production and in the conditions of life corresponding thereto.

The supremacy of the proletariat will cause them to vanish still faster. United action of the leading civilized countries, at least, is one of the first conditions for the emancipation of the proletariat.

In proportion as the exploitation of one individual by another is put an end to, the exploitation of one nation by another will also be put an end to. In proportion as the antagonism between classes within the nation vanishes, the hostility of one nation to another will come to an end.

The charges against Communism made from a religious, a philosophical and, generally, from an ideological standpoint, are not deserving of serious examination.

Does it require deep intuition to comprehend that man's ideas, views, and conceptions, in one word, man's consciousness, changes with every change in the conditions of his material existence, in his social relations and in his social life?

What else does the history of ideas prove than that intellectual production changes its character in proportion as material production is changed? The ruling ideas of each age have ever been the ideas of its ruling class.

When people speak of ideas that revolutionize society, they do but express the fact that within the old society the elements of a new one have been created and that the dissolution of the old ideas keeps even pace with the dissolution of the old conditions of existence.

When the ancient world was in its last throes, the ancient religions were overcome by Christianity. When Christian ideas succumbed in the eighteenth century to rationalist ideas, feudal society fought its death battle with the then revolutionary bourgeoisie. The ideas of religious liberty and freedom of conscience merely gave expression to the sway of free competition within the domain of knowledge.

"Undoubtedly," it will be said, "religious, moral, philosophical, and juridical ideas have been modified in the course of historical development. But religion, morality, philosophy, political science, and law constantly survived this change."

"There are, besides, eternal truths, such as Freedom, Justice, and so on, that are common to all states of society. But Communism abolishes eternal truths; it abolishes all religion, and all morality, instead of constituting them on a new basis; it therefore acts in contradiction to all past historical experience."

What does this accusation reduce itself to? The history of all past society has consisted in the development of class antagonisms, antagonisms that assumed different forms at different epochs.

But whatever form they may have taken, one fact is common to all past ages, namely, the exploitation of one part of society by the other. No wonder, then, that the social consciousness of past ages, despite all the multiplicity and variety it displays, moves within certain common forms, or general ideas, which cannot completely vanish except with the total disappearance of class antagonisms.

The Communist revolution is the most radical rupture with traditional property relations; no wonder that its development involves the most radical rupture with traditional ideas.

But let us have done with the bourgeois objections to Communism.

We have seen above that the first step in the revolution by the working class is to raise the proletariat to the position of ruling class, to win the battle of democracy.

The proletariat will use its political supremacy to wrest, by degrees, all capital from the bourgeoisie, to centralize all instruments of production in the hands of the state, that is, of the proletariat organized as the ruling class; and to increase the total of productive forces as rapidly as possible.

Of course, in the beginning, this cannot be effected except by means of despotic inroads on the rights of property and on the conditions of bourgeois production; by means of measures, therefore, which appear economically insufficient and untenable but which, in the course of the movement, outstrip themselves, necessitate further inroads upon the old social order, and are unavoidable as a means of entirely revolutionizing the mode of production.

These measures will of course be different in different countries.

Nevertheless in the most advanced countries, the following will be pretty generally applicable.

1. Abolition of property in land and application of all rents of land to public purposes.

2. A heavy progressive or graduated income tax.

3. Abolition of all right of inheritance.

4. Confiscation of the property of all emigrants and rebels.

5. Centralization of credit in the hands of the state by means of a national bank with state capital and an exclusive monopoly.

6. Centralization of the means of communication and transport in the hands of the state.

7. Extension of factories and instruments of production owned by the state; the bringing into cultivation of wastelands, and the improvement of the soil generally in accordance with a common plan.

8. Equal obligation of all to work. Establishment of industrial armies, especially for agriculture.

9. Combination of agriculture with manufacturing industries; gradual abolition of the distinction between town and country by a more equable distribution of the population over the country.

10. Free education for all children in public schools. Abo-

lition of children's factory labor in its present form. Combination of education with industrial production, and so on.

When, in the course of development, class distinctions have disappeared, and all production has been concentrated in the hands of a vast association of the whole nation, the public power will lose its political character. Political power, properly so called, is merely the organized power of one class for oppressing another. If the proletariat during its contest with the bourgeoisie is compelled, by the force of circumstances, to organize itself as a class; if, by means of a revolution, it makes itself the ruling class, and, as such, sweeps away by force the old conditions of production, then it will, along with these conditions, have swept away the conditions for the existence of class antagonisms and of classes generally, and will thereby have abolished its own supremacy as a class.

In place of the old bourgeois society, with its classes and class antagonisms, we shall have an association in which the free development of each is the condition for the free development of all.

Gabriel Tarde
(1843–1904)

SOCIAL LAWS

Gabriel Tarde's contribution to sociology and social psychology centers around the importance of imitation. Hume had already given his attention to the idea of imitation as a socializing force, but Tarde's analysis is by far the most exhaustive. Tarde makes a distinction between three social processes: imitation, opposition, and adaptation.

Tarde was most influenced by the philosopher and economist Augustin Cournot. Cournot saw imitation as an important social factor and distinguished three main aspects of imitation: a) form of repetition, b) habit in the individual, and c) analogy to reproduction or generation in organic life. Tarde recognized his debt to Cournot by dedicating his The Laws of Imitation *to him.*

Tarde arrived at his theories by way of his interest in criminology. He believed that criminal acts were committed in waves, and he discovered that imitation is a significant factor influencing criminal behavior. He also found that much of the human conduct arises out of opposition to existing behavior patterns, and decided that both imitation and opposition provide the basis for a third social factor: invention. In observing the social process we see, according to Tarde, an ever-widening imitation of inventions, the opposition of conflicting circles of imitation, and the rise of new inventions which in turn become new imitations.

The reader should realize that Tarde's sociology is essentially psychological. He also should take into consideration that most of his theories are in disrepute today. Many psychologists discredit in particular his laws of imitation. Though contemporary sociologists accept imitation as a part of the social structure, they do not consider it important.

Tarde was born in Sarlat, a village near Bordeaux in France. He received his education at the Jesuit College of Sarlat and studied philosophy and the classics. A long illness increased his interest in philosophy, but he took law as a career, for financial reasons. After completion of his legal studies he became a magistrate in his home town and re-

mained in this post for fifteen years. During this period he acquired an insight into the fields of penology and criminology and he found time to do his first writing. He was called to Paris in 1892 to become the head of the Bureau of Statistics in the Department of Justice. In that capacity he was able to undertake extensive studies of criminality. In the meantime he also served as a professor in the School of Political Science and taught criminology and economic psychology. In 1900 he relinquished his government post and became professor of modern philosophy at the Collège de France, which post he held until his death in 1904.

Of his many writings we mention here his two most important works The Laws of Imitation *(1890) and* Social Laws *(1898), the latter giving the best presentation of his philosophy and sociology.*

SOCIAL LAWS

INTRODUCTION

WHEN we traverse the gallery of history, and observe its motley succession of fantastic paintings—when we examine in a cursory way the successive races of mankind, all different and constantly changing, our first impression is apt to be that the phenomena of social life are incapable of any general expression or scientific law and that the attempt to found a system of sociology is wholly chimerical. But the first herdsmen who scanned the starry heavens, and the first tillers of the soil who essayed to discover the secrets of plant life, must have been impressed in much the same way by the sparkling disorder of the firmament, with its manifold meteors, as well as by the exuberant diversity of vegetable and animal forms. The idea of explaining sky or forest by a small number of logically concatenated notions, under the name of astronomy or biology, had it occurred to them, would have appeared in their eyes the height of extravagance. And there is no less complexity—no less real irregularity and apparent caprice— in the world of meteors and in the interior of the virgin forest, than in the recesses of human history.

How is it, then, that in spite of this changing diversity in the domain of sky and forest, among physical objects and living beings, we have seen the birth and gradual growth of the sciences of physics and biology? There are three essential elements involved in the development of these branches, and these must be carefully distinguished before we can form a complete and exact notion of what is meant by a certain noun and adjective that are very widely used, namely, *science* and *scientific*.

In the first place, then, men began to perceive some similarities in the midst of these differences, some *repetitions* among these variations. Such are the periodic return of the same conditions of the heavens, the cycle of the seasons, the regularly repeated succession of ages among living creatures—youth, maturity, and old age—and the traits common to individuals of the same species. There is no science of the individual as such; all science is general; that is, it considers the individual as repeated, or as capable of indefinite repetition.

Science is the coordination of phenomena regarded from the side of their *repetitions*. But this does not mean that differentiation is not an essential mode of procedure for the scientific mind. It is the duty of science to differentiate, as well as to assimilate; but only to the extent that the object differentiated is a *type* in nature yielding a certain number of copies, and capable of indefinite reproduction. A specific type may be discovered and carefully defined; but, if it be found to belong to a single individual only, and to be incapable of transmission to posterity, it fails to interest the scientist, except as a curious monstrosity. Repetition means the production of something that at the same time preserves the original; it implies simple and elementary causation without creation. The effect reproduces the cause point by point, just as in the case of transmission of movement from one body to another, or in the transmission of life from a living being to its progeny.

But in addition to the question of *reproduction*, the phenomena involved in *destruction* are of interest to science. And hence, in every sphere of fact to which she directs her attention, science must endeavor to discover, in the second place, the *oppositions* that exist there and are germane to her object. Thus, she must consider the equilibrium of forces, the symmetry of forms, the struggles of living organisms, and the strife among all creatures.

But this is not all, nor even the most important element. The *adaptations* of phenomena, and their relations in creative production, must above all be dealt with. The scientist labors continually to detect, disentangle, and explain these harmonies. With their discovery, he succeeds in establishing a higher adaptation, namely, the harmony of his system of notions and hypotheses with the interrelations of facts.

Thus science consists in viewing any fact whatsoever under three aspects, corresponding, respectively, to the repetitions, oppositions, and adaptations which it contains and which are obscured by a mass of variations, dissymmetries, and disharmonies. The relation of cause to effect, in fact, is not the only element which properly constitutes scientific knowledge. If it were so, pragmatic history, the mere concatenation of causes and effects, which simply teaches that certain battles and certain insurrections had such and such consequences, would be the most perfect example of science. Yet history, as we know, becomes a science only when the relations of causality which it reveals are shown to exist between a general cause, capable of repetition or actually repeating itself, and a general effect, also repeated or capable of repetition.

Again, mathematics never reveals causality in operation. When a cause is postulated under the name of *function*, it is always disguised as an equation. Yet mathematics is certainly a science; in fact, it is the prototype of all science. And why? Because nowhere has a more complete elimination of the dissimilar and individual side of phenomena been effected, and nowhere do they present a more exact and definite repetition, and a more symmetrical opposition. The great fault of mathematics lies in its not perceiving, or taking adequately into account, the adaptations of phenomena. Hence arises that insufficiency of the science, so strongly felt by philosophers, especially the geometricians among them, such as Descartes, Comte, and Cournot.

Repetition, opposition, and adaptation, I repeat, are the three keys which science employs to open up the arcana of the universe. She seeks, before all else, not the mere causes, but the laws that govern the repetition, opposition, and adaptation of phenomena. These are three different species of laws, which must certainly not be confounded; yet they are quite as closely connected as they are distinct. In biology, for example, the tendency of species to multiply in geometric progression (a law of repetition) forms the basis of the struggle for existence and natural selection (a law of opposition); and the appearance of individual variations, the production of various individual aptitudes and harmonies, and the correlation of parts in growth (laws of adaptation) are necessary to the proper functioning of both.[1]

But, of these three keys, the first and third are far more important than the second. The first is the great passkey; while the third, of finer construction, gives access to treasures deeply hidden and most precious. The second, an intermediary, of lesser importance, reveals certain strifes and collisions of temporary utility, which are destined to fade away little by little, though never completely, even this partial disappearance being effected only after numerous transformations and attenuations.

These reflections were needed in order to show what sociology must be, if it is to deserve the name of science, and along what paths sociologists must guide its course, if they wish to see it assume, unchallenged, its proper rank. Like every other science, it will attain this only when it has gained, and is conscious of possessing, its own domain of repetitions, its own domain of oppositions, and its own domain of adaptations, each characteristic of itself and belonging wholly to itself. Sociology can make progress only when it succeeds in substituting true repetitions, oppositions, and harmonies for false ones, as all the other sciences have done before it. And in place of repetitions, oppositions, and adaptations that are true but vague, it must find others that become ever more exact as it advances.

Let us place ourselves at each of these standpoints in turn, first of all to ascertain whether or not the evolution of science in general, and sociology in particular, has taken place in the manner which I have already imperfectly defined, and which I shall be able to define more fully as we proceed; in the second place, to point out the laws of social development under each of these three aspects.

THE REPETITION OF PHENOMENA

IMAGINE ourselves in the presence of some great object, such as the starry sky, the sea, a forest, a crowd, or a city. From

[1] It will be noted that Cuvier and the naturalists of his time, including even his opponent Lamarck, sought out primarily the laws of adaptation, while, on the other hand, Darwin and his evolutionist disciples preferred to consider the phenomena of life from the standpoint of repetitions and oppositions (the Malthusian law and the law of the struggle for existence), though they certainly took into account organic adaptation also, which is the most important fact of all.

every part of such an object emanate impressions which strike the senses of the savage as well as those of the scientist; but to the latter these manifold and incoherent sensations suggest certain logically correlated notions, which together make up a bundle of explanatory principles. How has this gradual elaboration of mere sensations into notions and laws come about? By what process has our knowledge of such phenomena become more and more scientific? The change, I contend, has come about, in the first place, because we have been constantly discovering a greater number of resemblances among these phenomena and because, in place of the merely superficial, apparent, and deceptive resemblances among them, we have come to discern certain other resemblances, at once deeper and more real. In fact, we have passed from complex and confused resemblances and repetitions of the whole to resemblances and repetitions of the parts. These latter are more difficult to discover, but, once found, they prove to be more exact and elementary; they are at once infinitely numerous and infinitely small. It is only after these elementary resemblances are perceived that the higher, broader, more complex, and vaguer resemblances can be explained and assigned their proper value. Such an advance occurs whenever a number of fundamental differences that have previously been considered *sui generis* are resolved into combinations of resemblances. By this we do not mean to say that science, as it advances, tends to eliminate the fundamental differences, or to diminish in number the unrepeated aspects of phenomena. For, while the grosser and more obvious distinctions of the mass dissolve under the searching glance of the scientific observer, their place is taken by others which are at once more subtle and more profound, and which multiply indefinitely, thus keeping pace with the uniformities among the elements.

To apply this principle to the realm of stars. The science of astronomy dates its origin from the moment when idle or curious herdsmen noticed the periodicity of the apparent revolutions of the heavens, the rising and setting of the stars, the circular courses of the sun and moon, and the regular succession and recurrence of their positions in the sky. But in those early times certain stars appeared to be exceptions to the general order of this one magnificent revolution, namely, the *wandering* stars, or planets; each of these was supposed to follow a capricious course, which varied at every moment from its own previous course and that of the rest; later on it was observed that there was some regularity even in these anomalies. Moreover, all stars—fixed and wandering, suns and planets, including even the shooting stars—were held to be essentially alike; the only striking difference admitted was between the sun and moon, on the one hand, and all the others, on the other; the two former being considered the only really distinctive bodies in the firmament.

Now astronomy made its first step in advance when for this one immense, apparent rotation of the entire heavens there was substituted the conception of a host of lesser real rotations, which differed greatly from one another, and were in no wise synchronous, but each of which repeated itself indefinitely. The second step occurred when the peculiar distinctiveness of the sun vanished, to be replaced by a more subtle differentiation of each separate star, as the luminary of an invisible system, and center of a planetary world analogous to the whirling concourse of our own planets. A still greater step in advance was made when the differences of apparent sidereal rotation which, though general and without exception, admitted irregularities in velocity, radius, eccentricity of orbit, et cetera, vanished before the Newtonian law of attraction—the latter representing all these periodicities of movement, from the most minute up to the greatest, and from the swiftest to the most slow, as due to endless and continual repetitions of one and the same fact, namely, attraction directly proportional to the mass and inversely to the square of the distance. And it were far better could we explain this fact in turn by the bold hypothesis, constantly rejected, yet ever besetting us anew, which attributes gravitation to the impacts of ether atoms, resulting from atomic vibrations of inconceivable minuteness and multiplicity.

Am I not correct, then, in saying that the science of astronomy has ever been concerned with resemblances and repetitions; that it started out with a single resemblance and repetition, immense and obvious in character, or with a small number at most, to arrive ultimately at an infinite number of infinitesimal resemblances and repetitions, real and elementary in character, which, when they appeared, furnished an explanation of the former?

Now does this necessarily imply, by the way, that the sky has lost any of its picturesqueness with the advances of astronomy? By no means. For, in the first place, the increased precision of apparatus and exactness of observations have enabled us to discern among the repetitions of stellar movements many differences, hitherto unperceived, which have led to many new discoveries—notably that of Leverrier. And in the second place, our celestial horizon has been constantly extended, and as its vastness has increased, the differences existing among various stars and groups of stars in respect to size, velocity, and physical characteristics have become much more marked. The varieties of form among the nebulae have multiplied, and when, at length, the spectroscope enabled us to analyze in so extraordinary a manner the chemical composition of the heavenly bodies, such differences were found among them that men were led to believe in the existence of radical differences between their respective inhabitants. Finally, the geography of the nearest planets has been revealed more clearly, and, judging the rest from these (after studying the canals of Mars, for instance), we may conclude that each of the countless planets which circle above and beneath us possesses its own special characteristics, its own world chart, and its own local features, and that these individual peculiarities give, there as here, a distinctive charm to each particular region, and no doubt engrave the love of country on the hearts of its inhabitants, whoever they may be.

Nor is this, in my opinion, all, though I shall only whisper it, lest I incur the serious charge of becoming a metaphysician. I believe that none of the above-mentioned differences, including even the mere variety of arrangement and random distribution of matter throughout space, can be explained on the theory of exactly similar atomic elements—a hypothesis so dear to chemists, who are in this respect the real metaphysicians; I do not see that Spencer's so-called law of the *instability of the homogeneous* explains anything. And hence, I believe that the only means of explaining this exuberant growth of individual differences upon the surface of phenomena is by assuming that they spring from a motley array of elements, each possessing its own individual characteristics. Thus in the same way that the mass *resemblances* have been resolved into resemblances of detail, so the gross and obvious mass *differences* have been transformed into infinitely minute differences of detail. And, just as resemblances among the details alone furnish an adequate explanation of whatever resemblances appear in the whole, so the elementary and invisible distinctions, which I believe exist, alone furnish an adequate explanation of those greater and more apparent differences that lend picturesqueness to the visible universe.

So much for the physical world. In the world of life the

same is true. Imagine ourselves placed, like primitive man, in the midst of a forest. All the fauna and flora of a certain zone are there, and we now know that the phenomena revealed by these divers plants and animals, however dissimilar they may seem, resolve themselves ultimately into a multitude of infinitesimal facts which are summed up in the laws of biology —whether it be animal or vegetable biology matters little, since the two are at present classed together. But at the outset men drew broad distinctions between many things that we now place in the same category, while they associated together many that we now differentiate. The resemblances and repetitions which were then perceived, and on which the infant science of the organism was nourished, were superficial and deceptive. Men classed together plants that had no kinship, because their leaves and general form revealed some rough similarity; while they drew sharp distinctions between plants of the same family which were of different shape and outline. The science of botany made an advance when it learned the relative value of different characteristics, and discovered that the most important of these (that is, the most repeated and significant, because accompanied by a host of other resemblances) are not those which are most obvious, but rather those which are most subtle and minute, especially those pertaining to the generative organs, such as the fact of having one cotyledon, two, or none at all.

And *biology*, the synthesis of zoology and botany, was born when the cell theory demonstrated that in both animals and plants the constantly repeated element is the cell—in the first place, the germ cell and then the others that proceed from it—when it showed that the fundamental phenomenon of life is an indefinite repetition by each cell of the functions of nutrition and activity, growth and fertilization, whose mold or cast each cell inherits and transmits in turn to its own posterity. This conformity to precedent may be called either habit or heredity. For simplicity's sake, let us call it all heredity, since habit is merely a sort of internal heredity, just as heredity is only externalized habit. Heredity, then, is the form of repetition appropriate to life, just as undulation, or periodic movement, is its physical, and imitation (as we shall find) its social form.

Thus we see that the progress of the science of living things has resulted in gradually removing all barriers raised on the side of their resemblances and repetitions, and substituting for these few, gross, and obvious resemblances, countless others, far more exact, though infinitely minute, which alone serve to explain the former. But at the same time hosts of new distinctions appear, and not only does the distinctive individuality of each organism become more salient, but we are forced also to admit certain differentiations of the cells themselves, and primarily of the germ cells; for while nothing is more similar in appearance than two germs, there is in reality scarcely anything more different than their contents. After experiencing the insufficiency of the explanations proposed by Darwin and Lamarck to account for the origin of species—whose kinship, descent, and evolution, however, is beyond dispute—we must admit that the real cause of species lies hidden with the cells, the invention, as it were, of some primitive germ possessing an exceptionally fruitful individuality.

Well, then if we proceed to examine a city, a crowd, or an army, in place of the sky or forest, I maintain that the above reflections can be applied to the growth of social science as well as to astronomy and biology. Here, too, men have passed from hasty generalizations, founded on splendid analogies that were at once artificial and illusory, to generalizations supported by a mass of minute facts, whose resemblance to one another was comparatively clear and exact. Sociology has long been in process of construction. The first incoherent attempts were made when, amid the distracting chaos of social data, men discerned, or believed that they discerned, something periodic and regular. An early groping after sociology appeared in the ancient conception of a great cyclic year, at the completion of which everything, in both the social and natural worlds, should recur in the same order. In place of this erroneously conceived single repetition of the whole, which was welcomed by the fanciful genius of Plato, Aristotle developed in his *Politics* certain repetitions of detail (which, though often true, were vague and difficult to grasp) concerning what is most superficial, or certainly most unimportant, in the social life, namely, the order of succession of the several forms of government. Arrested at this point, the evolution of sociology began again *ab ovo* in modern times. The *ricorsi* of Vico are the cycles of antiquity, taken up and traced out anew, with somewhat less of the fantastic element. This hypothesis and that of Montesquieu, on the supposed similarity of civilizations developed in the same climate, are good examples of the superficial and illusory repetitions and resemblances on which the science of sociology had to feed before it was fitted to receive more substantial nourishment. Chateaubriand, in his *Essai sur les révolutions*, drew a lengthy parallel between the English Revolution and the French Revolution, and took pleasure in dwelling on even the most superficial resemblances. Others founded elaborate theories on absurd analogies drawn between the Punic and English character, or between the Roman and British empires. This attempt to confine social facts within lines of development which would compel them to repeat themselves *en masse* with merely insignificant variations, has hitherto been the chief pitfall of sociology, and that, whether under the more rigid form conceived by Hegel, consisting of successions of triads, or under the more exact and scientific form that it has since received at the hands of the modern evolutionists. The latter, in discussing the transformations of laws (particularly the laws of family and of property) and the transformations of language, religion, industry, and art, have ventured to formulate general laws that would confine the progress of society, under these different aspects, to a constant passing and repassing along successive portions of the same arbitrary path. It remained to be discovered later that these supposed rules are honeycombed with exceptions, and that evolution, whether linguistic, legal, religious, political, economic, artistic, or moral, is not a single road, but a network of routes with many intersecting crossways.

Fortunately, screened and sheltered from view by these ambitious generalizations, certain less venturesome workers strove, with greater success, to formulate other, more substantial laws concerning the details. Among these should be mentioned the linguists, the mythologists, and above all the economists. These specialists in sociological fields discovered various interesting relations among successive and simultaneous facts, which recurred constantly within the limits of the narrow domain they were examining. In Adam Smith's *Wealth of Nations*, Bopp's *Comparative Grammar of the Indo-European Languages*, and Dietz's work, to cite but three instances, we find a mass of observations of this sort, in which are pointed out the resemblances running through countless human actions—resemblances in the pronunciation of certain consonants and vowels, in buying and selling, in the production and consumption of certain articles, et cetera. It is true that these resemblances, when linguists endeavored to formulate them further, gave rise to very imperfect laws, conforming to a majority of cases only. But this is because the authors were in too great haste to formulate them, and did not wait to remove from its husk of partial truths the real kernel of absolute truth; to wit, the fundamental social fact which sociology is blindly pursuing, and which it must attain before it can really develop into a science.

In some quarters the feeling has existed that we must look to psychology for any general explanation of the laws and pseudolaws of economics, language, mythology, et cetera. No man held to this view with greater force and clearness than John Stuart Mill. At the end of his *Logic* he represents sociology as a species of applied psychology. Unfortunately he did not analyze the concept carefully enough; and the psychology to which he looked for the key to social phenomena was merely individual psychology—the branch which studies the interrelations of impressions and imagery in a single mind, believing that everything within this domain can be explained according to the *laws of association* of these elements. Thus conceived, sociology became a sort of enlarged and externalized English associationism, and was in a fair way to lose its originality. But it is not alone, nor chiefly to this *intra*cerebral psychology that we must look for the fundamental fact of sociology, whose groupings and manifold combinations make up our so-called simple phenomena, and form the data of the particular social sciences; it is rather in an *inter*cerebral psychology, which studies the rise of conscious relations between two or more individuals, that we must seek it. The relation of one mind with another is, in fact, a distinctive event in the life of each; it is absolutely different from all their relations with the rest of the universe, giving rise to certain most unexpected states of mind, that cannot be explained at all according to the laws of physiological psychology.[2]

[2] The experiments that have been made on hypnotic suggestion, and suggestion in the waking state, already furnish abundant material for the construction of an *inter*cerebral psychology. I may be allowed to refer the reader to the applications of this still-embryonic psychology which I have proposed throughout my works; more especially to the chapter in my *Laws of Imitation* (1890), entitled "What Is a Society?" which appeared previously, in November, 1884, in the *Revue philosophique;* also to some pages of my *Philosophie pénale* (Philosophy of Punishment, 1890), on the formation of criminal crowds (in the chapter on "Crime," p. 324 f., 1st French edition); my report entitled *Les crimes des foules* (The Crimes of Crowds), submitted at the Congress for Criminal Anthropology at Brussels, in August, 1892, and an article published in the *Revue des Deux Mondes* for December, 1893, under the title of *Foules et sectes* (Crowds and Sects). The

This relation between a subject and an object which is itself a subject—and not a perception in no way resembling the thing perceived—will not allow the idealistic skeptic to call in question the reality of the latter; on the contrary, it means that we experience the sensation of a sentient thing, the volition of a conating thing, and the belief in a believing thing—the perception, in short, of a personality in which the perceiving personality is reflected and which the latter cannot deny without denying itself. This consciousness of a consciousness is the *inconcussum quid* which Descartes sought, and which the individual Self could not give him. Moreover, this unique relation is not a physical impulse given or received, nor is it the transmission of motor energy from the subject to an inanimate object or *vice versa*, according as we are dealing with an active or passive state; it is rather the transmission of something internal and mental, which passes from one to other of the two subjects, and that, curiously enough, without being lost or in the slightest degree diminished in the first. But what manner of thing is it that can thus be transmitted from one mind to another when they enter into psychological relation? Is it their sensations or affective states? Evidently not; for these are essentially incommunicable. The only material that two subjects can communicate to each other and consciously share, with the result that they feel themselves more closely united and more similar thereby, are their notions and volitions, their conclusions and aims. These are forms which may still remain the same, in spite of changes in content; they are products of that mental elaboration which reacts almost equally well to any sensory data. Neither does such a form alter perceptibly when it passes from a mind of the visual type to one of the auditory or motor

---

two latter studies were reprinted without change in my *Essais et mélanges sociologiques* (Sociological Essays and Miscellanies), which appeared in 1895 (Storck and Masson, publishers, Paris and Lyons). I may observe, by the way, that the passage from the *Philosophie pénale*, cited above, which is merely a corollary of the chapter cited also from the *Laws of Imitation*, contains in substance, and very explicitly, the explanation of the phenomena of crowds which was developed afterward in the two other works mentioned; this passage was published prior to the many interesting works that have recently appeared in France and abroad on the psychology of crowds. While this does not detract from their merit, it serves to answer a certain number of insinuations against me, which I have, moreover, fully met elsewhere.

type. Thus the geometrical ideas of one blind from birth are precisely the same as those of geometricians endowed with the sense of sight. And similarly, a plan of campaign proposed by one general whose temperament is choleric and melancholy to others of mercurial and sanguine or passive and phlegmatic dispositions may still remain the same, if only the plan be concerned with the same series of operations, and be desired by all with equal force, in spite of the special and distinctive kinds of feeling that move each one separately to desire it. The strength of subjective tendency, or mental eagerness, which I call desire, like the strength of intellectual grasp, or mental adhesion and constraint, which I call belief, forms one homogeneous and continuous stream. Though variously tinged with the different shades of affectivity pertaining to each separate mind, it nevertheless flows identically in each, now spreading and dividing, now uniting and contracting, and passing freely from one person to another, and from one perception to another in each person, without change.

To say that every real science possesses its own peculiar domain of elementary, countless, and infinitely small repetitions is equivalent to saying that every real science is based on its own special qualities. Quantity, indeed, implies the possibility of one or more infinite series of infinitely small resemblances and repetitions. For this reason I have thought it well to insist, elsewhere, on the quantitative character of the two mental energies which, like two diverging rivers, water the two opposite slopes of the Self—its intellectual and its voluntary activity. If we deny their quantitative character, we declare sociology to be impossible. But we cannot deny it without ignoring the evidence; and a proof that the quantities in question are really social factors is seen in the fact that their quantitative character becomes more evident, and is grasped by the mind with greater clearness, the larger the quantities in which we see them, as when they manifest themselves in the shape of currents of popular belief or passion, or in traditional convictions and obstinacies of custom, embracing large groups of men. The more a group increases in size, the more the rise or fall of opinion, whether affirmative or negative, with respect to a given object, becomes capable of measurement. Such fluctuations of national belief or volition, indicated, for example, by the rise or fall of shares on the exchanges, then become comparable to the changes of temperature or atmospheric pressure, or to the varying force of a waterfall. It is for this reason that a science of statistics is more easily developed as states grow larger. The particular aim of statistics being to discover and separate real quantities from the confused general mass of social facts, the success of the science is greater the more it strives to reach beyond the particular human acts which it collects, and to measure the total mass of beliefs and desires. The statistics of stock-exchange values express the variations of public confidence regarding the success of certain enterprises, such as the solvency of a certain borrowing state, and the changes in public desires and interests, to which these loans or enterprises appeal. Industrial and agricultural statistics indicate the importance of the general needs which demand the production of certain articles, or the probable suitability of the means set in operation to meet the demand. Judicial statistics, with their dry enumerations of trials or offenses, are of interest to consult only because, between their lines, we read the yearly increase or decrease in the amount of public desires engaged in proscribed or criminal channels, such as the tendency to divorce or theft; here, too, we see the degree in which public hopes are affected by certain kinds of trial or crime. The statistics of population constitute, in most respects, merely a biological study, having to do with the numerical growth of the race quite as much as with the duration and progress of social institutions. But they have a sociological import, in that they indicate the increase or decrease of the desire for paternity, maternity, and matrimony, as well as of the prevailing belief that happiness is to be found in marriage and the formation of fertile unions.

Under what conditions, then, is it legitimate to add together these forces of belief and desire that lie stored up in different individuals? Evidently, on condition that they possess the same object;—that they have regard to the same idea to be asserted, or the same action to be executed. And what brought about this convergence, which renders the individual energies capable of combining to form a social unit? Can it have occurred spontaneously, by a chance encounter, or by some sort of preestablished harmony? Decidedly not, except in a few instances; and even these apparent exceptions, were there time to follow them out, would be found to confirm the rule. This minute interagreement of minds and wills, which forms the basis of the social life, even in troublous times—this presence of so many common ideas, ends, and means, in the minds and wills of all members of the same society at any given moment—is not due, I maintain, to organic heredity, which ensures the birth of men quite similar to one another, nor to mere identity of geographical environment, which offers very similar resources to talents that are nearly equal; it is rather the effect of that suggestion-imitation process which, starting from one primitive creature possessed of a single idea or act, passed this copy on to one of its neighbors, then to another, and so on. Organic needs and spiritual tendencies exist in us only as potentialities which are realizable under the most diverse forms, in spite of their primitive similarity; and, among all these possible realizations, the indications furnished by some first initiator who is imitated determine which one is actually chosen.

Let us return, then, to the fundamental social couple, to which I alluded just now; not the couple consisting of a man and woman in love, for this couple, in so far as it is sexual, is a purely vital phenomenon; but rather a couple composed of two persons, of either sex, one of whom exerts a mental influence upon the other. I maintain that the relation between these two persons is the one essential element in the social life and that it always consists, at bottom, in an imitation of one by the other. But this fact must be correctly interpreted, lest it fall before the onslaught of foolish and superficial objections. No one will deny that whatever we say, do, or think, once we are launched in the social life, we are forever imitating someone else, unless, indeed, we are ourselves making an innovation—an event that rarely happens; it is easy, moreover, to show that our innovations are, for the most part, combinations of previous examples, and that they remain outside the social life so long as they are not imitated. There is not a word that you say which is not the reproduction, now unconscious, but formerly conscious and voluntary, of verbal articulations reaching back to the most distant past, with some special accent due to your immediate surroundings. There is not a religious rite that you fulfill, such as praying, kissing the icon, or making the sign of the cross, which does not reproduce certain traditional gestures and expressions, established through imitation of your ancestors. There is not a military or civil requirement that you obey, nor an act that you perform in your business, which has not been taught you and which you have not copied from some living model. There is not a stroke of the brush that you make, if you are a painter, nor a verse that you write, if you are a poet, which does not conform to the customs or the prosody of your

school, and even your very originality itself is made up of
accumulated commonplaces, and aspires to become commonplace in its turn.

Thus, the unvarying characteristic of every social fact
whatsoever is that it is imitative. And this characteristic belongs exclusively to social facts. On this point, however, a
specious objection has been urged against me by Professor
Giddings, who, nevertheless, with remarkable ability, frequently adopts my own sociological standpoint. One society,
he declares, copies another; even enemies will imitate one
another; we borrow each other's armaments, ruses of war,
and secrets of trade. Hence, the domain of *imitativeness* goes
beyond that of *sociality*, and cannot be a special characteristic
of the latter.[3] But I am astonished at such an objection on
the part of an author who regards the struggle between
societies as a potent agency looking toward their ultimate

---

[3] Giving to the word *imitation* the very wide meaning accorded
to it in a recent and already celebrated book on *Mental Development in the Child and the Race,* by Mr. Baldwin, professor of
psychology at Princeton University (U.S.A.), one might regard
imitation as the fundamental fact not only of social and psychological life but of organic life as well, where it would appear as
the necessary condition of habit and heredity. As a matter of fact,
however, the position of this keen psychologist, far from contradicting my own view, is a most striking illustration and confirmation of it. Imitation between man and man, as I understand it, is
the consequence of imitation between one state and another in
the same man; the latter is a species of internal imitation which
I had myself previously named *habit,* and is evidently distinguished from the former by characteristics clear enough to allow
of their differentiation. Professor Baldwin, who is first of all a
biological psychologist, explains very correctly the organic and
mental genesis of imitation, and his task comes to an end where
that of the psychological sociologist begins. It is a pity that his
book did not precede my own on the *Laws of Imitation,* which
would have gained by using his analyses. Nevertheless, the latter
do not oblige me to amend in any way the laws and arguments
formulated in my work. But in any case his book is the best answer I can make to those who accuse me of extending too widely
the meaning of the word *imitation*. Professor Baldwin proves the
contrary by extending it much further still. I learn, as these proofs
are being corrected, that Professor Baldwin has recently applied
his conceptions to sociology and that by an independent route he
has been led spontaneously to a position very analogous to that
developed in my *Laws of Imitation.* [The work by Professor Baldwin referred to is his *Social and Ethical Interpretations in Mental
Development* (Macmillan). In the second English edition of that
work the author speaks of the relation of his researches to those
of M. Tarde.—TR.]

socialization and merger into a broader society built up by their very battles. For is it not obvious that, to the extent that rival or hostile peoples assimilate their institutions, they themselves tend to coalesce? And hence, while it is perfectly true that each new act of imitation between individuals already associated tends to preserve and strengthen the social bond, it is no less certain that such an act between individuals not yet associated prepares them for an association that may take place in the future, weaving by invisible threads something that will in time become a palpable bond. As regards some other objections that have been raised against me, I need not stop to consider them, since they arise from a very imperfect understanding of my ideas. They will disappear of their own accord if one will but place himself squarely at my standpoint. I refer the reader to my works for the elucidation of this matter.

But it is not enough merely to recognize the imitative character of every social phenomenon. I go further, and maintain that this imitative relation was not, in the beginning, as it often is later, a connection binding one individual to a confused mass of men, but merely a relation between two individuals, one of whom, the child, is in process of being introduced into the social life, while the other, an adult, long since socialized, serves as the child's personal model. As we advance in life, it is true, we are often governed by collective and impersonal models, which are usually not consciously chosen. But before we speak, think, or act as "they" speak, think, or act in our world, we begin by speaking, thinking, and acting as "he" or "she" does. And this *he* or *she* is always one of our own near acquaintances. Beneath the indefinite *they*, however carefully we search, we never find anything but a certain number of *he's* and *she's* which, as they have increased in number, have become mingled together and confused. Simple though this distinction be, it is nevertheless overlooked by those who deny that individual initiative plays the leading role in any social institution or undertaking. These writers imagine they are stating a weighty truth when they assert, for instance, that languages and religions are *collective* productions; that crowds, without a leader, constructed Greek, Sanskrit, and Hebrew, as well as Buddhism and Christianity; and that the formations and transformations of societies are always to be explained by the coercive action of the group upon its individual members (so that the latter, great and small alike, are always molded and made subordinate to the former), rather than by the suggestive and contagious influence of certain select individuals upon the group as a whole. In reality, such explanations are quite illusory, and their authors fail to perceive that, in thus postulating a collective force, which implies the conformity of millions of men acting together under certain relations, they overlook the greatest difficulty, namely, the problem of explaining how such a general assimilation could ever have taken place. But this question is solved if we extend the analysis, as I have done, to the intercerebral relation of two minds, the one reflecting the other. Only thus can we explain the partial agreements, the beating of hearts in unison, and the communions of soul, which, once brought about, and afterward perpetuated by tradition and the imitation of our ancestors, exert on the individual a pressure that is often tyrannical, but oftener still most salutary.[4] It is this relation, then, that the sociologist must adopt as his own peculiar data, just as the astronomer adopts the relation between two masses, the attracting and the attracted; it is here that he must seek the key to the social mystery; it is from this that he must endeavor to derive the few simple but universal laws, which may be distinguished amid the seeming chaos of history and human life.

What I wish to call attention to at present is that sociology, thus understood, differs from the older conceptions that passed under the same name in the same way that our modern astronomy differs from that of the Greeks, or that biology, since the introduction of the cell theory, differs from the older natural history.[5] In other words, it rests on a foundation

[4] And do not forget this simple fact, that we enter upon the social life at a very early age. Hence the child, who turns to others as a flower turns to the sun, feels the attraction of his family environment much more than its constraint. And in the same way, throughout his entire life, he continues to drink in these examples with avidity.

[5] This conception is, in fact, almost the exact opposite of the *unilinear evolutionists'* notion and of M. Durkheim's. Instead of explaining everything by the supposed supremacy of a *law of evolution*, which compels collective phenomena to reproduce and repeat themselves indefinitely in a certain order—instead of thus explaining lesser facts by greater, and the part by the whole—I explain collective resemblances of the whole by the massing together of minute elementary acts—the greater by the lesser and the whole by the part. This way of regarding phenomena is destined to work a transformation in sociology similar to that brought about in mathematics by the introduction of the infinitesimal calculus.

composed of real and elementary resemblances and repetitions which are infinitely numerous and extremely exact; these have replaced a very small number of erroneous, or at least vague and deceptive, analogies as primary material for scientific elaboration. And I may add, also, that, while social similarity has gained in extent and depth by this substitution, social differentiation has gained no less by the change. We must, from now on, no doubt, abandon such artificial differences as the "philosophy of history" established between successive peoples, each of which, like the chief actors of an immense drama, had his own predetermined role to play. Hence, it is no longer allowable to interpret those much-abused expressions: "the genius of a people or race," "the genius of a language," or "the genius of a religion," in the way that some of our predecessors, including even Renan and Taine, understood them. These embodiments of collective character, appearing under the guise of metaphysical entities or *idols*, were endowed with a fictitious personal identity, which was, however, rather indefinite. Certain predispositions, supposed to be invincible, for some particular grammatical types, religious conceptions, or governmental forms, were freely attributed to them. On the other hand, they were supposed to have an insuperable repugnance to borrowing conceptions or institutions from certain of their rivals. The Semitic genius, for instance, was held to be absolutely irreconcilable with polytheism, parliamentary government, and the analytic scheme of modern languages; the Greek genius with monotheism; the Chinese and Japanese genius with all our European institutions and conceptions generally. If the facts protested against such an ontological theory, they were tortured to compel them to acknowledge its truth. It was useless to call the attention of these theorists to the radical transformations which a proselyting religion, a language, or an institution such as the jury system, undergoes, when it spreads far beyond the boundaries of its original race or people, in spite of invincible obstacles that the "genius" of other nations or races may seem to rear against it. They replied by revising the notion and distinguishing, at least, between noble and inventive races, which were alone endowed with the privilege of discovering and spreading discoveries, and races born to be in subjection, which had no understanding of language, religion, or ideas, and borrowed this material, or appeared to borrow it, from the former. Moreover, they denied that such a proselyting conquest of one civilization or race genius over another could pass certain bounds, as, for example, in the Europeanization of China and Japan. As regards the last, the contrary has since proved itself true, and it will soon prove true of the Middle Kingdom also.

Sooner or later, one must open his eyes to the evidence, and recognize that the genius of a people or race, instead of being a factor superior to and dominating the characters of the individuals (who have been considered its offshoots and ephemeral manifestations), is simply a convenient label, or impersonal synthesis, of these individual characteristics; the latter alone are real, effective, and ever in activity; they are in a state of continual fermentation in the bosom of every society, thanks to the examples borrowed and exchanged with neighboring societies to their great mutual profit. The impersonal, collective character is thus the product rather than the producer of the infinitely numerous individual characters; it is their composite photograph, and must not be taken for their mask. We shall certainly lose nothing of that social picturesqueness which makes the historian an artist, when, having cleared up, rather than cleared away, this phantasmagoria of great historic actors called Egypt, Rome, Athens, et cetera, we perceive behind it a swarm of individual innovators, each *sui generis*, stamped with his own distinctive mark, and recognizable among a thousand. Hence I conclude, once more, that in adopting this sociological standpoint we shall have done precisely what all the other sciences have done as they progressed, namely, replaced the small number of erroneous or uncertain resemblances and differences by countless real and exact ones; this is a great gain for both the artist and the scientist; but it is a still greater gain for the philosopher, who, if he is to retain a distinctive function, must undertake a synthesis of the two.

A few remarks more. So long as none of the elementary astronomical facts, such as the Newtonian Law, or at least that of elliptical orbits, had been discovered, there were many heterogeneous bits of astronomical knowledge—a science of the moon, *selenology*, and a science of the sun, *heliology*— but there was no astronomy. So long as there had been no discovery of the elementary facts of chemistry (affinity and combination in definite proportions), there were many bits of chemical knowledge, and the special chemistries of iron, tin, copper, et cetera, but no science of chemistry. So long as men had not discovered the essential fact of physics, the undulatory transmission of molecular movement, there were many bits of physical knowledge—optics, acoustics, thermology, electrology—but no physics. Physics became physico-chemistry, the science of all inorganic nature, when the possibility was seen of explaining all things by the fundamental laws of mechanics; that is, when men believed that they had discovered the elementary inorganic facts, in the equality and contrariety of action and reaction, the conservation of energy, the reduction of all forces to forms of motion, the mechanical equivalent of heat, electricity, light, et cetera. Finally, before the discovery of the analogies existing between animals and plants from the standpoint of reproduction, there was not a single botany and a single zoology, but different botanies and zoologies, which might have been named hippology, cynology, et cetera. The discovery of the above-mentioned resemblances gave only partial unity to these various scattered sciences—these *disjecta membra* of the coming biology. Biology was really born when the cell theory appeared, exhibiting the elementary fact of life; namely, that the functions of the cell (or histological element) and its proliferation are continued by the germ, itself a cell, so that nutrition and generation were thus seen from the same angle of vision.

And now we are about to construct, in like manner, a social science, to succeed the social sciences. For there were social sciences, at least in outline—the beginnings of political science, linguistics, comparative mythology, aesthetics, and ethics, together with a political economy already well advanced—long before even an embryo of sociology existed. Sociology requires a fundamental social fact. She requires it so urgently that, so long as she had not succeeded in discovering any (possibly because the fact was tearing out her eyes, if I may be pardoned the expression), she was dreaming of such a fact, and imagining it in the form of one of those idle, imaginary resemblances that beset the cradle of every science; she believed herself to be asserting a highly instructive fact when she pictured society as a great organism, where the individual (or, according to others, the family) was the social cell, and every form of social activity represented some sort of cellular function. I have already made many efforts, in company with most other sociologists, to sweep away this obstructive notion from the path of the new science. Yet a word further on the subject may be in place.

Scientific knowledge feels so strongly the need of relying on resemblances and repetitions before all else, that, when none are within its grasp, it actually creates imaginary ones to supply the place of the real; among these we must class the famous simile of the social organism, together with many other symbolic concepts that have attained a like ephemeral usefulness. At the starting point of every science, as at the starting point of every literature, allegory plays an important role. In mathematics, we find the allegorical vision of Pythagoras and Plato preceding the solid generalizations of Archimedes. Astrology and magic—the one the gateway to astronomy, the other the early babblings of chemistry—are founded on the postulate of *universal allegory* rather than on that of universal analogy; they assume a preestablished harmony between the positions of certain planets and the destinies of certain men, between some fictitious act and some real one, between the nature of a chemical substance and that of the heavenly body whose name it bears, and so on. We must not forget the symbolic character of primitive proceedings, for example, the *actio legis*, in the Roman Code, that early groping after jurisprudence. We should note also (since theology, like jurisprudence, became a science some time ago, the excessive application of figurative meanings to biblical stories by the earlier theologians, who saw in the history of Jacob a copy by anticipation of the history of Christ, or regarded the love of the husband and wife in the *Song of Solomon* as symbolic of the love of Christ and his church. The mediæval science of theology began in this way, just as modern literature began with the *Romance of the Rose*. It is a long step from such notions to the *Summa* of St. Thomas Aquinas. Even down to the present century we find lingering traces of this symbolic mysticism; they appear in good Father Gratry's works, now long forgotten, yet worthy to be resurrected on account of their Fénelonian grace of style. Father Gratry believed that the solar system symbolized the successive relations of the soul and God, as the former, according to his notion, revolved around the latter. For him, again, the circle and the ellipse symbolized the whole of ethics, a science which he believed to be inscribed in hieroglyphics upon the conic sections.

I have no desire, of course, to compare these eccentric views with the partly substantial and always serious development which Herbert Spencer and, more recently, M. René Worms and M. Novikov, following Comte, have effected in the theory of the "social organism." I appreciate fully the merit and temporary usefulness of such work, even though I

criticize it. But, to generalize now what precedes, I believe
I have the right to lay down the following proposition: The
advance of every science consists in suppressing *external* likenesses and repetitions—that is, comparisons of the peculiar
material of that science with other things—and replacing them
by *internal* likenesses and repetitions—that is, comparisons of
that material with itself, as it appears in its many copies and
under its different aspects. The notion of the social organism,
which regards the nation as a plant or animal, corresponds to
that of vital automatism, which regards the plant or animal
as a piece of mechanism. It is not this hollow and farfetched
comparison of the living body with a piece of mechanism that
has advanced biology, but rather a comparison of plants with
one another, animals with one another, and living bodies
with one another.[6] So, too, it is not by comparing societies
with organisms that sociology has already made great steps
in advance and is destined to make still greater ones in the
future, but by comparing various societies with one another;
by noting the endless coincidences between distinct national
evolutions, from the standpoint of language, jurisprudence,
religion, industry, art, and custom; and above all by attending to those imitations between man and man which furnish
an analytic explanation of the collective facts.

After these lengthy preliminaries, the time has come when
it would be in place to set forth the general laws governing
imitative repetition, which are to sociology what the laws of
habit and heredity are to biology, the laws of gravitation to
astronomy, and the laws of vibration to physics. But I have
fully treated this subject in one of my works, *The Laws of
Imitation*, to which I may refer those who are interested in
the subject. Nevertheless, I think it important to bring out
here what I did not make sufficiently clear, namely, that in
the last analysis all these laws flow from a higher principle—
the tendency of an example, once started in a social group, to
spread through it in geometrical progression, provided the
group remains homogeneous. By this term *tendency*, however,

[6] Similarly, it was not the Pythagorean comparisons between
mathematics and various other sciences that advanced mathematics; such comparisons were absolutely sterile, while the bringing together of two branches of mathematics, geometry and alge-
bra, under the guidance of Descartes, was most fruitful. And it
was only when the infinitesimal calculus was invented and men
went back to the indecomposable mathematical element whose
continuous repetition explains all, that the immense fertility of
mathematics fully appeared.

I do not mean anything mysterious; on the contrary, it denotes a very simple thing. When, for instance, in a group, the need is felt of expressing a new idea by a new word, the first individual who finds an expressive image fitted to meet that need has only to pronounce it, when immediately it is echoed from one neighbor to another, till soon it trembles on every lip in the group in question, and later spreads even to neighboring groups. Not that we mean by this, in the least, that the expression is endowed with a soul which causes it to send forth rays in this manner, any more than the physicist, in saying that a sound wave tends to radiate in the air, means to endow this mere form with a personal, eager, and ambitious force.[7] It is only another way of saying, in the one case, that the motor forces inherent in the molecules of air have found, in this vibratory repetition, a channel into which they drain; and, in the other case, that a special need felt by the human beings of the group in question has found satisfaction in this imitative repetition, which enables them, as a concession to their indolence (the analogue of physical *inertia*), to escape the trouble of inventing for themselves. However, there is no doubt of the tendency to spread in geometrical proportion, though this tendency is often hindered by obstacles of various sorts, so that it is quite rare, though not extremely so, for statistical diagrams relating to the spread of a new industrial invention to show a regular progression. Now what are the obstacles referred to? There are some that arise from differences of climate and race, but these are not the most important. The greatest impediment to the spread of a social innovation and its consolidation into a traditional custom is some other equally expansive innovation which it encounters during its course and which, to employ a physical metaphor, interferes with it. In fact, every time any one of us hesitates between two modes of verbal expression, two ideas, two beliefs, or two modes of action, it means that an interference between two imitation-rays takes place in him; these rays have started from different generating centers, often widely separated in space and time (namely, certain individual inventors and imitators of primitive times), and have spread onward, till they reached the individual in question.

[7] Or any more than the naturalist, when he says that a species tends to increase in geometrical proportion, regards the type-form as possessing an energy and aim independent of the sun, the chemical affinities, and the various forms of physical energy, instead of being simply their channel.

And how is his difficulty solved? What are the influences that decide his course? There are influences, as I have said elsewhere, of two kinds: logical and extralogical. I should add that even the latter are logical in one sense of the term; for while, between two examples, the plebeian selects blindly that of the patrician, the countryman that of the townsman, and the provincial that of the Parisian—a phenomenon which I have called the descent of imitation from the top to the bottom of the social ladder—this very imitation, however blind it be, is influenced in every case by the superiority attributed to the model, which makes the example of the latter appear in the eyes of the form to possess some social authority over him. The same is true when, as between his ancestors and some foreign innovator, primitive man does not hesitate to prefer the example of the former, whom he esteems infallible; and the same is true, only conversely, when, in a similar perplexity, the denizen of our modern cities, persuaded in advance that the new is always preferable to the old, makes precisely the opposite choice. Nevertheless, the case where the opinion of the individual is founded on reasons extrinsic to the nature of the models compared and to the two ideas or acts in opposition should be carefully distinguished from the case where he chooses in virtue of a judgment resting on the intrinsic character of these two ideas or volitions; hence, the term *logical* should be reserved for the influences that decide him in the latter case.

I need not discuss this question further at present, since in the next chapter I shall have occasion to speak again of these logical and teleological duels, which constitute the fundamental terms of social opposition. Let me only add here that the interferences of imitation-rays are not always impediments to each other's progress; often they result in mutual alliances, which serve to accelerate and enlarge the radiation; sometimes they are even responsible for the rise of some generic idea, which is born of their encounter and combination within a single head, as we shall see in the chapter devoted to social adaptation.

Herbert Spencer
(1820–1903)

A SOCIETY IS AN ORGANISM

In a recently published study by Abram Kardiner and Edward Preble entitled They Studied Man, *the reader will find the following description of Herbert Spencer:*

"*Herbert Spencer was one of the tidiest men who ever lived. He could not tolerate an inefficient saltcellar any more than he could abide a disorderly universe. His life was obsessed with the need to fit all of nature—the inorganic, the organic, and the "super-organic"—into a neat, perfectly axiomatized system. His great intellect focused on the most insignificant details of daily life at the same time that it explored the phenomena of nature which have stimulated the creations of artists, philosophers, and scientists through the centuries.*[1]

The keyphrase with which to describe Spencer's sociology is "social evolution." He advanced the scientific basis for sociology, as it was founded by Auguste Comte, although Spencer did not regard Comte as his scientific precursor, and introduced the concept of the evolution of society. He was one of the foremost commentators on the theory of universal evolution in general. Seven years before Darwin's publication of The Origin of Species *Spencer published a paper called "Development Hypothesis," in which he developed and defended the theory of organic evolution. He applied the concept of evolution to the fields of biology, psychology, ethics, and sociology.*

One finds Spencer's laws of universal evolution best expressed in the second part of his book First Principles. *He distinguishes three basic propositions. The first is the law of the persistence of force, which in Spencer's interpretation means the existence of an ultimate cause transcending knowledge. The second principle is the indestructibility of matter, and the third proposition is the continuity of motion. The last two propositions are derived from the first principle.*

Herbert Spencer was born in Derby, England and was the

[1] P. 37, *They Studied Man*, Abram Kardiner and Edward Preble, Cleveland, World Publishing Company, 1961.

eldest and only surviving child in a family of nine. Since Spencer was a frail child, he was taught at home and never went to school. As a child he was fascinated by all natural phenomena and his inquiring, speculative mind was appreciated by his elders, especially by his father, who encouraged his interest in science.

However, he declined an uncle's offer to send him to Cambridge and later in his life experienced the disadvantages of not having attended the university and thus acquiring academic discipline.

At the age of seventeen he became chief engineer of the London and Birmingham Railroad and was quite successful in this work. Four years later he quit and became the sub-editor of the Economist, *but resigned this position also after a few years. In the meantime he had published his first important book,* Social Statics (1850). *The rest of his life he devoted to writing.*

The essay, "A Society is an Organism," which follows here, forms a chapter of the first volume of Principles of Sociology, *which was published by Spencer in 1874. The conception of society as an organism, which is one of the main themes in his "Inductions of Sociology," can be traced from his book* Social Statics (1850).

A SOCIETY IS AN ORGANISM

When we say that growth is common to social aggregates and organic aggregates, we do not thus entirely exclude community with inorganic aggregates. Some of these, as crystals, grow in a visible manner; and all of them, on the hypothesis of evolution, have arisen by integration at some time or other. Nevertheless, compared with things we call inanimate, living bodies and societies so conspicuously exhibit augmentation of mass that we may fairly regard this as characterizing them both. Many organisms grow throughout their lives; and the rest grow throughout considerable parts of their lives. Social growth usually continues either up to times when the societies divide, or up to times when they are overwhelmed.

Here, then, is the first trait by which societies ally themselves with the organic world and substantially distinguish themselves from the inorganic world.

It is also a character of social bodies, as of living bodies, that while they increase in size they increase in structure. Like a low animal, the embryo of a high one has few distinguishable parts; but while it is acquiring greater mass, its parts multiply and differentiate. It is thus with a society. At first the unlikenesses among its groups of units are inconspicuous in number and degree; but as population augments, divisions and subdivisions become more numerous and more decided. Further, in the social organism as in the individual organism, differentiations cease only with that completion of the type which marks maturity and precedes decay.

Though in inorganic aggregates also, as in the entire solar system and in each of its members, structural differentiations accompany the integrations; yet these are so relatively slow, and so relatively simple, that they may be disregarded. The multiplication of contrasted parts in bodies politic and in living bodies is so great that it substantially constitutes another common character which marks them off from inorganic bodies.

This community will be more fully appreciated on observing that progressive differentiation of structures is accompanied by progressive differentiation of functions.

The divisions, primary, secondary, and tertiary, which arise in a developing animal, do not assume their major and minor unlikenesses to no purpose. Along with diversities in their shapes and compositions go diversities in the actions they perform: they grow into unlike organs having unlike duties. Assuming the entire function of absorbing nutriment at the same time that it takes on its structural characters, the alimentary system becomes gradually marked off into contrasted portions; each of which has a special function forming part of the general function. A limb, instrumental to locomotion or prehension, acquires divisions and subdivisions which perform their leading and their subsidiary shares in this office. So is it with the parts into which a society divides. A dominant class arising does not simply become unlike the rest, but assumes control over the rest; and when this class separates into the more and the less dominant, these, again, begin to discharge distinct parts of the entire control. With the classes whose actions are controlled it is the same. The various groups into which they fall have various occupations: each of such groups also, within itself, acquiring minor contrasts of parts along with minor contrasts of duties.

And here we see more clearly how the two classes of things we are comparing distinguish themselves from things of other classes; for such differences of structures as slowly arise in inorganic aggregates are not accompanied by what we can fairly call differences of function.

Why in a body politic and in a living body, these unlike actions of unlike parts are properly regarded by us as functions, while we cannot so regard the unlike actions of unlike parts in an inorganic body, we shall perceive on turning to the next and most distinctive common trait.

Evolution establishes in them both, not differences simply, but definitely connected differences—differences such that each makes the others possible. The parts of an organic aggregate are so related that one may change greatly without appreciably affecting the rest. It is otherwise with the parts of an organic aggregate or of a social aggregate. In either of these, the changes in the parts are mutually determined, and the changed actions of the parts are mutually dependent. In both, too, this mutuality increases as the evolution advances. The lowest type of animal is all stomach, all respiratory surface, all limb. Development of a type having appendages by which to move about or lay hold of food can take place only if these appendages, losing power to absorb nutriment directly from surrounding bodies, are supplied with nutriment by parts which retain the power of absorption. A respiratory surface to which the circulating fluids are brought to be aerated can be formed only on condition that the concomitant loss of ability to supply itself with materials for repair and growth is made good by the development of a structure bringing these materials. Similarly in a society. What we call with perfect propriety its organization necessarily implies traits of the same kind. While rudimentary, a society is all warrior, all hunter, all hunt builder, all toolmaker: every part fulfills for itself all needs. Progress to a stage characterized by a permanent army, can go on only as there arise arrangements for supplying that army with food, clothes, and munitions of war by the rest. If here the population occupies itself solely with agriculture and there with mining—if these manufacture goods while those distribute them, it must be on condition that in exchange for a special kind of service rendered by each part to other parts, these other parts severally give due proportions of their services.

This division of labor, first dwelt on by political economists as a social phenomenon, and thereupon recognized by biologists as a phenomenon of living bodies, which they called the "physiological division of labor," is that which in the society, as in the animal, makes it a living whole. Scarcely can I emphasize enough the truth that in respect of this fundamental trait, a social organism and an individual organism are entirely alike. When we see that in a mammal, arresting the lungs quickly brings the heart to a stand; that if the stomach fails absolutely in its office all other parts by and by cease to act; that paralysis of its limbs entails on the body at large death from want of food or inability to escape; that loss of even such small organs as the eyes deprives the rest of a service essential to their preservation; we cannot but admit that mutual dependence of parts is an essential characteristic. And when, in a society, we see that the workers in iron stop if the miners do not supply materials; that makers of clothes cannot carry on their business in the absence of those who spin and weave textile fabrics; that the manufacturing community will cease to act unless the food-producing and food-distributing agencies are acting; that the controlling powers, governments, bureaus, judicial officers, police, must fail to keep order when the necessaries of life are not supplied to them by the parts kept in order; we are obliged to say that this mutual dependence of parts is similarly rigorous. Unlike as the two kinds of aggregates otherwise are, they are unlike in respect of this fundamental character, and the characters implied by it.

How the combined actions of mutually dependent parts constitute life of the whole, and how there hence results a parallelism between social life and animal life, we see still more clearly on learning that the life of every visible organism is constituted by the lives of units too minute to be seen by the unaided eye.

An undeniable illustration is furnished by the strange order *Myxomycetes*. The spores or germs produced by one of these forms become ciliated monads, which after a time of active locomotion change into shapes like those of amoebæ, move about, take in nutriment, grow, multiply by fission. Then these amoeba-form individuals swarm together, begin to coalesce into groups, and these groups to coalesce with one another: making a mass sometimes barely visible, sometimes as big as the hand. This *plasmodium*, irregular, mostly reticulated, and in substance gelatinous, itself exhibits movements of its parts like those of a gigantic rhizopod, creeping slowly over surfaces of decaying matters, and even up the stems of plants. Here, then, union of many minute living individuals to form a relatively vast aggregate in which their individualities are apparently lost, but the life of which results from combination of their lives, is demonstrable.

In other cases, instead of units which, originally discrete, lose their individualities by aggregation, we have units which, arising by multiplication from the same germ, do not part company, but nevertheless display their separate lives very clearly. A growing sponge has its horny fibers clothed with a gelatinous substance, and the microscope shows this to consist of moving monads. We cannot deny life to the sponge as a whole, for it shows us some corporate actions. The outer amoeba-form units partially lose their individualities by fusion into a protective layer or skin; the supporting framework of fibers is produced by the joint agency of the monads; and from their joint agency also result those currents of water which are drawn in through the smaller orifices and expelled through the larger. But while there is thus shown a feeble aggregate life, the lives of the myriads of component units are very little subordinated: these units form, as it were, a nation having scarcely any subdivision of functions. Or, in the words of Professor Huxley, "The sponge represents a kind of subaqueous city, where the people are arranged about the streets and roads in such a manner that each can easily appropriate his food from the water as it passes along." Again, in the hydroid polyp *Myriothela*, "pseudopodial processes are being constantly projected from the walls of the alimentary canal into its cavity"; and these Dr. Allman regards as processes from the cells forming the walls, which lay hold of alimentary matter just as those of an amoeba do. The like may be seen in certain planarian worms.

Even in the highest animals there remains traceable this relation between the aggregate life and the lives of components. Blood is a liquid in which, along with nutritive matters, circulate innumerable living units—the blood corpuscles. These have severally their life histories. During its first stage each of them, then known as a white corpuscle, makes independent movements like those of an amoeba; it "may be fed with colored food, which will then be seen to have accumulated in the interior"; "and in some cases the colorless blood corpuscles have actually been seen to devour their more diminutive companions, the red ones." Nor is this individual life of the units provable only where flotation in a liquid allows its signs to be readily seen. Sundry mucous surfaces, as those of the air passages, are covered with what is called ciliated epithelium—a layer of minute elongated cells packed side by side, and each bearing on its exposed end several cilia continually in motion. The wavings of these cilia are essentially like those of the monads which live in the passages running through a sponge; and just as the joint action of these ciliated sponge-monads propels the current of water, so does the joint action of the ciliated epithelium cells move forward the mucous secretion covering them. If there needs further proof that these epithelium cells have independent lives, we have it in the fact that when detached and placed in a fit menstruum, they "move about with considerable rapidity for some time, by the continued vibrations of the cilia with which they are furnished."

On thus seeing that an ordinary living organism may be regarded as a nation of units which live individually, and have many of them considerable degrees of independence, we shall have the less difficulty in regarding a nation of human beings as an organism.

The relation between the lives of the units and the life of the aggregate has a further character common to the two cases. By a catastrophe the life of the aggregate may be destroyed without immediately destroying the lives of all its units; while, on the other hand, if no catastrophe abridges it, the life of the aggregate is far longer than the live of its units.

In a coldblooded animal ciliated cells perform their motions with perfect regularity long after the creature they are part of has become motionless. Muscular fibers retain their power of contracting under stimulation. The cells of secreting organs go on pouring out their product if blood is artificially supplied to them. And the components of an entire organ, as the heart, continue their cooperation for many hours after its detachment. Similarly, arrest of those commercial activities, governmental coordinations, and so on, which constitute the corporate life of a nation, may be caused, say, by an inroad of barbarians, without immediately stopping the actions of all the units. Certain classes of these, especially the widely diffused ones engaged in food production, may long survive and carry on their individual occupations.

On the other hand, the minute living elements composing a developed animal severally evolve, play their parts, decay, and are replaced, while the animal as a whole continues. In the deep layer of the skin, cells are formed by fission which, as they enlarge, are thrust outward, and, becoming flattened to form the epidermis, eventually exfoliate, while the younger ones beneath take their places. Liver cells, growing by imbibition of matters from which they separate the bile, presently die, and their vacant seats are occupied by another generation. Even bone, though so dense and seemingly inert, is permeated by blood vessels carrying materials to replace old components by new ones. And the replacement, rapid in some tissues and in others slow, goes on at such rate that during the continued existence of the entire body, each portion of it has been many times over produced and destroyed. Thus it is also with a society and its units. Integrity of the whole as of each large division is perennially maintained, notwithstanding the deaths of component citizens. The fabric of living persons which, in a manufacturing town, produces some commodity for national use remains after a century as large a fabric, though all the masters and workers who a century ago composed it have long since disappeared. Even with minor parts of this industrial structure the like holds. A firm that dates from past generations, still carrying on business in the name of its founder, has had all its members and *employees* changed one by one, perhaps several times over; while the firm has continued to occupy the same place and to maintain like relations with buyers and sellers. Throughout we find this. Governing bodies, general and local, ecclesiastical corporations, armies, institutions of all orders down to guilds, clubs, philanthropic associations, and so on, show us a continuity of life exceeding that of the persons constituting them. Nay, more. As part of the same law, we see that the existence of the society at large exceeds in duration that of some of these compound parts. Private unions, local public bodies, secondary national institutions, towns carrying on special industries may decay, while the nation, maintaining its integrity, evolves in mass and structure.

In both cases, too, the mutually dependent functions of the various divisions, being severally made up of the actions of many units, it results that these units, dying one by one, are replaced without the function in which they share being sensibly affected. In a muscle, each sarcous element wearing out in its turn is removed and a substitution made while the rest carry on their combined contractions as usual; and the retirement of a public official or death of a shopman perturbs inappreciably the business of the department, or activity of the industry, in which he had a share.

Hence arises in the social organism, as in the individual organism, a life of the whole quite unlike the lives of the units, though it is a life produced by them.

From these likenesses between the social organism and the individual organism, we must now turn to an extreme unlikeness. The parts of an animal form a concrete whole; but the parts of a society form a whole which is discrete. While the living units composing the one are bound together in close contact, the living units composing the other are free, are not in contact, and are more or less widely dispersed. How, then, can there be any parallelism?

Though this difference is fundamental and apparently puts comparison out of the question, yet examination proves it to be less than it seems. Presently I shall have to point out that complete admission of it consists with maintenance of the alleged analogy; but we shall first observe how one who thought it needful, might argue that even in this respect there is a smaller contrast than a cursory glance shows.

He might urge that the physically coherent body of an animal is not composed all through of living units but that it consists in large measure of differentiated parts which the vitally active parts have formed and which thereafter become semivital and in some cases unvital. Taking as an example the protoplasmic layer underlying the skin, he might say that while this consists of truly living units, the cells produced in it, changing into epithelium scales, become inert protective structures; and pointing to the insensitive nails, hair, horns, and so on, arising from this layer, he might show that such parts, though components of the organism, are hardly living components. Carrying out the argument, he would contend that elsewhere in the body there exist such protoplasmic layers, from which grow the tissues composing the various organs—layers which alone remain fully alive, while the structures evolved from them lose their vitality in proportion as they are specialized: instancing cartilage, tendon, and connective tissue, as showing this in conspicuous ways. From all which he would draw the inference that though the body forms a coherent whole, its essential units, taken by themselves, form a whole which is coherent only throughout the protoplasmic layers.

And then would follow the facts showing that the social organism, rightly conceived, is much less discontinuous than it seems. He would contend that as in the individual organism we include with the fully living parts the less living and not living parts which cooperate in the total activities, so in the social organism we must include not only those most highly vitalized units, the human beings, who chiefly determine its phenomena but also the various kinds of domestic animals, lower in the scale of life, which, under the control of man, cooperate with him, and even those far inferior structures, the plants, which, propagated by human agency, supply materials for animal and human activities. In defense of this view he would point out how largely these lower classes of organisms, coexisting with men in societies, affect the structures and activities of the societies—how the traits of the pastoral type depend on the natures of the creatures reared; and how in settled societies the plants producing food, materials for textile fabrics, and so on, determine certain kinds of social arrangements and actions. After which he might insist that since the physical characters, mental natures, and daily doings of the human units are, in part, molded by relations to these animals and vegetals which, living by their aid and aiding them to live, enter so much into social life as even to be cared for by legislation, these lower forms cannot rightly be excluded from the conception of the social organism. Hence would come his conclusion that when with human beings are incorporated the less vitalized beings, animal and vegetal, covering the surface occupied by the society, there results an aggregate having a continuity of parts more nearly approaching to that of an individual organism, and which is also like it in being composed of local aggregations of highly vitalized units, embedded in a vast aggregation of units of various lower degrees of vitality, which are, in a sense, produced by, modified by, and arranged by the higher units.

But without accepting this view, and admitting that the discreteness of the social organism stands in marked contrast with the concreteness of the individual organism, the objection may still be adequately met.

Though coherence among its parts is a prerequisite to that cooperation by which the life of an individual organism is carried on, and though the members of a social organism, not forming a concrete whole, cannot maintain cooperation by means of physical influences directly propagated from part to part, yet they can and do maintain cooperation by another agency. Not in contact, they nevertheless affect one another through intervening spaces, both by emotional language and by the language, oral and written, of the intellect. For carrying on mutually dependent actions, it is requisite that impulses, adjusted in their kinds, amounts, and times, shall be conveyed from part to part. This requisite is fulfilled in living bodies by molecular waves that are indefinitely diffused in low types, and in high types are carried along definite channels (the function of which has been significantly called *internuncial*). It is fulfilled in societies by the signs of feelings and thoughts, conveyed from person to person; at first in vague ways and only through short distances, but afterward more definitely and through greater distances. That is to say, the inter-nuncial function, not achievable by stimuli physically transferred, is nevertheless achieved by language—emotional and intellectual.

That mutual dependence of parts which constitutes organization is thus effectually established. Though discrete instead of concrete, the social aggregate is rendered a living whole.

But now, on pursuing the course of thought opened by this objection and the answer to it, we arrive at an implied contrast of great significance—a contrast fundamentally affecting our idea of the ends to be achieved by social life.

Though the discreteness of a social organism does not prevent subdivision of functions and mutual dependence of parts, yet it does prevent that differentiation by which one part becomes an organ of feeling and thought, while other parts become insensitive. High animals of whatever class are distinguished from low ones by complex and well-integrated nervous systems. While in inferior types the minute scattered ganglia may be said to exist for the benefit of other structures, the concentrated ganglia in superior types are the structures for the benefit of which the rest may be said to exist. Though a developed nervous system so directs the actions of the whole body as to preserve its integrity, yet the welfare of the nervous system is the ultimate object of all these actions: damage to any other organ being serious in proportion as it immediately or remotely entails that pain or loss of pleasure which the nervous system suffers. But the discreteness of a society negatives differentiations carried to this extreme. In an individual organism the minute living units, most of them permanently localized, growing up, working, reproducing, and dying away in their respective places, are in successive generations molded to their respective functions, so that some become specially sentient and others entirely insentient. But it is otherwise in a social organism. The units of this, out of contact and much less rigidly held in their relative positions, cannot be so much differentiated as to become feelingless units and units which monopolize feeling. There are, indeed, traces of such a differentiation. Human beings are unlike in the amounts of sensation and emotion producible in them by like causes: here callousness, here susceptibility, is a characteristic. The mechanically working and hard-living units are less sensitive than the mentally working and more protected units. But while the regulative structures of the social organism tend, like those of the individual organism, to become specialized as seats of feeling, the tendency is checked by want of that physical cohesion which brings fixity of function; and it is also checked by the continued need for feeling in the mechanically working units for the due discharge of their functions.

Hence, then, a cardinal difference in the two kinds of organisms. In the one, consciousness is concentrated in a small part of the aggregate. In the other, it is diffused throughout the aggregate: all the units possess the capacities for happiness and misery, if not in equal degrees, still in degrees that approximate. As, then, there is no social sensorium, the welfare of the aggregate, considered apart from that of the units, is not an end to be sought. The society exists for the benefit of its members; not its members for the benefit of the society. It has ever to be remembered that great as may be the efforts made for the prosperity of the body politic, yet the claims of the body politic are nothing in themselves, and become something only insofar as they embody the claims of its component individuals.

From this last consideration, which is a digression rather than a part of the argument, let us now return and sum up the reasons for regarding a society as an organism.

It undergoes continuous growth. As it grows, its parts become unlike: it exhibits increase of structure. The unlike parts simultaneously assume activities of unlike kinds. These activities are not simply different, but their differences are so related as to make one another possible. The reciprocal aid thus given causes mutual dependence of the parts. And the mutually dependent parts, living by and for one another, form an aggregate constituted on the same general principle as is an individual organism. The analogy of a society to an organism becomes still clearer on learning that every organism of appreciable size is a society; and on further learning that in both, the lives of the units continue for some time if the life of the aggregate is suddenly arrested, while if the aggregate is not destroyed by violence, its life greatly exceeds in duration the lives of its units. Though the two are contrasted as respectively discrete and concrete, and though there results a difference in the ends subserved by the organization, there does not result a difference in the laws of the organization: the required mutual influences of the parts, not transmissible in a direct way, being, in a society, transmitted in an indirect way.

Having thus considered in their most general forms the reasons for regarding a society as an organism, we are prepared for following out the comparison in detail.

Ferdinand Tönnies
(1855–1936)

COMMUNITY AND SOCIETY

Ferdinand Tönnies was born in Eiderstedt in the Frisian region of Schleswig-Holstein. The family moved in 1864 to the small town of Husum where young Tönnies became acquainted with the poet Theodor Sturm, who remained a great influence in his life. He was not yet seventeen years old when he graduated from the Gymnasium and went to the University of Jena, where he studied classical philology and philosophy. Soon he moved on to the University of Leipzig and later attended the universities of Bonn and Berlin. He received his doctorate in philosophy at the University of Tübingen in 1877

Those who influenced Tönnies most during his student years were Friedrich Paulsen, the philosopher, Adolph Wagner, the economist, and Wilhelm Wundt, the famous social psychologist.

In 1881 he became lecturer at the University of Kiel and remained with this institution until his removal by the Nazis in 1933. His connection with the University of Kiel, though he served the University for more than fifty years, was a loose one. He served only eight years in the rank of full professor and preferred research, writing, and travel to teaching.

His interest in sociology was greatly influenced by his early studies of Thomas Hobbes' philosophy of law and his theory of the state. One sometimes tends to forget that Tönnies, in addition to his major sociological works Gemeinschaft und Gesellschaft *and* Einführung in die Soziologie, *also made significant contributions to the philosophy of law, and wrote a comprehensive work on public opinion,* Kritik der öffentlichen Meinung (1922).

There is, however, no doubt that Ferdinand Tönnies will best be remembered for his major work, Gemeinschaft und Gesellschaft (Community and Society). *His conception of social theory was unusual in that he considered social theory as sociological data, mere expressions of social volition and reflections of actual social conditions.*[1]

His main purpose was to develop scientific concepts which could be used as tools with which to grasp the historical process. We certainly should not consider Gemeinschaft und Gesellschaft *as an attempt to describe the development from primitive, original communism to socialism, but much more as an exposition of categories which have been used by social scientists ever since Tönnies introduced them to us.*

Beside being the founder of the German Sociological Society Ferdinand Tönnies was also an honorary member of the American Sociological Society. He died in 1936 at eighty-one and, as Rudolf Heberle has said, was "one of the last scholars in our time who could be said to possess a truly universal erudition in the humanities and the cultural and social sciences."[2]

COMMUNITY AND SOCIETY

Knowledge and Nonknowledge

Sociology is the study of man, not of his bodily nor of his psychical, but of his social nature. His bodily and psychical beings are considered only in so far as they condition his social nature. It is our purpose to study the sentiments and motives which draw people to each other, keep them together, and induce them to joint action. We wish especially to investigate the products of human thought which, resulting therefrom, make possible and sustain a common existence. They find their consummation in such important forms as community, state, and church, which are often felt to be realities or even supernatural beings.

Nosce te ipsum (know yourself); if you want to understand others, look into your own heart. Every one of us has manifold relationships, direct and indirect, with other people. Every one of us knows many people, but only few in proportion to their total number. Thus the question arises, how do I know other people?

[1] *An Introduction to the History of Sociology,* edited by Harry Elmer Barnes, University of Chicago Press, Chicago, 1948. See p. 228.

[2] P. 229, ibid.

We shall first study the distinction between all people and those we know, without regard to the question as to how we come to know people. The distinction will head a list of four dichotomies dealing with one's relation to one's fellow beings. This distinction is:

1. *Acquaintanceship and Strangeness.* It is not necessary to do more than simply indicate the great importance of this distinction. In a crowd of strangers, in a strange city, one may meet by chance an acquaintance, perhaps even a familiar acquaintance or at least an acquaintance of long standing. This is usually a pleasant experience. One is likely to strike up a conversation with him at once, something one is seldom inclined to do with a complete stranger. Often what little inclination one has to converse with strangers is impeded by a foreign language. If the individual is only a casual acquaintance, it may be the first (and possibly the last) time that one shakes hands with him. Such a casual acquaintance may be a stranger except for the fact that he is known in some special capacity such as that of being engaged in the same profession or line of work; or it may be that the two persons have met once before and exchanged a few words. A casual acquaintance of mine may be a citizen of another country and have a different mother tongue, but he is known to me and is an acquaintance even if we had and still have difficulty in understanding each other. In the German language there is a subtle distinction between an acquaintance and a person whom one only "knows." An acquaintance, my acquaintance, knows me, too; someone whom I only know does not, in all probability, know me or, at least, will not necessarily know me. An individual occupying a high position is seen and known by many whom he himself overlooks, whom he does not know and very often does not wish to know. The person whom I know may not remember me or, even if he should, may not wish to take notice of me. I may not mean anything to him, or he may not like me. In contradistinction, an acquaintance is considered by many as being among their "friends." This may often be a sign of a superficial intellectual attitude or manner of speech, although, of course, acquaintanceship implies a slight tendency toward mutual approval just as strangeness implies a tendency toward mutual negation. This is, to be sure, only a tendency, but tendencies are important.

2. *Sympathy and Antipathy.* The fact that one knows a person or is acquainted with him does not necessarily imply that one likes him or is fond of him or (a rarer occurrence)

loves him. There is, of course, tremendous difference between those who are congenial to us and those whom we regard with antipathy. Sympathy and antipathy are feelings; they are often defined as instincts, that is, as something subhuman. In reality, they are frequently connected with thought and knowledge and thus with higher and nobler feelings which distinguish the human being. Indeed, they often spring from such feelings and from our thoughts and knowledge. A certain relationship of some significance exists, as has already been pointed out, between acquaintance and sympathy on the one hand and between strangeness and antipathy on the other. The more sympathy and antipathy are instinctive, the more they are related to outward appearance, especially where women are concerned. This holds true, above all, for the feelings resulting from the impression made upon them by a man. Such impression may be produced by his figure, his face and expression, his dress, his behavior, his manners, his way of speech, even the sound of his voice. Men, too, often fall in love with women at first sight. For some a beautiful figure, for others a lovely face, is the decisive factor; for some it is the expression of the eyes alone or the polished way of speaking, for still others the elegant dress or the smart hat. Immediate and instinctive sympathy or antipathy may, however, be counteracted in actual experience, by a more intimate knowledge of the hitherto strange person. One finds, for instance, that someone who gave one an unfavorable impression at first turns out to be quite a nice person, perhaps interesting or positively charming. It even happens that women and girls may develop a passionate affection for a man who, in the beginning, was as repulsive to them as was Richard the Third to the widowed queen. It is another question whether a steadfast, faithful love can spring from such a root. In many cases experience may prove the first impression to have been correct; but the reverse is also well known and practically a daily occurrence. An excellent impression may so bias one in favor of an individual that after more intimate acquaintance one may reproach oneself for having been taken in by a brilliant outward appearance.

But our souls, our feelings, are indifferent to the great mass of people, not only to those who are unknown to us, the strangers, but also even to those whom we know reasonably well. This indifference is, however, not immovably fixed; there may easily develop a tendency fluctuating between antipathy and sympathy. Sympathies and antipathies can be of many different degrees, especially if we take into consideration the above-mentioned intelligent sympathy and antipathy which are rooted in our thinking consciousness. We shall usually have a certain degree of sympathy, even though this may be small, for those who side with us, whether we have known them before or came to know them only as fellow fighters, comrades, countrymen, or even home folks, or as colleagues, or as persons of the same faith, same political party, same profession. Sympathy may also be engendered by the fact that individuals belong to the same estate, as in the case of the nobility, or the same class, as in the case of the proletariat or the propertied class. In the same way there exists, on the other hand, some antipathy toward all those who are in the opposite camp. Such antipathy often increases to the point of hatred, especially if a real conflict exists between the opposing sides. In other instances such antipathy manifests itself only in, and is reduced to, greater indifference, so that it can easily, as a result of close acquaintance or other motives, be transformed into real sympathy. However, the same or similar interests are sufficient to arouse sympathy to the extent that such similarities are in the consciousness of those involved, and by the same token contrary interests will evoke antipathy. For example, at times the masses have and are conscious of common interests as consumers. At such times they will feel a slight sympathy for one another. Their interests are opposed to those of producers and merchants, toward whom their antipathy is directed, and such antipathy is stronger than their mutual sympathy.

3. *Confidence and Mistrust.* The third difference to which I wish to draw attention is that of confidence or mistrust toward other people. An individual whom we know will inspire in us a certain confidence, however slight; a stranger, on the other hand, is likely to create in us a certain feeling, often quite strong, of mistrust. Furthermore, sympathy may easily and rather quickly lead to a feeling of confidence which is often just as quickly regretted, whereas antipathy may arouse, strengthen, and further a mistrust which sometimes proves to be unwarranted. But here again, how many gradations exist! Only in a chosen few do we have such great and abiding confidence that we rely on their absolute sincerity, affection, and faithfulness toward ourselves and our nearest, and feel we can build upon their devotion. As is well known, these chosen few are not always our "equals." When not, they have no claim to that sympathy which is characteristic of those of the

same class, the same estate. The faithful servant, the faithful maid, are not only figures of sagas and fiction, although they are more frequent under simpler and more rural than under modern conditions. Confidence betrayed—this is indeed a terrible, embittering experience which often leads to despair. But even mistrust can change into confidence, just as abused confidence, apart from arousing indignation, anger, and embitterment, will immediately turn into mistrust directed toward those formerly honored with confidence. Not only one's own but also other people's experience may lead one either to confidence in or mistrust of a person, thus investing him with either a reliable or a dubious reputation.

On the other hand, confidence has become highly impersonalized through modern trade. Personality has come to be of little or no importance. Only the "wealth" of a person counts, for it is assumed, and usually on valid grounds, that self-interest will induce even the personally less reliable businessman to pay his debts as long as he is able to do so. Personal reliability fades as it is transformed into reliability as debtor. As a rule, it is the business or manufacturing firm (irrespective of the moral qualities of its owner or manager) which has financial credit and is sound, or at least is supposed to be sound. In fact, as a result of this kind of confidence in the financial standing of the firm, the moral quality of its head may still be considered intact even though there may exist good reasons for a contrary judgment. Thus, confidence in the financial credit of the person or firm, like confidence in personal qualities, is often betrayed.

Moreover, without being conscious of it, we often trust many people on the strength of very slight knowledge concerning the persons involved. Sometimes we do not even know them or anything about them except that they are at their posts. This, too, is impersonalized confidence. Personal confidence is essentially conditioned by the personalities of those who confide; that is, by their intelligence, their knowledge of human nature, and their experience, on which the latter is based. Thus, in the case of personal confidence, simple-minded and inexperienced people are in general inclined to be trustful, whereas the intelligent and experienced persons are inclined to doubt. However, this difference all but disappears where rationalized confidence is concerned. We do not know the engineer who runs our train or the captain and the pilots who direct the course of our ship; in many cases we do not know the doctor whom we ask for advice, to whom we even entrust body and life for a surgical operation. Very often we do not know the lawyer whom we request to take our case, still less do we know the judge who will decide the case for or against us and who, we hope and expect, will restore our rights and our honor and do justice to our claims. In all these cases we rely (*a*) on skill (or knowledge), or (*b*) on volition. As far as that skill (or knowledge) is concerned, we are justified in trusting an individual because (1) skill (or knowledge) is bound up with his profession. How could he dare call himself a doctor, a lawyer, or a judge, if he were not such? The shoemaker, the locksmith, and the tailor also know their trades, their arts. The greater the importance of a matter, the more we rely on (2) examinations, (3) experience, (4) reputation, and (5) the personal advice or recommendation which opened the door for a man or woman to this activity or this office. In many cases, however, as, for instance, in that of the engineer or pilot, only the qualifications (2) and (3) are required.

As far as volition is concerned, we put our trust in (*a*) certain normal moral qualities and the assumption that the individual in whose care we entrust ourselves could not possibly follow this profession if he did not possess at least a modicum of such qualities. Closely connected therewith is (*b*) his own self-interest, either material or nonmaterial, both of which usually merge into each other.

But it can easily be seen that something else besides these reasons underlies our peace of mind, our feeling of security. Our confidence in that which is regular and safe, although we are rarely aware of it, rests upon the three great systems of social will which I define as order, law, and morality. The two functions last mentioned, the legal and the moral orders or systems, are the fully developed types of the first one.

4. *Interdependence.* And now I come to the fourth difference, which is closely related to and partly contained in the first three. This is the difference between my condition in case I am "bound" in some way to other people and my condition in case I am completely independent and free from them. The condition of being bound to others is the exact opposite of freedom, the former implying a moral obligation, a moral imperative, or a prohibition. There exists a great variety of such "ties," which involve an individual through different types of relationships. These ties may also be called types of social entities (*soziale Wesenheiten*) or forms which link him to his fellow beings. He is bound in these social entities if he

is conscious of being linked to them. His consciousness of the tie is either predominantly emotional or predominantly intellectual. From this consciousness there results a feeling or a realization of moral obligation, moral imperative, or prohibition, and a righteous aversion to the consequences of incorrect, illegal, and unlawful, as well as of immoral and indecent conduct and action.

To talk of such relationships as "bonds" implies, of course, a figurative use of the term, just as no social ties or associations are to be interpreted in terms of the literal meaning of the words. That a human being is tied to another human being can indicate a state of complete dependence. This, however, is a figurative expression indicating that one of the two beings involved does not or cannot have a will of his own, but depends for whatever he may desire on the volition of the other one. Thus, the dependence of the infant, and, in a diminishing degree, of the small child, on his mother or any other person who takes care of him, is an obvious fact. Of similar character are those types of dependence in which the well-being of a person is determined less by his own will than by the will of others. Such dependence is most typically exemplified by servitude, slavery, and the like. It finds its most visible and thus most forceful expression in such physical constraint as was used with slaves and is still practiced in transporting hardened criminals. Referring to an inability to act on one's own will which may result from a completely weak will we also speak of hypnotized persons, sexual slavery, and the like.

5. *Social Relationship or Bond; Connection.* Social relationship or bond implies interdependence, and it means that the will of the one person influences that of the other, either furthering or impeding, or both. If the volition of the one meets and combines with the volition of the other, there results a common volition which may be interpreted as unified because it is mutual. This common volition postulates or requires, and thus controls, the volition of A in accordance with the volition of B as well as the volition of B in accordance with the volition of A. This is the simplest case of the social will of two individuals, whom I prefer to call persons when referring to volition and action of each toward the other. In the same way as a person can be linked with another person, he can be united with many persons, and these again can be connected with one another; thus, the will of each single person who belongs to a group is part of and at the same time

conditioned by the group's collective will, which is to say he is dependent on it. Such collective will can take various forms, determined by the number of persons involved, its own character, and the mode of its existence, that is, the way in which it is expressed. Also, the individuals become conscious of it in many different ways. The collective will can remain the same for an indefinite period, but it can also from time to time undergo change by renewed acts. It can affect the persons involved either directly or indirectly in that a more comprehensive collective will may influence a smaller group and this, in turn, exert its influence upon the smallest unit. Every collective will can represent itself in a single natural person or in a number of those whose common will is conceived as the representative of a higher collective will.

Every collective will can be given a special name, but it can also bear the name of a thinking agent which designates the united multitude. What this name stands for is then conceived and thought of by the persons of this group as a person like themselves. That is to say, a collective person is one on whom either other collective persons or, in the simplest case, natural persons ultimately depend. They all know of their dependence on one another and thereby on the collective will which, in the simplest case, represents their own interrelationship or unity, and it is through this very knowledge that they are connected with one another. All following discussions in which such names are used must be interpreted in this sense. These names are taken from everyday language, where they were given a fixed meaning long ago, although very often without the proper insight into their real character. No clear and conscious distinction was made between a meaning that points only to the external form or significance as a group, a crowd, a band, and so on, and a meaning which is given to them by a scientific system of concepts, in which they are to be conceived as personalities and agents of a collective or social will; in other words, as social entities or phenomena.

That all these social entities have both similarities and differences in meaning and form can be easily deduced. Similarity exists in so far as they contain a social will which determines the cooperating individual wills by giving them rights as well as imposing duties on them and by defining the right of one person as the duty of another, and vice versa. The difference among them lies in the fact that each finds its most perfect form as an imaginary (artificial) social person. Such a collective person consists of single persons, first individuals

or, possibly, other subordinated collective persons. Even in
the simplest possible case for every person concerned there
is imposed a moral imperative by the collective (joint) will
as well as by his own will.

BARTER AND EXCHANGE AS SIMPLIEST TYPE OF SOCIAL RELATION OR BOND

WE shall most easily understand the diverse *modus operandi*
of social relationships or bonds if we relate all the varieties to
the simplest type, which is also the most rational one. Here
we are thinking of the case of simple barter or mutual promis-
sory obligations, which may be conceived of as prolonged
barter. Barter presents a typical and clear case because, in its
simplest form, it involves two separate objects which are related in no way other than that each is a means with respect
to the other, which is considered an end; each of them is useful and thus of value as a means to obtain the other.

If we agree to conceive of all acts of mutual aid and assistance as barter or exchange, it will be evident that all living
together is a continuous exchange of such aid and assistance
and that the degree of its intimacy depends upon its frequency. However, the character of these relationships is
determined by the underlying motives involved, which motives will manifest definite differences. In the simple case
where only two persons are considered, the essential motive
on the part of those involved can be characterized as follows:
from one side there may be expectation of and desire for
assistance, from the other there may be expectation, desire,
and restraint. This condition resembles the expectation and
demands of a collective entity which binds the individual;
that is to say, so connects him to others and constrains him
that this entitiy may take the place of and represent these
others. In distinct contrast is the case in which one's motives
to satisfy one's volition and desires take the form of satisfying
those of another individual, others, or whole groups, even
though one's own volition and desire may apparently be fostered by the similar volition and desires of the other or
others. Such volition and desire necessarily result in a different attitude toward the other individual or individuals. It is
essentially unconditional, like the love of the mother for her
infant, from whom she does not expect or require anything so
long as he has not reached the age of reason. Love alone does

not bind. Thus, definite liking and benevolence, even though it be love, becomes atrophied when one party fails to return it. Such love may be allowed to continue its pitiful existence on the basis of the faintest hope or mere knowledge of the presence of the other loved one because one party may make the welfare of the other his own will, as is especially true in the case of sexual love. However, such love can also turn to hate (the more passionate, the earlier) which then becomes an inverted love, just as self-love frequently leads to self-destruction.

The derived and higher type of social bond always contains that element which we may designate, on the one hand, as containing mutual advantage, assistance, or amicable activity, and, on the other, as always containing an element of binding social will which works on and controls the individual will. Always the obligation and reciprocity makes itself felt and is thereby recognizable in that an inadequate and opposing action of a partner (participant or fellow member) calls forth a counteraction of one or the other and consequently of the whole if this latter continues to exist, which will be the more likely the less this whole's continuity depends upon the action of one person. Thus, for example, a friendship of two and frequently a marriage, even though this latter is conditioned by an existing social will of a higher type, is dependent upon the behavior of both partners and may be broken. On the other hand, in an association the individual cannot as a rule accomplish this, and only the action of a group strengthens or endangers its existence. The opposition between a majority and a minority makes itself felt in such a group, and thus it may differ from the condition in which two individuals are involved. This difference is apparent if the majority wishes to retain or change the whole and if it is strong enough, as opposed to the minority, to make its will prevail over the whole. One must conceive as a normal case the condition in which individuals or parts, such as a minority, which act against the social will call forth the indignation of the majority, and the latter is in possession of sufficient power to react accordingly and, insofar as this is the case, will objectively represent the will of the whole even when the will of an important minority is opposed. Sociologically more important, however, is the case in which the principle prevails, perhaps having been recorded in expressed form, that the will of the majority or, at least, an especially large majority, shall prevail as the will of the whole corporation, social organization, or commission, so that after a resolution is passed the opposition is dissolved, at least for the time being.

BASES OF SOCIAL RELATIONS

1. *Social Entities* (soziale Wesenheiten). Sociology as a special science has as its subject the "things" which result from social life, and only from social life. They are products of human thinking and exist only for such thinking; that is, primarily for individuals themselves who are bound together and who think of their collective existence as dominating them and as a something which is represented as a person capable of volition and action, to which they give a name. The existence of such a something, a social person, can be recognized and acknowledged by outsiders, who may themselves be single or associated individuals, or by a social entity formed by such persons. Such recognition, if mutual, may create a new, essentially similar entity, in the most perfect case, a new social person, which again is existent immediately for its founders but can also be observed, recognized, and acknowledged by outsiders. The manner of existence of this social thing or person is not unlike that of the gods, which, being imagined and thought of by men who are bound together, are also created in order to be glorified, whether the form be that of an animal, a human being, or mixed being. There is, however, an obvious difference in that the gods disappear for the people to whom they belong when their existence is no longer believed in, even though they remain as subjects of the theoretical, historical, and sociological thinking. In contradistinction, social "entities," as we call them, do not require such belief or delusion. They can be thought of as subjects of common volition and operation in clear perception of their imaginary nature. Of course, it is also possible, indeed not an infrequent occurrence, that to the social entities, just as in the case of the gods, a supernatural or, better stated, a metaphysical nature will be ascribed. The fanciful mythological thinking to which man has always been inclined constantly prevails in this sense and will, therefore, often confuse the inventions and fantasies of one or the other type; the social entities, especially the collective persons, are superior, powerful, and exalted, and so are the gods. Thus, in the social entity there exists at least some of the godlike characteristics. They stand under the special protection of the gods, espe-

cially when to such an entity a supernatural origin is ascribed, as in the case of the church.

When the god is himself represented as a powerful and feared or as a benevolent and kind ruler, he is ruler over the earthly ruler, giving the latter his consecration, confirming and befriending him, establishing his right, especially the right of hereditary succession, as a god-given right. By the grace of God the earthly ruler reigns, enjoying a godlike veneration. All kinds of veneration, as they spring from natural feeling as childish adoration or as awe of the weak for the strong, who may be hated and detested, are interwoven one with another and with the gods in whom they find their consummation and shine forth as religion. As obedient servants of the gods, powerful men are agents and interpreters of the will of God and thereby increase their own power.

Even though this mere creature of thought does not live in the clouds or on Olympus but has ascribed to it an existence such as that which is perhaps embodied in the assembly of an armed force or other meeting of the people, it will not easily avoid that condition in which its existence is brought into relationship with that of the gods. The belief in the gods can support the belief in the republic just as the belief in the church and the veneration of the priesthood are directly related. The scientific critical attitude destroys all these illusions. It recognizes that only human thought and human will are contained in all these imaginary realms, that they are based upon human hopes and fears, requirements and needs, and that in their exalted forms they are comparable to poetical works of art on which the spirit of the ages has worked.

Thus, we return to the simple problem and thought: What, why, and how do thinking human beings will and want? The simple and most general answer is: They want to attain an end and seek the most appropriate means of attaining it. They strive toward a goal and seek the correct way leading thereto. This is the action, the behavior, which in the affairs of practical life, of daily work, of struggle, of trade, has through the ages been directed and made easier by pleasure and devotion, by hope and fear, by practice and habit, by model and precept.

2. *Human Volition.* The general human volition, which we may conceive as natural and original, is fulfilled through knowledge and ability and is also fundamentally conditioned through reciprocal interaction with them. The whole intellect, even in the plainest man, expresses itself in his knowledge

and correspondingly in his volition. Not only what he has learned but also the inherited mode of thought and perception of the forefathers influences his sentiment, his mind and heart, his conscience. Consequently I name the will thought of in this latter sense natural will *(Wesenwille)*, contrasting it with the type of rational will *(Kürwille)*, in which the thinking has gained predominance and come to be the directing agent. The rational will is to be differentiated from intellectual will. Intellectual will gets along well with subconscious motives which lie deep in man's nature and at the base of his natural will, whereas rational will eliminates such disturbing elements and is as clearly conscious as possible.

Deliberation, the thought form of ends and means, can separate the two, one from the other. From this results the inference that the means are not fundamentally connected to the end; that is to say, the means and end are not allied, interwoven, or identical. The means may rather be completely isolated and therefore possibly even stand in strong opposition to the ends. In this case the end under consideration requires that the means be as suitable to it as possible, that no means or segment thereof be used which is not conditioned by the end, but that the means most suitable for the attainment of a given end be chosen and used. This implies a definite divorce and differentiation of end and means which, therefore, permits no consideration of means other than that of their perfect suitability for the attaining of the end. The principle of the rationalization of the means develops everywhere as a necessary consequence the more thought, in accordance with the desire and intention, is intensively focused on the end or the goal. This signifies, therefore, an attitude of indifference to the means with respect to every consideration other than their greatest effectiveness in attaining the end. This indifference is frequently attained only by overcoming resistance resulting from motives other than the consideration of the end, which motives may hinder, dissuade, or frighten one from the application of this means. Thus, action which adjusts the means to the end desired may be viewed with definite reluctance, also with fear and anxiety, or, more characteristically, with aversion and, what is akin thereto, with feelings of opposition such as come with remorse. With some exaggeration, Goethe says the acting man is always "without conscience." In reality, the acting person often finds it necessary, if he "unscrupulously" follows his goal, to repress or overcome his conscientiousness. On account of this necessity, many consider themselves justified in despising or disowning such feelings, and sometimes they even find their satisfaction in bravado and arrogance, making themselves free from all such considerations.

This means, therefore, that on the one hand there is the simple emotional (impulsive) and, therefore, irrational volition and action, whereas on the other there is the simple rational volition and action in which the means are arranged, a condition which often stands in conflict with the feelings. Between these two extremes all real volition and action takes place. The consideration that most volition and action resembles or is inclined toward either one or the other makes it possible to establish the concepts of natural will and rational will, which concepts are rightly applied in this sense. I call them normal concepts. What they represent are ideal types, and they should serve as standards by which reality may be recognized and described.

3. *Gemeinschaft and Gesellschaft.* It is not a question of contrasting the rational will with the nonrational will, because intellect and reason belong to natural will as well as to rational will. Indeed, intellect in natural will attains its fruition in the creative, formative, and artistic ability and works and in the spirit of the genius. This is true even though in its elementary forms natural will means nothing more than a direct, naïve, and therefore emotional volition and action, whereas, on the other hand, rational will is most frequently characterized by consciousness. To the latter belongs manufacturing as contrasted with creation; therefore, we speak of mechanical work (as expressed in the German and other languages) referring to forging plans, machinations, weaving intrigues, or fabrications which are directed to the objective of bringing forth the means, the exclusive determination of which is that of producing the outward effects necessary to attain our desired ends.

When these concepts are applied to associations, it should not be understood that we are thinking only of the regular motives leading to the entrance into an association, creating of a confederation, or organizing of a union or special-interest group, or even the founding of a commonwealth. It is, however, of importance to recognize what motives lie at the basis of and explain the existence of all kinds of association or cause their persistence; and while we are here interested only in positive bases, this holds also for negative motives upon which persistence may be based. In this connection it is not to be

understood that the bases belong fundamentally and persist-
ently either to the one or the other category, that is, of natural
will or rational will. On the contrary a dynamic condition or
process is assumed which corresponds to the changeable elements of human feeling and thinking. The motives fluctuate
so that they are now of one category, then of the other. However, wherever such development takes place a certain regularity or even "law," in the sense of a tendency toward
abstract rational forms, may be observed.

I call all kinds of association in which natural will pre-
dominates Gemeinschaft, all those which are formed and
fundamentally conditioned by rational will, Gesellschaft.
Thus, these concepts signify the model qualities of the essence
and the tendencies of being bound together. Thus, both
names are in the present context stripped of their connotation
as designating social entities or groups, or even collective or
artificial persons; the essence of both Gemeinschaft and
Gesellschaft is found interwoven in all kinds of associations,
as will be shown.

SOCIAL SYSTEMS

1. *Relationships, Collectives, Social Organizations.* As social entities or forms, I differentiate: (1) Social relationships
(Verhältnisse), (2) Collectives *(Samtschaften),* (3) Social
organizations or corporate bodies *(Körperschaften)* (leagues,
fellowships, associations, or special-interest groups).

The third form is always thought of as a kind of human
person capable of creating a definite unified will which, as the
will of the natural or artificial persons belonging to it, binds
and constrains them to act in conformity with such will,
which may be directed inwardly or outwardly. In the social
relationship it is not the relationship itself which is so considered, even though it be designated by a special name.
However, it is essential that its subjects or bearers, who may
be considered as "members" of the relationship, are conscious
of it as a relationship which they will affirmatively and thus
establish as an existing reality. This manner of establishing
a social relationship represents in embryonic or emergent form
what is evolved to perfection in the establishment of a social
organization or corporation capable of willing and acting.

The collective lies between the social relationship and the
social organization. It is thought of as a plurality which, like
the social organization, includes a multitude of persons so

held together that there result common intentions, desires, inclinations, disinclinations—in short, common feelings and ways of thinking. However, the collective is not capable of real volition. It can reach no decision as long as it does not "organize" itself into a committee, special-interest group, or council.

2. *The Social Relationship.* The social relationship is the most general and simplest social entity or form. It also has the deepest foundation, because it rests partly upon the original, natural, and actual conditions as the causes of connections, of mutual dependence, and of attachment among men, and because it rests partly on the most fundamental, most universal, and most necessary requirements of human beings. The one basis, like the other, is raised to consciousness with different effects. If a natural relationship exists, as for example between my brother and me, on one hand, or between my brother-in-law, my stepbrother, adopted or foster brother and me, on the other, I have the feeling that we are intimate, that we affirm each other's existence, that ties exist between us, that we know each other and to a certain extent are sympathetic toward each other, trusting and wishing each other well. This is true although in the latter case, involving persons who are not blood brothers, the relationship is not so natural as in the first where I know the same mother gave birth to both my brother and me. From this it follows that we have certain values in common, whether it be that we are obliged to manage an estate together, or that we divide possessions as inheritances between us, or that the matter of intellectual goods or ideals is involved. At any rate, out of each such relationship, even between two, there result the recognition and acknowledgment of the social relationship as such on the part of each and therefore the knowledge of each that definite mutual action must regularly result therefrom. This action is expected and demanded of each by the other, and each expects and demands of himself that it be carried out in relation to the other. In this lies the embryo of "rights" which each claims for himself but also concedes to the other, as well as "duties" to which one feels obligated but which one puts upon oneself knowing that the other party wills that he be and considers that he is so obligated.

However, when I become conscious of my most urgent needs and find that I can neither satisfy them out of my own volition nor out of a natural relation, this means that I must do something to satisfy my need; that is, engage in free activity which is bound only by the requirement or possibly conditioned by the need but not by consideration for other people. Soon I perceive that I must work on other people in order to influence them to deliver or give something to me which I need. Possibly in restricted individual cases my mere requests will be granted, as, for example, in the case of a piece of bread or a glass of water. However, as a rule when one is not receiving something in a Gemeinschaft-like relationship, such as from within the family, one must earn or buy it by labor, service, or money which has been earned previously as payment for labor or service.

I now enter or have already entered into a social relationship, but it is of a different kind. Its prototype is barter or exchange, including the more highly developed form of exchange, the sale and purchase of things or services, which are the same as things and are therefore thought of as capable of being exchanged for things or for other services. All action which is of an intellectual nature, and consequently oriented by reason, is of this type because comparison and thinking are necessary to it and furnish a basis for it. Social relationships which result from such barter or exchange are primarily momentary in that they involve a momentary common volition. However, they come to have duration partly through repetition resulting in regularity of the exchange act and partly through the lengthening of the individual act by the postponement of fulfillment on the part of one or both sides. In this latter case there results a relationship, the distinguishing characteristic of which is a one-sided or mutual "promise." It is a real social relationship of obligation or mutual dependence resulting first of all from mutual promises, even though they may be expressly stated by one side and only tacitly understood by the other as such an eventual promise.

Also, the relationships which come to us from nature are in their essence mutual, are fulfilled in mutual performance. The relations produce this mutuality and demand, require, or make it necessary. Having these characteristics, they resemble the exchange relationship. However, the natural relationship is, by its very essence, of earlier origin than its subjects or members. In such natural relationships it is self-evident that action will take place and be willed in accordance with the relationship, whether it be what is contained on the one hand in the simplest relationships resulting from desire and inclination, from love or habit, or on the other hand from reason or intellect contained in the feeling of duty. These latter types of natural will change into one another, and each can be the basis of Gemeinschaft.

On the other hand, in the purest and most abstract contract relationship the contracting parties are thought of as separate, hitherto and otherwise independent, as strangers to each other, and perhaps even as hitherto and in other respects inimical persons. *Do, ut des* (I give, so that you will give) is the only principle of such a relationship. What I do for you I do only as a means to effect your simultaneous, previous, or later service for me. Actually and really I want and desire only this. To get something from you is my end; my service is the means thereto, which I naturally contribute unwillingly. Only the aforesaid and anticipated result is the cause which determines my volition. This is the simplest form of rational will.

Relationships of the first type are to be classified under the concept Gemeinschaft, those of the other type under the concept of Gesellschaft, thus differentiating Gemeinschaft-like and Gesellschaft-like relationships. Gemeinschaft-like relationships differ to the extent that there is assumed, on the one hand, a real, even if not complete, equality in knowledge or volition, in power and in authority on the part of the participants, and on the other hand, an essential inequality in these respects. This also holds for the relations of Gesellschaft. In accordance with this distinction we shall differentiate between the fellowship type and the authoritative type of social relationship. Let us now consider this difference.

A. In Gemeinschaft-Like Relationships. (*a*) The Fellowship Type. The simplest fellowship type is represented by a pair who live together in a brotherly, comradely, and friendly manner, and it is most likely to exist when those involved are of the same age, sex, and sentiment, are engaged in the same activity or have the same intentions, or when they are united by one idea.

In legend and history such pairs occur frequently. The Greeks used to honor such friendships as those of Achilles and Patroclus, Orestes and Pylades, Epaminondas and Pelopidas, to the extent that to Aristotle is ascribed the paradox: He who has friends has no friend. In the German language and literature it is customary to designate such sentiments, the nature of which the Greeks glorified as mutual happiness and sorrow, as a brotherly relationship. This characterization is based more on the thought of the ideal than on actual observation, but it is correct insofar as brothers actually make the most natural as well as the most probable pairs of friends, more because of their origin than because of a motive.

(*b*) Authoritative Type. The relationship of father to child, as observations in everyday life will prove, is to be found in all the strata of society in all stages of culture. The weaker the child and the more it is in need of help, the greater the extent to which the relationship is represented by protection. Protection of necessity always carries with it authority as a condition, because protection regularly can be carried out only when the protected party follows the directions and even the commands of the protector. Although all authority has a tendency to change into the use of force, in the case of the father as well as the mother relationship such a tendency is arrested by love and tenderness. These sentiments, being of animal and vegetative origin, are more likely to be regularly accorded to a child born to a parent than to any other possessed and protected person. The general character of the father relationship can be easily extended to include similar relationships involving protection, examples of which are the stepfather, foster father, the general house father, and the guardian, even though these, as representatives of the father, do not necessarily legally stand in Gemeinschaft-like relation to the ward. The authority of the father is the prototype of all Gemeinschaft-like authority. It is especially true in the case of the priesthood, even though the basis may be different. This rests primarily upon mythological conceptions which place the father in Olympus or in heaven and perhaps ascribe numberless children to the father of the gods and men. Or in a less sensual, more refined form, the father may be represented by an only son whom the struggle against polytheism tends almost to identify with the father. Little wonder that the title Pope (*Papa*, literally "father") in the original church of all bishops was raised to the pinnacle of spiritual dignity in the Roman Church and that in the Oriental Church the especially high priests are called fathers (*Popen*) in the language of the common people. Also, world and political authority, which is often mixed with and may not be less sanctified than the spiritual, easily takes on the character of the well-wishing father, as is most plainly expressed in the term "father" of a country. The fatherly authority, however, is the special case of authority of age, and the prestige-giving quality of age expresses itself most perfectly in the authority of the father. This easily explains the eminence which is attributed to the senator in the worldly and the presbyter in the spiritual commonwealth.

(c) Mixed Relationships. In many Gemeinschaft-like relationships the essence of authority and that of fellowship are mixed. This is the case in the most important of the relationships of Gemeinschaft, the lasting relation between man and woman which is conditioned through sexual needs and reproduction, whether or not the relationship is called marriage.

B. In Gesellschaft-Like Relationships. The difference between the fellowship and authoritative types is also to be found in the Gesellschaft-like relationships. It can, however, be derived only from the fact that the authority is based upon a free contract whether between individuals, as service contracts, or by agreement of many to recognize and place a master or head over them and to obey him conditionally or unconditionally. This may be a natural person or a collective person which results directly from individuals uniting in a society, social organization, or corporate body which is capable of volition and action and can be represented through its own totality. The Gesellschaft-like authority attains its consummation in the modern state, a consummation which many predecessors strove to attain until the democratic republic came into existence and allowed for development beyond the Gesellschaft-like foundation. The actual authority results, however, in the simple Gesellschaft-like relationship, from the difference in the power of two parties, as in the labor contract. Such authority results from contracts made between the individual "employer" and individual "employee," and also from the condition out of which come "peace treaties" between victor and conquered. Apparently it is a contract, but in actuality it is coercion and abuse.

3. *The Collective.* The second concept of social entity or form is that of the collective. I make distinctions between natural, psychical, and social collectives. Our concept concerns only social collectives, but these rest partly on natural and partly on psychical collectives, partly on both. This is because the essence of a social collective is to be found in the natural and psychological relationships forming the basis of the collective and are consciously affirmed and willed. This phenomenon appears everywhere in the life of a people and in many forms of mutualities, as, for example, in forms of life and customs, superstitions and religion. It is especially in evidence in the distinguishing characteristic through which a

segment of a people, that is, certain classes, are given prominence, nobility, and authority. A distinguishing characteristic which has this function is partly an objective phenomenon and partly something positive in the people's consciousness. The consciousness of belonging to a controlling estate makes its appearance in a distinct manner as pride and haughtiness —feelings which in turn are coupled with the submission and modesty of those "lower" classes over which authority is exercised so long as the controlling estates, as such, are honored, and so long as their excellence, or even their divinity, is believed in.

In the case of the collective the concepts of Gemeinschaft and Gesellschaft should also be applied. The social collective has the characteristics of Gemeinschaft insofar as the members think of such a grouping as a gift of nature or created by a supernatural will, as is expressed in the simplest and most naïve manner in the Indian caste system. Here, to be fixed to a given calling is just as necessary and natural as being born, and the professional estate or group has the same significance as a large family for which the pursuit and means of making a livelihood, even if this should be accomplished by thievery, is represented as something inherited which it is a duty to retain and nurture. In all systems of ranks or estates, traces of this condition are to be found because (and to the extent that) a complete emancipation from the social relationships established at birth seldom occurred and was often impossible. Thus, man as a rule submits to the social status in which parents and forebears, or, as it is wont to be expressed, "God," has placed him as if it were his lot to bear, even though it be felt as a burden, which, however, is habit and is lightened by the recognition that it cannot be changed. Indeed, within these limits there can exist an intellectual self-consciousness which affirms this estate (rank) even though it be recognized as one of the less significant. This intellectual basis manifests itself partly as the group extols itself for certain superiorities or virtues, the lack of which in the dominating estate is noticed and complained about. Also, the intellectual basis is to be found partly in the consciousness of special knowledge and skill of the group, as, for example, its art, craftsmanship, and skill, which are thought of as being at least the equivalent of the other honored or ruling estates.

Consciousness of a social collective has different results when directed toward the attainment of definite and important ends which it knows to be and claims are its own characteristics. This happens in a pronounced way in the political and intellectual struggle in which the social strata of a people stand against each other as classes. The more the consciousness of authority as a feeling of superiority results in putting one class in such a position of power as to force the lower class to stay in its place, the more this latter will strive toward the attainment of equality and therefore the more indignant it becomes concerning oppression and arrogance on the part of the controlling class, which it attempts to restrict and displace.

Whether this process is called class struggle *(Klassenkampf)* or struggle of estates *(Ständekampf)* is not important. The struggle among the estates usually takes place earlier, is less radical, and can be allayed. The lower estates strive only for the opportunity to participate in the satisfactions of life and fundamentals of authority, allowing the controlling estate to remain in power. This latter remains in power by proclaiming its own fitness and disparaging that of the lower estates and by exerting effort to reduce these lower strata to submission.

The class struggle is more unconditional. It recognizes no estates, no natural masters. In the foreground of the consciousness of the whole class which feels that it is propertyless and therefore oppressed, stands the ideal of the Gemeinschaft of property in field and soil and all the implements of labor. These latter have been acquired through the art of trade or as inherited property belonging by "law" to the small minority which, as the propertied class, is set off against the propertyless class. Therefore, the class struggle becomes more conscious and general than the struggle among the estates. However, even though there be no definite form of struggle there is a corresponding consciousness which makes itself felt in many ways. The great propertyless masses prefer to think of themselves as the people *(Volk)*, and the narrow class which is in control of property and its use thinks of itself as society, even though each expression is all inclusive. "The" people *(Volk)*, as in the case of the estate, resembles the Gemeinschaft; "the" society, like the class, has, in the sense in which it is here used, the basic characteristic of Gesellschaft.

4. *The Social Organization.* The third and most important category of pure or theoretical sociology is the social organization or corporate body, a social body or union known by many other names. It is never anything natural, neither can it be understood as a mere psychical phenomenon. It is completely and essentially a social phenomenon, and must be

considered as composed of several individuals. Capacity for
unified volition and action, a capacity which is demonstrated
most clearly as competency to pass resolutions, characterizes
it. Just as the thinking individual is capable of making decisions, so is a group of several individuals when they continuously agree or agree to the extent that there prevails and is
recognized a definite will as the will of all or sufficient consensus to be the will of the social organization or corporate
body. Thus, the volition of such a group can be represented
by the will of a natural person behind whom the will of the
whole social organization or corporate body stands. Continuing our discussion of social organizations or corporate bodies,
we may make the following observations:

(1) A social organization or corporate body can originate
from natural relationships provided these are social relationships. In this connection, kinship, the most universal and
natural bond which embraces human beings, comes to our
attention. The most important social organization or corporate
body which originates therefrom and which among all known
peoples occurs as the original form of a common life is the
kinship group, the gens, clan, or whatever name is applied to
designate this ancient union or unity.

Whether or not the totality of adult persons includes the
women, whether their council ends in agreement which is
sanctioned by a supposed will of God, or whether they rejoice
in and willingly accept the decisions of a leader and head, it
is under these conditions that there is formed the embryo of
a consciousness which matures into something beyond a mere
feeling of belonging together, and there is established and
affirmed an enduring self or ego in the totality.

(2) A common relation to the soil tends to associate people
who may be kinsfolk or believe themselves to be such. Neighborhood, the fact that they live together, is the basis of their
union; it leads to counseling and through deliberations to
resolutions. Here again the two principles of fellowship and
authority will be involved. The outstanding example of an
association of this type is the rural village community, which
attains its consummation in the cultivation of the soil practiced in common and the possession of common property in
village fields or land held in common by the village, and in
the Mark-community which comes to represent the unity of
several neighboring village communities which originally may
have formed one unit.

The rural village community is frequently identical with a

great family or clan, but the more alien elements are taken in, the more it loses its kinship characteristics. The bond of field and soil and living together first takes its place along with, and later more and more supplants, the bond of common ancestry. Especially when an alien tribe and its leaders become the conquerors of a territory and establish themselves in the seats of control without extirpating or driving out all the former residents and owners does this tendency manifest itself, molding a new people *(Volk)* from the two groups, even though the one was subjected to new masters. The existence of the village community as a social organization or corporate body ordinarily continues in the form of a fellowship. Such a village community, however, may be modified by the power and rights of feudal lords.

(3) In the more intimate and close living together in the town, the fellowship and cooperative quality attains a new level. Living together tends to depend less on common nature. People not related by blood tend to assemble in the towns, since these originally were walled-in villages or strongholds whose inhabitants were forced to cooperate for defense and for the maintenance of peace and order among themselves and thereby to form a political community, either under the rule of a lord or as citizens of equal rights. This was the great mission and service of the town *(Stadt)* community, the *"Polis"* which grew to be that commonwealth which later in Europe and elsewhere up to our time has bequeathed its character and name to the state *(Staat)*, the mightiest of all corporate bodies. That assembly of the sovereign people, the religious association *(Ekklesia)*, the other great commonwealth of the Roman and post-Roman period, loaned its name to the Church and spread its glory throughout the world in a similar manner.

These social bodies and communities retain their common root in that original state of belonging together, which according to our concept is the Gemeinschaft. Indeed, although the original state of common being, living, and working is changed, it retains and is able to renew its mental and political form and its cooperative functions. Thus, a people *(Volk)* which feels itself bound together by a common language, when held together within a national association or even when only striving to become a nation, will desire to be represented in a unity or *Volksgemeinschaft*, which may become intensified by national consciousness and pride, but may also thereby lose its original genuineness.

5. *Capitalistic, Middle-Class, or Bourgeois Society* (bürger-

liche Gesellschaft). During this development, the original qualities of Gemeinschaft may be lost because there takes place a continued change in the original basis upon which living together rests. This change reaches its consummation in what is frequently designated as individualism. Through this development social life in and of itself is not diminished, but social life of the Gemeinschaft is impaired and a new phenomenon develops out of the needs, interests, desires, and decisions of persons who previously worked cooperatively together and are acting and dealing one with another. This new phenomenon, the "capitalistic society," increases in power and gradually attains the ascendancy. Tending as it does to be cosmopolitan and unlimited in size, it is the most distinct form of the many phenomena represented by the sociological concept of the Gesellschaft.

A great transformation takes place. Whereas previously the whole of life was nurtured and arose from the profoundness of the people *(Volk)*, the capitalistic society through a long process spreads itself over the totality of this people, indeed over the whole of mankind. As a totality of individuals and families it is essentially a collective of economic character composed primarily of those who partake in that wealth which, as land and capital, represents the necessary means to the production of goods of all kinds. Within narrow or far-flung borders which are determined by actual or supposed kinship bonds, of the existence of which the language group is the most valuable sign, it constructs its state, that is to say, a kind of unity resembling a town community which is capable of willing and acting. It develops as the capitalistic middle-class republic and apparently finally attains its perfection in the social republic. It considers the state a means of attaining its ends, of which not the least important is protecting its person and property as well as the intellectual attitude which gives status and honor to its supporters.

However, since this capitalistic middle-class society cannot, without betraying itself, admit its uniqueness as a collective of Gesellschaft in contradistinction to the people *(Volk)* or, so to speak, herald this difference by raising its own flag, it can assert its existence only through claiming to be identical with, as well as representative and advocate of, the whole people to which it furnishes guidance. This process, which does not stop with conferring equal political rights on all citizens, to a certain extent closes the always widening hiatus between the wealth monopoly of the narrow and real Gesellschaft and the poverty of the people, but it cannot change the essential character of the hiatus. Indeed, it deepens it, spreading and strengthening the consciousness of the "social question."

By means of political and other intellectual organization promoted by town and, to a greater extent, by city life, the consciousness of the Gesellschaft gradually becomes the consciousness of an increasing mass of the people. The people come more and more to think of the state as a means and tool to be used in bettering their condition, destroying the monopoly of wealth of the few, winning a share in the products. Thus, the laborer would be allowed a share in proper proportion to his reasonable needs, and the leaders in production their share of certain goods which are to be divided for consumption, and those things suitable for continued common utilization would be retained as common property of the Gesellschaft, which is to say of the people or their organized association, the state.

Werner Sombart

(1863–1941)

THE SOCIOLOGY OF CAPITALISM

Werner Sombart was born the son of a self-made industrialist and landowner in Ermsleven-am-Harz, a small town near Magdeburg in Germany. His father, who took an active part in the social and political affairs of his time, was a member of the Reichstag and because of this the family moved to Berlin in 1875. Sombart studied at the University of Berlin and spent two years at the University of Pisa preparing his dissertation. He returned to the University of Berlin in 1888 and took his doctorate from that university in the same year.

In 1890 he accepted his first academic appointment at the University of Breslau and left in 1906 to accept a chair at the newly created Handelshochschule in Berlin. In 1917 he accepted the chair in economics at the University of Berlin, which had been vacated by the noted economist Adolph Wagner. He remained in this position until 1931, when he retired. As a professor he was well known for his lucidity and vigor in the classroom. He continued to write until his death in 1941.

At first, Sombart had been interested in agricultural problems. His doctoral dissertation was a study of Italian agricultural conditions and was entitled Die Römische Campagna. *But soon Sombart turned his attention to the problems of modern capitalism, which then became his lifework. His first book in this field was* Der Moderne Kapitalismus *(1902), and it was subjected to severe criticism. As a result Sombart revised this work over the years and published several studies which were in a sense preparatory to the final revision, which appeared in the years 1916–17.*

In the first part of his academic career Sombart was interested in and a sympathizer with the socialistic movement. A series of lectures on socialism, which he had given in 1896 in Zurich, were published in the same year under the title Sozialismus und soziale Bewegung. *The work was translated into many languages. But in his book* Der proletarische Sozialismus *(1924) Sombart drastically revised his views on*

*socialism as given in his original booklet, and, in effect, he
denounced his former socialistic beliefs.*

Among his many works two other studies stand out: Die
Juden und das Wirtschaftsleben *(1911) and* Die drei nationalekonomien *(1929), in which he expressed his views on
methodology.*

*In his methodology Werner Sombart was close to his col-
league and contemporary, Max Weber. He used the method
of "verstehen," which is sometimes described as a "grasping
of meanings"* (Sinnerfassen). *The quintessence of this method
is the scientific study of phenomena by relating them to a
system of clear relationships.*[1]

SOCIOLOGY OF CAPITALISM

The Spirit of Capitalistic Enterprise

"UNDERTAKING"[2] in its broadest conception means the realization of a well-considered plan, for the carrying out of which it
is needful to have the continued cooperation of many individuals under the guidance of a single will.

The plan must be well defined. Hence sudden instinctive
actions are excluded. You don't talk of an "undertaking" when
a few tramps quickly resolve there and then to set upon and
rob a passing traveler. On the other hand, it is distinctly an
"undertaking" when a gang of desperadoes calmly decide on
a burglary on a certain day, and resolve to meet to do the job.

Item, the plan must needs be realized. It is not enough
merely to conceive the idea, or even to decide its realization.
The action must be consummated.

Item, it must be a plan "for the carrying out of which it is
needful to have the continued cooperation of many individuals." Your plan may be ever so well considered, but if
only a single person carries it out it is not an "undertaking."
Accordingly, every artistic effort and every handicraft production is thus excluded from the conception.

And the plan must be carried out under the guidance of a

[1] For Sombart's position on the concept of "verstehen," see *Die
drei Nationalekonomien,* München, 1930, Ch. XIII "Das Verstehen."

[2] In the German, *die Unternehmung* connotes an undertaking,
or enterprise, of a definite economic character.

single will, which may be embodied in more than one person. If a number of friends plan to take a walk, that is not an "undertaking." But an African expedition, or a Cook's tour, undoubtedly is.

Note that the possibilities of undertaking are coextensive with all human activities, and are not by any means limited to those only that have reference to wealth. Undertaking in the economic sense is merely a subdivision of undertaking as a whole; and capitalist undertaking is a branch of undertaking in the economic sense.

And how shall we describe the spirit of enterprise? It is the resultant of the combination of all the qualities of the soul necessary for the successful consummation of an undertaking. These qualities may be divided, on the one hand, according to the different functions an undertaker has to carry out; and on the other, according to their importance, which varies with the varying work of the undertaker. But in every case, the successful undertaker must be a trinity composed of (1) conqueror, (2) organizer, (3) trader.

1. *The Conqueror.* What are the psychological qualities necessary for carrying out an enterprise? I should say they are three in number. (1) To make plans is one. Which is to say, that you must have ideas. The undertaker must thus possess a certain measure of intellectual freedom. (2) The will to carry out the plan—the will to do. The inventor does not possess this characteristic. For him the discovery or invention suffices. But the undertaker must needs reproduce the invention, must duplicate and multiply it. His one thought is the realization of his plan. What he needs above all is intellectual energy. (3) But he must also have the capacity to carry his scheme through. In other words, he must possess diligent application, turning from his goal neither to the right nor the left. Your true undertaker, who is a conqueror, will have sufficient determination and strength to break down any obstacle that stands in his way. But he must be a conqueror also in his ability to take high risks, and to stake his all in order to achieve greatly. In this he is akin to the gambler.

Sum it all up, and what is his mental outfit? Intellectual elasticity, mental energy, and intensity and constancy of will.

2. *The Organizer.* Seeing that the work on which an undertaker is engaged always requires other people to work with him and be subservient to his will, it follows that the undertaker must above all be a successful organizer. And organizing means so to dovetail the work of many persons as to produce

the most efficient results; so to dispose of human beings and commodities as to effect the desired creation of utilities. Now, obviously, this requires a complex of qualities for its achievement. For one thing, your successful organizer must have the knack of taking exact stock of people, that is, he must be able to pick out of a crowd just those individuals that are going to serve his purpose. For another, he must have the capacity of letting others do his work, putting each one in the place best suited for him, in order to obtain the maximum possible result, and also of getting the most from each. Third, and last, it is the organizer's business to see to it that the cooperating individual units form a productive whole, that the complex relationships are properly co-related. As Clausewitz says of the ideal military commander, what he needs is to gather his forces in the right place, and to have them ready at the right time.

3. *The Trader.* But organizing ability does not complete the undertaker's outfit. His contact with human beings calls for much besides. In the first place, he must obtain the services of his employees. Next, he must by peaceful means influence masses of people whom he does not know, so to shape their conduct that he will derive benefits from it. That is precisely what is done by the leader of an expedition who obtains leave to pass through a strange territory or get provisions for his party; or by a capitalist undertaker who disposes of his goods; or by a statesman who arranges a commercial treaty. In all these cases negotiation is necessary, and negotiation means to confer with another, and, by making the best of your own case and demonstrating the weakness of his, get him to adopt what you propose. Negotiation is but an intellectual sparring match.

Thus, the undertaker must be a skillful negotiator and dealer; and a dealer in the broadest economic sense is a trader. Trading, then, means negotiating concerning the buying and selling of commodities, shares, capital, or businesses. The rag-and-bone man at the backdoor, higgling with cook for a rabbit skin; the old-clo' dealer who spends his eloquence for hours together in order to get the country yokel to buy a pair of his trousers; a Rothschild conferring with an agent of some South American Republic in order to arrange for the floating of a large loan; the representative of the Standard Oil Trust obtaining special freight rates from all the railways in the States; Carnegie and his associates discussing with J. Pierpont Morgan a plan for the taking over by the latter of the

Carnegie Works, at a price that ran into thousands of millions, and of which the historian of the United States Steel Corporation remarks, "It was the most masterly piece of diplomacy in the history of American industry"—all these are instances of trading. The difference between them is merely quantitative; the thing is the same in each case. For the essence of all modern trading is negotiating, though not necessarily face to face. It may even be achieved impersonally, as when a shopkeeper resorts to all manner of tricks in order to try to induce the public to buy his wares. What else is advertising?

In every case, the end in view is to convince buyer or seller of the advantage of the contract. And when the populace is convinced, and hastens in crowds to some particular shop, the shopkeeper's ideal has been realized. To arouse interest, to win confidence, to stir up the desire to purchase—such is the goal of the successful trader. How he reaches it is immaterial, so long as he does reach it by any method except the appeal to force. He must make the other party eager to complete the bargain. The trader must work by suggestion; and one of the most effective suggestions is to convey to the mind the vital importance of closing with the deal at once. " 'It looks like snow, boys,' said the Finns, for they had Aander [a kind of snowshoe] to sell." So we read in the Magnus Barford Saga (A.D. 1006), and the story summarizes all trading, and is an instance of one of the earliest advertisements—that weapon of every modern trader, who no longer dwells in a strongly fortified house, as did his predecessors in Genoa in the days of Benjamin of Tudela; nor does he use cannon to force the natives of some newly discovered territory to trade with him, as did the East India merchants in the seventeenth century. . . .

That every enterprise may be affected by unforeseen circumstances goes without saying. Hence the undertaker must be capable of accommodating himself to changing conditions, must keep his nerve, must be able to do the right thing at the right time. *Coup d'oeil* Frederick the Great called the quality, which he regarded as an essential in his generals (and a general, remember, is also an undertaker in the broad sense); and its realization is assured by determination. . . .

THE BOURGEOIS—OLD STYLE

. . . Is the capitalist spirit constant? Does the bourgeois remain immutably the same? In other words, is there anything common to all the types . . . and to all the national expressions of capitalism, so that it may be possible to sketch the picture of the bourgeois from them?

With one qualification the answer is in the affirmative. And the qualification is that we should be allowed to divide one age of capitalist growth from another according to its characteristic spirit, for it was this that marked off one type of bourgeois or undertaker from another. This means that there was not one persistent type of undertaker at all times, but different sorts at different times.

Now, so far as I can judge, capitalist undertakers from the first dawn of capitalism to about the middle of the eighteenth century—the period which I have christened that of early capitalism—had, with all their variation in details, a good many characteristics in common. These were so definite that they form a clear dividing line between the undertaker of the early capitalist period and his prototype in modern times. What manner of man, then, was he, this bourgeois of old?

To begin with, he also was a capitalist undertaker. Profit was his end, undertakings his means; he speculated and calculated; and ultimately he cultivated the middle-class virtues, though not all in the same degree. What, then, was his distinguishing mark, you ask? How did he differ from his modern brother? You may sum it up in a sentence: In all his thoughts and actions, in all that he did or left undone, he was actuated by the weal or woe of the living, breathing human being. The central doctrine of the precapitalist period had not lost its efficacy. *Omnium rerum mensura homo;* man still continued to be the measure of all things. Life was still natural. Even the bourgeois as yet walked bolt upright on his two feet; he did not yet run about on all fours.

Of course, only fragments remained of the precapitalist man who was still met with in the first faint beginnings of capitalism, when the Genoese noble merchants built them towers, or when Sir Walter Raleigh sallied forth in search of El Dorado. These fragments you may come across in Defoe or Benjamin Franklin. But the remainder of that early natural man with his healthy appetites has disappeared; he has been forced to accustom himself to the straitjacket of middle-class respectability and the tyranny of the calculating habit. His claws have been trimmed, his carnivorous teeth blunted, and his horns encased in leather.

But all those who bowed the knee to capitalism—the rich landowner and the great oversea trader, the banker and the speculator, the manufacturer and the draper—all these never ceased to accommodate their economic activities to the healthy demands of life; for all of them business was but a means of livelihood. Their own interests and those of their fellowmen, for whom and with whom they labored, determined the extent and direction of what they did. In support of this, you need only examine the views of these old-fashioned bourgeois.

1. First and foremost, consider their conception of riches and their attitude toward profit. Wealth was undoubtedly prized, and to obtain it was the passionate desire of every heart. But wealth was not an end in itself. Its only virtue lay in the creation or preservation of life values. This is the tune on which all our informants harp, from Alberti to Defoe and Franklin.

The true value of money, says Alberti, can be appreciated only by him who has at any time been obliged to say to another "that bitter word, which all free spirits hate—'I pray thee.' " Riches should bring you independence and liberty, should get you friends, should make you honored and renowned. On the other hand, "What you cannot make use of is but a heavy burden."

It will suffice to add to these expressions of opinion, dating from the childhood of capitalism, others that were current in the latest period of this early capitalist era. The similarity in sentiment will be apparent.

Our first witness shall be Benjamin Franklin. A man, he says, who has been granted wealth and a soul to use it aright has received a special and splendid gift of grace. Once in possession of riches it is a paramount duty to use them well. "A wise man will desire no more than what he may get justly, use soberly, distribute cheerfully, and live upon contentedly." Riches must be constantly increasing through industry and skillful application. They should never be allowed to lie fallow, but always be adding to their owner's wealth and spreading happiness all around. It is sensible to accumulate goods and money; but to use them well is wise. It is not riches that give happiness, but rather their proper utilization. Riches bring fame, guarantee security, and provide means for many an honorable and useful undertaking. Moreover, wealth must be acquired in just and right ways, for only those riches bring joy that are gotten honestly, or *onestamente*, as Alberti says. If you are selling anything for profit, hearken to the still, small voice of conscience, and be content with fair gain; and take no advantage of the buyer's ignorance.

Now, it may quite rightly be objected that this wise counsel is easily given. In all probability it is the leisure thought of the writers; possibly the voice of conscience heard in the quiet of the study but neglected in the stress and heat of the day. Consequently, it is evidence that must be ruled out of court.

2. To see that such an objection would be invalid, observe (and this is the second point) the attitude of all our authorities to business itself, their conduct as businessmen, the way they carried on their affairs; in a word, their "style" (as it may be called), and you shall find the same spirit in it as that in their attitude toward wealth.

Their business pace was as yet slow; their whole activity was calm and unruffled. There was no stormy whirlwind in their work. Recall Franklin's decision to spend his time as profitably as possible and his view that industry was the prime virtue. His working day was mapped out thus: six full hours were devoted to his business; seven to sleep; and the rest he gave up to prayer, reading, and social diversions. And this was the type of the diligent undertaker, though Franklin was then only in a small way of business.

Leisure was thus appreciated. And just the same as you left yourself an abundance of it during the day and during the year, so, too, you sought to obtain the maximum amount of leisure for life as a whole. It was a common practice for people who had amassed a fortune in business or in industry (even though it were not of great proportions) to retire in middle age, and if possible purchase a country seat where they might end their days in contemplative ease. Jakob Fugger with his "Let me earn so long as I am able"—a dictum typically characteristic for a full-blown capitalist economic outlook—was undoubtedly far in advance of his age. It was for holding such a view that Anton Fugger described him as a queer fish. He was regarded as abnormal. And so he was, judged from the standpoint of those who in their demands on life placed the ideal of the retired private gentleman first and foremost.

This yearning for a peaceful existence in a country house may be found in all the Italian books on trade; in the German Renaissance there was the same tendency to feudalize the traders; and in the eighteenth century the English commercial world still continued to look longingly at this end-all of business. The ideal of the retired private gentleman may thus be regarded as an article of faith in the early capitalist economic creed everywhere. That it had yet another significance we shall see presently.

The domination of this ideal in England in the first half of the eighteenth century is attested by Defoe's remarks on the common English practice to retire from business comparatively early. When a man has amassed £20,000, "why should he trade any farther? and what need he desire any more that has such a bank? 'Tis time to leave off and have done; 'tis time to leave labouring for the world, when he has the world, as they call it, on a string." Such a one "changes his situation in the world, that is to say, he lays down the tradesman and takes up the gentleman with a £1,000 a year estate." Defoe gives him two "seasonable hints." Let him live within the compass of his income. Of his £1,000 a year he should spend half and lay up the remainder, thus ensuring "a rising family under him." Second, he should keep far from speculation, for has he not retired from business to enjoy what he has got? Why then adventure it? All he has to do is to be "quiet when he is arrived at this station of life." After all, "if a tradesman is leaving off, it is with the usual saying of the rich men that withdraw from the world—That he may enjoy himself; that he may live in quiet and peace at the latter end of his days, without noise and without hurry."

That was all very well when they had made their fortune. But while making it, what of their work? Let it be said at once that it was slow. Business methods were such that in any given time you accomplished the least possible transactions. The extensive development of commerce was small; its intensive development was only in accord with it. The spirit in which business was carried on appears to me to be exemplified in the ancient saw to demand as high prices as possible so as to obtain a great rate of profit on a small capital. Small turnover, large profits, seems to have been the ruling principle of the undertakers of those days. And not merely of the lesser men, some of whom had not yet thrown off entirely the shackles of the gild system; the very big trading companies had it too. Thus it was the policy of the Dutch East India Company to carry on "small transactions that brought in a great deal." That was why it always destroyed spice plants, burned rich harvests and the like; though another motive was to deprive the poor of the opportunity of enjoying colonial products.

Quite generally it was the aim of all business to satisfy the demands of the wealthy, which is always easier than to deal with the demand on a large scale. This was quite justifiable according to the economic theory of the seventeenth and eighteenth centuries, which made out a good case for high prices.

The dignified aspect of the old-fashioned bourgeois, his stiff and pedantic bearing, were only the outward garb of his inward calm. Can you imagine a man in the long fur cloak of the Renaissance, or in the knee breeches and powdered wig of the subsequent centuries, as ever being in a hurry? Reliable authorities, indeed, describe the old-fashioned tradesman as one who walks with careful step and slow, who is never in haste just because he is occupied. Messer Alberti, himself a very busy man, tells us that he had never observed a busy person walking otherwise than at a slow pace, and this applied to fifteenth century Florence. Of eighteenth century Lyons a contemporary tells the same tale. "Here," he says, "our walk is slow because everyone is busy; in Paris people are in one continuous haste—because there is nothing to do there." So in Glasgow about the same time. We read of its merchants "how in scarlet coats, cocked hats, and powdered wigs, they strutted up and down the Planistanes, the only bit of pavement then in Glasgow, covering three or four hundred yards of road in front of the Town Hall and the adjoining offices, talking grandly to one another and nodding haughtily to the humbler folk who came to do them homage."

3. The attitude of the old-fashioned traders toward competition and to their customers sprang naturally from their business style. Above all else they wanted quiet. This "static principle," which had dominated the whole of precapitalist economic activities, had not yet lost all its influence in the early capitalist period. And the circle of your customers was like a fenced-off preserve; it was wholly yours—to be compared to the territory assigned to the trading company in lands beyond the sea for its exclusive exploitation.

. . . Let me refer to one or two business principles, all of them naturally resulting from a static economic order, all of them included in the economic outlook of the old-fashioned bourgeois.

All "custom hunting" was looked at askance; to take away your neighbor's customers was contemptible, unchristian, and immoral. A rule for "Merchants who traded in commodities" was: "Turn no man's customers away from him, either by word of mouth or by letter, and do not to another what you would not have another do to you." It was, however, more than a rule; it became an ordinance, and is met with over and over again. In Mayence its wording was as follows: "No one shall prevent another from buying, or by offering a higher price make a commodity dearer, on pain of losing his purchase; no one shall interfere in another's business undertaking or carry on his own on so large a scale as to ruin other traders." In Saxony it was much the same. In the Ordinances of 1672, 1682, and 1692, Paragraph 18 reads: "No shop-keeper shall call away the customers from another's shop, nor shall he by signs or motions keep them from buying."

It followed from this that all tricks to increase your custom, of whatever sort they were, were rather despised. Right into the nineteenth century there was still a certain prejudice in many a high-class firm against even the simplest form of advertisement. Some houses in New York had not got rid of the prejudice by the middle of the century. "No respectable house would overdo the thing. There was a sort of self-respect about the articles advertised."

But even in an advertising age it was for long considered nefarious to praise your goods or to point out wherein your business was superior to others. The last word in commercial impropriety was to announce that your prices were lower than those of the man opposite. "To undersell" was most ungentlemanly: "No blessing will come from harming your neighbour by underselling and cutting prices."

Bad as underselling itself was, it was beneath contempt to advertise it. "Since the days of our author," remark the editors of the fifth edition (1745) of Defoe's *Complete English Tradesman* (Defoe died in 1731), "this underselling practice is grown to such a shameful height that particular persons publicly advertise that they undersell the rest of the trade."

For France there is extant a particularly valuable document, dating from the second half of the eighteenth century, which proves even more strikingly how heinous this offense was thought to be, even in Paris. It is an ordinance of the year 1761, and it proclaims to all and sundry in the French capital that to advertise that you are selling your goods at a price below the customary one must be regarded as the last resource of a merchant in difficulties and that such action deserved severe condemnation. The ordinance proceeded to forbid the wholesale and retail traders of Paris and its suburbs "to run after one another" trying to find customers, and above all to distribute handbills calling attention to their wares.

Other methods of drawing advantages for yourself at the expense of your neighbors or of poaching on others' preserves were equally disreputable. The author of *The Complete English Tradesman* has some reflections on this manner of competition which help us exceedingly in gaining a true estimate of the business ethics of those days. They prove that economic activities were still in a static state and that tradition and custom ruled them. Remember that Defoe was not unskilled as a trader and that generally he is filled with the capitalist spirit.

This is his story. Before Wiltshire broadcloth reaches Northampton, where it is retailed, four people find employment.

The clothier, when it is finished, sends it up by the carrier to London to Mr. A, the Blackwell Hall factor, to be sold. Mr. A, the factor, sells it to Mr. B, the woollen-draper; Mr. B, the woollen-draper, sells it to Mr. C, the shopkeeper at Northampton, and he cuts it out in his shop and sells it to the country gentlemen about him . . . also 'tis sent down by the carrier from London to Northampton.

Now, in Northampton is another shopkeeper, "perhaps an Alderman, a rich overgrown Tradesman," who has more money than his neighbors and therefore wants no credit. "Prying about into all the secrets of the trade," he discovers where the cloth comes from, communicates with the clothier in Wiltshire, and buys his goods direct, then has them brought by horsepacks to Northampton. Possibly by tempting the clothier with ready money he obtains the cloth a penny per yard cheaper than the factor in London sold it to the woolen draper. What is the result? The overgrown tradesman will save in cost of transport, so much so that his cloth will cost him half a crown per yard less than his neighbor. Hence he will be able to undersell, and thus obtain his neighbor's custom. Not only that, but he will have taken away the occupation of several people: the carrier who brought the goods to London from Wiltshire, the carrier who took them from London to Northampton, and finally Mr. A, the Blackwell Hall factor, who "also loses his employment and may sit and blow his fingers for want of trade." Mr. B likewise is ruined by the loss of his wholesale trade. "And what is all the benefit which is made by this spoil upon trade? Only this, that Squire D. E. of Northamptonshire buys his suits half-a-crown a yard cheaper," and a covetous man has been made richer. And the moral? "This is cutting off the circulation of trade; this is managing trade with a few hands; and if this practice, which is indeed evidently begun, was to come to be universal, a million of people in England that now live handsomely by trade would be destitute of employment and their families in time might want bread."

This passage speaks volumes. How utterly inconceivable must the line of thought appear to a modern businessman!

Like the producers, the consumers also received attention. In a certain sense the consumer received even more, for the conception that all production was in the interests of consumption had not yet disappeared. It was the old "natural" view; production for use was still the rule of all economic activities. Hence the stress laid throughout the whole of the early capitalist period on *good* wares, and on the principle that commodities should really be what they pretended. Innumerable were the ordinances that were everywhere promulgated to this intent, more especially in the seventeenth and eighteenth centuries; and the state deemed it part of its work itself to regulate the quality of wares. It is idle to assert that this very state control is evidence of the decline of the "natural" view; in other words, that the custom of producing for us was on the decline. Such was not the case. The interference of the state was intended to check the conduct of some few unscrupulous manufacturers. For the rest, the old tradition prevailed that you should make good and genuine commodities; it was the tradition of the gild system, and industry in the early capitalist period continued to be tinged with it.

It was long before the purely capitalist notion gained acceptance that the exchange value of any commodity was what influenced the undertaker most. We may observe how slow its progress was from the conflicting opinions on the subject in the eighteenth century. Sir Josiah Child appears to have been in the minority on this, as on most other questions, when he formulated the demand that every manufacturer should be allowed to judge for himself as to the kind of commodity, and the quality, that he brought into the market. It is curious enough nowadays to read Child's plea for the right of the manufacturer to make shoddy goods. "If we intend to have the trade of the world," he cries, "we must imitate the Dutch, who make the worst as well as the best of all manufactures, that we may be in a capacity of serving all markets and all humors."

4. Finally, the attitude of the old-fashioned bourgeois to technical inventions is significant for the spirit within him. The old view of life appears once more: technical improvements are to be welcomed only if they do not overthrow man's happiness. True, they may cheapen commodities; but the odd pence thus gained are too high a price for the tears and the sufferings of the families of the workmen who are thrown out of employment. Once more, then, human welfare is the pivot of the whole economic organism, even though this time it be but the welfare of the wage-earning class. The interests of this class were by no means absent from men's thoughts in those days, although the reason for this may have been a selfish one.

There is abundant testimony to the dislike of labor-saving machinery in the early capitalist period. Let us glance at one or two instances.

In the second year of Elizabeth's reign a Venetian inventor . . . offered a labor-saving machine to the Court of the London Clothworkers' Company (whose industry by that time was already capitalistic in its organization). The Court carefully considered the offer and decided to refuse it, for the new invention would probably have deprived many a workman of his living. "It wolde be a grete decay unto the companye, whereupon the Master and Wardens gave the stranger grete thanks and also xxs. in money towards his charge, and so parted."

In 1684 the knitting frame for stockings was forbidden to be used (again in a capitalistically organized industry), and once more the reason was that it might reduce the wages of the craftsmen. Even a professional "projector" and inventor like Johann Joachim Becher shared this view. "I should certainly advise no one to invent instruments that might do away with human labor or reduce wages; but there can be no objection to such as are of advantage and utility, especially in those places where there is more work than workers can accomplish." Colbert's language is stronger still; the inventor of timesaving devices is a "foe of work." And these are the sentiments of Frederick the Great: "It is not by any means my intention that the spinning machine should be generally used. . . . If it were, a large number of people who depended for their livelihood on spinning would be thrown out of employ-

ment into starvation—which cannot possibly be tolerated."
After all this we shall not be surprised to find that a man of
such noble sentiments and good taste as Montesquieu should
be conservative in this respect. He believed that machines,
even including water mills, were not an unmixed blessing.
Finally, so thorough a businessman as Postlethwayt is very
reserved in his judgment on new inventions. A people without
commerce may safely refuse to admit machines, but commercial states should allow them only after careful scrutiny
and should anyhow exclude such as manufacture goods for
home consumption. "What we gain in expedition, we lose in
strength."

What comes to the fore throughout? The old conception of
producing in order to satisfy wants, no more and no less, the
traditional way of life, or moral scruples. But be the reason
what it may, it is always a stumbling block to the unfettered
development of acquisitiveness, of the undertaking spirit, and
of economic rationalism.

With the dawn of the nineteenth century all this changed,
at first slowly, then with a rush. . . .

The Modern Businessman

How has the economic outlook changed in the last century?
What characterizes the capitalist spirit of our own day—the
zenith of capitalism; and how does that spirit differ from the
one which filled the old-fashioned bourgeois?

Before attempting to answer these questions, let us realize
that there is no one single type of undertaker today, any more
than in earlier epochs; that, as in the early capitalist period, a
different spirit moves different capitalist undertakers. Let us,
then, place the various types in groups. Surprising as it may
seem, they are the types we already know as having existed in
the past. Today, too, we find the freebooter, the ground landlord, the bureaucrat, the speculator, the trader, and the manufacturer.

Recall the career of a Cecil Rhodes. Does it not remind
you of the Genoese merchants on their towers, or possibly
even more of Sir Walter Raleigh and Sir Francis Drake? Cecil
Rhodes was of the stuff that robber-knights were made of.
He was a discoverer and a conqueror whom no stumbling
blocks could retard; besides the sword and the rifle he wielded
another mighty weapon—modern stock-exchange gambling.
He was partly politician, partly capitalist undertaker; rather

more of a diplomat than a trader; he recognized no power other than brute force. It is strange to find in him even one iota of the Puritan spirit. And if we are to compare him with earlier generations, he must be placed alongside the men of the Renaissance.

How different from Cecil Rhodes' world is that of (say) Stumm, or some Silesian mineowner! Here we are in the atmosphere of the old feudal landed nobility; the ancient relationship between master and man is still met with; the staff of the establishments are arranged in a kind of hierarchy, and business is deliberate and cumbersome. Such are a few of the characteristics of these concerns, the directors of which have much in common with the capitalist landed proprietor of days gone by.

Then there is a third kind of undertaker nowadays who reminds us of the bureaucrat of old—exact in his work, methodical to a degree, nicely balanced in his judgments, highly gifted as an organizer, very careful before committing himself, an excellent executive official, who today may be town clerk of a large town and tomorrow manager of a bank, who frequently enough gives up the control of a government department for that of a trust. You will find him at the head of state and municipal enterprises.

Different from all these is the speculator of our time, who appears to be twin brother to the eighteenth century projector. Recently the daily papers reported the exploits of a French speculator, and the story is worth recalling. Rochette was the man's name, his age scarcely thirty. Yet he had allowed millions to slip between his fingers. He started life as an underwaiter in a railway-station restaurant; before long he was a full-fledged waiter in a café in Melun. Coming to Paris, he made himself acquainted with bookkeeping, and entered the service of Berger, the financial swindler. On his master's bankruptcy Rochette took over the business with the 5,000 francs' dowry brought him by a typist whom he married. He then began to float companies, and in the space of four years no less than 13 came into existence. There was the Crédit Minier, with a capital of 500,000 francs; the Laviana Coal Mines, with 2 millions; the Liat Coal Mines, with the same amount; the Banque Franco-Espagnole, with 20 millions; the Minier Trust, with 10 millions; the Union Franco-Belge, with 2½ millions; the financial paper *Le Financier*, with 2 millions; a number of copper and tin companies; a Moroccan Fishery Company; an incandescent lamp company, with 4½ millions; and many more. He issued altogether some 60 million francs' worth of shares, which by skillful manipulation rose to 200 millions, though a tenth of that figure was more nearly their true value. He had opened no less than 57 branch establishments in France; and the total number of people who participated in his scheme was close upon 40,000. Most of them were ruined, their total losses amounting to more than 150 millions. Why, it may be asked, was Rochette able to take in so many people? The explanation will be found in his marvelous power of surrounding himself with "solid," respectable folk. Just to show how cunning he was in blinding his victims, it may be mentioned that he founded a large factory for utilizing a filament-lamp patent. Everybody rushed to get shares in the company; the huge factory was the talk of the town; its tall chimneys belched forth smoke day and night, to the great satisfaction of the shareholders. In reality, however, there was only a solitary individual working in the building, and he was the stoker!

Does not this story read like a report of doings in England in the 1720's?

How different is the persevering tradesman who makes a fortune because of his sure eye for the right conjuncture, or by clever calculations and advantageous agreements with his wholesale house, his customers, and his employees. What has such a man, say a Berlin draper, in common with Cecil Rhodes? What the director of a multiple shop with a gold-mine speculator? And what all these with the manufacturer who runs his factory as was done 100 or 200 years ago, in Bradford or Sedan?

These old friends are still among us, and seemingly their form is unchanged. Nor are they the only types of the modern undertaker. Others have joined the group, which thus becomes quite picturesque. A very common one, usually found in America, may be termed the master undertaker (since superundertaker is an ugly word). His great characteristic is that he unites within himself several independent types. He may be freebooter, unscrupulous calculator, landlord, and speculator all in one. Any trust magnate will serve as an illustration.

Finally, a phenomenon of our age is the collective undertaker, who is not an individual at all, but a group of capitalist undertakers at the head of a giant enterprise. They form a kind of syndicated undertaker, each of them exercising special functions, and in their corporate capacity they represent undertaking in all its comprehensiveness. We need think only of such industrial organizations as our electrical concerns, our iron foundries, our cannon factories.

In short, modern undertaking in all its types presents a variegated picture. But in our own days, as in those of long ago, all the types have certain features in common, all are filled with the same spirit. It is only a difference of degree that distinguishes the one from the other. In olden times, as we saw, the undertakers were children of the early capitalist spirit; in modern times they are the children of the perfected capitalist spirit.

What manner of thing is this perfected capitalist spirit? And what have all the types of the modern capitalist undertaker in common?

1. The ideal of both must be our first consideration. What is it? What are the life values that govern the latter-day businessman? What strikes us here is that there has been a peculiar change of perspective in the evaluation of man, a change of perspective which seems to have affected the whole of the rest of life. Man, the flesh-and-blood man, with his joys and sorrows, with his needs and demands, has been forced from his place as the center round which all economic activities rotate; his throne is now occupied by a few abstractions, such as Acquisitiveness and Business. Man has ceased to be what he was until the end of the early capitalist period—the measure of all things. The economic subjective agent now aims at as high a profit as he can, and strives to make his business flourish exceedingly. The two aims are closely intertwined, as we shall presently observe. Their relationship may be expressed thus: The undertakers wish to see business thriving; as for acquisitiveness, it is forced upon them, even though they may never have set out with that as their goal.

The real interest of undertaking does not always lie in mere gain, certainly not for the dominating personalities who determine the type. Walter Rathenau was, as I think, perfectly right when he once said: "I have never yet met with a businessman whose chief aim was to acquire wealth. I will even go so far as to assert that he who is out to make money cannot possibly be a great businessman." Something very different occupies the thoughts of the undertaker. His heart is set on seeing his business thrive. Once more Walter Rathenau has expressed it well:

The object of the businessman's work, of his worries, his pride and his aspirations is just his undertaking, be it a commercial company, factory, bank, shipping concern, theatre or railway. The undertaking seems to take form and substance, and to be ever with him, having, as it were, by virtue of his book-keeping, his organization, and his branches, an independent economic existence. The businessman is wholly devoted to making his business a flourishing, healthy, living organism.

This view is shared by all the capitalist undertakers of the day insofar as they have expressed themselves on the inner meaning of their activity.

Now, what is really meant by making a business, that is, a capitalist undertaking, flourish? Observe that a business begins with a sum of money and ends with the same, and that therefore its existence is bound up with the realization of a surplus. Success in business can only mean success in realizing this surplus. No profits, no business success. A factory may make very dear or very cheap goods, and their quality may establish their maker's name as a household word throughout the globe, but if the business continues to show a deficit from year to year, it is a failure from the capitalist point of view. To flourish, a concern must be profitable; to prosper, it must pay.

You see now what I meant when I made the statement that the undertakers wish to see business thriving, and as for acquisitiveness, it is forced upon them.

Such being the goal of the capitalist undertaker, the end of his activities is necessarily projected into infinity. In earlier times, when the needs of the community determined economic activities, these had natural boundaries or limits. There can be no such limits when economic activities are determined by acquisitiveness and by flourishing businesses. There is never a point in the future when the total profits are sufficiently great for the undertaker to say: It is enough. Should the development of a business be such that its prosperity ceases to increase, the many-sidedness of modern enterprise will see to it that before long a second, and possibly a third, business is added to the original one. Thus it is that in modern days two equally strong tendencies show themselves—expansion of one and the same business, and the branching out into subsidiary or additional businesses. This very often leads to a kind of inner pressure in the mind of the undertaker. It frequently happens that he really does not want to expand further, but he must. Many a captain of industry has confessed as much. We were always hoping, says Andrew Carnegie in his *Autobiography*, that there would come a time when extension of business would no longer be necessary; but we invariably found that to put off expanding would mean retrogression. Rockefeller tells the same tale. The first reason for starting his trusts was the desire to unite his capital and his capacities

to carry on a business of some magnitude and importance in place of the small business that each separately had heretofore carried. After some time, when the possibilities of the new conditions became apparent, we found that more capital was necessary. This we provided, as also the people, and founded the Standard Oil Company with a capital of a million dollars. Later we discovered that even more money could be profitably invested, and we raised our capital to 3½ millions. The more the business grew the more capital we put into it, the object being always the same: to extend our business by furnishing the best and cheapest products.

A kind of monomania this; capital is piled on capital *because* the business grows. Extension of business is the end; furnishing cheap and good products the means. A famous German undertaker—Strousberg—says exactly the same thing. "The first wedge calls as a rule for a second, and so the great railway I was building made further demands upon me. To satisfy these I extended my activities, departed more and more from my original intention, and, finding so much promise in the new prospect, I devoted myself wholly to my business."

Most capitalist undertakers think of nothing else but this constant desire for extension and expansion, which to the outside observer appears so meaningless. If you ask them what purpose the expansion is intended to serve, they will regard you with a kind of mild surprise and reply a little testily that the purpose is self-evident; it is to make economic life more vigorous, and, moreover, is demanded by economic progress.

But what is meant by "economic progress" in this quite general and fairly stereotyped answer? What is the association of ideas in the minds of the people who give it? Examine carefully and you shall find that it means an expansion in what may be called the "economic apparatus"—the production of largely increased quantities at the cheapest possible price; enormous output; enormous extent of communications; the quickest transportation of goods, people, and news.

But the answer, like the phenomena that prompted the

question, sounds meaningless too. It is therefore unsatisfactory. There must be method in all this madness; it must surely be explicable. The people concerned in the activities do not seem to be alive to any life values at their base. But life values in them there must be, or you would not find whole generations of men intellectually sound and strong engaged in the activities mentioned. An analysis of the soul of the modern capitalist undertaker therefore repays the trouble, and at the very outset you stumble across—the child. In very truth, the psychology of the modern undertaker appears to me to resemble greatly that of the child. Understand the one and you will understand the other. For all the processes in the mind of the undertaker (and indeed of modern man generally), if reduced to their simplest elements, show a kind of relapse into the days of childhood.

Let us consider the matter more in detail.

The child possesses four elementary "values"; four ideals dominate its existence. They are—

(*a*) Physical bigness, as seen in grown-ups and imagined in giants;

(*b*) Quick movement—in running, bowling a hoop, riding on a roundabout;

(*c*) Novelty—it changes its toys very quickly; it begins something and never completes it because another occupation attracts it; and

(*d*) Sense of power—that is why it pulls out the legs of a fly, makes Towzer stand on his hind legs and beg nicely, and flies its kite as high as it can.

Curious as it may sound, these ideals, and these only, will be found in all modern "values." Let us take them in turn.

(*a*) We attach importance to quantities, to mere size. It is what interests us, what we admire most. That, I fancy, will be generally admitted. There is a universal tendency (to use the words of Lord Bryce) "to mistake bigness for greatness." It matters not wherein the bigness consists: it may be the population of a town or a country, the height of a monument, the breadth of a river, the frequency of suicide, the passengers carried by a railway, the size of a ship, the number of players in an orchestra, or what not. Of course, our greatest admiration is reserved for a huge sum of money. Besides, money makes it possible to measure the size of otherwise unmeasurable things and to compare them. It is a natural and easy step from this to the belief that that is valuable which costs much.

We say this picture or this jewelry is twice as valuable as
that. In America, where this modern tendency may be studied
better than anywhere else because there it has reached its
greatest perfection, people come to the point at once, and
prefix to every commodity its monetary value. "Have you seen
the 50,000-dollar Rembrandt at Mr. A's house?" is a not unusual question. "Today Mr. Carnegie's 500,000-dollar yacht
entered the harbor of" (say) Boston—so you may read in the
daily paper.

Get into the habit of looking at the mere quantity of things
and you will naturally tend to compare any two phenomena
that may come under your notice; you will weigh the one
against the other and pronounce the larger to be the more
valuable. Again, if of two things the one becomes larger than
the other in a given space of time, it is said to have been successful. So that the inclination toward what is measurably big
brings with it necessarily another tendency—worship of success. The modern businessman is appraised only in accordance
with his success. Now success means to overtake others; to
do more, to achieve more, to possess more than others; in a
word, to be great, The pursuit of success holds out the same
unlimited possibilities as the chase of profits; the one comple-
ments the other.

To illustrate the influence on the inner workings of the mind
of this quantitative valuation of things, so characteristic of
our day, let us refer to the attitude of people to sport. What
is invariably the main question of interest? Is it not, who will
win? Who will score most? A match is but a quantitative
balance between two results. Imagine such a standpoint in an
ancient Greek wrestling school! Imagine it at a Spanish bull-
fight! The thing is impossible. In both these cases qualitative
values were looked for, for example, the highest personal
artistic skill.

(b) Speed is of almost the same consequence to the modern man as massivity. To rush on in a 100-h.p. motorcar is
one of the supremest ideals of our age; and he who cannot
speed madly along contents himself with reading of record-
breaking velocity. Perhaps the express between Hamburg and
Berlin was ten minutes in advance of its scheduled time; perhaps the latest ocean liner reached New York three hours
earlier than it was expected; perhaps the postman now comes
at seven-thirty instead of at the customary eight o'clock;
perhaps one newspaper published a declaration of war (prob-

ably a fictitious one) an hour before its competitor—all these
things are of tremendous interest to the queerly constituted
folk of our day; they seem to be of vital importance to them.

Moreover, a curious concept has sprung into existence,
that of "beating the record." In terms of record-breaking you
impress on your memory the speediest achievements as the
most valuable ones. In its fullest meaning the new concept
refers to great size and great speed combined. All the mega-
lomania, all the mad hurry of our time, is expressed in record-
beating. I think it most likely that the future historian of our
time will speak of it as "The Age of Record-Breaking."

(c) Whatever is new nowadays attracts merely because it
is novelty. It attracts most when the assurance is possible,
"There never has been anything like it." Sensational we call
its effect on the mind. That the love of sensation is a marked
feature of the age requires no expatiation. Modern journalism
is perhaps the best proof. But recall also how fashions in
dances, no less than in clothes, change from season to season.
Is it not because nothing is so attractive as what is new?

(d) The sense of power is the fourth characteristic of the
modern spirit; it is felt in the consciousness of superiority over
others. But in reality it is only an expression of weakness;
hence its importance in the child's world. For, after all, anyone gifted with true greatness, which is usually inward, will
be hardly likely to estimate the outward semblance of power
at all highly. Power has no temptation for Siegfried; only a
Mime thirsts for it. Bismarck in all probability did not bother
much about the power he exercised; but in Lassalle the desire
for power must have been tremendous. A king possesses
power; it is therefore of small moment in his sight. But the
financier of humble origin, who keeps a kingly borrower waiting in his antechamber for some little time, suns himself in
this power because his soul has none of it. An undertaker who
employs 10,000 men and experiences a sense of power in
consequence is like a little boy who makes his doggie bring
back the stick he keeps on throwing from him. Moreover,
when neither by money nor any other outward force power
over mankind is given us, we talk of the conquest of nature.
That is why our age is so childishly delighted with epoch-
making discoveries—say, the mastery of the air, and suchlike
achievements. The truly great man, however, will be comparatively unmoved at the sight of a biplane in the air. A truly
great generation concerned with the deepest problems of life
will not be enraptured because it made some discoveries in

technical science. Power of this sort it will assuredly regard as "superficial." Our own age lacks true greatness; accordingly, like a child, it admires the power which new inventions bestow, and it overrates those who possess it. Hence the high esteem in which the populace holds inventors and millionaires.

It is just possible that these visions float before the gaze of the undertaker more or less clearly. But certain it is that they take form and substance in his goal—the expansion and growth of his business. Acquisitiveness and interest in his enterprise thus direct his activities as a capitalist undertaker.

2. His ideal we have reviewed. It remains now to review these activities as influenced by the ideal. In essence the activities of the modern capitalist undertaker remain the same as before. He must conquer, organize, deal, speculate, and calculate. But the extent of each of these factors varies, and consequently the resultant whole is not quite like that of an earlier age.

In modern times the trading function has become of more and more significance. I use the word "trading" in the sense . . . of dealing or negotiating. It is on this that commercial success now increasingly depends; on the skill and strength of suggestion in making contracts of all kinds. In olden days knots were cut; today they must be unraveled.

Next in importance to dealing comes skillful speculation—by which I mean stock-exchange manipulations. Modern undertakings are drawn more and more into the vortex of stock-exchange activities. Trust development such as we find in the United States is in reality only the transformation of manufacturing and commercial enterprises into purely stock-exchange speculative concerns. Consequently the directors and managers of such businesses have new problems to solve, and this opens up new activities for them.

As for calculation, it becomes more and more delicate as well as increasingly difficult, both because of the need for absolute exactitude and also because it has become so extensive.

Finally, the activities of the capitalist undertaker have become much more many-sided; that is to say, insofar as specialization has not set in. Economic activities have branched out in all directions; what wonder then that those who direct them should be called upon to be many-sided?

So much for the nature of the activity itself. What is new is its boundlessness. So long as the needs of the living human being governed economic activities, so long did these have a limit. But with the disappearance of the governing factor, the natural limit fell away. Accordingly the activities of the capitalist undertaker have no bounds. . . . Which means that the expenditure of human energy in modern economic activities, extensively and intensively, is strained to the uttermost. Every minute of the day, of the year, nay, of life itself, is devoted to work; and during this working period every power is occupied at highest pressure. Everybody is acquainted with the hard-worked man of today. Whether employer or employed, he is constantly on the verge of a breakdown owing to overwork. That he tends to be excited, that he is always on the move, is generally known too. Speed and yet more speed —such is the cry of the age. It rushes onward in one mad race.

The influence of such a life on body and soul is not difficult to gauge. It corrodes the former and dries up the latter. Everything is sacrificed to the Moloch of work; all the higher instincts of heart and mind are crushed out by devotion to business. How much the inner life of modern man has been shattered is best seen if we cast a glance at the kernel of all natural life—the relationship to women. These men have no time for the enjoyment of delicate passions, nor even for gallant flirtations. They seem to be quite incapable of deep erotic emotions. Either they are wholly apathetic so far as love is concerned, or they are content with a brief sensual intoxication. They either do not bother about women at all, or they buy what they require in this respect.

3. Business principles likewise have undergone a change. That was only to be expected when the goal of enterprise has become different. Today, it may be said, five main rules regulate economic activities.

(*a*) Absolute rationalism is the first. Economic activities are ruled by cold reason, by thought. . . . [That] has always been the case; it showed itself in the making of plans, in considering whether any policy was likely to be successful or no, and in calculation generally. The modern capitalist spirit differs from its predecessors only in the degree in which this rule is obeyed. Today the rule is strictly, one might almost say sternly, enforced. The last trace of traditionalism has vanished. The man of today (and the American undertaker may stand as the most perfect type) is filled with the will to apply cold reason to economic activities; moreover, he possesses the determination to make the will effective. Accordingly, he is ever ready to adopt a newer method if it is more rational, whether in the sphere of organization, of production, or of calculation. This naturally implies that, no matter what the cost may be, he is able to leave the old methods the moment the newer ones are available.

(*b*) Production for exchange (as opposed to production for use) is the motto of economic activities. As much profit as possible is their ideal; consequently what matters is not the goodness or the kind of commodities produced but their salability. How they are sold is secondary, so long as they are sold. Consequently the undertaker is wholly indifferent to the quality of his wares; he will make shoddy goods or cheap substitutes, if only it pays. If cheap and nasty boots yield more profit than good ones, it would be a deadly sin against the holy spirit of capitalism to manufacture good ones. It is no argument against the truth of this to point to a movement in certain industries (the chemical industry is one), the object of which is to improve quality. As well say that the bonuses which the general store offers to its employees on the sale of more expensive articles proves the same thing. What both instances do prove is that they are cases where there is more profit from high-class goods than from inferior articles. The greatest gain is the only criterion in these matters, and an undertaker will make now cheap goods, now dearer, according as the one or the other yields more profit. From the capitalist's standpoint that is only natural.

What follows from this is plain. Since it is inherent in acquisitiveness to enlarge incomings to the uttermost; and since, again, the greater the sale, the larger the profits, it is only to be expected that the undertaker will try all he can to increase his sales. Apart from the greater gain, more extended sales will give him certain advantages over competitors. Hence it is by no means remarkable that the desire for greater sales, for new markets, for more customers, is one of the mightiest motive powers in modern capitalism. It is directly responsible for a number of business principles, all of which have one end in view—to make the public buy. The more important of these principles deserve to be mentioned.

(*c*) The first (and the third in the general scheme) may be enunciated as follows: Search out the customer and attack him. That is today as self-evident a maxim in all branches of business as it was strange and wrong in the age of early capitalism. In practice it means that you set out to attract the customer's attention and to stir up within him the desire to purchase. You attract his attention by shouting in his ears or catching his eye, by loud, colored indicators; you strive to make him purchase by suggestion; you seek to convince him that the articles for sale are extraordinarily good or valuable. Advertisement serves both ends—as everyone knows; and advertisements, as everyone knows also, shatter all sense of propriety, of taste, of good manners, and of dignity. Is it not true to say that modern advertising in its extreme forms is both unaesthetic and immoral?

(*d*) Second, sell as cheaply as you can; reduce price to the lowest possible figure so as to attract the public. In the early capitalist age low prices were an abomination. The motto then was . . . little business but great profits. Today we are at the opposite extreme: as much business as possible but small profits. Small profits, quick returns—is not this nowadays the universal motto?

(*e*) Elbow room is demanded in order to arrive at the wished-for goal. Which means, first, that you require freedom of action, liberty to enter upon or to abstain from any course, as seems best to you. It means emancipation from the trammels of law or morality; it means that you should be allowed to poach on your neighbor's preserves just as he may be allowed to poach on yours; it means that you should be allowed to oust him if you can; it means that you object to interference either from the state or from workingmen's organizations in making your contracts. You want none of the restraints of an earlier age. The free exercise of your powers shall alone determine economic success or failure.

And in the second place it means—what follows quite naturally—unrestricted competition. If acquisition is the first consideration, unrestricted competition is a matter of course. You need no longer be bound by considerations of any kind, whether moral, aesthetic, or social. Unscrupulous is the adjective for your actions.

Look at the extensive American trusts and you will see what unrestricted competition means. The . . . doings of the American Tobacco Company are a case in point; they outdistanced the accepted practices of Europe, and illustrate to what lengths an unscrupulous undertaker will go. No considerations give him pause; he leaves no road untried that promises success. The trust threw its goods away at ridiculous prices in order to conquer new markets; middlemen received enormous commissions; well-known brands were imitated and poor quality wares were sold in wrappers that misled the public. If it became involved in litigation, the trust by its superior financial strength was able to draw out the cases until its opponents were utterly exhausted. Even retail trading received careful attention, for the trust opened shops at effective points, and by underselling forced the old-established tobacconists to close their doors. Finally, the trust monopolized the raw material, and so came into conflict with the tobacco growers of Kentucky. In 1911 the trust was proceeded against under the Sherman Law, and the presiding judge in delivering sentence characterized the activities of the undertaking against their competitors as having been carried on with extraordinary cunning, precaution, and devilry. Every human creature that by energy or skill threatened to stand in the way of the trust was mercilessly crushed.

Perhaps the most perfect type of unscrupulous, smart businessman was Edward H. Harriman . . . the secret of . . . [whose] victorious career was his utter lack of moral scruples. Had he not cast these overboard he would have stumbled almost at the very first step he took. He began by breaking the man who had opened for him the gates of the railway paradise; following this up by his brutal campaign against Morgan, who, however, knew how to utilize for his own ends the capacities of his opponent. Harriman's fight with Hill was as unscrupulous as the policy that brought him into the Standard Oil Trust. But Harriman's delinquencies were not merely personal; they form part and parcel of American speculation.

Of the great victors on the racecourse of modern capitalism it may be asserted, what was recently said of Rockefeller, that they know how to glide over every moral restraint with almost childlike disregard. The mirror of this naïve view of life will be found in the memoirs of John Rockefeller, who once summed up the faith within him by saying that he was willing to pay a substitute a salary of a million dollars, if beside other positive qualities he had no scruples whatsoever, and was ready to kill off thousands of victims without a murmur.

Another undertaker, this time a German, who considered himself rather backward in this respect because he was "too good-natured and considerate"—I refer to Werner Siemens—urged his brother Charles to become a smart businessman in these terms: "Always be determined and unscrupulous. That in so large a concern is called for. Once begin to be considerate of private interests and you will fall into a morass of demands and intrigues" (letter of March 31, 1856).

4. The middle-class virtues—industry, frugality, and honesty —are they of any consequence for the modern capitalist

undertaker? It is as difficult to reply to the question in the affirmative as in the negative. The place of these virtues in modern economic life is so very different from what they occupied in the early capitalist system. As a matter of fact, they have ceased to be necessary to the undertaker. Nevertheless, they still play their part in undertaking. Before these virtues were still in the sphere wherein personal willpower was exercised; now they have become part of the mechanism of business. Before, they were characteristic of living beings; now, they have turned into objective principles of business methods.

This may sound difficult. I shall explain my meaning by considering each of the virtues in turn.

In the olden days when industry was preached as a prime virtue in the tradesman, it was necessary to implant a solid foundation of duties in the inner consciousness of men. Everybody had to be urged to exercise his willpower in a certain direction, and when the habit was once formed the industrious tradesman went through his day's work in conscious self-mastery. Today all this is changed. The businessman works at high pressure because the stress of economic activities carries him along in spite of himself. He is no longer exercising a virtue; necessity drives him to this particular course. The general business pace determines what his own business pace shall be. He can no more be idle than a man at a machine, whereas a craftsman with his tools can be idle or industrious as he chooses.

The objectiveness of frugality is even more marked, for the private and the business "housekeeping" of the undertaker are now separate. In the latter, frugality is needful more than ever. "Extravagance even in the smallest things should be avoided. It is not petty to have a care of this, for extravagance is a consuming disease difficult to localize. There are great undertakings whose existence depends on whether all the sand is removed from the carts or whether one shovelful is left behind." Recall the careful, almost miserly, economy of Rockefeller in his management of the Standard Oil Company; recall how not a drop of oil was wasted; the wooden boxes in which tin was brought from Europe were sold to florists or were used as firewood. But in the private housekeeping of the undertaker you will find none of this fanatical thrift. Neither Rathenau's nor Rockefeller's castle is a center of that frugality so much beloved of Benjamin Franklin; and the festive boards of our rich undertakers know nothing of sufficiency and moderation. And if the head of the family is content to go on in the old-fashioned bourgeois style of his youth, his wife, his sons, and his daughters will all see to it that luxury and superfluity and pomp become part and parcel of the new bourgeois spirit. Bourgeois the style of life still is, even in the case of the wealthiest. The old doctrines of Alberti still hold sway. Never let your expenditure exceed your income, he urged his disciples. And calculate. Today this advice is faithfully obeyed by the modern bourgeois. Herein his mode of living differs from the seignorial. The seigneur scorns money.

Commercial honesty comes last. Can anyone doubt that honesty is today—today perhaps more than ever—a factor in business life? In business life only, however. For the conduct of the undertaker as a man may differ widely from his conduct as a tradesman. Commercial honesty is a complexity of principles that are intended to apply to business but not to the personal conduct of the business subject. An honest tradesman today may certainly be unmoral in his private life. When you say he is "good," you mean that he is reliable in his business; that he will pay; that his firm has a good name. You pass no judgment on his personal conduct, which is governed by other principles. Indeed, the firm may not have an individual head at all. It may be an impersonal limited company, the directors of which change from time to time. Their personal morality stands in no relationship to the business. The "name" of the business is all that matters. Thus, here, too, what before was a personal quality has now become a matter of business routine. You can see it best by considering modern credit. A bank in olden days was relied upon because it could point to an ancient and honored name; it was "good" for personal reasons. Today a bank inspires confidence by the size of its invested capital and its reserves. Today you assume that business is carried on honestly—anyhow until some swindle comes to light to prove the contrary. In this virtue then, as in the others, what before was organic has now become mechanical.

All this applies to the large undertakings. In the small and middle-sized enterprises, however, you may still find the principles prevalent in the early days of capitalism. The middle-class virtues are still cultivated, and the undertaker's personal characteristics determine his economic progress. It is in the large undertakings and their directors and managers that we find the spirit of capitalism fully developed in all its shining purity. . . .

Edward Tylor
(1832–1917)

THE SCIENCE OF CULTURE

Edward Tylor was born in Camberwell, England. His parents were Quakers, and since his father was the owner of a prosperous brass foundry, he grew up in comfortable surroundings. His formal education was brief. He attended a school which was conducted by the Society of Friends. His Quaker faith prevented him from entering a university, since he was unable to pass the tests of religious orthodoxy that were then required for admission to the universities.[1] For seven years he worked in his father's business until ill health forced him to quit work altogether, and he was advised to lead a life of leisure and travel.

While traveling in Cuba in 1856 he met Henry Christy, a fellow-Quaker and an archaeologist and ethnologist of considerable reputation.[2] Christy took him along on an archaeological expedition to Mexico, and it was this trip that began Tylor's interest and work in anthropology.

In 1858 he married Anna Fox. Lady Tylor accompanied her husband on his many lecture tours, and "on one occasion, before a large audience, Tylor turned toward his wife after a lengthy exposition and said absentmindedly, 'And so, my dear Anna, we observe . . .'"[3]

In 1861 he published Anahuac, *describing his experiences in Mexico with Christy. His second work,* Researches in the Early History of Mankind, *was published in 1865, and it was this book which really established Tylor in the field of anthropology.* Primitive Culture, *published in 1871, was a monumental work, and it is still one of the best studies to date of primitive man. Tylor's goal in anthropology was to embrace the entire field of man and his environment. He approached*

[1] Throughout this introduction I have drawn material from the excellent and perceptive essay on Edward Tylor in *They Studied Man* by Abram Kardiner and Edward Preble.

[2] P. 57, *They Studied Man*, Cleveland, World Publishing Company, 1961.

[3] P. 59, ibid.

the main subject of his study (primitive man) with "a sense of cultural relativity unusual for his time."[4]

Although Tylor was undoubtedly influenced by Darwin and Spencer both, he denied any direct influence. Many consider Tylor to be the founder of cultural anthropology, and Max Müller has even referred to ethnology as "Mr. Tylor's Science." As Paul Radin has written: "If Tylor was not the first to apply the notion of culture to the study of man or to primitive society, he was surely the first to achieve a coherent and compelling monument of the cultural approach to primitive society.[5]

THE SCIENCE OF CULTURE

CULTURE or Civilization, taken in its wide ethnographic sense, is that complex whole which includes knowledge, belief, art, morals, law, custom, and any other capabilities and habits acquired by man as a member of society. The condition of culture among the various societies of mankind, insofar as it is capable of being investigated on general principles, is a subject apt for the study of laws of human thought and action. On the one hand, the uniformity which so largely pervades civilization may be ascribed, in great measure, to the uniform action of uniform causes: while on the other hand its various grades may be regarded as stages of development or evolution, each the outcome of previous history, and about to do its proper part in shaping the history of the future. To the investigation of these two great principles in several departments of ethnography, with especial consideration of the civilization of the lower tribes as related to the civilization of the higher nations, the present volumes are devoted.

Our modern investigators in the sciences of inorganic nature are foremost to recognize, both within and without their special fields of work, the unity of nature, the fixity of its laws, the definite sequence of cause and effect through which every fact depends on what has gone before it, and acts upon what is to come after it. They grasp firmly the Pythagorean doctrine of pervading order in the universal Cosmos. They

---

[4] P. 63, ibid.

[5] See Paul Radin's introduction to Edward Tylor's *The Origins of Culture*, New York, Harper Torchbooks, 1958, p. xiv.

affirm, with Aristotle, that nature is not full of incoherent episodes, like a bad tragedy. They agree with Leibniz in what he calls "my axiom, that nature never acts by leaps (*la nature n'agit jamais par saut*)," as well as in his "great principle, commonly little employed, that nothing happens without sufficient reason." Nor again, in studying the structure and habits of plants and animals, or in investigating the lower functions even of man, are these leading ideas unacknowledged. But when we come to talk of the higher processes of human feeling and action, of thought and language, knowledge and art, a change appears in the prevalent tone of opinion. The world at large is scarcely prepared to accept the general study of human life as a branch of natural science, and to carry out, in a large sense, the poet's injunction to "account for moral as for natural things." To many educated minds there seems something presumptuous and repulsive in the view that the history of mankind is part and parcel of the history of nature, that our thoughts, wills, and actions accord with laws as definite as those which govern the motion of waves, the combination of acids and bases, and the growth of plants and animals.

The main reasons of this state of the popular judgment are not far to seek. There are many who would willingly accept a science of history if placed before them with substantial definiteness of principle and evidence but who not unreasonably reject the systems offered to them, as falling too far short of a scientific standard. Through resistance such as this, real knowledge always sooner or later makes its way, while the habit of opposition to novelty does such excellent service against the invasions of speculative dogmatism, that we may sometimes even wish it were stronger than it is. But other obstacles to the investigation of laws of human nature arise from considerations of metaphysics and theology. The popular notion of free human will involves not only freedom to act in accordance with motive but also a power of breaking loose from continuity and acting without cause—a combination which may be roughly illustrated by the simile of a balance sometimes acting in the usual way, but also possessed of the faculty of turning by itself without or against its weights. This view of an anomalous action of the will, which it need hardly be said is incompatible with scientific argument, subsists as an opinion patent or latent in men's minds, and strongly affecting their theoretic views of history, though it is not, as a rule, brought prominently forward in systematic reasoning. Indeed, the definition of human will, as strictly according with motive, is the only possible scientific basis in such inquiries. Happily, it is not needful to add here yet another to the list of dissertations on supernatural intervention and natural causation, on liberty, predestination, and accountability. We may hasten to escape from the regions of transcendental philosophy and theology, to start on a more hopeful journey over more practicable ground. None will deny that, as each man knows by the evidence of his own consciousness, definite and natural cause does, to a great extent, determine human action. Then, keeping aside from considerations of extranatural interference and causeless spontaneity, let us take this admitted existence of natural cause and effect as our standing ground, and travel on it as far as it will bear us. It is on this same basis that physical science pursues, with ever-increasing success, its quest of laws of nature. Nor need this restriction hamper the scientific study of human life, in which the real difficulties are the practical ones of enormous complexity of evidence, and imperfection of methods of observation.

Now, it appears that this view of human will and conduct as subject to definite law, is indeed recognized and acted upon by the very people who oppose it when stated in the abstract as a general principle and who then complain that it annihilates man's free will, destroys his sense of personal responsibility, and degrades him to a soulless machine. He who will say these things will nevertheless pass much of his own life in studying the motives which lead to human action, seeking to attain his wishes through them, framing in his mind theories of personal character, reckoning what are likely to be the effects of new combinations, and giving to his reasoning the crowning character of true scientific inquiry, by taking it for granted that insofar as his calculation turns out wrong, either his evidence must have been false or incomplete or his judgment upon it unsound. Such a one will sum up the experience of years spent in complex relations with society, by declaring his persuasion that there is a reason for everything in life and that where events look unaccountable, the rule is to wait and watch in hope that the key to the problem may someday be found. This man's observation may have been as narrow as his inferences are crude and prejudiced, but nevertheless he has been an inductive philosopher "more than forty years without knowing it." He has practically acknowledged definite laws of human thought and action, and has simply thrown out of account in his own studies of life the whole fabric of motiveless will and uncaused spontaneity. It is assumed here that they should be just so thrown out of account in wider studies and that the true philosophy of history lies in extending and improving the methods of the plain people who form their judgments upon facts, and check them upon new facts. Whether the doctrine be wholly or but partly true, it accepts the very condition under which we search for new knowledge in the lessons of experience, and in a word the whole course of our rational life is based upon it.

"One event is always the son of another, and we must never forget the parentage," was a remark made by a Bechuana chief to Casalis the African missionary. Thus at all times historians, so far as they have aimed at being more than mere chroniclers, have done their best to show not merely succession, but connection, among the events upon their record. Moreover, they have striven to elicit general principles of human action, and by these to explain particular events, stating expressly or taking tacitly for granted the existence of a philosophy of history. Should anyone deny the possibility of thus establishing historical laws, the answer is ready with which Boswell in such a case turned on Johnson: "Then, sir, you would reduce all history to no better than an almanack." That nevertheless the labors of so many eminent thinkers should have as yet brought history only to the threshold of science need cause no wonder to those who consider the bewildering complexity of the problems which come before the general historian. The evidence from which he is to draw his conclusions is at once so multifarious and so doubtful, that a full and distinct view of its bearing on a particular question is hardly to be attained, and thus the temptation becomes all but irresistible to garble it in support of some rough-and-ready theory of the course of events. The philosophy of history at large, explaining the past and predicting the future phenomena of man's life in the world by reference to general laws, is in fact a subject with which, in the present state of knowledge, even genius aided by wide research seems but hardly able to cope. Yet there are departments of it which, though difficult enough, seem comparatively accessible. If the field of inquiry be narrowed from History as a whole to that branch of it which is here called Culture, the history, not of tribes or nations, but of the condition of knowledge, religion, art, custom, and the like among them, the task of investigation proves to lie within far more moderate compass. We suffer still from the same kind of difficulties which beset the wider argument, but they are much diminished. The evidence is no longer so wildly heterogeneous, but may be more simply classified and compared, while the power of getting rid of extraneous matter, and treating each issue on its own proper set of facts, makes close reasoning on the whole more available than in general history. This may appear from a brief preliminary examination of the problem, how the phenomena of Culture may be classified and arranged, stage by stage, in a probable order of evolution.

Surveyed in a broad view, the character and habit of mankind at once display that similarity and consistency of phenomena which led the Italian proverb-maker to declare that "all the world is one country," (*tutto il mondo è paese*). To general likeness in human nature on the one hand, and to general likeness in the circumstances of life on the other, this similarity and consistency may no doubt be traced, and they may be studied with especial fitness in comparing races near the same grade of civilization. Little respect need be had in such comparisons for date in history or for place on the map; the ancient Swiss lakedweller may be set beside the medieval Aztec, and the Ojibwa of North America beside the Zulu of South Africa. As Dr. Johnson contemptuously said when he had read about Patagonians and South Sea Islanders in Hawkesworth's Voyages, "One set of savages is like another." How true a generalization this really is, any ethnological museum may show. Examine, for instance, the edged and pointed instruments in such a collection; the inventory includes hatchet, adze, chisel, knife, saw, scraper, awl, needle, spear and arrowhead, and of these most or all belong with only differences of detail to races the most various. So it is with savage occupations; the woodchopping, fishing with net and line, shooting and spearing game, fire making, cooking, twisting cord and plaiting baskets, repeat themselves with wonderful uniformity in the museum shelves which illustrate the life of the lower races from Kamchatka to Tierra del Fuego, and from Dahomey to Hawaii. Even when it comes to comparing barbarous hordes with civilized nations, the consideration thrusts itself upon our minds how far item after item of the life of the lower races passes into analogous proceedings of the higher, in forms not too far changed to be recognized, and sometimes hardly changed at all. Look at the modern European peasant using his hatchet and his hoe, see his food boiling or roasting over the log fire, observe the exact place beer holds in his calculation of happiness, hear his tale of the ghost in the nearest haunted house, and of the farmer's niece who was bewitched with knots in her inside till she fell into fits and died. If we choose out in this way things which have altered little in a long course of centuries, we may draw a picture where there shall be scarce a hand's breadth difference between an English plowman and a Negro of Central Africa. These pages will be so crowded with evidence of such correspondence among mankind, that there is no need to dwell upon its details here, but it may be used at once to override a problem which would complicate the argument, namely, the question of race. For the present purpose it appears both possible and desirable to eliminate considerations of hereditary varieties of races of man, and to treat mankind as homogeneous in nature, though placed in different grades of civilization. The details of the inquiry will, I think, prove that stages of culture may be compared without taking into account how far tribes who use the same implement follow the same custom or believe the same myth may differ in their bodily configuration and the color of their skin and hair.

A first step in the study of civilization is to dissect it into details, and to classify these in their proper groups. Thus, in examining weapons, they are to be classed under spear, club, sling, bow and arrow, and so forth; among textile arts are to be ranged matting, netting, and several grades of making and weaving threads; myths are divided under such headings as myths of sunrise and sunset, eclipse myths, earthquake myths, local myths which account for the names of places by some fanciful tale, eponymic myths which account for the parentage of a tribe by turning its name into the name of an imaginary ancestor; under rites and ceremonies occur such practices as the various kinds of sacrifice to the ghosts of the dead and to other spiritual beings, the turning to the east in worship, the purification of ceremonial or moral uncleanness by means of water or fire. Such are a few miscellaneous examples from a list of hundreds, and the ethnographer's business is to classify such details with a view to making out their distribution in geography and history, and the relations which exist among them. What this task is like may be almost perfectly illustrated by comparing these details of culture with the species of plants and animals as studied by the naturalist. To the ethnographer the bow and arrow is a species, the habit of flattening children's skulls is a species, the practice of reckoning numbers by tens is a species. The geographical distribution of these things, and their transmission from region to region, have to be studied as the naturalist studies the geography of his botanical and zoological species. Just as certain plants and animals are peculiar to certain districts, so it is with such instruments as the Australian boomerang, the Polynesian stick-and-groove for fire making, the tiny bow and arrow used as a lancet by tribes about the Isthmus of Panama, and in like manner with many an art, myth, or custom, found isolated in a particular field. Just as the catalogue of all the species of plants and animals of a district represents its flora and fauna, so the list of all the items of the general life of a people represents that whole which we call its culture. And just as distant regions so often produce vegetables and animals which are analogous, though by no means identical, so it is with the details of the civilization of their inhabitants. How good a working analogy there really is between the diffusion of plants and animals and the diffusion of civilization comes well into view when we notice how far the same causes have produced both at once. In district after district, the same causes which have introduced the cultivated plants and domesticated animals of civilization, have brought in with them a corresponding art and knowledge. The course of events which carried horses and wheat to America carried with them the use of the gun and the iron hatchet, while in return the whole world received not only maize, potatoes, and turkeys, but the habit of tobacco smoking and the sailor's hammock.

It is a matter worthy of consideration that the accounts of similar phenomena of culture, recurring in different parts of the world, actually supply incidental proof of their own authenticity. Some years since, a question which brings out this point was put to me by a great historian—"How can a statement as to customs, myths, beliefs, and so on, of a savage tribe be treated as evidence where it depends on the testimony of some traveler or missionary, who may be a superficial observer, more or less ignorant of the native language, a careless retailer of unsifted talk, a man prejudiced or even willfully deceitful?" This question is, indeed, one which every ethnographer ought to keep clearly and constantly before his mind. Of course, he is bound to use his best judgment as to the trustworthiness of all authors he quotes, and if possible to obtain several accounts to certify each point in each locality. But it is over and above these measures of precaution that the test of recurrence comes in. If two independent visitors to different countries, say a medieval Mohammedan in Tartary and a modern Englishman in Dahomey, or a Jesuit missionary in Brazil and a Wesleyan in the Fiji Islands, agree in describing some analogous art or rite or myth among the people they have visited, it becomes difficult or impossible to set down such correspondence to accident or willful fraud. A story by a bushranger in Australia may, perhaps, be objected to as a mistake or an invention, but did a Methodist minister in Guinea conspire with him to cheat the public by telling the same story there? The possibility of intentional or unintentional mystification is often barred by such a state of things as that a similar statement is made in two remote lands, by two witnesses, of whom A lived a century before B, and B appears never to have heard of A. How distant are the countries, how wide apart the dates, how different the creeds and characters of the observers, in the catalogue of facts of civilization, need no farther showing to anyone who will even glance at the footnotes of the present work. And the more odd the statement, the less likely that several people in several places should have made it wrongly. This being so, it seems reasonable to judge that the statements are in the main truly given and that their close and regular coincidence is due to the cropping up of similar facts in various districts of culture. Now, the most important facts of ethnography are vouched for in this way. Experience leads the student after a while to expect and find that the phenomena of culture, as resulting from widely acting similar causes, should recur again and again in the world. He even mistrusts isolated statements to which he knows of no parallel elsewhere, and waits for their genuineness to be shown by corresponding accounts from the other side of the earth, or the other end of history. So strong, indeed, is this means of authentication, that the ethnographer in his library may sometimes presume to decide not only whether a particular explorer is a shrewd, honest observer but also whether what he reports is conformable to the general rules of civilization. *Non quis sed quid.*

To turn from the distribution of culture in different countries to its diffusion within these countries. The quality of mankind which tends most to make the systematic study of civilization possible is that remarkable tacit consensus or agreement which so far induces whole populations to unite in the use of the same language, to follow the same religion and customary law, to settle down to the same general level of art and knowledge. It is this state of things which makes it so far possible to ignore exceptional facts and to describe nations by a sort of general average. It is this state of things which makes it so far possible to represent immense masses of details by a few typical facts, while, these once settled, new cases recorded by new observers simply fall into their places to prove the soundness of the classification. There is found to be such regularity in the composition of societies of men that we can drop individual differences out of sight, and thus can generalize on the arts and opinions of whole nations, just as, when looking down upon an army from a hill, we forget the individual soldier, whom, in fact, we can scarce distinguish in the mass, while we see each regiment as an organized body, spreading or concentrating, moving in advance or in retreat. In some branches of the study of social laws it is now possible to call in the aid of statistics, and to set apart special actions of large mixed communities of men by means of taxgatherers' schedules, or the tables of the insurance office. Among modern arguments on the laws of human action, none have had a deeper effect than generalizations such as those of M. Quételet, on the regularity not only of such matters as average stature and the annual rates of birth and death but also of the recurrence, year after year, of such obscure and seemingly incalculable products of national life as the numbers of murders and suicides, and the proportion of the very weapons of crime. Other striking cases are the annual regularity of persons killed accidentally in the London streets, and of undirected letters dropped into post-office letterboxes. But in examining the culture of the lower races, far from having at command the measured arithmetical facts of modern statistics, we may have to judge of the condition of tribes from the imperfect accounts supplied by travelers or missionaries, or even to reason upon relics of prehistoric races of whose very names and languages we are hopelessly ignorant. Now, these may seem at the first glance sadly indefinite and unpromising materials for scientific inquiry. But in fact they are neither indefinite nor unpromising, but give evidence that is good and definite so far as it goes. They are data which, for the distinct way in which they severally denote the condition of the tribe they belong to, will actually bear comparison with the statistician's returns. The fact is that a stone arrowhead, a carved club, an idol, a grave mound where slaves and property have been buried for the use of the dead, an account of a sorcerer's rites in making rain, a table of numerals, the conjugation of a verb, are things which each express the state of a people as to one particular point of culture, as truly as the tabulated numbers of deaths by poison, and of chests of tea imported, express in a different way other partial results of the general life of a whole community.

That a whole nation should have a special dress, special tools and weapons, special laws of marriage and property, special moral and religious doctrines, is a remarkable fact, which we notice so little because we have lived all our lives in the midst of it. It is with such general qualities of organized bodies of men that ethnography has especially to deal. Yet, while generalizing on the culture of a tribe or nation, and setting aside the peculiarities of the individuals composing it as unimportant to the main result, we must be careful not to forget what makes up this main result. There are people so intent on the separate life of individuals that they cannot grasp a notion of the action of a community as a whole—such an observer, incapable of a wide view of society, is aptly described in the saying that he "cannot see the forest for the trees." But, on the other hand, the philosopher may be so intent upon his general laws of society as to neglect the individual actors of whom that society is made up, and of him it may be said that he cannot see the trees for the forest. We know how arts, customs, and ideas are shaped among ourselves by the combined actions of many individuals, of which actions both motive and effect often come quite distinctly within our view. The history of an invention, an opinion, a ceremony, is a history of suggestion and modification, encouragement and opposition, personal gain and party prejudice, and the individuals concerned act each according to his own motives, as determined by his character and circumstances. Thus sometimes we watch individuals acting for their own ends with little thought of their effect on society at large, and sometimes we have to study movements of national life as a whole, where the individuals cooperating in them are utterly beyond our observation. But seeing that collective social action is the mere resultant of many individual actions, it is clear that these two methods of inquiry, if rightly followed, must be absolutely consistent.

In studying both the recurrence of special habits or ideas in several districts, and their prevalence within each district, there come before us ever-reiterated proofs of regular causation producing the phenomena of human life, and of laws of maintenance and diffusion according to which these phenomena settle into permanent standard conditions of society, at definite stages of culture. But, while giving full importance to the evidence bearing on these standard conditions of society, let us be careful to avoid a pitfall which may entrap the unwary student. Of course, the opinions and habits belonging in common to masses of mankind are to a great extent the results of sound judgment and practical wisdom. But to a great extent it is not so. That many numerous societies of men should have believed in the influence of the evil eye and the existence of a firmament, should have sacrificed slaves and goods to the ghosts of the departed, should have handed down traditions of giants slaying monsters and men turning into beasts—all this is ground for holding that such ideas were indeed produced in men's minds by efficient causes, but it is not ground for holding that the rites in question are profitable, the beliefs sound, and the history authentic. This may seem at the first glance a truism, but, in fact, it is the denial of a fallacy which deeply affects the minds of all but a small critical minority of mankind. Popularly, what everybody says must be true, what everybody does must be right—"Quod semper, quod ubique, quod ab omnibus creditum est, hoc est vere proprieque Catholicum"—and so forth. There are various topics, especially in history, law, philosophy, and theology, where even the educated people we live among can hardly be brought to see that the cause why men do hold an opinion or practice a custom is by no means necessarily a reason why they ought to do so. Now collections of ethnographic evidence bringing so prominently into view the agreement of immense multitudes of men as to certain traditions, beliefs, and usages, are peculiarly liable to be thus improperly used in direct defense of these institutions themselves, even old barbaric nations being polled to maintain their opinions against what are called modern ideas. As it has more than once happened to myself to find my collections of traditions and beliefs thus set up to prove their own objective truth, without proper examination of the grounds on which they were actually received, I take this occasion of remarking that the same line of argument will serve equally well to demonstrate, by the strong and wide consent of nations, that the earth is flat, and nightmare the visit of a demon.

It being shown that the details of Culture are capable of being classified in a great number of ethnographic groups of arts, beliefs, customs, and the rest, the consideration comes next how far the facts arranged in these groups are produced by evolution from one another. It need hardly be pointed out that the groups in question, though held together each by a common character, are by no means accurately defined. To take up again the natural-history illustration, it may be said that they are species which tend to run widely into varieties. And when it comes to the question what relations some of these groups bear to others, it is plain that the student of the habits of mankind has a great advantage over the student of the species of plants and animals. Among naturalists it is an open question whether a theory of development from species to species is a record of transitions which actually took place, or a mere ideal scheme serviceable in the classification of species whose origin was really independent. But among ethnographers there is no such question as to the possibility of species of implements or habits or beliefs being developed one out of another, for development in Culture is recognized by our most familiar knowledge. Mechanical invention supplies apt examples of the kind of development which affects civilization at large. In the history of firearms, the clumsy wheellock, in which a notched steel wheel revolved by means of a spring against a piece of pyrites till a spark caught the priming, led to the invention of the more serviceable flintlock, of which a few still hang in the kitchens of our farmhouses for the boys to shoot small birds with at Christmas; the flintlock in time passed by modification into the percussion lock, which is just now changing its old-fashioned arrangement to be adapted from muzzle-loading to breech-loading. The medieval astrolabe passed into the quadrant, now discarded in its turn by the seaman, who uses the more delicate sextant, and so it is through the history of one art and instrument after another. Such examples of progression are known to us as direct history, but so thoroughly is this notion of development at home in our minds, that by means of it we reconstruct lost history without scruple, trusting to general knowledge of the principles of human thought and action as a guide in putting the facts in their proper order. Whether chronicle speaks or is silent on the point, no one comparing a longbow and a crossbow would doubt that the crossbow was a development arising from the simpler instrument. So among the fire drills for igniting by friction, it seems clear on the face of the matter that the drill worked by a cord or bow is a later improvement on the clumsier primitive instrument twirled between the hands. That instructive class of specimens which antiquaries sometimes discover, bronze celts modeled on the heavy type of the stone hatchet, are scarcely explicable except as first steps in the transition from the Stone Age to the Bronze Age, to be followed soon by the next stage of progress, in which it is discovered that the new material is suited to a handier and less wasteful pattern. And thus, in the other branches of our history, there will come again and again into view series of facts which may be consistently arranged as having followed one another in a particular order of development, but which will hardly bear being turned round and made to follow in reversed order. Such for instance are the facts I have here brought forward in a chapter on the Art of Counting, which tend to prove that as to this point of culture at least, savage tribes reached their position by learning and not by unlearning, by elevation from a lower rather than by degradation from a higher state.

Among evidence aiding us to trace the course which the civilization of the world has actually followed is that great class of facts to denote which I have found it convenient to introduce the term "survivals." These are processes, customs, opinions, and so forth, which have been carried on by force of habit into a new state of society different from that in which they had their original home, and they thus remain as proofs and examples of an older condition of culture out of which a newer has been evolved. Thus, I know an old Somersetshire woman whose hand-loom dates from the time before the introduction of the "flying shuttle," which new-fangled appliance she has never even learned to use, and I have seen her throw her shuttle from hand to hand in true classic fashion; this old woman is not a century behind her times; she is a case of survival. Such examples often lead us back to the habits of hundreds and even thousands of years ago. The ordeal of the Key and Bible, still in use, is a survival; the Midsummer bonfire is a survival; the Breton peasants' All Souls' supper for the spirits of the dead is a survival. The simple keeping up of ancient habits is only one part of the transition from old into new and changing times. The serious business of ancient society may be seen to sink into the sport of later generations, and its serious belief to linger on in nursery folklore, while superseded habits of old-world life may be modified into new-world forms still powerful for good and evil. Sometimes old thoughts and practices will burst out afresh, to the amazement of a world that thought them long since dead or dying; here survival passes into revival, as has lately happened in so remarkable a way in the history of modern spiritualism, a subject full of instruction from the ethnographer's point of view. The study of the principles of survival has, indeed, no small practical importance, for most of what we call superstition is included within survival, and in this way lies open to the attack of its deadliest enemy, a reasonable explanation. Insignificant, moreover, as multitudes of the facts of survival are in themselves, their study is so effective for tracing the course of the historical development through which alone it is possible to understand their meaning, that it becomes a vital point of ethnographic research to gain the clearest possible insight into their nature. This importance must justify the detail here devoted to an examination of survival, on the evidence of such games, popular sayings, customs, superstitions, and the like, as may serve well to bring into view the manner of its operation.

Progress, degradation, survival, revival, modification, are all modes of the connection that binds together the complex network of civilization. It needs but a glance into the trivial details of our own daily life to set us thinking how far we are really its originators, and how far but the transmitters and modifiers of the results of long-past ages. Looking round the rooms we live in, we may try here how far he who knows only his own time can be capable of rightly comprehending even that. Here is the "honeysuckle" of Assyria, there the fleur-de-lis of Anjou, a cornice with a Greek border runs round the ceiling, the style of Louis XIV and its parent the Renaissance share the looking glass between them. Transformed, shifted, or mutilated, such elements of art still carry their history plainly stamped upon them; and if the history yet farther behind is less easy to read, we are not to say that because we cannot clearly discern it there is therefore no history there. It is thus even with the fashion of the clothes men wear. The ridiculous little tails of the German postilion's coat show of themselves how they came to dwindle to such absurd rudiments; but the English clergyman's bands no longer so convey their history to the eye, and look unaccountable enough till one has seen the intermediate stages through which they came down from the more serviceable wide collars, such as Milton wears in his portrait, and which gave their name to the "bandbox" they used to be kept in. In fact, the books of costume, showing how one garment grew or shrank by gradual stages and passed into another, illustrate with much force and clearness the nature of the change and growth, revival and decay, which go on from year to year in more important matters of life. In books, again, we see each writer not for and by himself, but occupying his proper place in history; we look through each philosopher, mathematician, chemist, poet, into the background of his education,—through Leibniz into Descartes, through Dalton into Priestley, through Milton into Homer. The study of language has, perhaps, done more than any other in removing from our view of human thought and action the ideas of chance and arbitrary invention, and in substituting for them a theory of development by the cooperation of individual men, through processes ever reasonable and intelligible where the facts are fully known. Rudimentary as the science of culture still is, the symptoms are becoming very strong that even what seem its most spontaneous and motiveless phenomena will, nevertheless, be shown to come within the range of distinct cause and effect as certainly as the facts of mechanics. What would be popularly thought more indefinite and uncontrolled than the products of the imagination in myths and fables? Yet any systematic investigation of mythology, on the basis of a wide collection of evidence, will show plainly enough in such efforts of fancy at once a development from stage to stage, and a production of uniformity of result from uniformity of cause. Here, as elsewhere, causeless spontaneity is seen to recede farther and farther into shelter within the dark precincts of ignorance; like chance, that still holds its place among the vulgar as a real cause of events otherwise unaccountable, while to educated men it has long consciously meant nothing but this ignorance itself. It is only when men fail to see the line of connection in events that they are prone to fall upon the notions of arbitrary impulses, causeless freaks, chance and nonsense and indefinite unaccountability. If childish games, purposeless customs, absurd superstitions are set down as spontaneous because no one can say exactly how they came to be, the assertion may remind us of the like effect that the eccentric habits of the wild rice plant had on the philosophy of a Red Indian tribe, otherwise disposed to see in the harmony of nature the effects of one controlling personal will. The Great Spirit, said these Sioux theologians, made all things except the wild rice; but the wild rice came by chance.

"Man," said Wilhelm von Humboldt, "ever connects on from what lies at hand" (*der Mensch knüpft immer an Vorhandenes an*). The notion of the continuity of civilization contained in this maxim is no barren philosophic principle, but is at once made practical by the consideration that they who wish to understand their own lives ought to know the stages through which their opinions and habits have become what they are. Auguste Comte scarcely overstated the necessity of this study of development when he declared at the beginning of his *Positive Philosophy* that "no conception can be understood except through its history," and his phrase will bear extension to culture at large. To expect to look modern life in the face and comprehend it by mere inspection is a philosophy whose weakness can easily be tested. Imagine anyone explaining the trivial saying "A little bird told me," without knowing of the old belief in the language of birds and beasts, to which Dr. Dasent, in the introduction to the Norse Tales, so reasonably traces its origin. Attempts to explain by the light of reason things which want the light of history to show their meaning, may be instanced from Blackstone's *Commentaries.* To Blackstone's mind, the very right of the commoner to turn his beast out to graze on the common finds its origin and explanation in the feudal system: "For, when lords of manors granted out parcels of land to tenants, for services either done or to be done, these tenants could not plough or manure the land without beasts; these beasts could not be sustained without pasture; and pasture could not be had but in the lord's wastes, and on the uninclosed fallow grounds of themselves and the other tenants. The law therefore annexed this right of common, as inseparably incident, to the grant of the lands; and this was the original of common appendant." Now, though there is nothing irrational in this explanation, it does not agree at all with the Teutonic land law which prevailed in England long before the Norman Conquest and of which the remains have never wholly disappeared. In the old village community even the arable land, lying in the great common fields which may still be traced in our country, had not yet passed into separate property, while the pasturage in the fallows and stubbles and on the waste belonged to the householders in common. Since those days, the change from communal to individual ownership has mostly transformed this old-world system, but the right which the peasant enjoys of pasturing his cattle on the common still remains, not as a concession to feudal tenants but as possessed by the commoners before the lord ever claimed the ownership of the waste. It is always unsafe to detach a custom from its hold on past events, treating it as an isolated fact to be simply disposed of by some plausible explanation. . . .

Not merely as a matter of curious research, but as an important practical guide to the understanding of the present and the shaping of the future, the investigation into the origin and early development of civilization must be pushed on zealously. Every possible avenue of knowledge must be explored, every door tried to see if it is open. No kind of evidence need be left untouched on the score of remoteness or complexity, of minuteness or triviality. The tendency of modern inquiry is more and more toward the conclusion that if law is anywhere, it is everywhere. To despair of what a conscientious collection and study of facts may lead to, and to declare any problem insoluble because difficult and far off, is distinctly to be on the wrong side in science; and he who will choose a hopeless task may set himself to discover the limits of discovery. One remembers Comte starting in his account of astronomy with a remark on the necessary limitation of our knowledge of the stars: we conceive, he tells us, the possibility of determining their form, distance, size, and movement, whilst we should never by any method be able to study their chemical composition, their mineralogical structure, and so on. Had the philosopher lived to see the application of spectrum analysis to this very problem, his proclamation of the dispiriting doctrine of necessary ignorance would perhaps have been recanted in favor of a more hopeful view. And it seems to be with the philosophy of remote human life somewhat as with the study of the nature of the celestial bodies. The processes to be made out in the early stages of our mental evolution lie distant from us in time as the stars lie distant from us in space, but the laws of the universe are not limited with the direct observation of our senses. There is vast material to be used in our inquiry; many workers are now busied in bringing this material into shape, though little may have yet been done in proportion to what remains to do; and already it seems not too much to say that the vague outlines of a philosophy of primeval history are beginning to come within our view.

Ernst Troeltsch
(1866–1923)

THE SOCIOLOGY OF RELIGION

Karl Mannheim has said that Ernst Troeltsch had set himself the task "of solving the problem of how far the origin, growth, and modifications of Christianity as well as the arrest of that growth in modern times were sociologically determined."[1]

Ernst Troeltsch, who was born in Augsburg, Germany, was one of the most outstanding scholars in the field of the sociology of religion.

Troeltsch studied philosophy and theology and during his studies he met Gusstav Class, who introduced him to Fichte, Hegel, Kant, and Schleiermacher. He was also very much influenced by his teachers, Rulolph Harnack, Ritschl, and Lagarde. But it was Max Weber who was mainly responsible for the shift of Troeltsch's interest from theology to the philosophy and sociology of religion.[2]

In 1891 he was appointed as a lecturer at the University of Göttingen and served the University of Bonn from 1892 until 1894 as professor of theology. He taught at the University of Heidelberg (1894–1915), and there he became closely associated with Max Weber. In 1915 he became professor of philosophy at the University of Berlin, where he involved himself in political activities and was a member of the Prussian Parliament. He also served the Prussian minister of education as parliamentary undersecretary.

One of his first works was Die Soziallehren der christlichen Kirchen und Gruppen (1911), translated into English as The Social Teaching of the Christian Churches. The origin of this book was actually a book review that the editors of a journal had asked Troeltsch to write. The book he reviewed was The Cooperation of the Church in the Solution of the Social Problem by Nathusius, a theologian. According to Troeltsch it was a "miserable book." It completely lacked the

[1] P. 310, An Introduction to the History of Sociology, ed. by Harry Elmer Barnes, Chicago, 1948.
[2] P. 309, ibid.

understanding of the problem for which the church was to help find a solution.[3]

The picture of history that Troeltsch deliberated in The Social Teaching of the Christian Churches *is, according to Richard Niebuhr, "like a multi-perspectival painting. In one perspective it is a book about the church, presenting a double rebuttal to the Marxian thesis and to the orthodox; in another it is a book about Western history which uses the story of the churches' social teachings as an illustration of the whole complex process; in still another, it is a prolegomenon to the work of modern social construction or to the effort, as Troeltsch liked to say, of damming the stream of history for a while and of achieving a synthesis of culture, which, of course, again would pass away.*[4]

In his famous Der Historismus und seine Probleme (1922) *one encounters Troeltsch the historian. This book was strongly influenced by Dilthey and is considered one of the most outstanding works in the philosophy of history.*

In his methodology Troeltsch was close to Max Weber and his analysis of religious organizations as sociological types is extremely important for the contemporary student of the sociology of religion.

THE SOCIOLOGY OF RELIGION

THE beginnings of the economic ethic of Calvinism were insignificant, but it developed into a factor of the greatest historical importance, both in the development of the modern economic spirit and in that of Calvinism itself.

From the outset, in its main features the economic ethic of Calvinism was also related to the corresponding aspects of Lutheranism. The Calvinistic ethic shared the Lutheran view about work, to which it assigned a high value, regarding it as the practical exercise of a calling appointed by God, and therefore as divine worship; it also regarded it as a method of self-discipline and of diverting evil desires. Both Calvin and Luther advocated labor as a universal duty, and abolished monasticism and mendicancy. The Calvinistic economic ethic

[3] Pp. 7-8, *The Social Teaching of the Christian Churches*, Introduction by H. Richard Niebuhr, New York, Harper Torchbooks, 1960.

[4] Pp. 10-11, ibid.

also agreed with the Lutheran ethic in its "anti-Mammon"
spirit, its urgent desire for modesty and moderation, its observance of distinctions in rank, its campaign against luxury,
which in this respect was prosecuted with unexampled severity by laws against luxury, and which was supported ec-
clesiastically by the moral tribunal. Calvin also believed that
poverty fostered the Christian virtues more effectively than
wealth, and he launched out into violent denunciations of the
great commercial cities like Venice and Antwerp. In spite of
all this, however, Calvin influenced the "Reformed" economic
ethic from the very beginning in such a way that, as in the
political sphere, it developed an utterly different spirit from
that which animated the Lutheran ethic, both in its primitive and in its present form. This took place, however, without any special and conscious intention on Calvin's part. To
a very large extent indeed, the direction in which this ethic
evolved was determined by the conditions which governed
the practical situation in Geneva.

This was the decisive turning point: Calvin was convinced
that this "anti-Mammon" Christian spirit could express itself
and maintain its existence within the sphere of a society
which was based essentially upon a money economy, upon
trade and industry. Unlike Lutheranism in similar circumstances, Calvin did not hark back to the agrarian patriarchal
form of life as the ideal with its closely knit self-contained
family life, based as far as possible on primitive methods of
production, but he recognized industrial production based on
a money economy as the natural foundation and form of professional work alongside agrarian labor. Calvin himself had a
great deal to do with questions of industrial production, and
he quite approved of the fact that greater profits were made
in trade than in agriculture, since they were simply the reward of carefulness and industry. It is, of course, true that
he urged the abolition of certain kinds of business which
were questionable from the Christian point of view, such as
the manufacture of playing cards, but in general he was in
favor of movement and progress. It was at Calvin's instigation that, with the aid of a state loan, the manufacture of
cloth and velvet was introduced into Geneva as a home industry, in order to give work to the poor and unemployed. Later
on, when this industry had to be given up on account of the
competition of Lyons, the manufacture of watches was introduced with the same aim. He had no desire merely to uphold
existing customs and methods of gaining a livelihood. He

never denied the necessity for the mobility of an economic system based on industry and trade. All this, however, was due to the Genevan situation and the Genevan atmosphere, which even affected his correspondence; his letters, indeed, deal constantly with the interests of finance, trade, and industry (from the point of view of the manual laborer).

As a jurist and a townsman, from the beginning he may have felt differently about these things than Luther who was a monk, but from the sources it is plain that, in any case, in Geneva he could not think or feel otherwise, if he were to have a practical influence, and that he accepted this necessity without scruple or difficulty. The reason why Calvin was able to accept this situation as he did was probably due to the peculiar character of his practical active ethic, which embraced the whole sphere of public life and which set in the forefront those elements of behavior which were practically possible to achieve, while the radical commandments about love and suffering were relegated to the background. If Luther had lived in Geneva under the same conditions we can hardly imagine that he would have thought and felt otherwise than in Wittenberg. If Geneva had been a specially large and active commercial town it is of course probable that even Calvin would have felt it much more difficult to submit to the claims of capitalism. In Geneva, however, which was surrounded by hostile and rival neighbors, and whose territory was very small, the conditions were narrow and provincial. But it was precisely in this form that Calvin found capitalism acceptable, as a calling which suited the existing conditions in the city and which was capable of being combined with loyalty, seriousness, honesty, thrift, and consideration for one's neighbor. It was just because the economic conditions at Geneva were so bourgeois, and on such a small scale, that capitalism was able to steal into the Calvinistic ethic, while it was rejected by the Catholic and the Lutheran ethic.

That is officially expressed, properly speaking, in the important fact that Calvin and the Calvinistic ethic rejected the canonical veto on usury and the scholastic theory of money, and on the contrary supported a doctrine of money, credit, and usury which were nearer to the modern economic idea, with limitations, certainly, with which we shall have to deal presently. In this, Calvin abandoned the purely consumer's standpoint of the previous Christian ethic, and recognized the productive power of money and of credit. Calvin's cooperation with the economic administration of the State, and his conception of the importance of a social life which was well ordered from the economic point of view, for the holy community, shows that he felt an inner connection between economic progress and moral elevation. Calvin's successors at Geneva went forward in the path which he had traced. Beza and the Vénérable Compagnie devoted much detailed care and thought to questions of economic prosperity and efficiency. They also watched to see that wealth was rightly distributed, and that proper relief was given to the poor, and work to the unemployed. In questions of this kind the government of the state continually turned to them for their opinions and advice. They took an interest in taxation and in state loans, and in the rate of interest, which was always fixed with their approval. They gave their judgment in favor of the erection of a state bank, both in order to bring to the state the gain of exchange of business and to create cheap credit for the trades which were needing assistance.

Thus this economic practice of Geneva became the starting point from which capitalism was incorporated into the Calvinistic ethic all over the world, though with caution and under certain limitations. Conditions among the French Huguenots, in the Netherlands, and in England, each with their own characteristics, also helped to adjust modern business life to the religious point of view. One very important aspect of the situation is the fact that the Calvinists in France and England, and at the outset also in the Netherlands, and, above all, during their period of exile on the Lower Rhine, as minorities were forced out of public life and official positions in the state; they were thus obliged, in the main, to go into business life. Apart from this, however, the Calvinists displayed a strong tendency in this direction, even in circumstances which were not particularly favorable to business life; their industrious habits, their detachment from the world, and their rational and utilitarian spirit certainly strengthened this tendency.

The economic situation in Geneva, however, contained the germ of logical developments which went beyond the intention of Calvin and the Genevese. Once capitalism had been accepted, even with many precautions, given the right milieu, everywhere it led to results which increased its power; while the specifically Calvinistic habits of piety and industry justified its existence and helped to increase its strength, which gave it in the Calvinistic communities a special character and a peculiar intensity.[5] The exhortation to continual industry in labor, combined with the limitation of consumption and of luxury, produced a tendency to pile up capital, which for its part—in the necessity of its further utilization in work and not in enjoyment—necessitated an ever-increasing turnover. The duty of labor, coupled with the ban on luxury, worked out "economically as the impulse to save," and the impulse to save had the effect of building up capital. To what extent these developments took place everywhere is a separate question. Upon the whole, however, this result be-

[5] No one has ever asserted that capitalism is the direct product of Calvinism. We can, however, say that both possessed a certain affinity for each other, that Calvinistic ethic of the "calling" and of work, which declares that the earning of money with certain precautions is allowable, was able to give it an intellectual and ethical backbone, and that, therefore, thus organized and inwardly supported it vigorously developed, even though within the limits of antimammon. "There is no doubt that where an economic system and a 'spirit' with which it has a certain affinity meet, there ensues a development along uniform lines which is also inwardly unbroken (that is, where the spirit and the economic system agree, which is not always the case), of the kind which I had begun to analyse (that is, like the Calvinistic development)." The conjunction of these two elements itself is a historic accident, as I have said already in describing the similarly comparatively close affinity between the medieval system and the Catholic ethic. But out of such accidents (*Weber: Schlusswort*, XXXI, p. 580): "Humanity which through the meeting of religious and economic elements was created"; p. 583: "Protestant asceticism created for it [bourgeois capitalism] a positive ethic, a soul which needed that restless activity in order that 'spirit' and 'form' might be one"; p. 588: A current of psychic elements which arose from a very specific moral and religious source, combined with capitalistic possibilities of development from which the great historical developments proceed. The Christian ethic only attained a great actual importance for world history when it was supported by an "accident" of this kind. In itself alone, when it did not receive this support, it simply remained in the realm of theory. The combination of these elements then reacted, however, upon the religious and ethical spirit, as I prove in both instances. In the history of the Christian ethic there have only been two "accidents" of this kind, the medieval system and the Calvinistic system, whose expansion through the bourgeois sect will be demonstrated in the next section. There are other certainly often finer and deeper conceptions of the Christian ethos to whom an historic influence of this kind was denied, because they were not favored by such an "accident" or in their very nature were unable to find such support. If I speak here of "accident," this is naturally meant logically, i.e. that here there is no immanent development, not that these things have happened *sine Deo.*

longed to the very nature of the case, and it is the general opinion that this is what actually took place among the most important Calvinistic peoples.

This, however, is not the main point at issue. The contribution of Calvinism to the formation of the capitalist system itself is not the most important aspect of the question. This only becomes clear when, with Weber and Sombart, we inquire into the ethical "spirit" and the world outlook, or the "economic temper" which gave the system its firm hold over the minds of men and which, in spite of its opposition to natural human instincts, has been able to strike root in human minds as a firm conviction. Economic traditionalism, interrupted by unscrupulous individuals who are simply out for gain, is much more in line with ordinary human instincts than the concrete and abstract dominion of labor and profit, as ends in themselves, the continual increase of work produced by every fresh profit from labor. It is here that we perceive the importance (together with related, yet different, effects of Judaism) which the peculiar Calvinistic type of the inward ethical attitude has gained toward the performance of labor in business life, and its religious estimate of the earning of money. The Protestant ethic of the "calling," with its Calvinistic assimilation of the capitalist system, with its severity and its control of the labor rendered as a sign of the assurance of election, made service in one's "calling," the systematic exercise of one's energies, into a service both necessary in itself and appointed by God, in which profit is regarded as the sign of the divine approval. This conception of the "calling" and of labor, with its taboo on idleness of every kind, with its utilization of every chance of gain, and its confidence in the blessing of God, now, however, to a great extent approached the commercial professions and the business of making money. It laid the foundation of a world of specialized labor, which taught men to work for work's sake, and in so doing it produced our present-day bourgeois way of life, the fundamental psychological principles which gave it birth, which, however, it was not bound to perpetuate once this way of life had become the constitution of the modern world.

Thus there arose a current—definite, particularly powerful, and influential—of the bourgeois capitalistic spirit, which was preeminently typical of the bourgeois way of life in general. This was the predominance of labor and of the "calling," of industry for its own sake, a process of objectifying work and the results of work, which was only possible where work was exalted by means of an escetic vocational ethic of that kind, into the sphere of that which is *necessary in itself* by means of the underlying religious conception. Calvinism, which in its early days included a good many groups of the aristocracy, was at first indifferent to social questions, but in the course of the political development in various countries it become bourgeois; this social transformation, however, was entirely in line with certain elements in its spirit. . . .

The significant point which is important even today for our subject is this: that in these Christian circles, and in them alone, was it possible to combine modern economic activity with Christian thought, and, indeed, that down to the present day it is possible to do this with a clear conscience. In this connection we need only to recall the circumlocutions with which Catholicism tries to make this modern form of economic life tolerable, and how, at bottom, it continually attempts to restrain it, or the revulsion with which early Lutheranism and contemporary German Conservatism officially regard capitalism. Seen in this light, the significance of this new Calvinistic form of Christianity for the whole modern development, and especially for the position of Protestantism within it, becomes plain. It is the only form of Christian social doctrine which accepts the basis of the modern economic situation without reserve. The reason for this does not lie in any supposed "greater insight" into the essence of the economic processes, but in the fact that here the superidealistic and pietistic hindrances in the fundamental ethical idea have fallen away, which would have otherwise hindered or restrained this development; because, on the contrary, the Calvinistic ethic contains energies which directly further this economic development.

Whether a Christian ethic of this kind, contrasted with that of Catholicism and of Lutheranism, is entirely an advantage whether it is not tinged rather strongly with the spirit of "business" and the avidity of a materialistic outlook on life, is another question. The main point is that it is peculiar to the leading modern nations, or at least to majority groups among them, and that it here effects an adjustment to the modern economic world which has not been achieved by the Christian piety of other nations.

The Christian element in this Calvinistic justification of capitalism would, however, be greatly misunderstood if one did not at the same time remember the limits with which the real Christian idea of love here also surrounds the ethic of industry and which have continued to exert a beneficent influence right down to the present day, wherever, in all capitalistic labor, the main Calvinistic ideas have remained vitally alive. Labor is asceticism, an asceticism which is absolutely necessary. Profit is the sign of the blessing of God on the faithful exercise of one's calling. But labor and profit were never intended for purely personal interest. The capitalist is always a steward of the gifts of God, whose duty it is to increase his capital and utilize it for the good of Society as a whole, retaining for himself only that amount which is necessary to provide for his own needs. All surplus wealth should be used for works of public utility, and especially for purposes of ecclesiastical philanthropy. Thus the Genevese assessed themselves to the furthest possible limit for special cases of need, and gave regularly in support of the local poor as well as for the numerous refugees. The charitable activity of the Church which was exercised by the board of deacons was part of the requirement of the Church order instituted by God, was organized with great energy, and, with the aid of voluntary gifts which were often amazingly large, it was able to cope with the demands made upon it. This is the origin of the practice known among us through the example of American millionaires—in which even men who have become quite indifferent to religion will give a large portion of their profits for public purposes. The actual theory and practice of money and interest has also been determined by this spirit of philanthropy.

Only "productive credit" for business purposes is allowed, not "usury credit," which is simply used for living on interest. From poor men, or people who have been otherwise harassed by misfortune, no interest is to be taken; loans also were not to be refused for lack of securities. Arrangements of that kind are only to be carried out with reference to the good of the community as a whole. The debtor ought to gain just as much from the money as the creditor. The law of cheapness ought to prevail everywhere, in accordance with the principle of the Gospel and of the natural law, that "whatsoever ye would that they should do unto you, do ye also unto them." Finally, the rate of interest ought not to exceed a maximum, which is to be legally fixed according to the needs of the situation. This was the theory. In Geneva practical life was regulated in accordance with these principles. The fight against usury and the exploitation of the poor fill the protocols of the Council and of the Consistory, and these Christian-

Social elements of Calvinistic doctrine have also left their mark upon ethics. Thus we can understand how it is that within Calvinism, in the face of the modern development of capitalism, there has always been, and still is, a tendency to merge into a form of Christian Socialism. We have already seen that a Socialism of this kind was contained, from the very outset, in the Genevan ideal of the Holy Community. It was continued in the "communities under the Cross," where the religious idea developed freely. How far it helped to determine the state legislation of Calvinistic countries has still to be discovered.

The great English system of legislation which deals with the poor, with workmen and with wages—in the guild-professional sense and, above all, with respect to education for work—bore traces of its spirit. In opposition to the "Manchester" conception of the state and of economics, Carlyle deliberately asserted the old Puritan ideas. The Christian Socialism of the English people at the present day is essentially of Calvinistic origin, and the activity of the American churches is often of a Christian Socialist kind directed against the abuses of capitalism. In Switzerland, in the Netherlands, in England, and in America there are today Socialist clergy, whereas within the sphere of Lutheranism such a phenomenon is regarded as an offense against the sacred foundation of the divine order, as taking part in purely secular matters, as a reprehensible revolutionary spirit, and a human intervention in the order of Providence; among us social heresies are more dangerous and more objectionable than doctrinal heresies. The meaning of that is, however, that Calvinism is in closer agreement with modern tendencies of social life than Lutheranism, or than Catholicism, which, at least in the Latin lands of its origin, likewise holds these heresies at arm's length. This also is the basis of that intense self-consciousness of Calvinism, the sense that it is the only form of Christianity adapted to modern life, because, on the one hand, it is able to justify modern forms of economic production before the tribunal of conscience, and because, on the other hand, by means of Christian Socialism, it strives to rectify the abuses of the system when they occur. It is very conscious of representing "modern Christianity"—not because it is in touch with modern theological thought (for its theological tendency inclines to conservatism, and it is only its overwhelmingly practical character which leads to dogmatism being relegated to a secondary position), but because it is in harmony with

the political and economic way of life, and understands how
to further and yet to define its problems, whereas it considers
that Lutheranism is philosophically diseased, unpractical, and
remote from the problems of ordinary life. . . .

It has already been made abundantly clear that Lutheranism taught that labor in a calling was both a service rendered
to God and an outward expression of brotherly love. On the
other hand, by its emphasis upon the purely inward aspect of
religion, its lack of a clear standard of moral behavior, and
its acquiescence in the conditions of life which were created
by natural law, but were often extremely unchristian, it was
not able, on its own initiative, to bring about a coherent and
systematic transformation of social life in general. Neither in
theory nor in its attitude to life does it possess a systematic
ethic. Again and again Lutheranism casts aside its aseticism
(which it also possesses as the corollary of the doctrine of
Original Sin), and gives itself up to repose in the blessedness
of the divine mercy, and to the thankful enjoyment of divine
gifts in all that is good and beautiful, and whenever it becomes dubious about the world and about sin it withdraws
into the refuge of its inner happiness of justification through
faith.

Catholicism, on the other hand, likewise values the cosmos
of the vocational system as the means of natural existence
appointed by natural law. But this system of callings is applicable to the conditions of natural existence, and is thus
merely the lower degree of that higher supernatural ethic,
which inwardly is no longer connected with the claims of the
active life, but which in the life of contemplation attains the
highest degree of supernature or grace.

Ascetic Protestantism, however, regards the "calling" as a
proof, and the ardent fulfillment of one's professional duty as
the sign and token of the state of grace. Accordingly it
gathers all the work of the "calling" into a coherent system of
the utmost concentration of human faculties on the aim of the
"calling," which is appointed to the individual through his
providential position within the system. The principles and
ideals of Ascetic Protestantism may therefore be summarized
thus: the inner severance of feeling and enjoyment from all
the objects of labor; the unceasing harnessing of labor to an
aim which lies in the other world, and therefore must occupy
us till death; the depreciation of possessions, of all things
earthly, to the level of expediency; the habit of industry in
order to suppress all distracting and idle impulses; and the

willing use of profit for the religious community and for public welfare; these principles, which may vary in detail, are all in the main similar in character, and to a considerable extent also they have been and are being realized. . . .

The economic ethic, finally, teaches (likewise from the general Christian point of view) that labor is the result of the Fall, and is to be regarded as the penalty and the discipline of sin. But this idea is here developed into that of a rational, systematic discipline of labor, evolved, above all, in Puritanism, and thence taken over in a more or less logical manner; this ethic regards laziness and idleness as the source of all evil, and the result of a failure to impose discipline. With this systematic view of work (to which, incidentally, other than Puritan motives were sometimes added, as, for instance, among the Quakers the waiting and self-preparation for the divine illumination), a strong and systematic impulse was given to production, while, on the other hand, with the same asceticism there is united a considerable limitation of consumption and a complete avoidance of all luxury (at least, of all that is obvious and that ministers to vanity and arrogance). It is only at this point that we see the full effect of that which has already been described as the favorable ethical disposition of Calvinism for bourgeois capitalism. Thus this economic ethic became middle-class, one might almost say lower-middle-class-capitalist, and it bore all the signs of the results of the capitalistic attitude toward life: systematic division of labor, emphasis upon specialization, the feeling for advantage and profit, the abstract duty of work, the obligation toward property as toward something great, which ought to be maintained and increased for its own sake. The owner of wealth or property is "the Lord's steward," and administers a divine gift which has been entrusted to him. An ethic of this kind placed at the disposal of the nascent modern bourgeois capitalism both energetic and courageous entrepreneurs, and men who were willing to endure exploitation if they could only get work. This ethic differs from the capitalism of antiquity and of the later Middle Ages by those very features which have just been described; and alongside it the other existing kinds of capitalism, of course, must not be overlooked.

This type of capitalism, however, preserves its special Christian character by its taboo on pleasure seeking and self-glorification, the sense of the duty of work for the service of God, strict honesty and reliability, the humane obligation to make provision for the workers and to give respect to em-

ployers, and the extensive use of wealth for philanthropic
ends.

The system of fixed prices, the standardization and classification of goods according to their quality, the building up
of business upon the strictest formal honesty, the principle
"honesty is the best policy"—all arose at this point. It is the
expression of a spiritual and moralistic opposition to the guild
system and to unfair dealing in individual cases; it means that
the life of business is constructed upon the calculation of the
individual in relation to an abstract circle of purchasers, and
upon the absolute necessity for correctness and honesty as
regards estimates and deliveries. The inscription on the Bre-
men Exchange, which states that the merchant is the most
honest man, should be interpreted from this point of view.
The justification for the economic life lies in its value to the
community, and in this sense it can be considered a blessing;
in itself, however, the ideal attitude is that of the man whose
spirit is inwardly entirely independent of possessions. It is
even possible to go a step farther and to exalt poverty, which
preserves from the dangers of wealth, just as, on the other
hand, wealth, used in a Christian way, preserves the community from misery and want. Thus here also there is no idea
of equality. This is prevented by the whole idea of Providence, and above all, where it was still a vital force, by the
idea of predestination. The conception is always that of a
cosmos directed by God, in which the Christian ethos works
itself out only through reciprocal activities, division of labor,
a variety of gifts and capacities. Thus, as Calvinism and the
sects are of one mind on the question of the development of
a voluntary Church, and on the question of separation between Church and state, so also their views coincide in the
economic ethic of secular asceticism which determines the
ethic of ascetic Protestantism, renouncing its greater earlier
freedom: Calvinism reaches this point of view under the
urgent sense of need to prove in daily life the reality of its
faith, and it therefore produces the systematic asceticism
of labor; the passive, persecuted sect comes to this point by
giving up its hostility toward the world, and by fusing its
ascetic detachment from the world with the Protestant idea
of the "calling." Further, both movements shared the following experience: on account of their nonconformity and their
freedom from the state, they were forcibly excluded from all
official positions in the state and from its dignities; thus they
were thrust out of the ruling classes and obliged to join the

bourgeois middle class; this still further intensified the bourgeois capitalist element. Agriculture was not excluded, but it was practiced by the people of this class only by farming and by trading in property in land; but it has nothing to do with the feudal ownership of land.

Thus the difference between this ethic and that of the theoretical traditional economic ethic of Catholicism is clear. In this ethic, work and possessions belong to the natural sphere alone; the desire for gain does not directly concern the religious ethic at all; gain is regarded merely as a method of providing for one's needs according to one's rank in society; whatever is earned beyond that should be used for charity; the most genuine charity, however, is actually exercised by those who possess nothing at all, by those who stand outside the ordinary work of the world altogether.

The difference between this economic ethic and that of Lutheranism is equally clear. Lutheranism, it is true, makes the task of earning a living part of the "calling" to brotherly love, but, in spite of this, it gives preference to the callings which belong to a settled order of society consisting of agricultural laborers, manual workers, and officials; capitalism and the calculating spirit which is continually striving to make more money is regarded by Lutheranism with detachment and extreme misgiving.

But even contrasted with primitive Calvinism, to which, with its state-Church point of view, all methods of gaining a livelihood were of equal importance, which had not developed the asceticism of labor to this extent, and which had no trace of the lower-middle-class spirit at all—this was something new. This was the result of that asceticism in which the Puritan, legalistic, organizing Calvinism came into contact with those sects which were comparatively ready to accept secular civilization; it was also the result of the social and political situation in which both Calvinism and the sects found themselves over against the official world.

Max Weber
(1864–1920)

THE FUNDAMENTAL CONCEPTS
OF SOCIOLOGY

Max Weber, one of the founders of modern social science, was born in Berlin in 1864. His father was a wealthy lawyer and prominent in German politics; for many years he served as a member of the Reichstag and belonged to the National Liberal Party. The Weber house was a meeting place for many prominent liberal politicians and renowned scholars from the University of Berlin.

In 1882, after finishing at the Gymnasium, Max Weber enrolled at the University of Heidelberg, where he took up the study of law. He passed his law exams in 1886. He finished his doctoral thesis, A Contribution to the History of Medieval Business Organizations, *in 1889 and started his in-service training required for the German bench or bar. He published his second work,* Roman Agrarian History and its Significance for Public and Private Law, *in 1891. Soon he was made Privatdozent in Roman, German, and commercial law at the University of Berlin. In 1894 he was offered a chair of economics at the University of Freiburg, which he accepted. He did not stay long in Freiburg, for the University of Heidelberg appointed him as professor of economics in 1896. He fell seriously ill in 1897, however, and it was this illness which suspended his regular academic activities. During the remainder of his life Weber remained in feeble health. For many years he lived the life of a private scholar and only toward the end of his life did he resume teaching.*

Max Weber first became known in the United States for his work The Protestant Ethic and the Spirit of Capitalism. *This book was translated and introduced by Talcott Parsons, who has been chiefly responsible for the interest in Weber in this country. In this book Weber linked the development of modern capitalism to the Protestant Ethic of the Reformation. One can trace here the beginnings of Weber's sociology. From Weber's point of view, the discovery of laws is an end*

226

in itself in the study of the natural sciences; but in sociology, laws are only a means to aid in the study of the causal inter-relationships of historical phenomena.[1] The working hypotheses are "ideal types," for example, the "capitalist" and the "calvinist."[2] His views, as developed in The Protestant Ethic, *encountered many rebuttals from his contemporaries.[3]*

In addition to his work in the sociology of religion, he also did brilliant work in political sociology (note his studies on leadership), and his theories concerning large-scale organizations and modern bureaucracy were the first of their kind.

THE FUNDAMENTAL CONCEPTS OF SOCIOLOGY[4]

AN introductory discussion of concepts can hardly be dispensed with, in spite of the fact that it is unavoidably abstract and hence gives the impression of remoteness from reality. Its method, however, makes no claim to any kind of novelty. On the contrary it attempts only to formulate what all empirical sociology really means when it deals with the same problems, in what it is hoped is a more convenient and somewhat more exact terminology, even though on that account it may seem pedantic. This is true even where terms are used which are apparently new or unfamiliar. As compared to the author's essay in *Logos*,[5] the terminology has been simplified as far as possible and hence considerably changed in order to render it more easily understandable. Unfortunately, the most precise formulation cannot always be reconciled with a form which can readily be popularized. In such cases the latter aim has had to be sacrificed.

---

[1] P. 1, *Protestantism and Capitalism*, The Weber Thesis and Its Critics, by Arnold Green, Boston, 1959.

[2] Ibid.

[3] For an informative look at Weber's critics the collection of essays *Protestantism and Capitalism*, edited by Arnold Green, will prove very helpful to the reader.

[4] The following essay was translated by A. M. Anderson and Talcott Parsons. Parsons annotated the essay throughout. I have kept his notes, because they are essential to a full understanding of the semantics of this essay. I have omitted most cross-references.

[5] Vol. IV (1913, pp. 253 ff.); reprinted in *Gesammelte Aufsätze zur Wissenschaftslehre*, pp. 403-450 (Weber).

On the concept of "understanding"[6] compare the *Allgemeine Psychopathologie* of Karl Jaspers, also a few observations by Heinrich Rickert in the second edition of the *Grenzen der Naturwissenschaftlichen Begriffsbildung,* and particularly some of Simmel's discussions in the *Probleme der Geschichtsphilosophie.* For certain methodological considerations the reader may here be referred, as often before in the author's writings, to the procedure of Friedrich Gottl in his work *Die Herrschaft des Wortes.* This book, to be sure, is written in a somewhat difficult style and its argument does not appear everywhere to have been thoroughly thought through. As regards content, reference may be made especially to the fine work of Ferdinand Tönnies, *Gemeinschaft und Gesellschaft,* and also to the gravely misleading book of Rudolph Stammler, *Wirtschaft und Recht,* which may be compared with my criticism in the *Archiv für Sozialwissenschaft* (Vol. XXIV, 1907). This critical essay contains many of the fundamental ideas of the following exposition. The present work departs from Simmel's method (in the *Soziologie* and the *Philosophie des Geldes*) in drawing a sharp distinction between subjectively intended and objectively valid "meanings"; two different

---

[6] The German term is *Verstehen.* As Weber uses it, this is a technical term with a distinctly narrower meaning than either the German or the English in everyday usage. Its primary reference in this work is to the observation and theoretical interpretation of the subjective "states of mind" of actors. But it also extends to the grasp of the meaning of logical and other systems of symbols, a meaning which is usually thought of as in some sense "intended" by a mind or intelligent being of some sort. The most important point about this concept seems to the editor to be the fact that insofar as phenomena are "understood" in this technical sense, the relevant facts are stated and analyzed within a certain frame of reference, that of "action." For present purposes the most important feature of this frame of reference is its use of "subjective categories." The essential thing is the operational applicability of such categories, not the commonsense empirical question of whether the actor is conscious of the meanings imputed to him or in the ordinary sense "intended" a given course of action. For a further discussion of these problems, see Talcott Parsons, *The Structure of Social Action,* especially chaps. II and XIX.

It has not seemed advisable to attempt a rigorous use of a single English term whenever Weber employs *Verstehen.* "Understanding" has been most commonly used. Other expressions such as "subjectively understandable," "interpretation in subjective terms," "comprehension," etc., have been used from time to time as the context seemed to demand (Parsons).

things which Simmel not only fails to distinguish but often deliberately treats as belonging together.

1: THE DEFINITIONS OF SOCIOLOGY AND OF SOCIAL ACTION

1. Sociology (in the sense in which this highly ambiguous word is used here) is a science which attempts the interpretative understanding of social action in order thereby to arrive at a causal explanation of its course and effects. In "action" is included all human behavior when and insofar as the acting individual attaches a subjective meaning to it. Action in this sense may be either overt or purely inward or subjective; it may consist of positive intervention in a situation, or of deliberately refraining from such intervention or passively acquiescing in the situation. Action is social insofar as, by virtue of the subjective meaning attached to it by the acting individual (or individuals), it takes account of the behavior of others and is thereby oriented in its course.[7]

[7] In this series of definitions Weber employs several important terms which need discussion. In addition to *Verstehen*, which has already been commented upon, there are four important ones: *Deuten, Sinn, Handeln,* and *Verhalten. Deuten* has generally been translated as "interpret." As used by Weber in this context it refers to the interpretation of subjective states of mind and the meanings which can be imputed as intended by an actor. Any other meaning of the word "interpretation" is irrelevant to Weber's discussion. The term *Sinn* has generally been translated as "meaning"; and its variations, particularly the corresponding adjectives, *sinnhaft, sinnvoll, sinnfremd,* have been dealt with by appropriately modifying the term meaning. The reference here again is always to features of the content of subjective states of mind or of symbolic systems which are ultimately referable to such states of mind.

The terms *Handeln* and *Verhalten* are directly related. *Verhalten* is the broader term referring to any mode of behavior of human individuals, regardless of the frame of reference in terms of which it is analysed. "Behavior" has seemed to be the most appropriate English equivalent. *Handeln,* on the other hand, refers to the concrete phenomenon of human behavior only insofar as it is capable of "understanding," in Weber's technical sense, in terms of subjective categories. The most appropriate English equivalent has seemed to be "action." This corresponds to the editor's usage in *The Structure of Social Action,* and would seem to be fairly well established. "Conduct" is also closely similar and has sometimes been used. *Deuten, Verstehen,* and *Sinn* are thus applicable to human behavior only insofar as it constitutes action or conduct in this specific sense (Parsons).

(a) THE METHODOLOGICAL FOUNDATIONS OF SOCIOLOGY[8]

1. "Meaning" may be of two kinds. The term may refer first to the actual existing meaning in the given concrete case of a particular actor, or to the average or approximate meaning attributable to a given plurality of actors; or secondly to the theoretically conceived *pure type*[9] of subjective meaning attributed to the hypothetical actor or actors in a given type of action. In no case does it refer to an objectively "correct" meaning or one which is "true" in some metaphysical sense. It is this which distinguishes the empirical sciences of action, such as sociology and history, from the dogmatic disciplines in that area, such as jurisprudence, logic, ethics, and esthetics, which seek to ascertain the "true" and "valid" meanings associated with the objects of their investigation.

2. The line between meaningful action and merely reactive behavior to which no subjective meaning it attached cannot be sharply drawn empirically. A very considerable part of all

---

[8] Weber's text is organized in a somewhat unusual manner. He lays down certain fundamental definitions and then proceeds to comment upon them. The definitions themselves are in the original printed in large type, the subsidiary comments in smaller type. For the purposes of this translation it has not seemed best to make a distinction in type form, but the reader should be aware that the numbered paragraphs which follow a definition or group of them are in the nature of comments, rather than the continuous development of a general line of argument. This fact accounts for what is sometimes a relatively fragmentary character of the development and for the abrupt transition from one subject to another. Weber apparently did not intend this material to be "read" in the ordinary sense, but rather to serve as a reference work for the clarification and systematization of theoretical concepts and their implications. While the comments under most of the definitions are relatively brief, under the definitions of Sociology and of Social Action, Weber wrote what is essentially a methodological essay. This makes Sec. 1 out of proportion to the other sections of this and the following chapters. It has, however, seemed best to retain Weber's own plan for the subdivision of the material (Parsons).

[9] Weber means by "pure type" what he himself generally called and what has come to be known in the literature about his methodology as the "ideal type." The reader may be referred for general orientation to Weber's own Essay (to which he himself refers below), *Die Objektivität sozialwissenschaftlicher Erkenntnis;* to two works of Dr. Alexander von Schelting, "Die logische Theorie der historischen Kulturwissenschaften von Max Weber" (*Archiv fuer Sozialwissenschaft*, Vol. XLIX), and *Max Webers Wissenschaftslehre;* and to the editor's *Structure of Social Action,* Chap. XVI. A somewhat different interpretation is given in Theodore Abel, *Systematic Sociology in Germany,* Chap. IV (Parsons).

sociologically relevant behavior, especially purely traditional behavior, is marginal between the two. In the case of many psychophysical processes, meaningful, that is, subjectively understandable, action is not to be found at all; in others it is discernible only by the expert psychologist. Many mystical experiences which cannot be adequately communicated in words are, for a person who is not susceptible to such experiences, not fully understandable. At the same time the ability to imagine one's self performing a similar action is not a necessary prerequisite to understanding; "one need not have been Caesar in order to understand Caesar." For the verifiable accuracy[10] of interpretation of the meaning of a phenomenon, it is a great help to be able to put oneself imaginatively in the place of the actor and thus sympathetically to participate in his experiences, but this is not an essential condition of meaningful interpretation. Understandable and nonunderstandable components of a process are often intermingled and bound up altogether.

3. All interpretation of meaning, like all scientific observation, strives for clarity and verifiable accuracy of insight and comprehension (*Evidenz*). The basis for certainty in understanding can be either rational, which can be further subdivided into logical and mathematical, or it can be of an emotionally empathic or artistically appreciative quality. In the sphere of action things are rationally evident chiefly when we attain a completely clear intellectual grasp of the action

10 This is an imperfect rendering of the German term *Evidenz*, for which, unfortunately, there is no good English equivalent. It has hence been rendered in a number of different ways, varying with the particular context in which it occurs. The primary meaning refers to the basis on which a scientist or thinker becomes satisfied of the certainty or acceptability of a proposition. As Weber himself points out, there are two primary aspects of this. On the one hand a conclusion can be "seen" to follow from given premises by virtue of logical, mathematical, or possibly other modes of meaningful relation. In this sense one "sees" the solution of an arithmetical problem or the correctness of the proof of a geometrical theorem. The other aspect is concerned with empirical observation. If an act of observation is competently performed, in a similar sense one "sees" the truth of the relevant descriptive proposition. The term *Evidenz* does not refer to the process of observing, but to the quality of its result, by virtue of which the observer feels justified in affirming a given statement. Hence "certainty" has seemed a suitable translation in some contexts, "clarity" in others, "accuracy" in still others. The term "intuition" is not usable because it refers to the process rather than to the result (Parsons).

elements in their intended context of meaning. Empathic or appreciative accuracy is attained when, through sympathetic participation, we can adequately grasp the emotional context in which the action took place. The highest degree of rational understanding is attained in cases involving the meanings of logically or mathematically related propositions; their meaning may be immediately and unambiguously intelligible. We have a perfectly clear understanding of what it means when somebody employs the proposition $2 \times 2 = 4$ or the Pythagorean theorem in reasoning or argument, or when someone correctly carries out a logical train of reasoning according to our accepted modes of thinking. In the same way we also understand what a person is doing when he tries to achieve certain ends by choosing appropriate means on the basis of the facts of the situation as experience has accustomed us to interpret them. Such an interpretation of this type of rationally purposeful action possesses, for the understanding of the choice of means, the highest degree of verifiable certainty. With a lower degree of certainty, which is, however, adequate for most purposes of explanation, we are able to understand errors, including confusion of problems of the sort that we ourselves are liable to, or the origin of which we can detect by sympathetic self-analysis.

On the other hand, many ultimate ends or values toward which experience shows that human action may be oriented often cannot be understood completely, though sometimes we are able to grasp them intellectually. The more radically they differ from our own ultimate values, however, the more difficult it is for us to make them understandable by imaginatively participating in them. Depending upon the circumstances of the particular case we must be content either with a purely intellectual understanding of such values or, when even that fails, sometimes we must simply accept them as given data. Then we can try to understand the action motivated by them on the basis of whatever opportunities for approximate emotional and intellectual interpretation seem to be available at different points in its course. These difficulties apply, for instance, for people not susceptible to the relevant values, to many unusual acts of religious and charitable zeal; also certain kinds of extreme rationalistic fanaticism of the type involved in some forms of the ideology of the "rights of man" are in a similar position for people who radically repudiate such points of view.

The more we ourselves are susceptible to them, the more

readily can we imaginatively participate in such emotional reactions as anxiety, anger, ambition, envy, jealousy, love, enthusiasm, pride, vengefulness, loyalty, devotion, and appetites of all sorts, and thereby understand the irrational conduct which grows out of them. Such conduct is "irrational," that is, from the point of view of the rational pursuit of a given end. Even when such emotions are found in a degree of intensity of which the observer himself is completely incapable, he can still have a significant degree of emotional understanding of their meaning and can interpret intellectually their influence on the course of action and the selection of means.

For the purposes of a typological scientific analysis it is convenient to treat all irrational, affectually determined elements of behavior as factors of deviation from a conceptually pure type of rational action. For example, a panic on the stock exchange can be most conveniently analyzed by attempting to determine first what the course of action would have been if it had not been influenced by irrational affects; it is then possible to introduce the irrational components as accounting for the observed deviations from this hypothetical course. Similarly, in analyzing a political or military campaign, it is convenient to determine in the first place what would have been a rational course, given the ends of the participants and adequate knowledge of all the circumstances. Only in this way is it possible to assess the causal significance of irrational factors as accounting for the deviations from this type. The construction of a purely rational course of action in such cases serves the sociologist as a type ("ideal type") which has the merit of clear understandability and lack of ambiguity. By comparison with this it is possible to understand the ways in which actual action is influenced by irrational factors of all sorts, such as affects[11] and errors, in that they account for the deviation from the line of conduct which would be expected on the hypothesis that the action were purely rational.

Only in this respect, and for these reasons of methodological convenience, is the method of sociology "rationalistic." It is naturally not legitimate to interpret this procedure as involving a "rationalistic bias" of sociology, but only as a methodological device. It certainly does not involve a belief in the

---

[11] A term now much used in psychological literature, especially that of psychoanalysis. It is roughly equivalent to "emotion" but more precise (Parsons).

actual predominance of rational elements in human life, for on the question of how far this predominance does or does not exist, nothing whatever has been said. That there is, however, a danger of rationalistic interpretations where they are out of place naturally cannot be denied. All experience unfortunately confirms the existence of this danger.

4. In all the sciences of human action, account must be taken of processes and phenomena which are devoid of subjective meaning,[12] in the role of stimuli, results, favoring or hindering circumstances. To be devoid of meaning is not identical with being lifeless or nonhuman; every artifact, such as for example a machine, can be understood only in terms of the meaning which its production and use have had or will have for human action; a meaning which may derive from a relation to exceedingly various purposes. Without reference to this meaning such an object remains wholly unintelligible.[13] That which is intelligible or understandable about it is thus its relation to human action in the role either of means or of end; a relation of which the actor or actors can be said to have been aware and to which their action has been oriented. Only in terms of such categories is it possible to "understand" objects of this kind. On the other hand processes or conditions, whether they are animate or inanimate, human or nonhuman, are in the present sense devoid of meaning insofar as they cannot be related to an intended purpose. That is to say, they are devoid of meaning if they cannot be related to action in the role of means or ends but constitute only the stimulus, the favoring or hindering circumstances.[14] It may be that the incursion of the Dollart at the beginning of the twelfth

[12] The German term is *sinnfremd*. This should not be translated by "meaningless," but interpreted in the technical context of Weber's use of *Verstehen* and *Sinndeutung*. The essential criterion is the impossibility of placing the object in question in a complex of relations on the meaningful level (Parsons).

[13] *Unverstehbar* (Parsons).

[14] Surely this passage states too narrow a conception of the scope of meaningful interpretation. It is certainly not *only* in terms such as those of the rational means-end schema that it is possible to make action understandable in terms of subjective categories. This probably can actually be called a source of rationalistic bias in Weber's work. In practice he does not adhere at all rigorously to this methodological position. For certain possibilities in this broader field, see Talcott Parsons' *Structure of Social Action*, Chaps. VI and XI (Parsons).

century[15] had historical significance as a stimulus to the beginning of certain migrations of considerable importance. Human mortality, indeed the organic life cycle generally from the helplessness of infancy to that of old age, is naturally of the very greatest sociological importance through the various ways in which human action has been oriented to these facts. To still another category of facts devoid of meaning belong certain psychic or psychophysical phenomena such as fatigue, habituation, memory, and so on; also certain typical states of euphoria under some conditions of ascetic mortification; finally, typical variations in the reactions of individuals according to reaction-time, precision, and other modes. But in the last analysis the same principle applies to these as to other phenomena which are devoid of meaning. Both the actor and the sociologist must accept them as data to be taken into account.

It is altogether possible that future research may be able to discover nonunderstandable uniformities underlying what has appeared to be specifically meaningful action, though little has been accomplished in this direction thus far. Thus, for example, differences in hereditary biological constitution, as of "races," would have to be treated by sociology as given data in the same way as the physiological facts of the need of nutrition or the effect of senescence on action. This would be the case if, and insofar as, we had statistically conclusive proof of their influence on sociologically relevant behavior. The recognition of the causal significance of such factors would naturally not in the least alter the specific task of sociological analysis or of that of the other sciences of action, which is the interpretation of action in terms of its subjective meaning. The effect would be only to introduce certain nonunderstandable data of the same order as others which, it has been noted above, are already present, into the complex of subjectively understandable motivation at certain points. Thus it may come to be known that there are typical relations between the frequency of certain types of teleological orientation of action or of the degree of certain kinds of rationality and the cephalic index or skin color or any other biologically inherited characteristic.

5. Understanding may be of two kinds: the first is the

---

[15] A gulf of the North Sea which broke through the Netherlands coast, flooding an area (Parsons).

direct observational understanding[16] of the subjective meaning of a given act as such, including verbal utterances. We thus understand by direct observation, in this sense, the meaning of the proposition $2 \times 2 = 4$ when we hear or read it. This is a case of the direct rational understanding of ideas. We also understand an outbreak of anger as manifested by facial expression, exclamations, or irrational movements. This is direct observational understanding of irrational emotional reactions. We can understand in a similar observational way the action of a woodcutter or of somebody who reaches for the knob to shut a door or who aims a gun at an animal. This is rational observational understanding of actions.

Understanding may, however, be of another sort, namely, explanatory understanding. Thus we understand in terms of *motive* the meaning an actor attaches to the proposition twice two equals four, when he states it or writes it down, in that we understand what makes him do this at precisely this moment and in these circumstances. Understanding in this sense is attained if we know that he is engaged in balancing a ledger or in making a scientific demonstration, or is engaged in some other task of which this particular act would be an appropriate part. This is rational understanding of motivation, which consists in placing the act in an intelligible and more inclusive context of meaning.[17] Thus we understand the chopping of wood or aiming of a gun in terms of motive in

[16] Weber here uses the term *aktuelles Verstehen*, which he contrasts with *erklärendes Verstehen*. The latter he also refers to as *motivationsmaessig*. "Aktuell" in this context has been translated as "observational." It is clear from Weber's discussion that the primary criterion is the possibility of deriving the meaning of an act or symbolic expression from immediate observation without reference to any broader context. In *erklärendes Verstehen*, on the other hand, the particular act must be placed in a broader context of meaning involving facts which cannot be derived from immediate observation of a particular act or expression (Parsons).

[17] The German term is *Sinnzusammenhang*. It refers to a plurality of elements which form a coherent whole on the level of meaning. There are several possible modes of meaningful relation between such elements, such as logical consistency, the esthetic harmony of a style, or the appropriateness of means to an end. In any case, however, a *Sinnzusammenhang* must be distinguished from a system of elements which are causally interdependent. There seems to be no single English term or phrase which is always adequate. According to variations in the context, "context of meaning," "complex of meaning," and sometimes "meaningful system" have been employed (Parsons).

addition to direct observation if we know that the wood-chopper is working for a wage or is chopping a supply of firewood for his own use or possibly is doing it for recreation. But he might also be "working off" a fit of rage, an irrational case. Similarly we understand the motive of a person aiming a gun if we know that he has been commanded to shoot as a member of a firing squad, that he is fighting against an enemy, or that he is doing it for revenge. The last is affectually determined, and thus in a certain sense irrational. Finally, we have a motivational understanding of the outburst of anger if we know that it has been provoked by jealousy, injured pride, or an insult. The last examples are all affectually determined, and hence derived from irrational motives. In all the above cases the particular act has been placed in an understandable sequence of motivation, the understanding of which can be treated as an explanation of the actual course of behavior. Thus for a science which is concerned with the subjective meaning of action, explanation requires a grasp of the complex of meaning in which an actual course of understandable action thus interpreted belongs.[18] In all such cases, even where the processes are largely affectual, the subjective meaning of the action, including that also of the relevant meaning complexes, will be called the "intended" meaning.[19] This involves a departure from ordinary usage, which speaks of intention in this sense only in the case of rationally purposive action.

6. In all these cases understanding involves the interpreta-

[18] On the significance of this type of explanation for causal relationship, see para. 6, pp. 96 ff. below in the present section (Weber).

[19] The German is *gemeinter Sinn*. Weber departs from ordinary usage not only in broadening the meaning of this conception. As he states at the end of the present methodological discussion, he does not restrict the use of this concept to cases where a clear self-conscious awareness of such meaning can be reasonably attributed to every individual actor. Essentially, what Weber is doing is to formulate an operational concept. The question is not whether in a sense obvious to the ordinary person such an intended meaning "really exists," but whether the concept is capable of providing a logical framework within which scientifically important observations can be made. The test of validity of the observations is not whether their object is immediately clear to common sense, but whether the results of these technical observations can be satisfactorily organized and related to those of others in a systematic body of knowledge (Parsons).

tive grasp of the meaning present in one of the following contexts: (*a*) as in the historical approach, the actually intended meaning for concrete individual action; or (*b*) as in cases of sociological mass phenomena the average of, or an approximation to, the actually intended meaning; or (*c*) the meaning appropriate to a scientifically formulated pure type (an ideal type) of a common phenomenon. The concepts and "laws" of pure economic theory are examples of this kind of ideal type. They state what course a given type of human action would take if it were strictly rational, unaffected by errors or emotional factors and if, furthermore, it were completely and unequivocally directed to a single end, the maximization of economic advantage. In reality, action takes exactly this course only in unusual cases, as sometimes on the stock exchange; and even then there is usually only an approximation to the ideal type.[20]

Every interpretation attempts to attain clarity and certainty, but no matter how clear an interpretation as such appears to be from the point of view of meaning, it cannot on this account alone claim to be the causally valid interpretation. On this level it must remain only a peculiarly plausible hypothesis. In the first place the "conscious motives" may well, even to the actor himself, conceal the various "motives" and "repressions" which constitute the real driving force of his action. Thus in such cases even subjectively honest self-analysis has only a relative value. Then it is the task of the sociologist to be aware of this motivational situation and to describe and analyze it, even though it has not actually been concretely part of the conscious "intention" of the actor; possibly not at all, at least not fully. This is a borderline case of the interpretation of meaning. Second, processes of action which seem to an observer to be the same or similar may fit into exceedingly various complexes of motive in the case of the actual actor. Then even though the situations appear superficially to be very similar, we must actually understand them or interpret them as very different, perhaps, in terms of meaning, directly opposed.[21] Third, the actors in any given situation are often subject to opposing and conflicting impulses, all of which we

[20] The scientific functions of such construction have been discussed in the author's article in the *Archiv für Sozialwissenschaft*, Vol. XIX, pp. 64 ff. (Weber).

[21] Simmel, in his *Probleme der Geschichtsphilosophie*, gives a number of examples (Weber).

are able to understand. In a large number of cases we know from experience it is not possible to arrive at even an approximate estimate of the relative strength of conflicting motives, and very often we cannot be certain of our interpretation. Only the actual outcome of the conflict gives a solid basis of judgment.

More generally, verification of subjective interpretation by comparison with the concrete course of events is, as in the case of all hypotheses, indispensable. Unfortunately, this type of verification is feasible with relative accuracy only in the few very special cases susceptible of psychological experimentation. The approach to a satisfactory degree of accuracy is exceedingly various, even in the limited number of cases of mass phenomena which can be statistically described and unambiguously interpreted. For the rest there remains only the possibility of comparing the largest possible number of historical or contemporary processes which, while otherwise similar, differ in the one decisive point of their relation to the particular motive or factor the role of which is being investigated. This is a fundamental task of comparative sociology. Often, unfortunately, there is available only the dangerous and uncertain procedure of the "imaginary experiment" which consists in thinking away certain elements of a chain of motivation and working out the course of action which would then probably ensue, thus arriving at a causal judgment.[22]

For example, the generalization called Gresham's Law is a rationally clear interpretation of human action under certain conditions and under the assumption that it will follow a purely rational course. How far any actual course of action corresponds to this can be verified only by the available statistical evidence for the actual disappearance of undervalued monetary units from circulation. In this case our information serves to demonstrate a high degree of accuracy.

[22] The above passage is an exceedingly compact statement of Weber's theory of the logical conditions of proof of causal relationship. He developed this most fully in his essay *Die Objektivität sozialwissenschaftlicher Erkenntnis, op. cit.* It is also discussed in certain of the other essays which have been collected in the volume *Gesammelte Aufsätze zur Wissenschaftslehre.* The best and fullest secondary discussion is to be found in von Schelting's book *Max Webers Wissenschaftslehre.* There is a briefer discussion in Chap. XVI of Talcott Parsons' *Structure of Social Action* (Parsons).

The facts of experience were known before the generalization, which was formulated afterward; but without this successful interpretation our need for causal understanding would evidently be left unsatisfied. On the other hand, without the demonstration that what can here be assumed to be a theoretically adequate interpretation also is in some degree relevant to an actual course of action, a "law," no matter how fully demonstrated theoretically, would be worthless for the understanding of action in the real world. In this case the correspondence between the theoretical interpretation of motivation and its empirical verification is entirely satisfactory, and the cases are numerous enough so that verification can be considered established. But to take another example, Eduard Meyer has advanced an ingenious theory of the causal significance of the battles of Marathon, Salamis, and Platea for the development of the cultural peculiarities of Greek, and hence, more generally, Western, civilization.[23] This is derived from a meaningful interpretation of certain symptomatic facts having to do with the attitudes of the Greek oracles and prophets toward the Persians. It can be directly verified only by reference to the examples of the conduct of the Persians in cases where they were victorious, as in Jerusalem, Egypt, and Asia Minor, and even this verification must necessarily remain unsatisfactory in certain respects. The striking rational plausibility of the hypothesis must here necessarily be relied on as a support. In very many cases of historical interpretation which seem highly plausible, however, there is not even a possibility of the order of verification which was feasible in this case. Where this is true the interpretation must necessarily remain a hypothesis.

7. A motive is a complex of subjective meaning which seems to the actor himself or to the observer an adequate ground for the conduct in question. We apply the term "adequacy on the level of meaning"[24] to the subjective interpretation of a coherent course of conduct when and insofar as,

---

[23] See Eduard Meyer, *Geschichte des Altertums* (Stuttgart, 1901), Vol. III, pp. 420, 444 ff. (Weber).

[24] The expression *sinnhafte Adäquanz* is one of the most difficult of Weber's technical terms to translate. In most places the cumbrous phrase "adequacy on the level of meaning" has had to be employed. It should be clear from the progress of the discussion that what Weber refers to is a satisfying level of knowledge for the particular purposes of the subjective state of mind of the actor or actors. He is, however, careful to point out that *causal*

according to our habitual modes of thought and feeling, its component parts taken in their mutual relation are recognized to constitute a "typical" complex of meaning. It is more common to say "correct." The interpretation of a sequence of events will on the other hand be called *causally* adequate insofar as, according to established generalizations from experience, there is a probability that it will always actually occur in the same way. An example of adequacy on the level of meaning in this sense is what is, according to our current norms of calculation or thinking, the correct solution of an arithmetical problem. On the other hand, a causally adequate interpretation of the same phenomenon would concern the statistical probability that, according to verified generalizations from experience, there would be a correct or an erroneous solution of the same problem. This also refers to currently accepted norms but includes taking account of typical errors or of typical confusions. Thus causal explanation depends on being able to determine that there is a probability, which in the rare ideal case can be numerically stated, but is always in some sense calculable, that a given observable event (overt or subjective) will be followed or accompanied by another event.

A correct causal interpretation of a concrete course of action is arrived at when the overt action and the motives have both been correctly apprehended and at the same time their relation has become meaningfully comprehensible. A correct causal interpretation of typical action means that the process which is claimed to be typical is shown to be both adequately grasped on the level of meaning and at the same time the interpretation is to some degree causally adequate. If adequacy in respect to meaning is lacking, then no matter how high the degree of uniformity and how precisely its probability can be numerically determined, it is still an incomprehensible statistical probability, whether dealing with overt or subjective processes. On the other hand, even the most perfect adequacy on the level of meaning has causal

---

adequacy involves in addition to this a satisfactory correspondence between the results of observations from the subjective point of view and from the objective; that is, observations of the overt course of action which can be described without reference to the state of mind of the actor. For a discussion of the methodological problem involved here, see *Structure of Social Action*, Chaps. II and V (Parsons).

significance from a sociological point of view only insofar as there is some kind of proof for the existence of a probability[25] that action in fact normally takes the course which has been held to be meaningful. For this there must be some degree of determinable frequency of approximation to an average or a pure type.

Statistical uniformities constitute understandable types of action in the sense of this discussion, and thus constitute "sociological generalizations," only when they can be regarded as manifestations of the understandable subjective meaning of a course of social action. Conversely, formulations of a rational course of subjectively understandable action constitute sociological types of empirical process only when they can be empirically observed with a significant degree of approximation. It is unfortunately by no means the case that the actual likelihood of the occurrence of a given course of overt action is always directly proportional to the clarity of subjective interpretation. There are statistics of processes devoid of meaning such as death rates, phenomena of fatigue, the production rate of machines, the amount of rainfall, in exactly the same sense as there are statistics of meaningful phenomena. But only when the phenomena are meaningful is it convenient to speak of sociological statistics. Examples are such cases as crime rates, occupational distributions, price statistics, and statistics of crop acreage. Naturally there are many cases where both components are involved, as in crop statistics.

8. Processes and uniformities which it has here seemed convenient not to designate as (in the present case) sociological phenomena or uniformities because they are not "understandable," are naturally not on that account any the less important. This is true even for sociology in the present

_____

[25] This is the first occurrence in Weber's text of the term *Chance* which he uses very frequently. It is here translated by "probability," because he uses it as interchangeable with *Wahrscheinlichkeit*. As the term "probability" is used in a technical, mathematical and statistical sense, however, it implies the possibility of numerical statement. In most of the cases where Weber uses *Chance* this is out of the question. It is, however, possible to speak in terms of higher and lower degrees of probability. To avoid confusion with the technical mathematical concept, the term "likelihood" will often be used in the translation. It is by means of this concept that Weber, in a highly ingenious way, has bridged the gap between the interpretation of meaning and the inevitably more complex facts of overt action (Parsons).

sense which restricts it to subjectively understandable phenomena—a usage which there is no intention of attempting to impose on anyone else. Such phenomena, however important, are simply treated by a different method from the others; they become conditions, stimuli, furthering or hindering circumstances of action.

9. Action in the sense of a subjectively understandable orientation of behavior exists only as the behavior of one or more *individual* human beings. For other cognitive purposes it may be convenient or necessary to consider the individual, for instance, as a collection of cells, as a complex of biochemical reactions, or to conceive his "psychic" life as made up of a variety of different elements, however these may be defined. Undoubtedly such procedures yield valuable knowledge of causal relationships. But the behavior of these elements, as expressed in such uniformities, is not subjectively understandable. This is true even of psychic elements because the more precisely they are formulated from a point of view of natural science, the less they are accessible to subjective understanding. This is never the road to interpretation in terms of subjective meaning. On the contrary, both for sociology in the present sense, and for history, the object of cognition is the subjective meaning-complex of action. The behavior of physiological entities such as cells, or of any sort of psychic elements, may at least in principle be observed and an attempt made to derive uniformities from such observations. It is further possible to attempt, with their help, to obtain a causal explanation of individual phenomena, that is, to subsume them under uniformities. But the subjective understanding of action takes the same account of this type of fact and uniformity as of any others not capable of subjective interpretation. This is true, for example, of physical, astronomical, geological, meteorological, geographical, botanical, zoological, and anatomical facts and of such facts as those aspects of psychopathology which are devoid of subjective meaning or the facts of the natural conditions of technological processes.

For still other cognitive purposes as, for instance, juristic, or for practical ends, it may on the other hand be convenient or even indispensable to treat social collectivities, such as states, associations, business corporations, foundations, as if they were individual persons. Thus they may be treated as the subjects of rights and duties or as the performers of legally significant actions. But for the subjective interpretation of action in sociological work these collectivities must be treated as *solely* the resultants and modes of organization of the particular acts of individual persons, since these alone can be treated as agents in a course of subjectively understandable action. Nevertheless, the sociologist cannot for his purposes afford to ignore these collective concepts derived from other disciplines. For the subjective interpretation of action has at least two important relations to these concepts. In the first place it is often necessary to employ very similar collective concepts, indeed often using the same terms, in order to obtain an understandable terminology. Thus both in legal terminology and in everyday speech the term "state" is used both for the legal concept of the state and for the phenomena of social action to which its legal rules are relevant. For sociological purposes, however, the phenomenon "the state" does not consist necessarily or even primarily of the elements which are relevant to legal analysis; and for sociological purposes there is no such thing as a collective personality which "acts." When reference is made in a sociological context to a "state," a "nation," a "corporation," a "family," or an "army corps," or to similar collectivities, what is meant is, on the contrary, *only* a certain kind of development of actual or possible social actions of individual persons. Both because of its precision and because it is established in general usage the juristic concept is taken over, but is used in an entirely different meaning.

Second, the subjective interpretation of action must take account of a fundamentally important fact. These concepts of collective entities which are found both in common sense and in juristic and other technical forms of thought, have a meaning in the minds of individual persons, partly as of something actually existing, partly as something with normative authority. This is true not only of judges and officials but of ordinary private individuals as well. Actors thus in part orient their action to them, and in this role such ideas have a powerful, often a decisive, causal influence on the course of action of real individuals. This is above all true where the ideas concern a recognized positive or negative normative pattern.[26] Thus, for instance, one of the important aspects of the "existence" of a modern state, precisely as a complex of social interaction of individual persons, consists in the fact that the action

---

[26] By a negative normative pattern, Weber means one which prohibits certain possible modes of action (Parsons).

of various individuals is oriented to the belief that it exists or should exist, thus that its acts and laws are valid in the legal sense. This will be further discussed below. Though extremely pedantic and cumbersome, it would be possible, if purposes of sociological terminology alone were involved, to eliminate such terms entirely, and substitute newly coined words. This would be possible even though the word "state" is used ordinarily not only to designate the legal concept but also the real process of action. But in the above important connection, at least, this would naturally be impossible.

Third, it is the method of the so-called "organic" school of sociology[27] to attempt to understand social interaction by using as a point of departure the "whole" within which the individual acts. His action and behavior are then interpreted somewhat in the way that a physiologist would treat the role of an organ of the body in the "economy" of the organism, that is, from the point of view of the survival of the latter.[28] How far in other disciplines this type of functional analysis of the relation of "parts" to a "whole" can be regarded as definitive, cannot be discussed here; but it is well known that the biochemical and biophysical modes of analysis of the organism are on principle opposed to stopping there. For purposes of sociological analysis two things can be said. First, this functional frame of reference is convenient for purposes of practical illustration and for provisional orientation. In these respects it is not only useful but indispensable. But at the same time if its cognitive value is overestimated and its concepts illegitimately "reified,"[29] it can be highly dangerous.

---

[27] A classical example is Schäffle's brilliant work, *Bau und Leben des sozialen Körpers* (Weber).

[28] One of the most illuminating treatments of physiological problems from such a functional point of view, which is readily understandable to the layman, is W. B. Cannon, *The Wisdom of the Body*, second edition, 1938. The point of reference on this physiological level is not primarily survival value to the species in the sense o fthe Darwinian theory of evolution, but rather the maintenance of the individual organism as a "going concern" in carrying through its typical life cycle. What is the life cycle is to the physiologist essentially a matter of empirical observation (Parsons).

[29] The term "reification" as used by Professor Morris Cohen in his book *Reason and Nature* seems to fit Weber's meaning exactly. A concept or system of concepts, which critical analysis can show to be abstract, is "reified" when it is used naïvely, as though it provided an adequate total description of the concrete phenomenon in question. The fallacy of "reification" is virtually another

Second, in certain circumstances this is the only available way of determining just what processes of social action it is important to understand in order to explain a given phenomenon.[30] But this is only the beginning of sociological analysis as here understood. In the case of social collectivities, precisely as distinguished from organisms, we are in a position to go beyond merely demonstrating functional relationships and uniformities. We can accomplish something which is never attainable in the natural sciences, namely, the subjective understanding of the action of the component individuals. The natural sciences on the other hand cannot do this, being limited to the formulation of causal uniformities in objects and events and the explanation of individual facts by applying them. We do not "understand" the behavior of cells, but can only observe the relevant functional relationships and generalize on the basis of these observations. This additional achievement of explanation by interpretative understanding, as distinguished from external observation, is of course attained only at a price —the more hypothetical and fragmentary character of its results. Nevertheless, subjective understanding is the specific characteristic of sociological knowledge.

It would lead too far afield even to attempt to discuss how far the behavior of animals is subjectively understandable to us, and vice versa; in both cases the meaning of the term "understanding" and its extent of application would be highly problematical. But insofar as such understanding existed it would be theoretically possible to formulate a sociology of the relations of men to animals, both domestic and wild. Thus many animals "understand" commands, anger, love, hostility, and react to them in ways which are evidently often by no means purely instinctive and mechanical and in some sense both consciously meaningful and affected by experience. There is no *a priori* reason to suppose that our ability to share the

---

name for what Professor Whitehead has called "the fallacy of misplaced concreteness." See his *Science and the Modern World* (Parsons).

[30] Compare the famous dictum of a well-known physiologist: "Sec. 10. The spleen. Of the spleen, gentlemen, we know nothing. So much for the spleen." Actually, of course, he "knew" a good deal about the spleen—its position, size, shape, etc.; but he could say nothing about its function, and it was his inability to do this that he called "ignorance" (Weber).

feelings of primitive men is very much greater.[31] Unfortunately we either do not have any reliable means of determining the subjective state of mind of an animal or what we
have is at best very unsatisfactory. It is well known that the
problems of animal psychology, however interesting, are very
thorny ones. There are in particular various forms of social
organization among animals: "monogamous and polygamous
families," herds, flocks, and finally "state," with a functional
division of labor. The extent of functional differentiation
found in these animal societies is by no means, however,
entirely a matter of the degree of organic or morphological
differentiation of the individual members of the species. Thus,
the functional differentiation found among the termites, and
in consequence that of the products of their social activities,
is much more advanced than in the case of the bees and ants.
In this field it goes without saying that a purely functional
point of view is often the best that can, at least for the present, be attained, and the investigator must be content with it.
Thus it is possible to study the ways in which the species
provides for its survival; that is, for nutrition, defense, reproduction, and reconstruction of the social units. As the principal bearers of these functions, differentiated types of individuals can be identified: "kings," "queens," "workers," "soldiers," "drones," "propagators," "queen's substitutes," and so
on. Anything more than that was for a long time merely a

[31] The present state of anthropological research, which has advanced enormously since Weber wrote, would seem to throw considerable doubt on the validity of this statement. In making it,
Weber apparently does not adequately take account of the fundamental fact that no nonhuman species has even a primitive form
of language; whereas no human group is known without a "fully
developed" one. The ability to use language is on the one hand a
fundamental index of the state of development of the individual
himself, so far as it is relevant to the theory of action. On the
other hand, language is perhaps the most crucially important
source of evidence for subjective phenomena. What has seemed
to so many "civilized" men to be the strangeness and incompre-
hensibility of the behavior and throught of primitive peoples, is
apparently primarily a matter of the former's failure to submit the
latter to an adequately thorough and rigorous investigation. It can
be said with considerable confidence that a competently trained
anthropological fieldworker is in a position to obtain a level of
insight into the states of mind of a people whom he has carefully
studied, which is quite comparable, if not superior, to that of the
historian of a civilization at all widely different from his own
(Parsons).

matter of speculation or of an attempt to determine the extent
to which heredity on the one hand and environment on the
other would be involved in the development of these "social"
proclivities. This was particularly true of the controversies
between Götte and Weismann. The latter's conception of the
omnipotence of natural selection was largely based on wholly
nonempirical deductions. But all serious authorities are naturally fully agreed that the limitation of analysis to the functional level is only a necessity imposed by our present ignorance which it is hoped will be only temporary.[32]

It is relatively easy to grasp the significance of the functions of these various differentiated types for survival. It is
also not difficult to work out the bearing of the hypothesis of
the inheritance of acquired characteristics or its reverse on
the problem of explaining how these differentiations have
come about and further what is the bearing of different variants of the theory of heredity. But this is not enough. We
would like especially to know first what factors account for
the original differentiation of specialized types from the still
neutral undifferentiated species-type. Second, it would be
important to know what leads the differentiated individual in
the typical case to behave in a way which actually serves the
survival value of the organized group. Wherever research has
made any progress in the solution of these problems it has
been through the experimental demonstration of the probability or possibility of the role of chemical stimuli or physiological processes, such as nutritional states, the effects of
parasitic castration, et cetera, in the case of the individual
organism. How far there is even a hope that the existence of
"subjective" or "meaningful" orientation could be made ex-
perimentally probable, even the specialist today would hardly
be in a position to say. A verifiable conception of the state of
mind of these social animals accessible to meaningful understanding would seem to be attainable even as an ideal goal
only within narrow limits. However that may be, a contribution to the understanding of human social action is hardly to
be expected from this quarter. On the contrary, in the field
of animal psychology, human analogies are and must be continually employed. The most that can be hoped for is, then,
that these biological analogies may someday be useful in

---

[32] See, for example, for an account of the state of knowledge of
the termites, the study of Karl Escherich, *Die Ameise,* 1906
(Weber).

suggesting significant problems. For instance, they may throw light on the question of the relative role in the early stages of human social differentiation of mechanical and instinctive factors, as compared with that of the factors which are accessible to subjective interpretation generally, and more particularly to the role of consciously rational action. It is necessary for the sociologist to be thoroughly aware of the fact that in the early stages even of human development, the first set of factors is completely predominant. Even in the later stages he must take account of their continual interaction with the others in a role which is often of decisive importance. This is particularly true of all "traditional" action and of many aspects of charisma.[33] In the latter field of phenomena lie the seeds of certain types of psychic "contagion," and it is thus the bearer of many dynamic tendencies of social processes. These types of action are very closely related to phenomena which are understandable either only in biological terms or are subject to interpretation in terms of subjective motives only in fragments and with an almost imperceptible transition to the biological. But all these facts do not discharge sociology from the obligation, in full awareness of the narrow limits to which it is confined, to accomplish what it alone can do.

The various works of Othmar Spann are often full of suggestive ideas, though at the same time he is guilty of occasional misunderstandings and above all of arguing on the basis of pure value judgments which have no place in an empirical investigation. But he is undoubtedly correct in doing something (to which, however, no one seriously objects), namely, emphasizing the sociological significance of the functional point of view for preliminary orientation to problems. This is what he calls the "universalistic method." We certainly need to know what kind of action is functionally necessary for "survival," but further and above all for the maintenance of a cultural type and the continuity of the corresponding modes of social action, before it is possible even to inquire how this action has come about and what motives determine it. It is necessary to know what a "king," an "official," an "enterpreneur," a "procurer," or a "magician" does;

---

[33] Since the term "charisma" was, in its sociological usage, introduced by Weber himself from a different field, no attempt has been made to find an English equivalent, and it will be used directly throughout. Weber took it from the corresponding Greek which was used in the literature of early Christianity and means "the gift of grace" (Parsons).

that is, what kind of typical action, which justifies classifying an individual in one of these categories, is important and relevant for an analysis, before it is possible to undertake the analysis itself.[34] But it is only this analysis itself which can achieve the sociological understanding of the actions of typically differentiated human (and only human) individuals, and which hence constitutes the specific function of sociology. It is a monstrous misunderstanding to think that an "individualistic" *method* should involve what is in any conceivable sense an individualistic system of *values*. It is as important to avoid this error as the related one which confuses the unavoidable tendency of sociological concepts to assume a rationalistic character with a belief in the predominance of rational motives, or even a positive valuation of "rationalism." Even a socialistic economy would have to be understood sociologically in exactly the same kind of "individualistic" terms; that is, in terms of the action of individuals, the types of "officials" found in it, as would be the case with a system of free exchange analyzed in terms of the theory of marginal utility. It might be possible to find a better method, but in this respect it would be similar. The real empirical sociological investigation begins with the question: What motives determine and lead the individual members and participants in this socialistic community to behave in such a way that the community came into being in the first place and that it continues to exist? Any form of functional analysis which proceeds from the whole to the parts can accomplish only a preliminary preparation for this investigation—a preparation the utility and indispensability of which, if properly carried out, is naturally beyond question.

10. It is customary to designate various sociological generalizations, as for example "Gresham's Law," as scientific "laws." These are in fact typical probabilities confirmed by observation to the effect that under certain given conditions an expected course of social action will occur, which is understandable in terms of the typical motives and typical subjective intentions of the actors.[35] These generalizations are

---

[34] This is what Rickert means by *Wertbezogenheit* (Weber).

[35] It is desirable at this point to call attention to Weber's usage of the term "law" in a scientific sense. In conformity with his strong emphasis upon the role of ideal types among possible kinds of generalized concepts in the social sciences, by "law," or a German expression he frequently uses, *generelle Erfahrungsregel*, he usually means what is perhaps most conveniently called a "type

both understandable and definite in the highest degree in so far as the typically observed course of action can be understood in terms of the purely rational pursuit of an end, or where for reasons of methodological convenience such a theoretical type can be heuristically employed. In such cases the relations of means and end will be clearly understandable on grounds of experience, particularly where the choice of means was "inevitable." In such cases it is legitimate to assert that insofar as the action was rigorously rational it could not have taken any other course because for technical reasons, given their clearly defined ends, no other means were available to the actors. This very case demonstrates how erroneous it is to regard any kind of "psychology" as the ultimate foundation of the sociological interpretation of action. The term "psychology," to be sure, is today understood in a wide variety of senses. For certain quite specific methodological purposes the type of treatment which attempts to follow the procedures of the natural sciences employs a distinction between "physical" and "psychic" phenomena which is entirely foreign to the disciplines concerned with human action, at least in the present sense. The results of a type of psychological investigation which employs the methods of the natural sciences in any one of various possible ways may naturally, like the results of any other science, have, in specific contexts, outstanding significance for sociological problems; indeed this has often happened. But this use of the results of psychology is something quite different from the investigation of human behavior in terms of its subjective meaning. Hence sociology has no closer logical relationship on a general analytical level to this type

---

generalization." It is not an empirical generalization in the ordinary sense in that it does not adequately describe any particular concrete course of events but is abstract in the same sense as the ideal type. Where it is possible on the basis of ideal type analysis to construct not merely a structural form but, under certain conditions, a course of events which can be predicted if certain conditions are given, it is possible to formulate such generalizations. These generalizations are, however, not methodologically equivalent to most of the laws of physics, especially of analytical mechanics. The latter do not generally formulate a concrete course of events, but rather a uniform relationship between the values of two or more variables. Weber does not even consider the possibility of formulating laws of this latter type, essentially because he does not develop social theory explicitly in the direction of setting up a system of interdependent variables, but confines it to the ideal type level (Parsons).

of psychology than to any other science. The source of error lies in the concept of the "psychic." It is held that everything which is not physical is *ipso facto* psychic, but that the *meaning* of a train of mathematical reasoning which a person carries out is not in the relevant sense "psychic." Similarly the rational deliberation of an actor as to whether the results of a given proposed course of action will or will not promote certain specific interests, and the corresponding decision, do not become one bit more understandable by taking "psychological" considerations into account. But it is precisely on the basis of such rational assumptions that most of the laws of sociology, including those of economics, are built up. On the other hand, in explaining the irrationalities of action sociologically, that form of psychology which employs the method of subjective understanding undoubtedly can make decisively important contributions. But this does not alter the fundamental methodological situation.

11. It has continually been assumed as obvious that the science of sociology seeks to formulate type concepts and generalized uniformities of empirical process. This distinguishes it from history, which is oriented to the casual analysis and explanation of individual actions, structures, and personalities possessing cultural significance. The empirical material which underlies the concepts of sociology consists to a very large extent, though by no means exclusively, of the same concrete processes of action which are dealt with by historians. Among the various bases on which its concepts are formulated and its generalizations worked out is an attempt to justify its important claim to be able to make a contribution to the casual explanation of some historically and culturally important phenomenon.[36] As in the case of

[36] This is one of the most important problems with which Weber was concerned in his methodological studies. He insisted on the very great importance of the cultural significance of a problem for the values of the time in determining the direction of interest of the investigator. He formulated this relation in his important concept of the *Wertbeziehung* of social science concepts. But he went so far as to deny the legitimacy of the formulation of a generalized theoretical system as an aim of theoretical analysis in social science. This denial seems to rest on a failure on Weber's part to carry his criticism of certain aspects of German idealistic social thought through to its logical conclusion. For Weber's position, see *Die Objektivität sozialwissenschaftlicher Erkenntnis, op. cit.*, and von Schelting, *Max Webers Wissenschaftslehre.* For a criticism of Weber's position, see *Structure of Social Action*, Chap. XVI (Parsons).

every generalizing science, the abstract character of the concepts of sociology is responsible for the fact that, compared with actual historical reality, they are relatively lacking in fullness of concrete content. To compensate for this disadvantage, sociological analysis can offer a greater precision of concepts. This precision is obtained by striving for the highest possible degree of adequacy on the level of meaning in accordance with the definition of that concept put forward above. It has already been repeatedly stressed that this aim can be realized in a particularly high degree in the case of concepts and generalizations which formulate rational processes. But sociological investigation attempts to include in its scope various irrational phenomena, as well as prophetic, mystic, and affectual modes of action, formulated in terms of theoretical concepts which are adequate on the level of meaning. In *all* cases, rational or irrational, sociological analysis both abstracts from reality and at the same time helps us to understand it, in that it shows with what degree of approximation a concrete historical phenomenon can be subsumed under one or more of these concepts. For example, the same historical phenomenon may be in one aspect "feudal," in another "patrimonial," in another "bureaucratic," and in still another "charismatic." In order to give a precise meaning to these terms, it is necessary for the sociologist to formulate pure ideal types of the corresponding forms of action which in each case involve the highest possible degree of logical integration by virtue of their complete adequacy on the level of meaning. But precisely because this is true, it is probably seldom if ever that a real phenomenon can be found which corresponds exactly to one of these ideally constructed pure types. The case is similar to a physical reaction which has been calculated on the assumption of an absolute vacuum. Theoretical analysis in the field of sociology is possible only in terms of such pure types. It goes without saying that in addition it is convenient for the sociologist from time to time to employ average types of an empirical statistical character. There are concepts which do not require methodological discussion at this point. But when reference is made to "typical" cases, the term should always be understood, unless otherwise stated, as meaning *ideal* types, which may in turn be rational or irrational as the case may be (thus in economic theory they are always rational), but in any case are always constructed with a view to adequacy on the level of meaning.

It is important to realize that in the sociological field as elsewhere, averages, and hence average types, can be formulated with a relative degree of precision only where they are concerned with differences of degree in respect to action which remains qualitatively the same. Such cases do occur, but in the majority of cases of action important to history or sociology the motives which determine it are qualitatively heterogeneous. Then it is quite impossible to speak of an "average" in the true sense. The ideal types of social action which for instance are used in economic theory are thus "unrealistic" or abstract in that they always ask what course of action would take place if it were purely rational and oriented to economic ends alone. But this construction can be used to aid in the understanding of action not purely economically determined but which involve deviations arising from traditional restraints, affects, errors, and the intrusion of other than economic purposes or considerations. This can take place in two ways. First, in analyzing the extent to which in the concrete case, or on the average for a class of cases, the action was in part economically determined along with the other factors. Second, by throwing the discrepancy between the actual course of events and the ideal type into relief, the analysis of the noneconomic motives actually involved is facilitated. The procedure would be very similar in employing an ideal type of mystical orientation with its appropriate attitude of indifference to worldly things, as a tool for analyzing its consequences for the actor's relation to ordinary life; for instance, to political or economic affairs. The more sharply and precisely the ideal type has been constructed, thus the more abstract and unrealistic in this sense it is, the better it is able to perform its methodological functions in formulating the clarification of terminology, and in the formulation of classifications, and of hypotheses. In working out a concrete causal explanation of individual events, the procedure of the historian is essentially the same. Thus in attempting to explain the campaign of 1866, it is indispensable both in the case of Moltke and of Benedek to attempt to construct imaginatively how each, given fully adequate knowledge both of his own situation and of that of his opponent, would have acted. Then it is possible to compare with this the actual course of action and to arrive at a causal explanation of the observed deviations, which will be attributed to such factors as misinformation, strategical errors, logical fallacies, personal temperament, or considerations outside the realm of strategy. Here, too, an ideal-typical construction of rational action is actually employed even though it is not made explicit.

The theoretical concepts of sociology are ideal types not only from the objective point of view but also in their application to subjective processes. In the great majority of cases actual action goes on in a state of inarticulate half-consciousness or actual unconsciousness of its subjective meaning. The actor is more likely to "be aware" of it in a vague sense than he is to "know" what he is doing or be explicitly self-conscious about it. In most cases his action is governed by impulse or habit. Only occasionally and, in the uniform action of large numbers often only in the case of a few individuals, is the subjective meaning of the action, whether rational or irrational, brought clearly into consciousness. The ideal type of meaningful action where the meaning is fully conscious and explicit is a marginal case. Every sociological or historical investigation, in applying its analysis to the empirical facts, must take this fact into account. But the difficulty need not prevent the sociologist from systematizing his concepts by the classification of possible types of subjective meaning. That is, he may reason as if action actually proceeded on the basis of clearly self-conscious meaning. The resulting deviation from the concrete facts must continually be kept in mind whenever it is a question of this level of concreteness, and must be carefully studied with reference both to degree and kind. It is often necessary to choose between terms which are either clear or unclear. Those which are clear will, to be sure, have the abstractness of ideal types, but they are none the less preferable for scientific purposes.[37]

(b) THE CONCEPT OF SOCIAL ACTION[38]

1. Social action, which includes both failure to act and passive acquiescence, may be oriented to the past, present, or expected future behavior of others. Thus it may be motivated by revenge for a past attack, defense against present, or measures of defense against future aggression. The "others" may be individual persons, and may be known to the actor as such, or may constitute an indefinite plurality and may be entirely unknown as individuals. Thus "money"

[37] On all these questions see the author's article in *Archiv für Sozialwissenschaft*, Vol. XIX, *op. cit.* Reprinted in *Gesammelte Aufsätze zur Wissenschaftslehre*, pp. 176-214 (Weber).

[38] The definition of social action has been given above. See p. 229 (Weber).

is a means of exchange which the actor accepts in payment because he orients his action to the expectation that a large but unknown number of individuals he is personally unacquainted with will be ready to accept it in exchange on some future occasion.

2. Not every kind of action, even of overt action, is "social" in the sense of the present discussion. Overt action is nonsocial if it is oriented solely to the behavior of inanimate objects. Subjective attitudes constitute social action only so far as they are oriented to the behavior of others. For example, religious behavior is not social if it is simply a matter of contemplation or of solitary prayer. The economic activity of an individual is social only if, and then only insofar as, it takes account of the behavior of someone else. Thus very generally in formal terms it becomes social insofar as the actor's actual control over economic goods is respected by others. Concretely it is social, for instance, if in relation to the actor's own consumption the future wants of others are taken into account and this becomes one consideration affecting the actor's own saving. Or, in another connection, production may be oriented to the future wants of other people.

3. Not every type of contact of human beings has a social character; this is rather confined to cases where the actor's behavior is meaningfully oriented to that of others. For example, a mere collision of two cyclists may be compared to a natural event. On the other hand, their attempt to avoid hitting each other, or whatever insults, blows, or friendly discussion might follow the collision, would constitute "social action."

4. Social action is not identical either with the similar actions of many persons or with action influenced by other persons. Thus, if at the beginning of a shower a number of people on the street put up their umbrellas at the same time, this would not ordinarily be a case of action mutually oriented to that of each other, but rather of all reacting in the same way to the like need of protection from the rain. It is well known that the actions of the individual are strongly influenced by the mere fact that he is a member of a crowd confined within a limited space. Thus, the subject matter of studies of "crowd psychology," such as those of Le Bon, will be called "action conditioned by crowds." It is also possible for large numbers, though dispersed, to be influenced simultaneously or successively by a source of influence operating similarly on all the individuals, as by means of the press.

Here also the behavior of an individual is influenced by his membership in the crowd and by the fact that he is aware of being a member. Some types of reaction are only made possible by the mere fact that the individual acts as part of a crowd. Others become more difficult under these conditions. Hence it is possible that a particular event or mode of human behavior can give rise to the most diverse kinds of feeling—gaiety, anger, enthusiasm, despair, and passions of all sorts—in a crowd situation which would not occur at all or not nearly so readily if the individual were alone. But for this to happen there need not, at least in many cases, be any meaningful relation between the behavior of the individual and the fact that he is a member of a crowd. It is not proposed in the present sense to call action "social" when it is merely a result of the effect on the individual of the existence of a crowd as such and the action is not oriented to that fact on the level of meaning. At the same time the borderline is naturally highly indefinite. In such cases as that of the influence of the demagogue, there may be a wide variation in the extent to which mass clientele is affected by a meaningful reaction to the fact of its large numbers; and whatever this relation may be, it is open to varying interpretations.

But furthermore, mere "imitation" of the action of others, such as that on which Tarde has rightly laid emphasis, will not be considered a case of specifically social action if it is purely reactive so that there is no meaningful orientation to the actor imitated. The borderline is, however, so indefinite that it is often hardly possible to discriminate. The mere fact that a person is found to employ some apparently useful procedure which he learned from someone else does not, however, constitute, in the present sense, social action. Action such as this is not oriented to the action of the other person, but the actor has, through observing the other, become acquainted with certain objective facts; and it is these to which his action is oriented. His action is then *causally* determined by the action of others, but not meaningfully. On the other hand, if the action of others is imitated because it is "fashionable" or traditional or exemplary, or lends social distinction, or on similar grounds, it is meaningfully oriented either to the behavior of the source of imitation or of third persons or of both. There are of course all manner of transitional cases between the two types of imitation. Both the phenomena discussed above, the behavior of crowds and imitation, stand on the indefinite borderline of social action.

The same is true, as will often appear, of traditionalism and charisma. The reason for the indefiniteness of the line in these and other cases lies in the fact that both the orientation to the behavior of others and the meaning which can be imputed to the actor himself, are by no means always capable of clear determination and are often altogether unconscious and seldom fully self-conscious. Mere "influence" and meaningful orientations cannot therefore always be clearly differentiated on the empirical level. But conceptually it is essential to distinguish them, even though merely "reactive" imitation may well have a degree of sociological importance at least equal to that of the type which can be called social action in the strict sense. Sociology, it goes without saying, is by no means confined to the study of "social action"; this is only, at least for the kind of sociology being developed here, its central subject matter, that which may be said to be decisive for its status as a science. But this does not imply any judgment on the comparative importance of this and other factors.

Georg Simmel
(1858–1918)

THE SOCIOLOGY OF CONFLICT

Georg Simmel was born in Berlin in 1858, the youngest of seven children. His father, who had a partnership in a chocolate-factory, died when Simmel was still a boy. A friend of the family, who acted as Simmel's guardian, left him a considerable fortune, thus enabling Simmel to devote himself to research and writing.

In 1876, after graduating from the Gymnasium, Simmel entered the University of Berlin, where he studied philosophy and history. In 1881 he received his doctorate from Berlin, his thesis being The Nature of Matter according to Kant's Physical Monadology. *He was appointed in 1885 as a Privatdozent in philosophy at the University of Berlin, which post he held until 1900. Simmel encountered difficulties in his academic career because of his Jewish background. Paul Honigsheim comments on this and other difficulties in "The Time and Thought of the Young Simmel": and we quote:*

"Simmel began his career as a Jew in a Berlin and a university both of which were becoming increasingly anti-Semitic. This fact proved a handicap to his career throughout almost his entire life. He was a teacher at Berlin University, where he received little or no salary, until the age of fifty-six, and his Jewish background was one of the causes of his partial isolation. Another was his failure to identify himself with any of the political and social groups that characterized his time and place. None of them, he feared, granted the individual independence."[1]

In 1914, after having served for fourteen years as a Professor Extraordinary (ausserordentlicher Professor), he was called to a chair at the University of Strassburg, which post he held until his death in 1918.

Georg Simmel was primarily a philosopher, and his sociological interests form only a part of his total lifework. He had a strong interest in history, literature, and the fine arts. He

---

[1] See p. 167, *Georg Simmel (1858-1918)*, ed. Kurt H. Wolff, Columbus, Ohio State University Press, 1959.

*lectured on "logic, principles of philosophy, history of philoso-
phy, modern philosophy, Kant, Lotze, Schopenhauer, Darwin,
pessimism, ethics, philosophy of religion, philosophy of art,
psychology, social psychology, political pschology, and sociology,"*[2] *and Simmel's interest in these fields is amply shown in
his many writings.*[3] *One is not surprised to learn, therefore,
that his work has been described as "a philosophy of contemporary culture."*[4]

*He was one of the first German sociologists who received
early and wide recognition in the United States, and one may
find his publications in the early volumes of the* American
Journal of Sociology.

*Simmel's definition of the nature and scope of sociology re-
mains a challenge to this day. As Donald Levine has written,
"he delimited the province of sociology"*[5] *and cultivated many
of its special areas. Simmel has generally been considered the
founder of "formal sociology," and the key to an understanding of Simmel's sociology is the forms of social interaction
or "forms of sociation" which he considered the object of
sociology.*

THE SOCIOLOGY OF CONFLICT

I

THAT conflict has sociological significance, inasmuch as it
either produces or modifies communities of interest, unifications, organizations, is in principle never contested. On the
other hand, it must appear paradoxical to the ordinary mode
of thinking to ask whether conflict itself, without reference to
its consequences or its accompaniments, is not a form of
socialization. This seems, at first glance, to be merely a verbal
question. If every reaction among men is a socialization, of
course conflict must count as such, since it is one of the most
intense reactions, and is logically impossible if restricted to a
single element. The actually dissociating elements are the

---

[2] P. xxv, Nicholas J. Spykman, *The Social Theory of Georg Simmel,* Chicago, 1925.
[3] See the bibliography in this volume.
[4] P. xxvi, Nicholas J. Spykman, *The Social Theory of Georg
Simmel,* Chicago, 1925.
[5] See p. 9, "The Structure of Simmel's Social Thought" by Donald N. Levine in *Georg Simmel* cited above.

causes of the conflict—hatred and envy, want and desire. If, however, from these impulses conflict has once broken out, it is in reality the way to remove the dualism and to arrive at some form of unity, even if through annihilation of one of the parties. The case is, in a way, illustrated by the most violent symptoms of disease. They frequently represent the efforts of the organism to free itself from disorders and injuries. This is by no means equivalent merely to the triviality, *si vis pacem para bellum*, but it is the wide generalization of which that special case is a particular. Conflict itself is the resolution of the tension between the contraries. That it eventuates in peace is only a single, specially obvious and evident, expression of the fact that it is a conjunction of elements, an opposition, which belongs with the combination under one higher conception. This conception is characterized by the common contrast between both forms of relationship and the mere reciprocal indifference between elements. Repudiation and dissolution of social relation are also negatives, but conflict shows itself to be the positive factor in this very contrast with them; namely, shows negative factors in a unity which, in idea only, not at all in reality, is disjunctive. It is practically more correct to say, however, that every historically actual unification contains, along with the factors that are unifying in the narrower sense, others which primarily make against unity.

As the individual achieves the unity of his personality not in such fashion that its contents invariably harmonize according to logical or material, religious or ethical, standards, but rather as contradiction and strife not merely precede that unity, but are operative in it at every moment of life; so it is hardly to be expected that there should be any social unity in which the converging tendencies of the elements are not incessantly shot through with elements of divergence. A group which was entirely centripetal and harmonious—that is, "unification" merely—is not only impossible empirically, but it would also display no essential life process and no stable structure. As the cosmos requires *Liebe und Hass*, attraction and repulsion, in order to have a form, society likewise requires some quantitative relation of harmony and disharmony, association and dissociation, liking and disliking, in order to attain to a definite formation. Moreover, these enmities are by no means mere sociological passivities, negative factors, in the sense that actual society comes into existence only through the working of the other and positive social forces, and this, too, only insofar as the negative forces are powerless to hinder the process. This ordinary conception is entirely superficial. Society, as it is given in fact, is the result of both categories of reactions, and insofar both act in a completely positive way. The misconception that the one factor tears down what the other builds up and that what at last remains is the result of subtracting the one from the other (while in reality it is much rather to be regarded as the addition of one to the other) doubtless springs from the equivocal sense of the concept of unity. We describe as unity the agreement and the conjunction of social elements in contrast with their disjunctions, separations, disharmonies. We also use the term "unity," however, for the total synthesis of the persons, energies, and forms in a group, in which the final wholeness is made up not merely of those factors which are unifying in the narrower sense but also of those which are, in the narrower sense, dualistic. We associate a corresponding double meaning with disunity or opposition. Since the latter displays its nullifying or destructive sense *between the individual elements*, the conclusion is hastily drawn that it must work in the same manner upon the *total relationship*. In reality, however, it by no means follows that the factor which is something negative and diminutive in its action between individuals, considered in a given direction and separately, has the same working throughout the totality of its relationships. In this larger circle of relationships the perspective may be quite different. That which was negative and dualistic may, after deduction of its destructive action in particular relationships, on the whole, play an entirely positive role. This visibly appears especially in those instances where the social structure is characterized by exactness and carefully conserved purity of social divisions and gradations. For instance, the social system of India rests not only upon the hierarchy of the castes but also directly upon their reciprocal repulsion. Enmities not merely prevent gradual disappearance of the boundaries within the society—and for this reason these enmities may be consciously promoted, as guarantee of the existing social constitution—but more than this the enmities are directly productive sociologically. They give classes and personalities their position toward each other, which they would not have found if these objective *causes* of hostility had been present and effective in precisely the same way, but had not been accompanied by the feeling of enmity. It is by no means certain that a secure and complete community life would always result if these energies should disappear which, looked at in detail, seem repulsive and destructive, just as a qualitatively unchanged and richer property results when unproductive elements disappear; but there would ensue rather a condition as changed and often as unrealizable, as after the elimination of the forces of cooperation—sympathy, assistance, harmony of interests.

This applies not only in the large to that sort of competition which merely as a formal relation of tension, and entirely apart from its actual results, determines the form of the group, the reciprocal position, and the distance of the elements; but it applies also where the unification rests upon the agreement of the individual minds. For example, the opposition of one individual element to another in the same association is by no means merely a negative social factor, but it is in many ways the only means through which coexistence with individuals intolerable in themselves could be possible. If we had not power and right to oppose tyranny and obstinacy, caprice and tactlessness, we could not endure relations with people who betray such characteristics. We should be driven to deeds of desperation which would put the relationships to an end. This follows not alone for the self-evident reason—which, however, is not here essential—that such disagreeable circumstances tend to become intensified if they are endured quietly and without protest; but, more than this, opposition affords us a subjective satisfaction, diversion, relief, just as under other psychological conditions, whose variations need not here be discussed, the same results are brought about by humility and patience. Our opposition gives us the feeling that we are not completely crushed in the relationship. It permits us to preserve a consciousness of energy, and thus lends a vitality and a reciprocity to relationships from which, without this corrective, we should have extricated ourselves at any price. Moreover, opposition does this not alone when it does not lead to considerable consequences, but also when it does not even come to visible manifestation, when it remains purely subjective; also when it does not give itself a practical expression. Even in such cases it can often produce a balance in the case of *both* factors in the relationship, and it may thus bring about a quieting which may save relationships, the continuance of which is often incomprehensible to observers from the outside. In such case opposition is an integrating component of the relationship itself; it is entitled to quite equal rights with the other grounds of its existence. Opposition is not merely a means of conserving the total relationship, but it is one of the concrete functions in which the relationship in reality consists. In case the relationships are purely external, and consequently do not reach deeply into the practical, the latent form of conflict discharges this service: that is, aversion, the feeling of reciprocal alienation and repulsion, which in the moment of a more intimate contact of any sort is at once transformed into positive hatred and conflict. Without this aversion life in a great city, which daily brings each into contact with countless others, would have no thinkable form. The whole internal organization of this commerce rests on an extremely complicated gradation of sympathies, indifferences, and aversions of the most transient or most permanent sort. The sphere of indifference is in all this relatively restricted. The activity of our minds responds to almost every impression received from other people in some sort of a definite feeling, all the unconsciousness, transience, and variability of which seems to remain only in the form of a certain indifference. In fact, this latter would be as unnatural for us as it would be intolerable to be swamped under a multitude of suggestions among which we have no choice. Antipathy protects us against these two typical dangers of the great city. It is the initial stage of practical antagonism. It produces the distances and the buffers without which this kind of life could not be led at all. The mass and the mixtures of this life, the forms in which it is carried on, the rhythm of its rise and fall—these unite with the unifying motives, in the narrower sense, to give to a great city the character of an indissoluble whole. Whatever in this whole seems to be an element of division is thus in reality only one of its elementary forms of socialization.

If accordingly the hostile relationships do not of themselves alone produce a social structure, but only in correlation with unifying energies, so that only by the co-working of the two can the concrete life unity of the group arise, yet the former are to the above extent scarcely to be distinguished from the other forms of relationship which sociology abstracts from the manifoldness of actual existence. Neither love nor division of labor, neither good fellowship with a third person nor hostility to him, neither adhesion to a party nor organization into superiority and inferiority, could alone produce a historical unification or permanently support it; and wherever this result has come about, the process has contained a multiplicity of distinguishable forms of relationship. It is once for all the nature of the human mind not to be bound to other minds by a single thread. Scientific analysis must busy itself with the elementary unities, and their specific combining energies, but in fact they do not work in isolation. On the other hand, however, there are many, apparently composite, relationships between individuals, which in reality are probably quite unitary structures, although we may not directly designate them as such. We make them, consequently, in accordance with all sorts of analogies, because of anterior motives or subsequent external consequences, into a concert of manifold psychic elements. The distance, for example, between two related individuals—which distance gives character to their relation—often appears to us as the product of an inclination which should properly have produced a much closer intimacy, and of a disinclination which must have thrust them much further from each other. Since these two forces act as reciprocal limitation, the resultant is the degree of distance which we observe. This may, however, be an entire error. The relationship is destined from within to this particular degree of distance. It has, so to speak, from the beginning a certain temperature, which does not arise merely through the accommodation of an essentially warmer and an essentially cooler condition. The degree of superiority and suggestion which establishes itself between certain persons is often interpreted by us as though it were produced by the strength of the one party, which is crossed by a contemporary weakness on the other side. This strength and weakness may be present, but its duality frequently plays no part in the relationship as it actually exists; but this relationship is determined by the total nature of the elements; and only as a subsequent matter do we analyze its immediate character into these factors.

Erotic relationships furnish the most frequent examples. How often do they seem to us to be woven together out of love and respect, or even of contempt; out of love and conscious harmony of natures, or again out of the consciousness of complementing each other through complete contrast of nature; out of love and the instinct of dominance, or a clinging disposition. What the observer, or even the subject himself, analyzes thus as two commingling streams is in reality often only a single current. In the relationship, as it finally exists, the total personality of the one party works upon that of the other, and its reality is independent of the consideration that, if this particular relationship did not exist, the persons concerned would still be at least moved to respect or sympathy, or the opposite. We very often characterize such a combination as a mixed feeling or a mixed relationship, because we construe the consequences which the qualities of the one party would produce upon the other, *if they operated separately;* which, however, is not the case. It should also be remembered that this mixture of feelings and relationships, even when we may be most justified in using the expression, always remains a problematical phrase. In the expression we transfer an occurrence visible in space, by the use of somewhat thoughtless symbolism, to quite heterogeneous mental relationships.

In many respects the like is the case with the so-called commingling of converging and diverging currents in a society. The relationship is in such cases either entirely *sui generis;* that is, its motive and form is in itself quite unitary, and only in order to describe and classify it do we subsequently construct it out of a monistic and an antagonistic current; or these two factors are present from the beginning indeed, but so to speak before the relationship came into being at all. In this relationship itself they have grown into an organic unity, in which the separate factor with its specific energy is no longer observable at all. In saying this we, of course, do not overlook the enormous number of relationships in which the antithetical partial relationships actually persist side by side, and are constantly to be recognized within the total situation. It is a special shade of the historical development of relationships that the same frequently in an early stadium show undifferentiated tendencies which only later separate into complete difference. As late as the thirteenth century there were at the courts of central Europe permanent assemblages of noblemen who constituted a kind of council of the prince. They lived as his guests, and yet at the same time they were a semiclass representation of the nobility. They championed the interests of the nobility *against* the prince. The community of interests with the king, the administration of which they incidentally served, and the action as a sort of opposition guarding the peculiar rights of their rank, took place in this social structure, not merely in an undifferentiated way side by side, but involved with each other. The position was surely felt to be a unity, however incompatible its elements may appear to us to have been. In England, at this time, the parliament of the barons can still hardly be distinguished from an extended royal council. Membership in it and critical or partisan opposition are here still combined in embryonic unity. So long as the real process in hand is the working out of institutions which have the task of adjusting the increasingly complex relationships involved in the internal equilibrium of the gorup, so long will it often be undetermined whether concurrence for the good of the whole shall take place in the form of opposition, competition, criticism, or in that of immediate unity and harmony. Accordingly, an original condition of indifference may exist, which, judged from the standpoint of the later differentiated condition, may seem logically contradictory, yet may quite harmonize with the undeveloped character of the organism.

The subjective attitudes of persons toward each other develop, in many ways, in the opposite direction. The decisiveness of attachment or opposition is likely to be relatively great in relatively primitive culture epochs. Indefinite relationships between persons, made possible by a sort of dawning condition of the sensibilities, the final word of which may mean almost as well love as hate; the indifference of which, indeed, often betrays itself in a sort of oscillation between the two sorts of feeling—such relationships are much more characteristic of mature or of overripe than of youthful periods. For instance, it is merely a reflection of these forms of feeling when uncultured persons and belated art can see only angelic virtue or devilish malignity in men. Theoretical judgment, like æsthetic taste, overcomes as it advances, this entanglement between the alternative of love or hate. The change does not mean that men come to be judged as mixtures of good and evil, or of worth and worthlessness, but as in themselves beyond either judgment. The individual has in himself, to be sure, the germs of both characters, which develop according to historical circumstances, stimuli, and judgments in many and various ways. He is originally, and he also remains to a certain degree, the undifferentiated unity of those antitheses. If in many objective social structures the unlimited opposition or unity distinguishes precisely the later stage of development, this is only one of the frequent cases in which the last stage of an evolution reproduces the form of its earliest stage, only in a maturer, more conscious, and more voluntary fashion; and so they exhibit more clearly, in the similarity of the external phenomena, the progress of the essential meaning.

Although antagonism in itself alone does not constitute socialization, no more is it likely to be lacking as a sociological element in the formation of societies (marginal cases being neglected); and its function may be extended indefinitely; that is, up to the exclusion of all unifying factors. The scale of relationships thus resulting is also one that may be described from the standpoint of ethical categories. The latter, however, furnish in general no sufficient point of attachment from which to exhibit completely and without prejudice the sociological element in the phenomena. The judgments of value with which we accompany the voluntary actions of individuals produce series which have only a purely accidental relationship to the arrangement of their forms in accordance with real criteria. To represent ethics as a species of sociology would deprive it of its profoundest and purest content: the attitude of the soul in and toward itself, which does not at all enter into its external relationships; its religious exercises, which affect only its own weal or woe; its devotion to the objective values of knowledge, of beauty, of significance of things, which are entirely outside all alliances with other men. The combination of harmonious and hostile relationships, however, allows the sociological and the ethical series to coincide. It begins here with the action of A to the advantage of B; continues in the action of A for private advantage, but by means of the utility to B; then to private advantage by means of B without any advantage to him, but also without inflicting upon him any injury; and ends at last in egoistic action at the expense of B. Since this now is reciprocated from the side of B, but scarcely ever in precisely the same manner and in equal measure, there result the countless mixtures of convergence and divergence in human relationships.

To be sure, there are struggles which appear to exclude every other element, for example, between the robber or the thug and his victim. When a struggle of this sort goes to the extreme of annihilation, it is surely the marginal case in which the share of the unifying element has become a nullity; in which, however the concept of reciprocal action really no longer finds any application, because this extreme case really assumes the nonexistence of the other party to a reaction. So soon, on the other hand, as any sort of consideration, any limitation of violence, is present, there comes into play by virtue of that fact a socializing factor, if it is only in the form of a restraint. Kant declares that every war in which the parties do not lay upon themselves any reservations in the use of possible means must, on psychological grounds, become a war of extermination; since when men do not at least restrain themselves from assassination, from treachery, from instigation of treason, they thereby destroy that confidence in the mental processes of the enemy which is the one necessary condition to make possible a conclusion of peace.

Almost unavoidably an element of community weaves itself into the hostility where the stage of open violence has given place to some other relation, which perhaps shows a completely undiminished aggregate of enmity between the parties. When the Lombards in the sixth century had conquered northern Italy, they imposed upon the conquered a tribute of one-third the product of the soil. They did it in such a manner that each individual among the conquerors had assigned to him the tribute of defined individuals in the population. In the case of the type thus distinguished it is impossible that the hatred of the conquered toward their oppressors may grow to such a degree that it may even be stronger than during the struggle itself, and that it may even be reciprocated not less intensively by the oppressors, because hatred toward him who hates us is a sort of instinctive means of protection, perhaps because we are accustomed to hating him whom we have injured. Nevertheless, there was still in the relationship a certain community, namely, that which begot the hostility. The common property assumed by the Lombards in the products of the previous inhabitants was at the same time an indisputable parallelism of interests. Inasmuch as divergence and harmony intertwined inextricably with each other at this point, the content of the former developed itself actually as the germ of later community. This form-type realized itself most generally in the enslavement of the captured enemy, in place of his destruction. In this slavery resides, to be sure, in countless instances, the marginal case of that absolute hostility of temper the occasion for which, however, brings about a sociological relation, and therewith frequently enough its own amelioration. The sharpening of the antithesis can, therefore, be directly provoked for the sake of its own removal. This not merely as heroic treatment, in confidence that the antagonism beyond a certain degree will be modified either by exhaustion or by insight into its foolishness; but in monarchies sometimes a prince is given to the opposition as a leader. For example, this was done by Gustav Vasa. The opposition is strengthened thereby indeed; this new center of gravity attracts elements which would otherwise have held themselves apart; at the same time, however, the opposition is by this very means held in certain check. While the government apparently gives the opposition intentional reinforcement, the force of the opposition is, nevertheless, by this means, actually broken.

Another marginal case appears to be given when the conflict is stimulated exclusively by love of fighting. The moment any stimulus prompts the struggle—a desire to possess or to control, some contempt or revenge—limitations arise not only from the object itself, or from the condition that is to be attained, to impress upon the struggle common norms or reciprocal restrictions; but this struggle, in which the stake is something exterior to struggle itself, will on general principles be colored by the fact that every end is to be reached by *various* means. The desire for a given possession, as well as for the subjugation, or even the annihilation, of an enemy, may be satisfied by other combinations and through occurrences other than fighting. Where struggle is merely a means determined by its *terminus ad quem,* there exists no ground for not limiting or omitting it, if with equal success another means can be used. To be sure, the most effective presupposition for preventing struggle, the exact knowledge of the comparative strength of the two parties, is very often only to be attained by the actual fighting out of the conflict. In case, however, the conflict is determined exclusively by the subjective *terminus a quo,* where inner energies are present which can be satisfied only by struggle as such, there is no possible alternative. Struggle is in that case its own end and purpose, and consequently is utterly free from admixture of any other form. Such a struggle for struggle's sake seems to have its natural basis in a certain formal impulse of hostility, which forces itself sometimes upon psychological observation, and in various forms. In the first place, it appears as that natural enmity between man and man which is often emphasized by skeptical moralists. The argument is: Since there is something not wholly displeasing to us in the misfortune of our best friends, and, since the presupposition excludes, in this instance, conflict of material interests, the phenomenon must be traced back to an a priori hostility, to that *homo homini lupus,* as the frequently veiled, but perhaps never inoperative, basis of all our relationships. The completely contrasted tendency in moral philosophy which derives ethical altruism from the transcendental foundations of our nature does not thereby, however, separate itself so very far from the former pessimism. It admits that within the circuit of our experience and our knowledge of volitions devotion to the *alter* is not to be discovered. Empirically, so far as our knowledge goes, man is accordingly a simple egoist, and every variation from this natural fact must occur, not by virtue of nature itself, but only because of a metaphysical reality which somehow or other breaks through the rationally conceivable. That we are inclined, however, to oppose to this radical egoism, which is at the outset merely a negation, a refusal to take any interest in a nonego, the counterpoise of altruism, indicates that the former, considered with reference to its significance and its expressions in practical life, instigates radical enmity between men; indeed, *is* such enmity. Since men, however, live in society, the function of absolute egoism is nothing else than absolute hostility, which, through the necessity of calling into existence a transcendency to be the *deus ex machina* for its conversion to altruism, betrays itself as the natural basis of empirical human relationships. As such basis this hostility seems at least to take its place by the side of the other factor, the a priori sympathy between them. The notably strong interest, for example, which men take even in the *sufferings* of others, is merely a phenomenon to be explained as a mixture of the two motives. The not infrequent phenomena of the spirit of contradiction point also toward this a priori antipathy. We refer by no means merely to the conduct of those chronic objectors who in friendly and family circles, committees, or theater audiences, for instance, are the despair of their neighbors. What we have in mind by no means celebrates its most characteristic triumphs upon the political field, in the ranks of the opposition, whose classical type Macaulay describes in the case of Robert Ferguson: "His hostility was not to popery or to Protestantism, to monarchical government or to republican government, to the house of Stuart or to the house of Nassau, but to whatever was, at the time, established." All such cases, usually held to be types of pure opposition, need not necessarily be this. Such obstructors usually give themselves out as champions of threatened rights, protectors of the objectively ethical, knightly defenders of the minority as such. Much less striking occurrences appear to me to betray even more clearly an abstract impulse of opposition: the gentle, often scarcely conscious, and even immediately vanishing inclination to answer with a negation an assertion or an appeal, especially when it is addressed to us in categorical form. Even in quite harmonious relationships, in the case of many altogether yielding natures, this impulse of opposition betrays itself with the inevitableness of reflex action, and it mingles, even if without very much effect, in the total situation. Even if we should characterize this as in reality an instinct of protection—as many animals, upon mere touch, bring their protective or defensive apparatus automatically into action—yet this would still tend to prove the primary, fundamental character of opposition; for it shows that the personality, even in case it is not at all attacked, but merely encountering purely objective manifestations of a third party, cannot assert itself otherwise than through opposition; in other words, that the first instinct with which it affirms itself is negation of the other party.

Finally, it seems to me that the *suggestibility* of the hostile temper, which is often so faint that it is uncanny, points to a primary need of hostility. It is much more difficult to influence the average man in general to take an interest in, or to feel an inclination of sympathy for, a third person previously indifferent, than to develop in him mistrust and antipathy. It seems to be particularly decisive that this difference is relatively crass in cases of the lower grades of either sentiment, of the first betrayals of feeling or judgment for or against a person. Over the higher grades of feeling, which approach precision, these fugitive impulses, betraying, nevertheless, the fundamental instinct, are not so decisive, but they are rather more conscious antipathies. The same fundamental reality is exhibited, only in another phase, in the fact that those indefinite prejudices with reference to another, which cross our minds sometimes like a shadow, may often be suggested by quite indifferent persons, while a *favorable* prejudice requires a source in some person of authority or one whose relation to us is that of agreeable confidence. Perhaps this *aliquid haeret* would not win its tragic truthfulness without this facility or frivolity with which the average man reacts precisely upon suggestions of an unfavorable sort. Observation of many antipathies and partisanships, alienations and open quarrels, might surely cause hostility to be classified among those primary human energies which are not set free by the external reality of their objects but which spontaneously create their object. Thus it has been said that man does not have religion because he believes in God, but because he has religion as an attitude of the soul, consequently he believes in God. In the case of love, it is very generally recognized that, especially in earlier years, it is not the mere reaction of our soul which proceeds directly from the influence of its object, as the sensation of color arises in our optical apparatus. On the contrary, the soul has an amatory impulse, and selects for itself an object which satisfies this need, although the soul itself under certain circumstances first clothes that object with the qualities which apparently evoke the love. With the modification to be introduced presently, nothing can be shown to disprove the assertion that the like is the case with hate: that the soul possesses also an autochthonous need of hating and of fighting, which often on its side projects their offensive qualities upon the objects which it selects. The reason why this case does not emerge so evidently as that of love may be that the love impulse, in connection with its intense physiological stimulation in youth, gives unmistakable evidence of its spontaneity, its impulse from the *terminus a quo*. The impulse to hate has in itself only in exceptional cases such acute stages, through which its subjective-spontaneous character would be equally evident. All relationships of one human being to others are in their ultimate ground to be distinguished by this question—although in countless variations between absolute affirmation and negation—namely, whether their psychical basis is an impulse of the subject, which develops itself as an impulse without any external stimulus, and then of itself seeks an adequate object, whether this object be originally presented as adequate, or by the fantasy of the subject reconstructed into adequacy; or, on the other hand, whether the psychical basis consists in the reaction which the being or the acting of a personality produces in us. Of course, the possibility of such reaction must be present in our mind, but such possibilities would in themselves have remained latent, and would never of themselves have taken the form of impulses. All relationships to human beings present themselves in terms of this antithesis, whether they are intellectual or æsthetic, sympathetic or antipathetic. It is often only from this basis that they may be formulated as to their intensity and their content.

If now there exists in men a formal impulse of hostility as the counterpart of the sympathetic impulse, it seems to me that historically it springs from one of those processes of distillation in the soul by which subjective motions, evoked by definite and manifold contents, finally leave behind in the soul the form common to them all, as an independent impulse. Interests of every sort impel so often to conflict over goods, to opposition against persons, that as a residuum of them a condition of irritability, impelling spontaneously toward antagonistic demonstrations, may quite easily have passed over into the inventory of the transmissible traits of our species.

The reciprocal relationship of primitive groups is notoriously, and for reasons frequently discussed, almost invariably, one of hostility. The decisive illustration is furnished perhaps by the Indians, among whom every tribe on general principles was supposed to be on a war footing toward every other tribe with which it had no express treaty of peace. It is, however, not to be forgotten that in early stages of culture war constitutes almost the only form in which contact with an alien group occurs. So long as interterritorial trade was undeveloped, individual journeys unknown, and intellectual community did not extend beyond the group boundaries, there was, outside war, no sociological relationship whatever between the various groups. In this case the relationship of the elements of the group to each other and that of the primitive groups to each other present completely contrasted forms. Within the closed circle hostility signifies, as a rule, the *severing* of relationships, voluntary isolation, and the avoidance of contact. Along with these negative phenomena there will also appear the phenomena of the passionate reaction of open struggle. On the other hand, the characteristic group as a whole remains indifferently side by side with similar groups so long as peace exists, and these groups become significant for each other only when war breaks out. On this account the very same impulse of expansion and enterprise which within the group promotes absolute peace, as the condition of the interaction and unhindered reciprocity of interests, may in its operation between groups operate as an instigator of war. That the impulse of hostility, considered also from this point of view, may attain an independent life in the soul is the less to be doubted since it represents here, as in many another easily observable combination, the embodiment of an impulse which is in the first place quite general but which also occurs in quite peculiar forms, namely, *the impulse to act in relationships with others.*

In spite of this independence in the soul, which we may thus attribute to the antagonistic impulse, there still remains the question whether it *suffices* to account for the total phenomena of hostility. This question must be answered in the negative. In the first place, the spontaneous impulse restrains its sovereignty to the extent that it does not exercise itself toward every object whatsoever but only upon those that are in some way promising. Hunger, for example, springs from the subject. It does not have its origin in the object. Nevertheless, it will not attempt to satisfy itself with wood or stone, but will select only edible objects. In the same way, love and hatred, however little their impulses may depend upon external stimuli, will yet need some sort of opposing structure or object, and only with such cooperation will the complete phenomena appear. On the other hand, it seems to me probable that the hostile impulse, on account of its formal character, in general only intervenes as a reinforcement of conflicts stimulated by material interest, and at the same time furnishes a foundation for the conflict. And where a struggle springs up from sheer formal love of fighting, which is also entirely impersonal, and indifferent both to the material at issue and to the personal opponent, hatred and fury against the opponent as a person unavoidably increase in the course of the conflict, and probably also the interest in the stake at issue, because these affections stimulate and feed the psychical energy of the struggle. It is *useful* to hate the opponent with whom one is for any reason struggling, as it is useful to love him with whom one's lot is united and with whom one must cooperate. The reciprocal attitude of men is often intelligible only on the basis of the perception that intimate adaptation teaches us those feelings which are appropriate to the given situation; feelings which are the most appropriate to the employment or the overcoming of the circumstances of the situation; feelings which bring us, through psychical association, the energies necessary for discharging the momentary task and for defeating the opposing impulses. Accordingly, no serious struggle can long continue without being supported by a complex of psychic impulses. These may, to be sure, gradually develop into effectiveness in the course of the struggle. The purity of conflict merely for conflict's sake, accordingly, undergoes adulteration, partly through the admixture of objective interests, partly by the introduction of impulses which may be satisfied otherwise than by struggle, and which, in practice, form a bridge between struggle and other forms of reciprocal relationship. I know in fact only a single case in which the stimulus of struggle and of victory in itself constitutes the exclusive motive, namely the war game, and only in the case that no further gain is to arise than is included in the outcome of the game itself. In this case the pure sociological attraction of self-assertion and predominance over another in a struggle of skill is combined with purely individual pleasure in the exercise of purposeful and successful activity, together with the excitement of taking risks with the hazard of fortune which stimulates us with a sense of mystic harmony of relationship to powers beyond the individual as well as the social occurrences. At all events, the war game, *in its sociological motivation*, contains absolutely nothing but struggle itself. The worthless markers, for the sake of which men often play with the same earnestness with which they play for gold pieces, indicate the formalism of this impulse which, even in the play for gold pieces, often far outweighs the material interest. The thing to be noticed, however, is that, in order that the foregoing situations may occur, certain sociological forms—in the narrower sense, unifications—are presupposed. There must be agreement in order to struggle, and the struggle occurs under reciprocal recognition of norms and rules. In the motivation of the whole procedure these unifications, as said above, do not appear, but the whole transaction shapes itself under the forms which these explicit or implicit agreements furnish. They create the technique. Without this, such a conflict, excluding all heterogeneous or objective factors, would not be possible. Indeed, the conduct of the war game is often so rigorous, so impersonal, and observed on both sides with such nice sense of honor, that unities of a corporate order can seldom in these respects compare with it.

The foregoing illustration exhibits the struggle principle and the unifying principle which bind antithetical elements into a unity with almost the clearness of abstract conceptions. It thus shows how each arrives at its complete sociological significance in cooperation with the other. The same form dominates, although not with the same distinctness and freedom from mixture of the elements, the struggle for legal victory. In this case, to be sure, an object of contention is present. Voluntary concession of this object might satisfactorily end the contention. This is not the case with struggle for struggle's sake. Moreover, what we are accustomed to calling the joy and passion of conflict in the case of a legal process is probably, in most cases, something quite different, namely, the energetic sense of justice, the impossibility of tolerating an actual or supposed invasion of the sphere of right with which the ego feels a sense of solidarity. The whole obstinacy and uncompromising persistence with which parties in such struggles often maintain the controversy to their own hurt has, even in the case of the aggressive party, scarcely the character of an attack in the proper sense, but rather that of a defense in a deeper significance. The point at issue is the self-preservation of the personality which so identifies itself with its possessions and its rights that any invasion of them seems to be a destruction of the personality; and the struggle to protect them at the risk of the whole existence is thoroughly consistent. This individualistic impulse, and not the sociological motive of struggle, will consequently characterize such cases. With respect to the form of the struggle itself, however, judicial conflict is, to be sure, of an absolute sort; that is, the reciprocal claims are asserted with a relentless objectivity and with employment of all available means, without being diverted or modified by personal or other extraneous considerations. The judicial conflict is, therefore, absolute conflict, insofar as nothing enters the whole action which does not properly belong in the conflict and which does not serve the ends of conflict; whereas, otherwise, even in the most savage struggles, something subjective, some pure freak of fortune, some sort of interposition from a third side, is at least possible. In the legal struggle everything of the kind is excluded by the matter-of-factness with which the contention, and absolutely nothing outside the contention, is kept in view. This exclusion from the judicial controversy of everything which is not material to the conflict may, to be sure, lead to a formalism of the struggle which may come to have an independent character in contrast with the content itself. This occurs, on the one hand, in the legal cabalistic, in which real elements are not weighed against each other at all, but only quite abstract notions maintain controversy with each other. On the other hand, the controversy is often shifted to elements which have no relation whatever to the subject which is to be decided by the struggle. In case legal controversies, accordingly, in higher civilizations, are fought out by attorneys, the device serves to abstract the controversy from all personal associations which are essentially irrelevant. If, on the other hand, Otto the Great ordains that a legal controversy shall be settled by judicial duel between professional fighters, there remains of the whole struggle of interests only the bare form, namely, that there shall be struggle and victory. This alone is, in the latter case, common between the struggle which is to be decided and the fighter who is to decide it. This latter case portrays, in the exaggeration of caricature, the reduction and limitation, here in question, of the judicial conflict to the mere struggle element. But precisely through its pure objectivity, because it stands quite beyond the subjective antitheses of pity and cruelty, this unpitying type of struggle, as a whole, rests on the presupposition of a unity and a community of the parties never elsewhere so severely and constantly maintained. The common subordination to the law, the reciprocal recognition that the decision can be made only according to the objective weight of the evidence, the observance of forms which are held to be inviolable by both parties, the consciousness throughout the whole procedure of being encompassed by a social power and order which are the means of giving to the procedure its significance and security—all this makes the legal controversy rest upon a broad basis of community and consensus between the opponents. It is really a unity of a lesser degree which is constituted by the parties to a compact or to a commercial transaction, a presupposition of which is the recognition, along with the antithesis of interests, that they are subject to certain common, constraining, and obligatory rules. The common presuppositions, which exclude everything that is merely personal from the legal controversy, have that character of pure objectivity to which, on its side, the sharpness, the inexorableness, and the absoluteness of the species of struggle correspond. The reciprocity between the dualism and the unity of the sociological relationship is accordingly shown by the judicial struggle not less than by the war game. Precisely the most extreme and unlimited phases of struggle occur in both cases, since the struggle is surrounded and maintained by the severe unity of common norms and limitations.

Finally, this emerges on all hands where the parties are moved by an objective interest; that is, where the struggle interest, and consequently the struggle itself, is differentiated from the personality. Under such circumstances two alternatives are possible: the struggle may turn about purely objective decisions and may leave everything personal undisturbed; or it may draw in the persons from their subjective side without thereby affecting the contemporary objective interests common to the parties. The latter type is illustrated by the saying of Leibniz, that he would become a follower of his deadly enemy if he could learn something from him. That this situation may compose and modify enmity is so evident that at present only the opposite consequence can be in question. It is certainly true that the hostility which runs its course in an objective sphere under definite terms of obligation and understanding has, so to speak, a definiteness of outline and a security of its right. The knowledge of such delimitation assures us that personal antipathy will not cross the boundaries thus drawn. The assurance which we derive only from such differentiation may, under certain circumstances, lead to an intensification of the enmity; for where the enmity thus confines itself to its own bounds—in this case the subjectivity of the personality—we may give ourselves over to it very often more absolutely than if its impulse had to carry a ballast of secondary animosities into territories which really are assailed only by those central motives. Where such differentiation leaves room, on the other hand, for struggle only on the side of impersonal interests, the minutest intensifications and embitterments usual when personal considerations enter into quarrels will also fall away. On the other hand, however, the consciousness of being merely the representative of super-individual claims—that is, of fighting, not for self but only for the thing itself—may lend to the struggle a radicalism and mercilessness which have their analogy in the total conduct of many very unselfish and high-minded men. Because they grant themselves no consideration, they likewise have none for others, and hold themselves entirely justified in sacrificing everybody else to the idea to which they are themselves a sacrifice. Such a struggle, into which all the powers of the person are thrown, while victory accrues only to the cause, carries the character of respectability, for the reputable man is the wholly personal, who, however, understands how to hold his personality entirely in check. Hence objectivity operates as *noblesse*. When, however, this differentiation is accomplished, and struggle is objectified, it is not subjected to a further reserve, which would be quite inconsistent; indeed, that would be a sin against the content of the interest itself upon which the struggle had been localized. On the basis of this common element between the parties—namely, that each defends merely the issue and its right, and excludes from consideration everything selfishly personal—the struggle is fought out without the sharpness, but also without the mollifyings, which come from intermingling of the personal element. Merely the imminent logic of the situation is obeyed with absolute precision. This form of antithesis between unity and antagonism intensifies conflict perhaps most perceptibly in cases where both parties actually pursue one and the same purpose; for example, in the case of scientific controversies, in which the issue is the establishment of the truth. In such a case every concession, every polite consent to stop short of exposing the errors of the opponent in the most unpitying fashion, every conclusion of peace previous to decisive victory, would be treason against that reality for the sake of which the personal element is excluded from the conflict.

With endless varieties otherwise, the social struggles since Marx have developed themselves in the above form. Since it is recognized that the situation of laborers is determined by the objective organization and formulas of the productive system, independent of the will and power of individual persons, the personal embitterment incident to the struggle in general, and to local conflicts exemplifying the general conflict, necessarily diminishes. The entrepreneur is no longer, as such, a bloodsucker and damnable egotist; the laborer is no longer universally assumed to act from sinful greed; both parties begin, at least, to abandon the program of charging the other with demands and tactics inspired by personal malevolence. This literalizing of the conflict has come about in Germany rather along the lines of theory; in England, through the operation of the trade unions, in the course of which the individually personal element of the antagonism has been overcome. In Germany this was effected largely through the more abstract generalization of the historical and class movement. In England it came about through the severe superindividual unity in the actions of the unions and of the combinations of employers. The intensity of the struggle, however, has not on that account diminished. On the contrary, it has become much more conscious of its purpose, more concentrated, and at the same time more aggressive, through the consciousness of the individual that he is struggling, not merely, and often not at all, for himself, but rather for a vast, superpersonal end.

A most interesting symptom of this correlation was presented by the boycotting of the Berlin breweries by the labor body in the year 1894. This was one of the most intense local struggles of the last decade. It was carried on by both sides with extraordinary energy, yet without any personal offensiveness on either side toward the other, although the stimulus was close at hand. Indeed, two of the party leaders, in the midst of the struggle, published their opinions about it in the same journal. They agreed in their formulation of the objective facts, and disagreed in a partisan spirit only in the practical conclusions drawn from the facts. Inasmuch as the struggle eliminated everything irrelevantly personal, and thereby restricted antagonism quantitatively, facilitating an understanding about everything personal, producing a recognition of being impelled on both sides by historical necessities, this common basis did not reduce, but rather increased, the intensity, the irreconcilability, and the obstinate consistency of the struggle.

Altogether, this logical relationship, so to speak, between the monism and the antagonism of social reactions operates as a means of organizing the latter. The struggle interests are the primary elements, and unity is a coordinating, and consequently modifying, addition. The synthesis of these two has the quite opposite consequence if the unity is the point of departure of the relationship, and conflict arises on that basis. Such a conflict is usually more passionate and more radical than in cases where no previous interdependence of the parties or other coherence exists. History is full of examples, from which I select a few to emphasize the similarity of the sociological form, along with the greatest differences of the motives which either unify or dissociate. In permitting bigamy the old Hebrew law nevertheless forbids marrying two sisters (although one might, after the death of the one, marry the other). The animus of the prohibition was that the forbidden relationship would be especially liable to stimulate jealousy. That is, the assumption is made, as matter of experience, that sharper antagonism arises on the foundation of community of relationship than on that between strangers. The reciprocal hatred of petty neighboring states, whose whole world, whose local concerns and interests, are unavoidably closely similar, and indeed often identical, is frequently much more passionate and irreconcilable than that between great nations which, geographically and actually, are completely alien to each other. This was at one time the misfortune of Greece and of post-Roman Italy, and an outbreak of the same convulsed England after the Norman conquest before the amalgamation of the races occurred. The hatred of the two races, living in the same territory, united to each other by persistent, actual life interests, and held together by a common civic idea, yet internally quite alien to each other, in their entire character lacking reciprocal understanding, in their power interests absolutely hostile to each other—hatred in this case, as has been rightly emphasized, was more bitter than could occur between races externally and internally distinct. Ecclesiastical relationships furnish the strongest illustrations, because in them the smallest divergence over fixing of dogma at once involves a logical irreconcilability. If any variation whatever occurs, it is conceptually indifferent whether it is great or small. Thus, in the confessional controversies between the Lutheran and the "Reformed" communions, particularly in the seventeenth century: scarcely had the great schism between Catholics and Protestants occurred when all Protestantism split into parties over the most trivial question. With reference to these the saying was often heard, "It is easier to hold with the Papists than with the members of the other confession." And when, in 1875, in Berne, a difficulty occurred with reference to the place for holding the Catholic service, the pope did not permit it in the church used by the Old Catholics, but sanctioned the service in a Reformed church.

It is of wide sociological interest to examine the two species of community which come into view, according to these and countless other examples, as bases of especially intense antagonism. Questions are presented as to the grounds of this consequence, and especially as to the operation of the forces concerned within the realm of everyday personal relationships. These two species are, namely, the community of qualities, on the one hand, and, on the other hand, community through subsumption under one and the same social interdependence. The former runs back exclusively to the fact that we are creatures of diversity (*Unterschiedswesen*). An enmity must excite consciousness the more deeply and energetically the greater the similarity between the parties among whom it originates. In case of peaceful or affectionate attitude, this is an excellent protective device within the association. It is analogous with the warning function of pain within the organism. For precisely the energetic consciousness with which the dissonance makes itself felt, where there is otherwise thorough harmony of the relationships, prescribes at the same time removal of the ground of difference, so that it may not half-unconsciously eat further and further, even to the foundation of the relationship. In case, however, this fundamental intention of holding together under all circumstances is lacking, that consciousness of antagonism which is otherwise made precise and pointed by similarity in other respects will sharpen the antagonism. People who have much in common often do each other worse and more unjust wrong than total strangers; in many cases because the large common territory between them has become matter of course, and consequently not this common factor, but that which is momentarily different, defines their reciprocal attitude; principally, however, simply because but very little is different between them, so that every most petty antagonism has a quite different relative significance from that between strangers who, of course, calculate upon all sorts of differences. Hence come the family quarrels over the most pitiful trifles. Hence the tragedy of the trifles, over which people who are in full agreement sometimes come to disruption. This by no means always proves that the harmonizing forces were already in decay. It can arise from such a degree of likeness of qualities, inclinations, and convictions that incompatibility at a quite insignificant point makes itself perceptibly intolerable on account of the very refinement of the antithesis. The foregoing may be further expressed in this way. With reference to the stranger with whom one shares neither qualities nor other interests, one stands in objective contrast, and one reserves the proper personality. On that account a difference in a single particular does not so easily carry the whole person with it. In the case of a person quite unlike ourselves, we come into contact only at the point of a single transaction or coincidence of interests. The accommodation of a conflict will consequently limit itself to this single issue. The more we have, however, as total personalities in common with another, the easier will our whole personality become involved in each separate contact with him. Hence the quite disproportionate intensity with which otherwise quite self-contained persons frequently allow themselves to become moved in their conduct toward their most intimate associates. The whole happiness and the whole depth in the relationship to a person with whom we feel ourselves, so to speak, identical; the condition in which no single reaction, no single word, no single common doing or withholding remains actually single, but each is an affair of the whole soul which manifests itself and is perceived without subtraction in it—all these make between such persons any outbreaking difference often so portentous. The persons in such a case are too much accustomed to putting into the phase of their action which they present to each other the totality of their being and feeling, not to equip conflict also with emphasis, and at the same time with ulterior bearings, through which it extends far beyond its provocation and its objective significance, and betrays the whole of the two personalities into disunion. On the highest psychical plane of development this may be avoided, for on this level it is characteristic to combine loyalty of soul to a person with reciprocal discrimination of the elements of the soul. While undifferentiated passion fuses the totality of a man with the excitement of a portion or an element, higher culture restrains one such portion or element from exerting an influence beyond its proper, definitely limited right. Culture consequently secures to the relationships of harmoniously developed personalities that, precisely in the midst of conflict, they are aware how insignificant conflict is in comparison with the unifying forces. Apart from this, however, in the case of the deeper natures, refined susceptibility of differences will make attractions and repulsions the more intense when they arise from past tendencies in opposite directions. This will appear in the case of irrevocable determinations of their relationship, entirely distinguished from the above-discussed oscillations within the everyday experience of a common condition, which on the whole is settled beyond question. Between husbands and wives a quite elemental aversion, or even more energetic repulsion, not traceable to specific grounds, but as the reciprocal reaction of the total personalities, is sometimes the first stadium of relationships of which the second is passionate love. We might, indeed, arrive at the paradoxical supposition that in the case of natures which are destined to the closest community of feeling this phenomenon is produced by an instinctive utility, that is, in order to give to the definitive feeling the most passionate refinement and consciousness of what has been achieved, by means of a contrasted prelude, as through an assault and retreat. The contrasted phenomenon presents a like form. The deepest hatred grows out of terminated love. In this case the decisive factor is not merely the susceptibility of difference, but principally the repudiation of one's own past, which is involved in such a revulsion of feeling. A profound love—one which is not merely sexual—recognized as a mistake and a misdirection of instinct, constitutes such an exposure of ourselves to ourselves, such a break in the security and unity of our self-consciousness, that we unavoidably make the object of this incompatibility the scapegoat of the error. It is a very convenient way to cover up the secret feeling of our own fault in the transaction, by the hatred which makes it easy for us to charge the whole responsibility upon the other party.

This peculiar bitterness of conflict in relationships in which from their very nature it is supposed that peace should reign appears to be a positive confirmation of the matter of course that relationships show their intimacy and strength by the absence of differences. This matter of course, however, is by no means without its exceptions.

That in very intimate relationships, which control, or at

least affect, the whole content of life—such, for example, as marriage—no occasions for conflicts emerge is unthinkable. Never to yield to them, but to anticipate them from a distance, to ensure against them in advance by reciprocal concession, is by no means always an affair of the most genuine and profound affinity, but it occurs rather in the case of sentiments which are affectionate to be sure, virtuous, and loyal, in which, however, the ultimate unlimited devotion of feeling is lacking. The individual in such instances may be conscious of inability to offer such devotion, and may be all the more anxious to preserve the relationship free from every shadow. He may consequently manifest the most extreme kindness, self-control, consideration, in order to compensate the other for any lack. All this may also be necessary, in particular, to quiet his own conscience because of slight or serious infidelity in his own attitude. Not even the most upright or even the most passionate will is always able to escape such affections. This is because the whole is a matter of feelings, which as such are not amenable to the will, but come or go as forces of destiny. The perceived insecurity in the basis of such relationships frequently influences us, because of our wish to preserve the relationships at all costs, to exercise quite exaggerated unselfishness, and even to use mechanical guarantees of the situation, through avoidance on principle of every threatening conflict. In case one is certain of the immovability and unreserve of his own feeling, this absolute assurance of peace is by no means necessary. One knows that no shock could penetrate to the foundation of the relationship upon which there would not always be a revival of the attachment. The strongest love can best endure a blow, and the fear which troubles lesser affections, that they will not be able to endure the consequences of such a blow and that it must consequently be avoided at all hazards, does not suggest itself to the stronger affection. In spite of the fact, therefore, that a feud between intimate friends may have more tragic consequences than between strangers, it appears from the foregoing analysis that the most deeply rooted relationship may come much easier to such a conflict, while many another which is good and moral, but rooted in inferior depths of feeling, may to all appearances run a course that is much more harmonious and free from conflict.

A special gradation of sociological distinction, and of emphasis of conflict upon the basis of equality, is given where the sundering of originally homogeneous elements is a conscious purpose, where the disunion is not properly the consequence of conflict, but the conflict arises from the disunion. The type in this instance is furnished by the hatred of apostates and against the heretical. The thought of the former consensus operates here so forcibly that the present antithesis is immeasurably sharper and more bitter than if no connection had ever existed. It is to be added that both parties have an interest in asserting their differences in contrast with the persisting tradition of similarity. It is of extreme importance for them to assert the unequivocal character of this difference. They are able to bring this about only by emphasizing the difference beyond its original importance. For this end of assuring the position, theoretical or religious dissent leads to a reciprocal accusing of heresy in every ethical, personal, subjective, or objective respect, which would not be at all necessary if precisely similar differences occurred between strangers. Indeed, that a difference of *convictions* should at all run into hatred and struggle occurs as a rule only in case of essential and original equality of the parties. The sociologically very significant phenomenon of "respect for the enemy" is usually absent when hostility has arisen where there was earlier community. Where so much similarity still exists that mistakes of identity and obliteration of boundaries are possible, the points of difference must be emphasized to an extent which is often not at all justified by the matter itself, but only by this danger. This was the case, for example, in the instance, cited above, of Catholicism in Berne. Roman Catholicism has no occasion to fear that its peculiarity is threatened by an external contact with a church so completely differentiated as the Reformed body. It could, however, be compromised by association with a body which is still so closely related with it as the Old Catholic church.

This illustration brings to view also the second type here in question, which in practice, to be sure, falls more or less into identity with the other. This is the case of that hostility, the intensity of which is based upon association and unity which is by no means always likeness. The occasion for separate discussion of this type is that here, instead of the consciousness of difference, an entirely new motive emerges—the peculiar phenomenon of social hatred, that is, of hatred toward a member of a group, not from personal motives, but because he threatens the existence of the group. Insofar as such a danger threatens through feud within the group, the one party hates the other not alone on the material ground which instigated the quarrel but also on the sociological ground, namely, that we hate the enemy of the group, as such; that is, the one from whom danger to its unity threatens. Inasmuch as this is a reciprocal matter, and each attributes the fault of endangering the whole to the other, the antagonism acquires a severity which does not occur when membership in a group unity is not a factor in the situation. Most characteristic in this connection are the cases in which an actual dismemberment of the group has not yet occurred. If this dismemberment has already taken place, it signifies a certain termination of the conflict. The individual difference has found its sociological termination, and the stimulus to constantly renewed friction is removed. To this result the tension between antagonism and still persisting unity must directly work. As it is fearful to be at enmity with a person to whom one is nevertheless bound, from whom one cannot be freed, whether externally or subjectively, even if one will, so there is increased bitterness if one will not detach himself from the community because he is not willing to give up the value of membership in the containing unity, or because he feels this unity as an objective good, the threatening of which deserves conflict and hatred. From such a correlation as this springs the embittering with which, for example, quarrels are fought out within a political faction or a trade union or a family. The individual soul offers an analogy. The feeling that a conflict between sensuous and ascetic feelings, or selfish and moral impulses, or practical and intellectual ambitions, within us, not merely lowers the claims of one or both parties, and permits neither to come to quite free self-realization, but also threatens the unity, the equilibrium, and the total energy of the soul as a whole—this feeling may in many cases repress conflict from the beginning. In case the feeling cannot avail to that extent, it, on the contrary, impresses upon the conflict a character of bitterness and desperation, an emphasis as though a struggle were really taking place for something much more essential than the immediate issue of the controversy. The energy with which each of these tendencies seeks to subdue the others is nourished not only by their egoistic interest, so to speak, but by the interest which goes much farther than that and attaches itself to the unity of the ego, for which this struggle means dismemberment and destruction, if it does not end with a victory for unity. Accordingly, struggle within a closely integrated group often enough grows beyond the measure which its object and its immediate interest for the parties could justify. The feeling accumulates that this struggle is an affair, not merely of the party, but of the group as a whole; that each party must hate in its opponent, not its opponent merely, but at the same time the enemy of its higher sociological unity.

Finally there is an apparently quite individual fact, which in reality is sociologically very significant, and which may unite the most extreme intensity of antagonistic excitement to closeness of personal association. This fact is jealousy, the universal significance of which it is now worthwhile to formulate. Our ordinary use of language is not unequivocal in dealing with this conception. We frequently fail to distinguish jealousy from envy. Both sentiments are undoubtedly of the widest significance for the molding of human relationships. With both there comes into question an object of value which a third party either actually or symbolically hinders us in attaining or controlling. When it is a case of attaining, we may more properly speak of envy; if it is a matter of retaining, jealousy is the passion involved. In this case, of course, the definitive division of the goods is quite insignificant, and only the discrimination of the psychosociological procedures is of importance. It is peculiar to the passion called jealousy that the subject claims to have a claim to the possession in question, while envy is concerned, not with the claim, but simply with the desirability of the withheld object. In the case of envy it is a matter of indifference whether the object is withheld because the third party possesses it, or whether even loss or renunciation of the object on the part of this third party would still fail to put the envious person in possession of it. Jealousy, on the contrary, is directly determined in its subjective direction and shading by the fact that the possession is withheld from it, *because* it is in the hands of a third party, and with the removal of this situation the desired object would at once come into our possession. The susceptibility of the envious turns rather upon the thing to be possessed, than of the jealous upon the possessor. One may envy another his fame, even when there is not the slightest claim to fame on the part of the envier. We are jealous of another when we are of the opinion that he enjoys a fame which we deserve as much or more than he. Jealousy is a feeling of a type and strength so specific that it may arise out of any sort of exceptional psychic combination. That which embitters and gnaws the jealous is a certain fiction of feeling, however unreasonable it may be, that the object of the jealousy has, so to speak, robbed him of the fame. In a certain degree midway between the phenomena of envy and of jealousy stands a third feeling, belonging in the same scale, which we may call disfavor—the envious desire for the object, not because it is in itself especially desirable for the subject, but only because the other possesses it. The passionate form of this feeling prefers rather to forego the object, or even to destroy it, rather than to have it in the possession of the other person. These variously specialized forms of disfavor run through the reciprocal attitudes of people in countless ways. The vast problem area, throughout which the relationships of people to things appear as the causes or the effects of their relationships to each other, is in very large measure covered by this type of affections. In the case of these factors the issue is not merely that money or power, love or social position, is desired, so that competition, or any other surpassing or eliminating of a person, is a mere technique in its essential meaning, not other than the surmounting of a physical difficulty. Rather do the accompanying feelings which attach themselves to such a merely external and secondary relationship of persons grow in these modifications of disfavor to independent sociological forms which merely have their content in the desire for the objects. This is confirmed by the circumstance that the last-mentioned steps of the series have completely canceled the interest for the objective content in question, and have retained it merely as material in and of itself quite indifferent, with reference to which the personal relationship is crystallized.

On this general basis is to be found the significance which jealousy has for our particular problem, that is, especially when the content of the jealousy is a person or the relationship of a subject to a person. It appears to me, furthermore, as though verbal usage does not recognize jealousy on account of a purely impersonal object. What we are now concerned with is the relationship between the jealous person and the person on whose account the jealousy is aroused toward a third person. The relationship to this third person has quite another, much less peculiar and complicated, sociological form. For toward this third person there arise scorn and hatred, contempt and cruelty, on the stimulus of the presupposition of reciprocal relationship, that is, of an external or internal, actual or supposed, claim to love, friendship, recognition, or consensus of some sort or other. In this case the tension of antagonism, whether reciprocal or one-sided, becomes the stronger and more comprehensive, the more un-limited the unity is from which it proceeds, and the more passionately its conquest is sought. If the consciousness of the jealous person often seems to vibrate between love and hate, this means that these two strata, of which the second is built upon the first over its whole extension, in turn gain the pre-ponderance in consciousness. Very important is the limitation suggested above; namely, the *right* which one claims to the psychical or physical possession, to the love or the respect, of the person who is the object of the jealousy. A man may *envy* another the possession of a woman; he only is jealous, how-ever, who has some sort of a *claim* to the possession of her. This claim may, to be sure, consist in the mere passion of the desire. From this to derive a claim is a very general touch of human nature. The child excuses himself for disobeying a command with the formula with reference to the forbidden thing, "I wanted it so much." The adulterer, supposing him to possess any trace of conscience at all, could not claim the right of meeting the aggrieved husband in a duel, if he did not see in his love for the wife a right which he might so defend against the mere legal right of the husband. Since everywhere mere possession counts as right to the possession, so even the approach, desire, grows into the character of such a right, and the equivocal sense of the term "claim," namely, as simple desire and as rightfully founded desire, points to the fact that will is strongly inclined to attribute to the right of its might the might of a right. To be sure, jealousy often comes to the most pitiable tragedy on account of this assump-tion. To justify rights on the basis of feelings like love and friendship is an attempt with quite inappropriate means. The level on which one may reach out from the basis of a right in no way coincides with the plane in which these feelings lie. To imagine that one can conquer them with a bare right, however deep and well won this may be in other directions, is senseless. It is as though one would order back into its cage the flown bird that is long since beyond sight and hearing. This inconsequence of the right to love produces the phe-nomena which so characterize jealousy. It insists finally on the external evidences of the desired feeling. These may be con-strained, to be sure, by appeal to the sense of duty. Such pitiful satisfaction and self-deception preserve the body of the relationship as though there still remained in it something of its spirit.

The claim which belongs with jealousy is as such often

enough recognized from the other side. It signifies or it produces, like every right between persons, a sort of unity. It is
the ideal or legal existence of an obligation, of a positive relationship of some sort or other, at least of the subjective anticipation of such relationship. Upon the so existing and further
operating unity, there arises now at the same time its negation, which creates the situation for jealousy. In this case it is
not the fact, as with many other reactions between unity and
antagonism, that the two have their reference to different territories, and are only held together or in opposition by the
total compass of the personalities. On the contrary, precisely
that unity which consists in some real or ideal form, or which
at least is on the one side thought of as so existing, is denied.
The feeling of jealousy interposes its quite unique, blinding,
uncompromising embitterment between the persons, because
the separating factor between them has taken possession of
precisely the point of their unification. Consequently the tension between them lends to the negative factor the utmost
possible intensity and force. From this fact, that this formal
sociological relationship dominates entirely the inner situation, we may explain the further fact, namely, the remarkable
and really altogether unlimited extent of the motives by
which jealousy may be nourished, and the frequent senseless-
ness of its manifestations. In case the structure of the relationship is either from the beginning built upon such a synthesis of synthesis and antithesis, or in case the soul of the
one party presents this structure within its own disposition,
every occasion whatsoever will produce the consequences of
the situation, and the easier the oftener this previous disposition has been in actual operation, because in this case, in the
relationship of the individuals, common destiny and antagonism revolve around one and the same point; consciousness
of the tension seems to be reciprocally aroused upon the most
inadequate material stimulus so soon as the fatal relationship
is once joined. That every human act and word is susceptible
of various interpretations, as to its purpose and motive, gives
to jealousy which will see everywhere only one interpretation
a perfectly complacent tool. Inasmuch as jealousy can associate the most passionate hatred with the contemporary persistence of the most passionate love, and can demand the
continuance of the most intimate common destiny at the cost
of the annihilation of both parties (for the relationship destroys the jealous person just as it stimulates him to the
destruction of his rival), jealousy is perhaps that sociological

phenomenon in which the erection of antagonism above unity reaches subjectively its most radical form.

II

Our discussion thus far has found evidence among the parties in conflict of many kinds of unification; minglings of antithesis and synthesis; the erection of the one above the other; reciprocal limitations as well as promotions. Parallel with this is to be found the further sociological significance of struggle; namely, the influence which it exercises, not upon the relation of the parties to each other, but rather upon the inner structure of each party. Daily experience shows how easily a conflict between two individuals changes the individual himself. Entirely apart from its distorting or purifying, weakening or strengthening, consequences for the individual, the change occurs through the preliminary conditions which struggle imposes. There must be inner alterations and adaptations demanded by the exigencies of conflict. The German language affords a peculiarly apposite and simple formula for these immanent alterations. The champion must "pull himself together" [*sich zusammennehmen*], that is, all his energies must be concentrated upon a single point at once, in order that at any moment they may be exerted in the direction demanded. In peace he may allow himself more latitude [*sich gehen lassen*, "let himself go"] that is, he may indulge the individual energy and interests of his nature which may take courses in various directions and somewhat independently of each other. In times of attack and defense, however, the consequence of this indulgence would be a waste of energy through counterefforts of the different impulses, and a loss of time through the necessity of assembling and organizing them in each instance. In such cases, therefore, the whole man must assume the form of concentration as his essential line of battle and means of defense. Conduct formally the same is demanded in the like situation of the group. This necessity of centralization, of energetic mobilization of all the elements, which alone guarantees their utilization for all possible demands without dissipation of strength and time, is a necessity so matter-of-course in a case of conflict that, as a whole, it calls for no discussion. The familiar reaction between despotic constitution and martial tendencies in a group rests upon this formal ground; war demands the centralized energizing of the group form, which despotism most easily guarantees. And on the other hand, if this has once taken place, the energies thus bound together and consolidated with each other strive very easily for the most natural discharge—for a foreign war. An illustration of this correlation may be cited from its opposite, on account of its characteristic precision. The Eskimos of Greenland are one of the anarchistic peoples; no sort of chieftainship exists among them. In fishing they are inclined, to be sure, to follow to some extent the most experienced man, but he possesses no sort of authority, and against one who separates himself from the community undertaking there is no means of constraint. Now, it is said of these people that the only way in which quarrels are fought out among them is by a singing duel. If one of them believes himself to have been injured by another, he composes some satirical verses and produces them in a popular gathering drawn together solely for this purpose. Thereupon the opponent answers in similar fashion. Accordingly, the absolute absence of all warlike instinct and the equally absolute absence of all political centralization correspond with each other. Among the organizations of the aggregate group, therefore, that of the army is always the most centralized, with perhaps the single exception of the fire guard, which encounters necessities absolutely the same in form. In such organization, through the unlimited command of the central authority, every independent movement of the elements is excluded, and therefore the impulse which proceeds from this source of command realizes itself without any dynamic loss in the movement of the whole. That which characterizes a federated state as such is its unity as a war-making power. In all other particulars each state may retain its independence; in its military system this is impossible, if a federated relationship is to exist at all. The perfectly federated state has, therefore, been described as the one which in its relation to other states—essentially in its military relation—constitutes an absolute unity, while its members in their relationship to each other possess complete independence.

In view of the incomparable utility of a unified organization for the purpose of war, it would be supposed that each party would have the utmost interest in the absence of that unity in the opposing party. Yet there are certain cases of the opposite. The form of the centralization into which the military situation forces the party grows beyond the party itself, and gives to this party occasion to prefer that the opponent should present himself in this form. In the struggles of recent decades between laborers and employers this has been most unmistakably the case. The Royal Labor Commission in England reached the conclusion, in 1894, that firm organization of laborers was favorable for the employers in an industry, and in like manner organization of employers for the laborers. This is for the reason that, although outbreaking struggle might reach large extension and duration, yet this is nevertheless for both parties more advantageous and more economical than many local quarrels, losses of labor, and petty conflicts which, in the absence of a firm organization for the parties, never ceased. This is parallel with a war between modern states, however destructive and expensive it may be. It still presents a more favorable balance than the incessant petty struggles and frictions in periods in which the governments were weaker and less centralized. In Germany also the laborers have recognized that a close and effective organization of the employers, precisely for the purpose of fighting out conflicts of interest, is entirely to the advantage of the laborers themselves; for only an organization of that sort can furnish representatives with whom one can treat with full security. Only in dealings with such an organization are the workmen in the given case sure that the result reached will not be at once jeopardized by the independent operators. The disadvantage which a party suffers through the unified organization of its opponent—because this organization is an advantage for the opponent—is in the foregoing cases far outweighed by the fact that under such constitution of both parties the struggle itself may be one that is concentrated, entirely within the field of vision, and capable of being brought to a conclusion that can assure a permanent and general peace. On the other hand, when one opposes a diffused crowd of enemies, one may oftener gain isolated victories, but it is very hard to arrive at decisive results which definitely fix the relationships of the contestants. This case is so profoundly instructive with reference to the fundamental interdependence between the unitary form and the aggressive action of the group because it exhibits the utility of this interdependence to the extent that it triumphs even over the immediate disadvantage in opposing a given enemy. The case exhibits that centripetalism as the objectively ideal form of aggressive constitution which in the surest and shortest way brings the essential issues of struggle face to face. This teleology extends alike over the parties and allows each individual party, finally, to find its advantage in it. It realizes the apparent paradox of enabling each opponent to see the advantage of his enemy as his own advantage.

For the sociological significance of the formation there is an essential difference whether the group as a whole enters into an antagonistic relationship to an external group, and, as a consequence, that concentration of its parts and increase of its unity of which we have been speaking occurs in consciousness and in action; or whether each element of a numerous body has an enemy for itself, and because this enemy is the same for all, a coalition of all ensues on that account—whether the individuals had previously been entirely independent of each other, or whether now at least new formations come into existence between them. The first case demands this further specification, that the quarrel or war of a group, on the one hand, may disregard many sorts of incidental discrepancies and individual enmities, and, on the other hand, may bring the relationships within the group very frequently to a clearness and definiteness otherwise never to be reached. This will be especially observed in groups of moderate size, and those which may not yet have attained objective existence, in contrast perhaps with a modern state. When a political party which unites many sorts of interests finds itself forced into a very definite and one-sided antagonism, this becomes at once an opportunity for secession. At such moments the only alternatives are, either to forget the inner antitheses or by exclusion of certain members to bring the interests involved to sharper expression. If a family contains individuals of strong but latent dissimilarity, the moment in which a danger or an attack demands of it the most possible coherence will be precisely the moment which assures its unity for a long time or which destroys it forever. Such a crisis will decide with precision how far a cooperation of such personalities is possible. If a school class has on hand a trick on the teacher or a fight with another class, this usually, to be sure, brings on the one side, all sorts of enmities to silence; on the other side, however, it stimulates certain pupils to separate themselves from the rest, not merely from motives material to the question, but because they are not willing to be led by the same string with this or that other pupil with whom, in other respects, they cooperate without further thought in the class structure but with whom they are unwilling to be drawn into closer union for such decided attacks. In short, the state of peace within the group permits antagonistic elements to live side by side in a somewhat undecided situation, because each may go his own way and may avoid collisions. The state of conflict, however, draws the elements so closely together, and subjects them to such a unified impulse, that they either tolerate each other with perfect reciprocity or they must completely repel each other. On this account foreign war, in the case of a state split by internal antitheses, is often the ultimate means of overcoming the same. It also happens that the foreign war may, however, give occasion for fatal developments of these antipathies.

Hence groups which find themselves in any sort of war are not tolerant. They cannot endure individual departures from the unity of the correlating principle beyond a certain definitely limited latitude. The technique for this purpose is sometimes an apparent tolerance, exercised, however, in order the more surely to exclude the elements which cannot be definitively brought into the general order. The Catholic Church, for instance, has from the beginning of its power found itself in a dual warfare. On the one hand, it has been opposed to the whole complex of involved philosophical opinions which together have constituted heresy; on the other hand, it has encountered the actual life interests and powers holding parallel competence and demanding some sort of dominion independent of the church. The compact unity of form which under these circumstances the church needed has been secured in this way: dissenters have been treated so long as possible as though belonging within the church. From the moment, however, that this was no longer possible, they have been thrust out of the church with an incomparable energy. For a structure of this sort a certain elasticity of its outward form is extremely important; not in order to facilitate transition and accommodation with the antagonistic powers, but rather, precisely for the sake of opposing them with the utmost vigor without sacrificing any still available elements. The elasticity is not in stretching out beyond the proper boundary. The latter, rather, circumscribes in this case the elastic body quite as unequivocally as it can bound a rigid one. This roominess characterizes, for example, the monastic orders through which the mystical or fanatical impulses that emerge in all religions in this case have expressed themselves in a way that has been harmless to the church and quite subordinate to it. On the contrary, in Protestantism, with its sometimes more intense dogmatic intolerance, the same factors have led to schism and disintegration. Sociological attitudes which specifically concern women seem to run back to the same motive. Among the highly manifold elements out of which the aggregate relationships between men and women are formed there occurs also a typical enmity springing from the two sources, first, that the women as the physically weaker are always in danger of economic and personal exploitation,[6] and, second, that women, as the objects of sensuous desire on the part of men, must hold themselves on the defensive. While this immanent and personal struggle, by which the history of the human race is filled, seldom comes to an immediate cooperation of women against men, yet there is a superpersonal form which serves as a protection against both dangers, and in which, consequently, the female sex is, so to speak, *in corpore* interested: morality (*die Sitte*). The strong personality is able to protect itself against encroachments, or at most requires the protection of the law. The weak, on the other hand, would be lost in spite of this support if the individuals who were superior in strength did not for some reason forego the exercise of this superiority. This occurs in part through morality. Since, however, this has no other executive than the conscience of the individual, it works insecurely enough and requires the reinforcement of the moral code. The latter has not, to be sure, the precision and sanction of the legal norm, yet it has a certain guarantee of observance through instinctive shame and through many perceptibly disagreeable consequences of transgression. The moral code is then the proper protection of the weak, who would go to the wall so soon as the struggle of individuals should break out unchecked by any restraint upon force. The character of this agency is consequently in essence that of prohibition, of restriction. It brings about a certain equality between the weak and the strong. It goes so far in its restraint of the purely natural relation between the two that it may even give the advantage to the weak, as, for example, chivalry shows. That in the insinuating encounter between men and women the former are the stronger, and the assailants, forces the latter under the protection of the moral code; it makes them the chosen—through their own interests chosen—guardians of the same. It follows that they are naturally, for

[6] I am here speaking of the relation as it has existed in the far largest part of known history, and I waive the question whether a change in the relation in the future is to be brought about through the modern development of the rights and powers of women, or whether the change is already partially accomplished.

themselves also, committed to severe observance of the whole complex of moral prescriptions, and not merely in cases which concern masculine excesses. All the standards of morality are in a condition of solidarity with each other. Violation of a single one weakens the principle, and consequently every other. It follows that women in this connection hold unreservedly together. Here a real unity actually corresponds with the peculiarly ideal one in which men conceptualize them when they speak of "the women" in general, and which has quite the character of a partisan antithesis. This solidarity which they have in contrast with the men, and which is expressed in the lines of Freidank—

> Der Mann trägt seine Schmach allein;
> Doch kommt ein Weib zu Falle,
> So schilt man auf sie alle—

this solidarity of sex has in its interest for morality, as its common means of struggle, a real vehicle. Consequently, there is repeated here again the sociological form which we have been discussing. Women recognize, as a rule, with reference to another woman, only complete inclusion or complete exclusion from the realm of morality. There exists among them the tendency so far as possible not to concede a breach of morality by a woman—to interpret it as harmless, except where love of scandal and other individual motives work in the other direction. If this assumption, however, is no longer possible, they render an irrevocable and severe judgment of exclusion from good society. If the violation of morality must be confessed, the culprit is also eliminated radically from that unity which is held together by the common interest for morality. We have seen, therefore, that women have sometimes passed the same condemnation upon Gretchen as upon Marguérite Gauthier, upon Stella as upon Messalina. Thus, by negation of differences in degree, they have made impossible an intermediation between those within and those outside the boundaries of morality. The defensive situation of women does not permit that the wall of morality be lowered at even a single point. Their party knows, in principle at least, no compromise, but only decisive acceptance of the individual into the ideal totality of "respectable women," or the equally decisive exclusion—an alternative whose abruptness cannot by any means be justified from the purely moral standpoint. It is only intelligible when understood in connection with the above-considered demand for inviolable unity, occasioned by the need of a party firmly consolidated against an opponent.

For the same reasons it may be advantageous for political parties to suffer even the diminution of their numbers, so soon as such change would remove elements inclined to mediation and compromise. In order that this procedure should be indicated, two conditions should usually coincide: in the first place, there should be a condition of acute conflict; in the second place, the struggling group should be relatively small. The type is the minority party, and in particular in cases in which it does not limit itself to defensive action. English parliamentary history has furnished many illustrations. In 1793, for instance, the Whig party was already greatly depleted, yet it operated as a renewal of strength when another defection of all the still somewhat mediating and irresolute elements occurred. The few remaining very resolute members could then pursue a quite coherent and radical policy. The majority group does not need to insist upon such certainty of acquiescence or opposition. Vacillating and equivocal adherents are less dangerous to it, because its greater extent can edure such phenomena at the periphery without suffering any serious effect at the center. In cases of more restricted groups, where center and circumference are not far apart, every insecurity with reference to a member at once threatens the nucleus, and therewith the coherence of the whole. On account of the limited span between the elements, there is lacking that elasticity of the group which in this case is the limit of tolerance.

Consequently groups, and especially minorities, that exist in struggle and persecution, frequently rebuff approaches and tolerance from the other side, because otherwise the solidity of their opposition would disappear, and without this they could not further struggle. This, for example, has occurred more than once in the struggles over creeds in England. Both under James II. and William and Mary the nonconformists, independents, Baptists, Quakers, repeatedly experienced attempted approaches on the part of government, which they met with no sort of response. Otherwise the possibility would have been offered to the more yielding and irresolute elements among them, and the temptation would have been furnished to build compromise parties, or at least to have modified their opposition. Every concession on the part of the government, *provided it is only partial,* threatens that uniformity in the opposition of all the members, and therewith that unity of coherence, upon which a struggling minority must uncompromisingly insist. Accordingly, the unity of groups so frequently disappears if they have no more enemies. This has often been pointed out from various directions in the case of Protestantism. Just because the protest was essential to Protestantism, the moment the opponent against whom it protested passed out of the range of active struggle, it lost its energy or its inner unity; this latter in such a degree, indeed, that in such circumstances Protestantism repeated the conflict with the enemy in its own camp, and divided itself into a liberal and an orthodox party. The same thing has occurred in the party history of the United States. More than once the complete inferiority of one of the great parties has had as a consequence the dissolution of the other in minor groups with party antipathies of their own. Moreover, it is by no means promotive of the unity of Protestantism that it has really no heretics. On the other hand, the consciousness of unity in the Catholic Church is decidedly strengthened by the fact of heresy and by its hostile attitude toward the same. The various elements of the church have always been able to orient themselves by the implacability of the antithesis with heresy, and in spite of many a centrifugal interest they have been by this fact able to preserve consciousness of unity. Hence the complete victory of a group over its enemies is not always fortunate in the sociological sense, for the consequence may be a decline of the energy which guarantees the coherence of the group, and, on the other hand, proportional activity of the disintegrating forces that are always at work. The fall of the Romano-Latin empire in the fifth century has been explained by the fact that the common enemies were all subdued. Perhaps its basis—namely, protection on the one side, and devotion on the other—had for a period been no longer of a natural sort; but this came to light only after there was no longer any common enemy to offset the essential contradictions in the structure. Indeed, it may be actual political sagacity within many a group to provide for enemies in order that the unity of the elements may remain active and conscious as the vital interest.

The example last cited leads to the following additional emphasis upon the meaning of struggle as a means of cohesion in the group: namely, through struggle not merely an existing unity concentrates itself more energetically, and excludes radically all elements which might tend to erase the sharp boundary distinctions against the enemy, but further struggle brings persons and groups that otherwise had nothing to do with each other into a coalition. The energy with which struggle operates in this direction will perhaps be most distinctly visible from the fact that the relationship between the two parties is strong enough to operate also in the reverse direction. Psychological associations in general display their strength in the fact that they are also retroactive. If, for example, a given personality is represented under the concept "hero," the connection between the two conceptions proves itself to be the strongest if it becomes impossible to think the notion "hero" in general without reproducing the image of that particular personality. In the same way, the combination for the purpose of struggle is a procedure so often experienced that frequently the mere combination of elements, even if it is not formed for any aggressive or other competitive purposes, seems to other groups to be a threatening or unfriendly act. The despotism of the modern state directed itself primarily against the mediæval conception of unity. At last every association, as such, between cities, ranks, nobles, or any other elements in the state, counted in the eyes of the government as a rebellion, as a latent struggle against itself. For instance, in Moravia an ordinance of 1628 provided: "Accordingly federations or coalitions, for whatever purpose, or against whomsoever directed, are the prerogative of no one else except the king." For the particular tendencies now in question historical instances are so close at hand that it would be superfluous to make any further inquiry, except as to the degree of unification which is feasible in this particular way. In the forefront must be placed the establishment of the unified state. France owes the consciousness of its national unity essentially to struggle against the English; the Moorish war was the means of converting the Spanish subdivisions into one community. The next lower grade is marked by the confederacies and leagues of states in the order of their coherence, and of the power of their central administration in manifold gradations. The United States required its War of the Rebellion, Switzerland its struggle against Austria, the Low Countries their uprising against Spain, the Achean League its war against Macedonia; and the founding of the new German Empire furnishes a parallel instance. In all these cases the characteristic element is that the unity came into being through the struggle and for the purposes of the same, to be sure; but, over and above the struggle, this unity persists, and develops ulterior interests and combinations, that have no connection with the warlike purpose. The significance of the struggle is in these cases virtually that it is only the reagent to set the latent relationship and unity into activity; it is thus much more the occasioning cause of essentially demanded unifications than their purpose. It is the latter, at the most, in the first moment. In the degree in which the unification is grounded in some necessity other than essential needs—that is, not in the immanent qualities and affinities of the elements—in precisely that degree does the meaning of the unity reduce, of course, to the militant purpose, as the externally exploited aim, which remains the irreducible element of the collectivity. However particularistic the component parts of a confederated state or a confederation of states may be, however small may be the proportion of their individual rights and liberties which they concede to the federation, they usually transfer to it at least the prerogative of waging war. This is the *pièce de résistance* of coherence; if this should fall away, the atoms would have to assume again their completely isolated life. *Within* the collective struggle-interest there is, to be sure, a still further gradation, namely, whether the unification for purposes of struggle is offensive and defensive, or only for defensive purposes. The latter is probably the case with the majority of coalitions between already existing groups, especially between numerous groups or those that are very different from each other. The defensive purpose is the collectivistic minimum, because for each particular group, and for each individual, it is the most inevitable form of the instinct of self-preservation. The more various the elements are which unite, the smaller is the visible number of the interests in which they coincide; and in the extreme case it reduces to the primitive impulse, namely, the ultimate instinct of self-preservation. In reply to expressions of anxiety on the part of the employers over the possible unification of all English trade organizations, one of their most ardent adherents asserted that even if it should go so far, it could be exclusively for defensive purposes alone.

Among the cases in which the solidifying effect of struggle is projected beyond the moment and the immediate purpose, which may occur in the case of the above-discussed minimum of the same, the extension again sinks to the cases in which the unification actually occurs only *ad hoc*. Here two types are to be distinguished, namely: the federated unification for a single action, which, however, frequently involves the total energies of the elements, as in the case of actual wars. In this case an unlimited unity is formed, which, however, after attaining, or failure in attaining, the definite purpose, releases the parties again for their previous separate existence, as, for instance, in the case of the Greeks, after the removal of the Persian danger. In the case of the other type the unity is less complete, but also less transient. The grouping takes place around a purpose which is less a matter of time than of content, and which occasions no disturbance of the other sides of the elements. Thus in England since 1873 there exists a federation of associated employers of labor, founded to antagonize the influence of the trade unions. In the same way, several years later, a combination of employers as such was formed in the United States, without reference to the various branches of business, in order, as a whole, to put an end to strikes. The character of both types appears, of course, most evidently when the elements of the struggling unity are, in other periods or in other relationships, not merely indifferent, but even hostile to each other. The unifying power of the struggle principle never shows itself stronger than when it produces a temporal or actual consensus out of relationships of competition or animosity.

The antithesis between violent antagonism and momentary comradeship in struggle may, under particular circumstances, reach such refinement that, for the parties concerned, the very absoluteness of their enmity may constitute the direct cause of their coalition. The opposition in the English Parliament has sometimes been constituted in the following manner: The ultras of the ministerial party were not satisfied by the administration, and they joined as a party with those who were their opponents on principle. This combination was held together by the common element of hostility to the ministry. For instance, the ultra-Whigs under Pulteney united with the high Tories against Robert Walpole. Thus the very radicalism of the principle which was nourished on hostility against the Tories fused its adherents with the latter. If they had not been so extremely anti-Tory, they would not have combined with the Tories in order to secure the fall of the Whig ministry which was not sufficiently Whiggish for them. This case is so vivid because the common enemy led individuals who were otherwise enemies to the point where he, in the view of each, seemed to stand too much on the side of the other. Further than this, the case is still only the clearest example of the vulgar experience that even the most bitter enmities do not hinder coalition, so soon as it may have a bearing upon a common enemy.

Finally, the lowest step in this scale, its least acute form, consists of those coalitions which are merely formed by a common tone of feeling (*Stimmung*). That is, in this case there is consciousness of belonging together only insofar as there is a similar aversion or a similar practical interest against a third; but this need not lead to a concerted struggle. In this case also we must distinguish two types. Concentrated industry, which has placed masses of laborers in opposition to a few employers has, as we know, not merely brought into existence separate coalitions of the former for struggle over the conditions of labor, but another consequence has been the quite general feeling that all wage laborers in some way belong together, because they are all in the struggle which is radically one against the employing class. This opinion crystallizes, to be sure, at certain points in distinct actions in the way of organizing political parties, or of wage struggle. Yet, as a whole, this feeling cannot, by reason of its very nature, become practical. It remains the feeling of an abstract principle of community, namely, that of common hostility against an abstract enemy. While in the former case the feeling of unity is abstract, but persistent, in the second case it is concrete, but temporary. This second case occurs, for instance, when strangers who, however, belong in the same plane of culture or the same sphere of sympathy, find themselves together in company, say in a railroad car or elsewhere, with other persons of uncouth and vulgar manners. Without any outbreak or scene, without any interchange of word or look, the former have certain awareness of themselves as a party joined by common aversion against what may be regarded as, at least in the ideal sense, the aggressive vulgarity of the others. Through its highly refined and sensitive character, with accompanying unequivocalness, this unification completes the structural grades of those who are brought from the condition of completely alien elements through the community of hostility. In case the synthetic energy of the latter is not in question, so far as the number of points of interest are concerned, but with reference to the permanence and intensity of the coalition, it is an especially favorable circumstance if, instead of actual struggle, permanent threatening by an enemy is present. From the first days of the Achean League, that is, about 270, it was emphasized that Achaia was surrounded by enemies, who all, however, for the time being were otherwise occupied than with attack upon Achaia. Such a period of danger which constantly threatened, but which was as constantly postponed, is said to have been especially favorable for the strengthening of the feeling of unity. This is a case of the unique type that a certain *distance* between the elements that are to be united, on the one hand, and the point and interest that unites them, on the other hand, is an especially favorable combination for the union. This is particularly the case when somewhat extended circles are concerned. This is true of religious relationships. In contrast with the tribal and national deities, the God of Christianity, who is equally related to all the world, is immeasurably removed from the faithful. He lacks entirely those traits which are attributed to the special divinities. On the other hand, for that very reason, he can unite the most heterogeneous peoples and personalities in an unprecedented religious community. Still further, the costume characterizes always distinct social strata as belonging together; and it often appears to fulfill this social function best when it is an imported costume. To dress as they dress in Paris signifies a close and exclusive community with a certain social stratum in other lands. The prophet Zephaniah spoke already of the superior classes, which as such wore foreign garments. The very manifold meanings which the notion of "distance" covers have still many sorts of psychological relationship. An image the object of which is presented as in any way "distant" appears to work in a certain degree more impersonally, the individual reaction which follows from immediate vicinity and contact is thereby less intense, it bears a less immediately subjective character, and may consequently be the same for a greater number of individuals. Just as the general notion which comprehends a number of particulars is the more abstract, that is, the more widely distant from each of these separate particulars, the more numerous and the more unlike each other the latter are, so also a social point of unification appears to exercise specifically consolidating and comprehensive influences, if it is somewhat widely removed from the elements to be combined. This interval may be also both spatial and of other sorts. Such unifications in consequence of a danger which, however, has rather a chronic than an acute character, through a struggle that is not fought out, but always latent, will be most effective in cases where a permanent unification of elements that are in some way antithetical is in question. This was the situation in the case of the Achean League to which I have already referred. Accordingly, Montesquieu observed that "while peace and confidence make the glory and the security of the monarchy, a republic needs to be in fear of somebody." Obviously the basis for this assertion is an undefined consciousness of the before-mentioned constellation. The monarchy as such takes care for the cohesion of elements in any wise antagonistic. Where these elements, however, have no one above them who brings them into unity, but possesses relative sovereignty, they will easily fall apart if not common sense of danger forces them together—a danger which evidently is not presented as a struggle already in existence, but as a permanent threat of such a struggle which exerts a constant menace.

While it is more a question of degree, the principle of connection between the coherence of the collectivity and hostility calls for the following addition: Aggressive enterprises tend much more than peaceful ones to draw into cooperation, from their very beginnings, the largest possible number of elements which are otherwise unrelated, and which would not of themselves have begun the undertaking. In the case of peaceful actions, it is the rule, on the whole, to be confined to those who in other respects are somewhat nearly associated. But for "allies," to which notion verbal usage has already imparted a martial coloring, one selects often enough elements with which one has scarcely anything in common, nor even wishes to have. Reasons for this fact are, in the first place, that war, and not merely the political type, frequently represents a case of desperation in which in selecting reinforcements one may not be finical. In the second place, the situation in question is likely to occur if the object of the action lies outside the territory or other immediate interest sphere of the allies, so that they may return after the end of the struggle to their former distance. In the third place, the gain to be made by struggle, although a precarious one, nevertheless under favorable circumstances is likely to be especially rapid and intensive, and consequently exercises upon certain natures a formal attraction which it is possible for peaceful enterprises to exert only through their content. In the fourth place, the struggle causes the essentially personal in the parties in conflict to take a position of relative insignificance, and thereby permits the unification of elements that are otherwise heterogeneous. There comes finally, in addition, the motive that hostilities are easily aroused on both sides. Even within one and the same group, if it maintains a feud with another, all sorts of hidden or half-forgotten enmities of the individual against individuals in the other group come to expression. Accordingly, struggle between two groups within a third group usually evokes in this third group all the malice and resentment against one of them which of themselves would not have come to expression; but now, while the other hostility has led the way, they are occasioned as a sort of annex to the operation of this instigating hostility. It is quite in accordance with this trait that, especially in earlier times, the unifying relationships of populations as wholes to each other were martial only, while the other assimilations, like commerce, hospitality, intermarriage, were relationships which affected merely the intercourse of individuals. Understandings between the peoples made these relationships possible, to be sure, but did not of themselves put them into effect.

III

IF an evolution occurs in the form of incessant rhythmical reaction of two periods, the one equally legitimate with the other, and attaining its proper meaning only in relationship and antithesis with the other, the image that we present to ourselves of such a procedure seldom reproduces its objective equilibrium and the persistent level upon which the one element always relieves the other. Almost inevitably, however, on the other hand, we give to the reaction between them a kind of teleological accent, so that the one element always counts as the point of departure, the essential premise out of which the other develops, while the transition in the opposite direction appears to be a retrogression. Assuming, for example, that the world process is a perpetual reaction between qualitative homogeneity of combined masses of matter, and differentiated hetrogeneity of the same matter; supposing also that we are convinced that one of these conditions always proceeds from the other, and then again the derived condition passes into another form of the primary condition; nevertheless, as our thought categories always function, we still regard the condition of homogeneity as first; that is, our demand for explanation requires much more the derivation of manifoldness from unity than the reverse, although it would perhaps be much more correct to assume neither of the two as the first, but to posit an unending rhythm, in which we can make no halt at any calculable stage, but must rather assume the stage as one derived from an earlier condition. The same thing is true of the principles of rest and motion. Although,

in the whole of nature as well as in its particular details, the
two constantly relieve each other, yet we are in the habit of
assuming that the condition of rest is original, or at least a
definitive condition which, so to speak, calls for no derivation.
Accordingly, inasmuch as we contemplate together a pair
of periods, the one always seems to be explanatory or needing
explanation; and only as we place them in this subordination
of rank do we seem to ourselves to have seized upon the
meaning of their reaction. With their mere reaction as the
phenomena present it, and which in itself designates neither
of the component elements as the primary and neither as the
secondary, we are not satisfied. Distinctions of difference of
value and of purpose are so much a part of the tendencies of
the human mind that we cannot refrain from representing to
ourselves the unbroken flow of alternating periods through
such distinctions as those just referred to, and from expressing
them at the same time under the forms of ruling and serving,
or of preparation and fulfillment, or of provisional and definitive situation. The same relationship may be asserted of
struggle and peace. Both in the serial and in the contemporary aspect of social life these conditions are so interwoven
that in every peaceful situation the conditions for future conflict, and in every struggle the conditions for future peace,
are developing. If we follow the stages of social development
backward under these categories, we can find no stopping
place. In historical reality each condition always has the other
as its corollary. Nevertheless, we always feel an essential
difference in the significance of the different members of this
series. Struggle seems to be the preliminary, the purpose of
which resides in the fact and in the contents of peace. While
the rhythm between the two elements, objectively considered,
plays its role upon a single level, our estimate of value constructs at the same time iambic periods out of the process,
with struggle as the thesis and with peace as the arsis. Thus
in the most ancient constitution of Rome, the king must first
appeal to the citizens for their consent if he wished to begin
a war, but he did not need this consent when it was a question of peace. In the latter case the consent is assumed as a
matter of course.

It is obvious that the transition from war to peace must
present a more considerable problem than the reverse. The
latter needs really no particular scrutiny. For the situations
within the condition of peace out of which struggle emerges
are themselves already struggle in diffuse, unobserved or latent

form. For instance, if the economic advantage which the southern states of the American Union had over the northern states before the Civil War, as a consequence of the slave system, was also the reason for this war, yet so long as no out-breaking antagonism arises, but there is nearly an imminent condition of the one portion of the nation as against another condition in another portion, this reason for conflict remains outside the specific question of war and peace. At the moment, however, in which the situation began to assume a color which meant war, this itself was an accumulation of antago-nisms; of hatred, feelings, newspaper arguments, frictions be-tween private persons, and on the borders, reciprocal moral equivocations in matters outside the central antithesis. The end of peace is thus not distinguished by a special sociological situation, but rather out of some sort of real relationships within a peaceful condition antagonism is developed im-mediately, if not at once in its most visible and energetic form. The case is different, however, in the reverse direction. Peace does not attach itself so immediately to struggle. The termination of strife is a special undertaking which belongs neither in the one category nor in the other, like a bridge which is of a different nature from that of either bank which it unites. The sociology of struggle demands, therefore, at least as an appendix, an analysis of the forms in which struggle comes to an end, and which present certain special forms of reaction not to be observed in other circumstances.

The particular motive which in most cases corresponds with the transition from war to peace is the simple longing for peace. With the emergence of this factor there comes into being, as a matter of fact, peace itself, at first in the form of the wish immediately parallel with the struggle itself, and it may without special transitional form displace struggle. We need not pause long to observe that the desire for peace may spring up both directly and indirectly; the former may occur either through the return to power of this peaceful character in the party which is essentially in favor of peace; or through the fact that, through the mere change of the formal stimulus of struggle and of peace which is peculiar to all natures, al-though in different rhythms, the latter comes to the surface and assumes a control which is sanctioned by its own nature alone. In the case of the indirect motive, however, we may distinguish, on the one hand, the exhaustion of resources which, without removal of the persistent contentiousness, may install the demand for peace; and, on the other hand, the withdrawal of interest from struggle through a higher interest in some other object. The latter case begets all sorts of hypocrisies and self-deceptions. It is asserted and believed that peace is desired from ideal interest in peace itself and the suppression of antagonism, while in reality only the object fought for has lost its interest and the fighters would prefer to have their powers free for other kinds of activity.

Beyond this special case, the disappearance of the original object of the struggle often gives peculiar shadings to the termination of conflict. Every conflict which is not of an absolutely impersonal sort draws the available energies of the individual into its service; it operates as a point of crystallization, around which the individual energies arrange themselves at greater or lesser distances—the form of the active and reserve army is essentially repeated—and conflict thus gives to the whole complex of personalities, so far as it is drawn into the struggle, a peculiar structure. So soon, now, as conflict of one of the ordinary sorts is ended, through victory and defeat, through conciliation, through compromise, this psychical structure reconstructs itself into that of the peaceful condition. The central point shares with the energies drawn into struggle its own transition from agitation to pacification. Instead of this organic—although incalculably varied—process of the quieting down of the hostile movement, there often occurs a quite irrational and turbulent process, if the object of struggle suddenly disappears, so that the whole movement, so to speak, swings into emptiness. Everywhere emerge confusion and harm if psychical movements, which have been brought into existence for the sake of a definite content, are suddenly robbed of this purpose, so that they can no longer further develop themselves and express themselves in a natural way, but are thrown back, without other recourse, upon themselves, or are forced to seek some meaningless substitute. If, therefore, while the conflict is in progress, accidents or a higher power spirit away its purpose—for instance, in the case of jealous rivalry, the object of which decides for a third party; or struggle for booty, which in the meanwhile is seized by another; or in the case of a theoretical controversy, in which a superior intelligence suddenly proves *both* contending assertions to be erroneous, et cetera—under such circumstances there frequently occur an empty continuance of hostility, a fruitless reciprocal accusing, a revival of earlier, long-buried differences. This is the continuation of the struggle movement, which must under these circumstances work itself off in senseless and tumultuous demonstrations before it can come to rest. This perhaps occurs most characteristically in the cases where the objective struggle is recognized by both parties as illusory and not worth the conflict. In such cases mortification over the blunder which neither of the parties is willing to confess to the other, draws out the struggle for a long time with an utterly groundless and painful expense of energy, but with the greater bitterness against the opponent who is the cause of committing us to this quixotism.

The simplest and most radical sort of passage from war to peace is victory—a quite unique phenomenon in life, of which there are, to be sure, countless individual forms and measures, which, however, has no resemblance to any of the otherwise mentioned forms which may occur between persons. Victory is a mere watershed between war and peace; when considered absolutely, only an ideal structure which extends itself over no considerable time. For so long as struggle endures there is no definitive victor, and when peace exists a victory *has been* gained, but the act of victory is no longer in continuance (*man siegt nicht mehr*). Of the many shadings of victory, through which it qualifies the following peace, I mention here merely as an illustration the one which is brought about, not exclusively by the preponderance of the one party, but, at least in part, through the resignation of the other. This confession of inferiority (*Klein-Beigeben*), this acknowledgment of defeat, or this consent that victory shall go to the other party without complete exhaustion of the resources and chances for struggle, is by no means always a simple phenomenon. A certain ascetic tendency may also enter in as a purely individual factor, the tendency to self-humiliation and to self-sacrifice, not strong enough to surrender one's self from the start without a struggle, but emerging so soon as the consciousness of being vanquished begins to take possession of the soul; or another variation may be that of finding its supreme charm in the contrast to the still vital and active disposition to struggle. Still further, there is impulse to the same conclusion in the feeling that it is worthier to yield rather than to trust to the last moment in the improbable chance of a fortunate turn of affairs. To throw away this chance and to elude at this price the final consequences that would be involved in utter defeat—this has something of the great and noble qualities of men who are sure not merely of their strengths but also of their weaknesses, without making it necessary for them in each case to make these perceptibly conscious. Finally, in this voluntariness of confessed defeat there is a last proof of power on the part of the agent; the latter has of himself been able to act. He has therewith virtually made a gift to the conqueror. Consequently, it is often to be observed in personal conflicts that the concession of the one party, before the other has actually been able to compel it, is regarded by the latter as a sort of insult, as though this latter party were really the weaker, to whom, however, for some reason or other, there is made a concession without its being really necessary. Behind the objective reasons for yielding, *um des lieben Friedens willen*, a mixture of these subjective motives is not seldom concealed. The latter may not be entirely without visible consequences, however, for the further sociological attitude of the parties. In complete antithesis with the end of strife by victory is its ending by compromise. One of the most characteristic ways of subdividing struggles is on the basis of whether they are of a nature which admits of compromise or not. This is by no means to be decided merely by the question whether the stake at issue is an indivisible unity, or whether it is capable of division between the parties. With reference to certain issues compromise by division is out of the question, as between rivals for a woman's favor, between possible purchasers of one and the same purchasable object that is a unit, and also in the case of struggles the motive of which is hatred and revenge. Nevertheless, struggles over indivisible objects are open to compromise in case these objects may be capable of representation, so that the literal stake may, indeed, fall only to the one, while this one, however, may indemnify the other for his concession by some equivalent value. Whether goods are exchangeable in this fashion depends, of course, not upon any objective equality of value between them, but exclusively upon the disposition of the parties to end the struggle which they have entered upon or which is imminent by any such concession or indemnification. This chance is present in case of sheer obstinacy, where the most rational and abundant indemnity, for which the party would otherwise eagerly sacrifice the issue involved in the struggle, is refused for the sole reason that it is tendered by the opponent—and at the other extreme those other cases in which the party seems to be drawn in at first through the individuality of the object at issue, and then complacently resigns it to the adversary, compensated by an object the competence of which to replace the other is entirely inexplicable to any third party.

On the whole, compromise, especially of that type which is brought to pass through negotiation, however commonplace and matter of fact it has come to be in the processes of modern life, is one of the most important inventions for the uses of civilization. The impulse of uncivilized men, like that of children, is to seize upon every desirable object without further consideration, even though it be already in the possession of another. Robbery and gift are the most naïve forms of transfer of possession, and under primitive conditions change of possession seldom takes place without a struggle. It is the beginning of all civilized industry and commerce to find a way of avoiding this struggle through a process in which there is offered to the possessor of a desired object some other object from the possessions of the person desiring the exchange. Through this arrangement a reduction is made in the total expenditure of energy as compared with the process of continuing or beginning a struggle. All exchange is a compromise. We are told of certain social conditions in which it is accounted as knightly to rob and to fight for the sake of robbery, while exchange and purchase are regarded in the same society as undignified and vulgar. The psychological explanation of this situation is to be found partly in the fact of the element of compromise in exchange, the factors of withdrawal and renunciation which make exchange the opposite pole to all struggle and conquest. Every exchange presupposes that values and interest have assumed an objective character. The decisive element is accordingly no longer the mere subjective passion of desire, to which struggle only corresponds, but the value of the object, which is recognized by both interested parties but which without essential modification may be represented by various objects. Renunciation of the valued object in question, because one receives in another form the quantum of value contained in the same, is an admirable reason, wonderful also in its simplicity, whereby opposed interests are brought to accommodation without struggle. It certainly required a long historical development to make such means available, because it presupposes a psychological generalization of the universal valuation of the individual object, which at first is identified with the valuation; that is, it presupposes ability to rise above the prejudices of immediate desire. Compromise by representation (*Vertretbarkeit*), of which exchange is a special case, signifies in principle, although realized only in part, the possibility of avoiding struggle, or of setting a limit to it before the mere force of the interested parties has decided the issue.

In distinction from the objective character of accommodation of struggle through compromise, we should notice that *conciliation* is a purely subjective method of avoiding struggle. I refer here, not to that sort of conciliation which is the consequence of a compromise or of any other adjournment of struggle, but rather to the reasons for this adjournment. The state of mind which makes conciliation possible (*Versöhnlichkeit*) is a primary attitude which, entirely apart from objective grounds, seeks to end struggle, just as, on the other hand, quarrelsomeness, even without any real occasion, promotes struggle. Probably both mental attitudes have been developed as matters of utility in connection with certain situations; at any rate, they have been developed psychologically to the measure of independent impulses, each of which often makes itself felt where the other would be more practically useful. We may even say that in the countless cases in which struggle is ended otherwise than in the most pitiless consistency of the exercise of force, this quite elementary and unreasoned tendency to conciliation is in play—that is, a factor quite distinct from weakness, or good-fellowship, from either social morality or love of the neighbor. This conciliating tendency is rather a quite specific sociological impulse which manifests itself exclusively as a pacificator, and is not even identical with the peaceful disposition in general. The latter avoids strife under all circumstances, or carries it on, if it is once undertaken, without going to extremes in the devotion of energy, and always with the undercurrents of longing for peace. The spirit of conciliation, however, manifests itself frequently in its full peculiarity precisely after complete devotion to the struggle, after the conflicting energies have exercised themselves to the full in the conflict.

Conciliation depends very intimately upon the external situation. It can occur both after the complete victory of the one party and after the progress of indecisive struggle, as well as after the arrangement of the compromise. Either of these situations may end the struggle without the added conciliation of the opponents. To bring about the latter it is not necessary that there shall be a supplementary repudiation or expression of regret with reference to the struggle. Moreover, conciliation is to be distinguished from the situation which may follow it. This may be either a relationship of attachment or alliance, and reciprocal respect, or a certain permanent distance which avoids all positive contacts. Conciliation is thus a removal of the roots of conflict, without reference to the fruits which these formerly bore, as well as to that which may later be planted in their place. On the other hand, these roots may continue to exist without putting forth any visible shoots.

A special problem is, furthermore, presented by the conciliated relationship in distinction from the relationship which has never been strained. We are not speaking here of cases whose inner rhythm vibrates between repulsion and conciliation, but of those that have suffered an actual breach and after it have come together again as upon a new basis. Such relationships may be characterized by various traits, as, for example, whether or not in this case they show increased or diminished intensity. This is at least the alternative for all deep and sensitive natures; in case of a relationship, after it has experienced a radical break, immediately reappears in precisely the same fashion as though nothing had happened, we may in general presuppose either frivolity or lack of refinement in the mental character of the persons concerned. The first-named case is the least complicated. That a once existing difference cannot ever be completely reconciled, not even when the parties are most frankly disposed to reconciliation, is intelligible without further comment. Under such circumstances it is not at all necessary that a remainder of the object at issue in the struggle shall as such still be present, but the mere fact that a breach has once occurred is alone decisive. To bring about this result, in the case of intimate relationships which have come to visible conflict, the following factor frequently cooperates. The parties have observed that it is possible to get along without each other, that life may perhaps not be quite so gay, but it still keeps on its course. This not merely reduces the value of the relationship, but the one party may, after the unity is restored, easily construe this fact as a species of betrayal and infidelity, which cannot be made good, and which unavoidably adulterates the newly adjusted relationship with a certain degree of indifference, or even mistrust, in spite of preferences to the contrary. To be sure, a certain self-deception is also often involved in this situation. The often surprising facility with which one endures the disruption of an intimate relationship comes from the excitement which we retain as one of the consequences of the catastrophe. This latter has made all our possible energies active, and their operation bears us along awhile and supports us. As, however, the death of a friend does not in the first moment dispose its whole sadness, because it takes the lapse of time to present all the situations in which he was an element, and because we must first live through these situations as though after the loss of one of our bodily members, and because no first moment can summarize these experiences—in the same way an important relationship cannot be properly appraised at the moment of dissolving it, for at that time the grounds for its dissolution control our consciousness. We rather discover the loss for each separate hour only by experience of case after case, and consequently our feeling with reference to the loss does not become wholly just until after a long time. Meanwhile, we have seemed to endure the loss with a certain equanimity. For this reason also the conciliation of many relationships is deep and passionate in proportion to the length of time during which the breach has continued.

That the degree of intensity of the conciliated relationship grows beyond that of the unbroken relationship has various causes. Principally a background is created through the experience, in contrast with which all value and all continuations of the unity come into consciousness and vividness. In addition to this, the discretion with which one avoids every reference to what is past brings a new gentleness, indeed, even a new unspoken community of feeling into the relation. As a general rule, the common avoidance of a too sensitive point may signify quite as great intimacy and reciprocal understanding as the sort of indifference (*Ungenicrtheit*) which makes each object of the inner life of the individual a matter on which to express opinion. Finally, the intensity of the wish to protect the newly enlivened relationship from every sort of shadow springs not merely from the experienced pains of the separation, but first of all from the consciousness that a second breach would not be so easily healed as the first. In countless cases such second reconciliation, at least between sensitive poeple, would reduce the whole relationship to the level of caricature. Even in the profoundest relationship a tragic breach and then a reconciliation may occur. This, however, belongs among the experiences which may not take place more than once. The repetition of the experience between the same parties would rob it of all dignity and earnestness. For, supposing that one such repetition has occurred, nothing then appears against a second and a third, which would reduce the whole situation to a contemptible and frivolous proceeding. Perhaps this feeling that a repetition of the breach would be final—a feeling to which previous to the first breach there is properly no analogy—is for the more refined natures the strongest bond through which the conciliated relationship distinguishes itself from that which has never been interrupted.

The degree of reconciliation after conflict, after pain inflicted on one or both sides, is for the development of all the relationships of the persons concerned, both in minor and in major matters, of decided significance. For this reason there is need of a few words about its negative extreme, that is, irreconcilability. So long as this has rather an external meaning, so long as it proceeds from hatred, love of fighting, extravagance of the claims urged, and so on, it is no further problem. It becomes an additional problem when, as in the case of the conciliatory attitude, it presents itself as a formal sociological factor. In this case it requires, to be sure, a purely external situation in which to actualize itself, but, this being given, it proceeds quite spontaneously, and not merely as the consequence of further mediating emotions. Both tendencies belong to the polar elements, the combination of which determines all relationships between men. It is often said, for instance, that if we could not forget, we could not forgive, or we could not become completely reconciled. This would obviously mean the most frightful irreconcilability, since it makes conciliation depend upon the disappearance from consciousness of every occasion for the contrary attitude. Moreover, it would also, like all other states of consciousness, be subject to the constant danger of being called into existence through a revival of memory. If this whole opinion is to have any meaning at all, it is to be found in the reverse direction. The state of conciliation, as a primary fact, is in itself the reason why the quarrel and the pain which the one party has occasioned for the other mounts no longer into consciousness. In a corresponding way, essential irreconcilability by no means consists in the fact that consciousness does not extend beyond the past conflict. The fact is rather that the soul has through the conflict undergone some sort of modification of itself, which cannot be recalled, which is not to be likened to a wound that can be healed, even though it leaves a scar, but rather to a lost member. This is the most tragic irreconcilability: neither a grudge nor a reservation nor secret spite needs to have remained in the soul and to have created a positive barrier between the two parties. The fact is merely that through the conflict which has been fought out something has been killed in the person in question which cannot be again brought to life, no matter how eager the efforts may be to that end. Here is a point at which the impotence of the will emerges most vividly in contrast with the actual personality. Wherever this is misunderstood there will be countless unjust judgments and self-martyrdoms. It is entirely useless to accuse a defective will for the impossibility of restoring the old relationship. While this is the form of irreconcilability in the case of very simple and not easily influenced natures, another form is observed in the case of persons who are subjectively highly differentiated. The image and aftereffects of the conflict, and of all those things which are laid to the charge of the other party, remain in consciousness, and the painful impression created by it cannot be removed; but undiminished love and attachment gather around this image nevertheless, while recollections of it and resignation with reference to the past do not constitute a diminution of the attachment, but are wrought into the image of the other party; we love him now, so to speak, inclusive of these passive elements in the balance of our total relationship to him, which our thoughts can no longer eliminate from our conception of him. The bitterness of the struggle, the points at which the personality of the other party asserted itself, which bring into the relationship either a prominent renunciation or a constantly renewed irritation—all this is forgotten and really unreconciled. It is, however, so to speak, localized; it is absorbed as a factor in the total relationship, the central identity of which need not suffer because of this factor. That the quarrel leaves behind such a dissociating element, which, however, is entirely drawn into the positive quality of the essential relationship, at the same time an organic member of the latter, which nevertheless does not immediately affect the soul of the whole—all this is not capable of further explanation on its conceptual side, but it must be psychologically experienced.

It is obvious, however, that these two manifestations of irreconcilability, which are so widely different from those usually designated by the term, still include the whole scale of this situation. The one permits the consequence of the conflict, utterly detached from its real content, to sink into the center of the soul. It completely makes over the personality in its profoundest depths, so far as it is related to the other. It leaves to the will for remedial action no access. In the other case, on the contrary, the psychological deposit of the struggle which seems to produce a sociological deficit, is also at the same time isolated; it remains a separate element which may be taken up into the image of the other, with the result that it is included in the total relationship to the other. Between this worst and this best case of irreconcilability—the former in which it vitiates the fundamental attitude, the latter in which it remains rigidly limited—stretches obviously the whole quantitative variety of degrees in which irreconcilability places peace still in the shadow of the conflict.

Emile Durkheim
(1858–1917)

SOCIETY AND ANOMIE

Emile Durkheim is considered one of the great founders of modern social science,[1] and his writings continue to exercise considerable influence on modern sociology.

He was born in 1858 at Epinal, Lorraine, France. His cultured parents came from rabbinical families, and this background supposedly had a decided effect on Durkheim's sociological work, especially in the realm of religion and morals. Durkheim received his education at the College d'Epinal, the Lycée Louis-le-Grand, and the Ecole Normale Supérieure de Paris which he entered in 1879. In the year 1885–86 he went to Germany and acquainted himself with the German school of social sciences; he concentrated especially on national economics, cultural anthropology and folk psychology. He also became quite impressed with the new psychology and methods as developed by Wilhelm Wundt. In 1892 the University of Paris granted him the first doctor's degree in sociology. The Division of Labor in Society, his doctoral thesis, was published the year after. He taught for five years as a lycée professor of philosophy.

In 1898 the Faculté des Lettres de Bordeaux appointed him to teach sociology. He was the first scholar in France to hold a chair in sociology, which had been created especially for him. The University of Paris called him to Paris in 1902 to teach social science. At first he held the chair of the Science of Education at the Sorbonne, but in 1906 he was named Professor of Sociology and Pedagogy.

His doctoral dissertation, The Division of Labor in Society, *is still one of his most important books. It is one of his most theoretical books and sets forth his theory of social evolution. Durkheim adopted the idea of sociology as an independent science from Comte, and in his book* The Rules of Sociological Method *Durkheim made a definite attempt to establish soci-*

---

[1] "In the deepest sense, our debt is to the work of the great founders of modern social science, among whom we may single out Durkheim, Freud, and Max Weber." Talcott Parsons and Edward A. Shills, *Toward a General Theory of Action*, Cambridge, Harvard University Press, 1951.

ology as an independent science and define its method and scope. His Suicide *is still in many respects a model for social research, and it is indeed an example of consistent and organized use of statistical method in social investigation.*[2]

Durkheim's impact on American sociology has been widely recognized. The noted sociologists Talcott Parsons and Robert Merton applied certain sociological methods as developed by Durkheim in their functional theory. Merton refined Durkheim's concept of anomie in his classic essay "Social Structure and Anomie,"[3] *and it should be noted that the significance of Durkheim's concept of anomie has been recently stressed in various publications.*[4]

The emphasis by contemporary social scientists on the study of anomie in modern mass society and the increasing awareness in sociological circles of the link between anomie and crime (and delinquency) were the main reasons for presenting Durkheim's views on this subject here.

SOCIETY AND ANOMIE

I

No living thing can be contented, or even go on living, unless its wants are sufficiently harmonized with the means at its disposal. If these wants require more or something different than is available, they will constantly be thwarted and will be unable to function without pain. Now, a movement which cannot occur without pain tends not to be repeated. Tendencies which fail of fulfillment atrophy, and, since the urge to live is merely the resultant of all other tendencies, it cannot but weaken if these other tendencies lose their force.

In the case of an animal, at least under normal circumstances, this equilibrium between wants and resources is established automatically and spontaneously because it depends upon purely material conditions. The organism requires

[2] George Simpson in his Preface to *Suicide,* Glencoe, The Free Press, 1951.

[3] Robert Merton, *Social Theory and Social Structure,* Glencoe, The Free Press, 1957, p. 131 ff. Also in *Varieties of Modern Social Theory,* edited by Hendrik M. Ruitenbeek, New York, Dutton Paperbacks, 1963.

[4] See *American Sociological Review,* April 1959, Vol. 24, no. 2 (special Anomie issue), and *The American Journal of Sociology,* May 1958, Vol. LXIII, no. 6.

only that the quantities of matter and energy which are endlessly consumed in the maintenance of life be periodically replaced by equivalent amounts, that is, that replacement be equal to wear and tear. When the hole which living digs in its own resources has been filled up again, the animal is satisfied and asks for nothing more. Its reflective powers are not sufficiently well developed to conceive of aims other than those implicit in its physical structure. On the other hand, as the work required of each organ itself depends on the general condition of the life processes and on the necessities of organic equilibrium, the wear and tear involved in the use of the organ is regulated by its replacement and thus a balance is struck automatically. The limits of the one are the limits of the other; they are both alike registered in the very constitution of the living organism, which has no way of going beyond them.

The situation of man is different, however, for most of his wants are not at all, or at least not to the same degree, dependent upon his body. At the most, one can conceive as determinable the physical quantity of material nourishment that is essential for the maintenance of a human life. However, even this determination would be less precise and the scope for variable combinations of desires greater than in the preceding case of lower animals. For, beyond the indispensable minimum with which nature is willing to content herself when she functions instinctively, reflective thought, being more vigorous in man than in animals, leads man to imagine better conditions which then appear as desirable goals and incite his activity. However, we may admit that desires of this kind [bodily desires][5] sooner or later reach a limit beyond which they cannot pass. Yet how is one to determine exactly the amount of well-being, of comfort, of luxury, to which a human being can legitimately aspire? In neither the organic nor the psychological constitution of man is anything to be found which sets a boundary to such propensities. The operation of the individual's life process does not require that those wants stop at one point rather than at another. This is proved by the fact that they have grown periodically since the beginning of history, that progressively fuller satisfaction has been given to them, and that, in spite of these changes, the average level of health has not declined. Above all, how is one to

---

[5] Brackets are used throughout where the translator has added a word or phrase to the text in the interests of clarity.

determine the manner in which these wants should vary according to social conditions, occupation, relative importance of services, et cetera? There is no society in which they are satisfied equally at the different levels of the social hierarchy. And yet, in its essential characteristics, human nature obviously is the same for all members of society. Thus, it is not human nature which would be capable of setting such a variable limit to human desires [for well-being, comfort, and luxury] as they require. Therefore, insofar as they depend upon the individual alone, these desires are boundless. In itself, disregarding all external forces which control it, our capacity for feeling (*sensibilité*) is a bottomless abyss which nothing could fill.

But then, if no external force limits our feeling, it can be by itself nothing but a source of pain. For unlimited desires are insatiable by definition, and it is not without reason that insatiability is regarded as a sign of morbidity. Since nothing restricts them, such wants are forever and infinitely outdistancing the means available for their satisfaction; hence nothing can appease them. An unquenchable thirst is a perpetually renewed agony. To be sure, the saying goes that it is characteristic of human activity to unfold without assignable end and to set up for itself aims which it cannot realize. But it is impossible to see how such a state of indeterminateness can be reconciled any more readily with the conditions of mental life than with the exigencies of physical life. Whatever pleasure man may experience in acting, moving, exerting effort, he still needs to feel that his efforts are not futile and that as he travels he gets somewhere. But one does not progress when one is moving toward no goal, or, what comes to the same thing, when the goal toward which one is moving is infinitely far away. If one's distance from the goal remains always the same, however far one has gone, the result is the same as if one were running on a treadmill. Even backward glances, and the feeling of pride which one may have as one looks over the ground already covered, can bring only an illusory satisfaction, since the distance still to be covered has not been reduced correspondingly. To pursue a goal that is by hypothesis unattainable is thus to condemn oneself to a perpetual state of discontent. No doubt man does hope against all reason; and, even when it is irrational, hope has its joys. Hence, it may sustain him for a while; but it cannot indefinitely survive the repeated disillusionments of experience. Now, what more can the future possibly offer than the past, since it is forever impossible to reach a place where a stand can be made, and since one cannot even approach the ideal at which one aims? Thus, the more one has and the more one wants, the more the satisfactions already attained have the effect only of stimulating, never of appeasing, one's wants. But in the first place, that is true only if one closes one's eyes sufficiently to remain unaware of the action's futility. Then, too, if this pleasure is to be felt and if it is even partly to assuage and disguise the painful anxiety by which it is accompanied, this endless striving must at least go on easily and without any obstacles. Let it be thwarted, and only the anxiety is left, together with the discomfort which it induces. Now, it would be miraculous if no insurmountable obstacle ever arose. Under these circumstances, one holds onto life only by an extremely slender thread, which may snap at any moment.

If the outcome is to be different, the first requisite is that bounds be set to the passions. Only then can they be harmonized with one's powers and consequently gratified. But since there is nothing within the individual which can set a limit to his propensities, any such limitation must come from a source outside himself. Some regulating power must play the same role with reference to the social wants that the physical organism plays reference to the biological wants. In other words, this power must itself be a moral [social] force. For it was the awakening of the mind which began to upset the equilibrium in which the animal lay sleeping; thus mind alone can provide the means for restoring it. Physical checks would be useless here; human passions cannot be changed by physicochemical forces. To the extent that appetites are not curbed automatically by physiological mechanisms, they cannot be halted except by a limitation which they themselves recognize as just. Men would not consent to limit their desires if they believed themselves justified in overriding the assigned boundaries. Yet they cannot prescribe this rule of justice to themselves, for the reasons we have indicated. They must receive it from an authority which they respect and before which they bow spontaneously. Only society, whether directly and as a whole, or indirectly through one of its agencies, is in a position to play this restraining role; for it is the only moral power which is superior to the individual and which he acknowledges as superior. Society alone has the authority necessary to say what is right, and set for the passions the point beyond which they are not to go. Furthermore, society alone can act as judge to determine what reward should be offered to each group for the performance of its particular social function, for the sake of the common interest.

And in fact, at every moment in history there exists in the mores (*conscience des sociétés*) a vague notion of what the various social functions are worth, of the relative remuneration due each of them, and, consequently, of the degree of comfort appropriate to the average worker in each occupation. The various functions are ranked by public opinion into a sort of hierarchy, and a certain coefficient of welfare is assigned to each according to the place it occupies in the hierarchy. Traditionally, for example, there is a certain mode of life which is regarded as the upper limit to which the manual worker may aspire in his efforts to improve his lot, and a lower limit below which we can hardly bear to see him fall unless he has forfeited our respect. Both these limits differ as between the urban and the rural worker, the domestic servant and the journeyman, the commercial employee and the public official, et cetera. Similarly, again, people find fault with the rich man who lives as if he were poor, but they condemn him also if he tries to acquire too many of the refinements of luxury. In vain do the economists protest; it will always offend public sentiment that any single person may consume in utterly needless waste an overlarge amount of wealth, and in fact it seems that this intolerance is relaxed only in periods of moral confusion.[6]

There is, consequently, a very real set of rules which, though it does not always have a legal form, nonetheless sets more or less precisely the maximum standard of living which each class may legitimately seek to attain. Yet the scale thus set up is by no means unalterable. It changes as the total social income grows or diminishes, and in accordance with the changes which occur in the mores of the society. So it happens that things which look like luxury to one age no longer look so to another; that a level of comfort which for a long time was granted to a particular class only as an exceptional and superfluous right now is regarded as absolutely necessary and a matter of strict equity.

Under this pressure, each person in his own orbit takes account in a general way of the extreme point to which his ambitions may go, and aspires to nothing beyond it. At least,

---

[6] This condemnation nowadays is entirely of an informal moral character, and seems to be scarcely capable of legal enforcement. We do not believe that any reintroduction of sumptuary laws would be desirable or even possible.

if he respects the rule and submits to group authority—that is, if he is of sound moral makeup—he feels that it is not right to demand more. An objective and a limit are thus marked out for human passions. To be sure, this determination has nothing either rigid or absolute about it. The economic ideal assigned to each category of citizens is defined by certain upper or lower limits between which there is a large area within which their desires may move about freely. But this area is not unlimited. It is just this relative limitation and the resulting moderation which make men content with their lot and at the same time spur them on moderately to improve it; and it is this contentment which gives birth to that feeling of serene yet active delight, to that enjoyment of being and living which, in societies as well as in individuals, is the sign of health. Generally speaking, everyone is then well adjusted to his station in life and desires only those things for which he can legitimately hope as the normal reward for his efforts. Moreover, a man is not thereby condemned to immobility. He can try to embellish or improve his life; but such attempts may fail without leaving him despondent. For, as he enjoys what he has, and does not put his whole soul into seeking what he has not, he may not succeed in getting all the new things he desired and hoped to acquire, without feeling that he has lost everything at the same time. The essentials he still has. The equilibrium of his happiness is stable because it is determinate, and a few disappointments are not enough to upset it.

However, it would not be sufficient that everyone accept as equitable the hierarchy of functions as it is set up by the mores, if he did not also consider equally equitable the manner in which the individuals who are to perform these social functions are recruited. The worker is not adjusted to his social position if he is not convinced that he really has the position he deserves. If he believes he should in justice hold some other rank, the one he occupies cannot satisfy him. Thus it is not enough that the general level of wants for each social rank should be regulated by public sentiment; there must exist along with this another, more precise system of regulation which determines the manner in which the various ranks are to be opened up to individuals. And as a matter of fact, there is no society in which such regulation does not exist. It varies with time and place. Formerly it made birth the almost exclusive principle of social stratification; today it recognizes no native inequalities but those which stem from inherited wealth or personal worth. Yet beneath these widely varying forms this type of regulation has the same purport everywhere. Everywhere, too, it is effective only if imposed upon individuals by an authority which is superior to them—that is, by collective authority. For this control cannot operate without requiring sacrifices and concessions from one group or another—or more generally from all groups—in the name of public interest.

Certain writers, to be sure, have argued that this social pressure would become useless as soon as economic position ceased to be transmitted by inheritance. If, they have said, the inheritance system has been abolished and each person begins life with the same resources, if, therefore, the competitive struggle is joined under conditions of perfect equality, no one could consider the results of this struggle unjust. Everyone would recognize spontaneously that things are as they ought to be.

As a matter of fact, there is no doubt that, the closer we approach to that ideal equality, the less necessary social control will be. But this is only a question of degree. For one kind of heritage will always remain, namely that of natural endowments. Intelligence, taste, scientific or artistic or literary or industrial ability, courage, manual dexterity are powers which each of us receives at birth, just as the property owner by inheritance receives his capital, or as the noble used to receive his title and feudal office. A moral discipline will still be needed to induce those least favored by nature to accept the inferior station in life which they owe to the accidents of birth. Some will go so far as to insist that everyone's share should be identical, that no advantage should be given to the more productive and deserving. But if that is to be the case, a very different yet equally vigorous discipline will be required to get these latter to accept treatment no better than that accorded to the mediocre and inefficient.

However, this discipline, like the type mentioned earlier, can be socially useful only if the people subjected to it believe it to be fair. When it is maintained only by habit and force, peace and harmony continue to exist only outwardly; the spirit of restlessness and discontent are latent; appetites, only superficially held in check, will soon break loose. This is what happened in Rome and in Greece when the beliefs on which rested the ancient organization of patriciate and plebs were shaken, and in our modern societies when the traditional aristocratic principles began to lose their former ascendancy.

But this state of disturbance is unusual; it occurs only when society is passing through some abnormally disturbed period of transition (*crise maladive*). Normally, the social order is acknowledged as equitable by the vast majority of its subjects. Thus, when we say that an authority is required to impose this order upon the individuals, we do not imply at all that violence is the only means by which it can be imposed. Because this control is to restrain the passions of individuals, it must emanate from a power which can master these individuals; but it is equally true that this power must be obeyed from respect and not from fear.

Accordingly, it is not true that human activity can be freed of every restraint. Nothing in this world can enjoy such a privilege. For every being, since it is part of the universe, is relative to the rest of the universe; its nature and the way in which it manifests that nature depend not only upon itself, but also upon the other beings, which as a natural consequence, restrain and control it. In this respect, the only differences between inorganic matter and thinking beings are differences of degree and form. The unique characteristic of man is the fact that the check to which he is subjected is not physical but moral, that is, social. He receives his law not from a material environment which imposes itself upon him by brute force, but from a mind that is superior to his own, and whose superiority he realizes. Because the greater and better part of his life transcends the life of the body, he escapes the yoke of the body but becomes subject to that of society.

However, when society is disturbed or disorganized, whether by a painful crisis or by a fortunate but too sudden turn of events, it is temporarily incapable of exercising this influence upon the individual; and such conditions lead to those abrupt rises in the suicide curve which we have proved in a preceding section of this book.

As a matter of fact, in severe economic depressions there occurs, so to speak, a lowering in the social scale (*déclassement*), a process that flings certain individuals suddenly into a social position lower than that which they had previously occupied. They must reduce their demands, restrain their wants, learn to control themselves even more than before. All the fruits of society's "moral" influence upon them are lost as far as they are concerned; their moral education has to be started all over again. But this social process of remolding them to fit into the conditions of their new life and of teaching them to exercise this unwonted additional self-restraint cannot be completed overnight. Consequently, they are not adjusted to the situation which is thrust upon them. Even the thought of it they find unbearable; and this is the source of sufferings which lead them to abandon an impaired life even before they have had much actual experience with it.

The results are not different if the disturbance originates in an abrupt increase in power and wealth. Then, indeed, as the conditions of life are changed, the scale in accordance with which people's wants were controlled cannot remain unchanged; for it varies with the resources of society, since it determines roughly the share which is to go to each class of producers. Its gradations are overthrown; yet on the other hand, no new pattern can be quickly improvised. It takes time for public sentiment to develop a new social classification of people and goods. As long as the social forces thus let loose have not attained a new equilibrium, their relative social values remain indeterminate, and consequently all coordination is lacking for a while. People no longer feel sure about what is possible and what is not, what is just and what is unjust, which claims or aspirations are legitimate and which go beyond the bounds of propriety. As a result, there is nothing to which men do not lay claim. If the disturbance is at all profound, it affects even the principles which govern the distribution of individuals among the various occupations. For as the relations among the different parts of society are necessarily modified, the ideas which express these relationships cannot remain the same. Whatever class has been especially favored by the disturbance is no longer disposed to its former self-restraint, and as a repercussion, the sight of its enhanced fortune awakens in the groups around and below it every manner of covetousness. Thus the appetites of men, unrestrained now by a public opinion which has become bewildered and disoriented, no longer know where the bounds are before which they ought to come to a halt. Furthermore, at just this moment they are in a state of abnormal excitement simply by virtue of the fact that general vitality is more intense. Because prosperity has increased, desires are inflamed. The richer prize offered to them stimulates them, makes them more exacting, more impatient of every rule, just at the time when the traditional rules have lost their authority. The state of rulelessness (*dérèglement*) or *anomie* is further heightened by the fact that human desires are less disciplined at the very moment when they would need a stronger discipline.

But under such circumstances their very unreasonableness renders it impossible to satisfy them. Overexcited ambitions always go on beyond the results achieved, whatever these may be, for they are not warned to go no further. Thus far nothing can appease them and all this excitement sustains itself perpetually without leading to any satiation. Above all, since this race toward an unattainable end can produce no pleasure but that of activity itself, if indeed there is any such pleasure at all, let it be blocked by an obstacle and one is left completely empty-handed. Now, it happens that at the same time the struggle becomes more violent and more painful, both because it is less regulated and because the competition is more intense. All classes are at grips with each other because there is no longer any established system of social stratification. Thus effort increases just when it becomes less productive of results. How, under these conditions, could the will to live do other than languish?

This explanation [of suicide] is confirmed by the singular immunity enjoyed by poor countries. If poverty protects people against suicide, it is because by its very nature it acts as a restraint. Whatever one may do, one's desires are obliged, in some measure, to reckon with the available resources; what one has acts in part as a guide in determining what one would like to have. Consequently, the less one possesses, the less he is inclined to extend endlessly the range of his wants. By subjecting us forcibly to moderation, poverty habituates us to it, and, besides, where mediocrity is a general condition, nothing occurs to excite envy. Wealth, on the other hand, by virtue of the power which it confers upon its possessor, creates the illusion that we can rise simply by our own efforts. By reducing the obstacles which are placed in our way, riches lead us to believe that such obstacles can be mastered indefinitely. Now the less a man feels himself restrained, the more intolerable any actual restraint seems to him. It is not without reason, then, that so many religions have glorified the benefits and the moral worth of poverty. Poverty is, indeed, the best school for teaching a man self-restraint. By obliging us to exercise constant discipline over our selves, it prepares us docilely to accept social discipline, while opulence, by overexciting the individual, always runs the risk of awakening that spirit of rebellion which is the very wellspring of immorality. To be sure, that is no reason for preventing humanity from improving its material condition. But if the moral danger entailed in every increase in comfort is not without remedy, it is still necessary not to lose sight of its existence.

II

IF anomie occurred only in the forms indicated above, that is, in intermittent attacks and in the form of sharp disturbances [that is, in depressions or sudden abnormal prosperity], anomie itself would not be a regular and constant factor in determining suicide rates, though it might well account for variations from time to time. However, there is one area of social life in which it is chronic, namely in the world of commerce and industry.

For a century, economic progress has consisted principally in liberating industrial relationships from all regulation. Until modern times, it was the function of a whole system of moral powers to control such relationships. In the first place, religion exerted an influence which was felt equally by workers and masters, poor and rich. It consoled the first, and taught them to rest content with their lot by teaching them that the social order is designed by Providence, that God himself has determined the share each class receives, and inducing them to hope for a future world in which just compensation will be made for the inequalities of this life. Religion restrained the rich and powerful by reminding them that worldly interests are not man's all but should be subordinated to other, higher interests, and therefore do not deserve to be pursued without rule or moderation. Second, the state, by virtue of the control it exercised over economic processes and the subordinate role it assigned to them, restricted the impetus of economic interests. Finally, at the very core of the economic world itself, the craft guilds, by regulating wages, prices of products, and production itself, indirectly established the average level of incomes through which wants are, in the nature of the case, in part determined. In describing this system of economic order we do not wish to suggest it as a model to be followed. Clearly, without profound changes it could not fit present-day societies. We assert merely that it did exist, that it had useful results, and that there is nothing taking its place today.

In fact, religion has lost the greater part of its power over men. Governmental authority, once the regulator of economic life, has become its instrument and servant. The most contradictory schools of thought, orthodox economists and extreme Socialists, are agreed upon reducing the state to the role of a more or less passive intermediary among the various groups in society. The former want to make it simply a guardian of private contracts; the latter leave to the government only the task of doing society's bookkeeping, that is, of recording the demands of consumers, passing them on to the producers, tallying the total income and distributing it according to a set formula. But both deny that it has any right to subordinate the other organs of society to itself and to coordinate all their activities for the attainment of any one dominant aim. On both sides it is asserted that the only, or at any rate the main, objective of nations should be industrial prosperity; this is implied in the dogma of economic materialism, which forms the basis of both these systems, ostensibly opposed though they are. And, as these theories merely reflect the state of public sentiment, industry, which was formerly regarded as one means toward a higher end, has become the supreme end for individuals as well as for whole societies. But then it came to pass that the appetites which [modern capitalistic] industry brings into play find themselves freed of all constraining authority. This apotheosis of material well-being, by so to speak sanctifying them, has placed economic appetites above every human law. People view any attempt to dam up the flood of their desires as a sort of sacrilege. Consequently, even that purely expediential control which the business world itself used to exert over them through the medium of guilds no longer remains in force. Finally, this unleashing of desires has been still further aggravated by the sheer development of industry and the virtually infinite expansion of the market area. As long as the producer could dispose of his output only in his own immediate neighborhood, the rather modest profit to be expected could not inflame any great surge of ambition. But now that he can almost claim the whole world as his customer, how can we expect that in the face of these limitless opportunities men will submit to such regulations of their wants as prevailed in an earlier day?

Thus arises the instability which is especially prevalent in this segment of society but which has spread from there through all activities and groups. The fact is that there [in the world of commerce and industry] a state of disturbance and of anomie is constant, and, so to speak, normal. From top to bottom of the social scale, violent but indefinite and unfocused desires are aroused. Nothing could possibly appease

them, since the goal they seek is infinitely far beyond anything they can attain. Reality seems worthless compared with
what these fevered imaginations conceive to be possible; thus
people abandon reality, only to abandon the possible when it
in turn becomes real. They thirst for novelty, for unknown
delights, for nameless sensations, which nevertheless lose all
their zest as soon as they are experienced. Then, let the slightest reverse occur and men are powerless to bear it. The whole
fever drops and people discover how futile the whole uproar
was, and realize that any number of these novel experiences
piled up indefinitely has not succeeded in accumulating a
solid capital of happiness on which they might live in times of
trial. The wise man, who knows how to enjoy the results he
has attained without constantly feeling a need to replace them
with others, finds in this mode of life something that helps
him to hold onto life when the hour of adversity has sounded.
But the man who always expected everything from the future,
who has lived with his eyes riveted on what is to come, has
nothing in his past to fortify him against the tribulations of
the present; for the past has been to him but a series of way
stations which he passed through impatiently. He was able to
blind himself about his own condition precisely because he
continually counted on finding around the next corner that
happiness which he had not yet encountered. But now his
progress is halted; from this time on, he has nothing either
behind or before him on which he can rest his gaze. Besides,
sheer fatigue is enough to produce disillusionment, for it is
difficult in the long run to avoid feeling the futility of an endless chase.

One might even ask whether it is not primarily this social-
psychological condition (*état moral*) which makes economic
crises so prolific of suicides. In societies where he is subjected
to a healthy discipline, man resigns himself more readily to
strokes of bad luck. Since he is already used to self-restraint
and self-control, the effort required to impose on himself a
little more forbearance costs him relatively little. But when
every limitation is in itself odious, how can we expect that a
more rigorous limitation should seem other than unbearable?
The feverish impatience in which men live scarcely disposes
them to resignation. When a man has no goal but that of
driving continually past the point he has just reached, how
grievous it is to be thrown back! Yet the very lack of organization [lack of social-moral control] which characterizes our
economic system opens the door to all kinds of risks. As imagi-

nations are avid for novelty and know no rule, they grope their way forward at random. Necessarily, the losses grow with the risks taken, and thus crises multiply at the very time when they are becoming more destructive.

And meanwhile, these tendencies have become so chronic that society has got itself used to regarding them as normal. People repeat endlessly that it is in the nature of man to be eternally discontented, to move ever forward without truce or rest toward an unknown destination. The passion for the infinite is presented every day as a mark of moral distinction, when in fact it can come into existence only in ruleless minds which elevate to the dignity of a rule the very rulelessness of which they are the victims. The doctrine of progress at any cost and as rapidly as possible has become an article of faith. But also, paralleling the theories which glorify the blessings of instability, there appear others which generalize the situation out of which they arise, declare that life is evil, and accuse it of producing more pain than pleasure and of seducing man with wholly delusive charms. And since it is in the economic world that this confusion is at its height, it is there also that it finds most of its victims.

The industrial and commercial occupations are, as a matter of fact, among those which produce the highest suicide rates. . . . Their rate is almost as high as that of the liberal professions, sometimes even exceeding it; above all, they are noticeably more afflicted than is agriculture. For farming is the occupation in which the old-time regulative forces still make themselves felt most powerfully and into which the feverish excitement of business has penetrated least. It is agriculture which best recalls the former structure of the economic order. And the difference would be still more marked if, among the suicides in industry, the employers were distinguished from the workers, for the former probably are the principal group very strongly affected by anomie. The enormous rate in the rentier class (720 per million) shows clearly enough that it is the most fortunate who suffer most from anomie. Whatever compels subordination mitigates the effects of that condition. The lower classes at least have their horizon limited by those who stand above them, and by virtue of that very fact their desires are more determinate. But those who have only the void above them are almost bound to lose themselves in it, if there is no force to hold them back.

Anomie in our modern societies is, then, a steady and specific factor in suicide; it is one of the sources from which the annual quota is fed. Consequently, we are faced with a new type of suicide, which must be distinguished from the others. It differs from them in that it depends not on the manner in which individuals are attached to society, but on the way in which society controls them. Egoistic suicide arises from the fact that men no longer see any reason for staying alive; altruistic suicide from the fact that this reason seems to them to lie outside life itself; the third type of suicide, the existence of which we have just established, arises from the fact that their actions become ruleless and that they suffer from this condition. Because of its origin, we shall give to this last species the name anomic suicide.

Assuredly, anomic and egoistic suicide are not without kinship resemblance. Both result from the fact that society is not sufficiently strongly present to the individuals concerned. But the sphere from which it is absent is not the same in both. In egoistic suicide, it is from specifically collective activity that [the claims of and regard for] society are absent, thus leaving such activity destitute of both object and meaning. In anomic suicide, [the claims of and regard for] society is [are] missing from specifically private activities, thus leaving them with a restraining harness. Consequently, despite their similarity, these two types of suicide remain distinct from one another. We can render unto society all that is social in us, and still be unable to limit our desires; without being an egoist, one can live in a state of anomie, and vice versa. Furthermore, these two types of suicide do not recruit their main clientele from the same social milieus: the one is found primarily in the intellectual occupations, the world of thought, the other in the world of industry and commerce.

III

UP to now, we have studied the division of labor only as a normal phenomenon, but, like all social facts, and, more generally, all biological facts, it presents pathological forms which must be analyzed. Though normally the division of labor produces social solidarity, it sometimes happens that it has different, and even contrary, results. Now, it is important to find out what makes it deviate from its natural course, for if we do not prove that these cases are exceptional, the division of labor might be accused of logically implying them. Moreover, the study of these devious forms will permit us to determine the conditions of existence of the normal state better. When we know the circumstances in which the division of labor ceases to bring forth solidarity, we shall better understand what is necessary for it to have that effect. Pathology, here as elsewhere, is a valuable aid of physiology.

One might be tempted to reckon as irregular forms of the division of labor criminal occupations and other harmful activities. They are the very negation of solidarity, and yet they take the form of special activities. But to speak with exactitude, there is no division of labor here, but differentiation pure and simple. The two terms must not be confused. Thus, cancer and tuberculosis increase the diversity of organic tissues without bringing forth a new specialization of biologic functions.[7] In all these cases, there is no partition of a common function, but, in the midst of the organism, whether individual or social, another is formed which seeks to live at the expense of the first. In reality, there is not even a function, for a way of acting merits this name only if it joins with others in maintaining general life. This question, then, does not enter into the body of our investigation.

We shall reduce to three types the exceptional forms of the phenomenon that we are studying. This is not because there can be no others, but rather because those of which we are going to speak are the most general and the most serious.

The first case of this kind is furnished us by industrial or commercial crises, by failures, which are so many partial breaks in organic solidarity. They evince, in effect, that at certain points in the organism certain social functions are not adjusted to one another. But, insofar as labor is divided more, these phenomena seem to become more frequent, at least in certain cases. From 1845 to 1869, failures increased 70%.[8] We cannot, however, attribute this fact to the growth in economic life, since enterprises have become a great deal more concentrated than numerous.

The conflict between capital and labor is another example, more striking, of the same phenomenon. Insofar as industrial functions become more specialized, the conflict becomes more lively, instead of solidarity increasing. In the Middle Ages, the worker everywhere lived at the side of his master, pursu-

---

[7] This is a distinction that Spencer does not make. It seems that, for him, the two terms are synonymous. The differentiation, however, which disintegrates (cancerous, microbic, criminal) is very different from that which brings vital forces together (division of labor).

[8] Block, *Statistique de la France.*

ing his tasks "in the same shop, in the same establishment."[9] Both were part of the same corporation and led the same existence. "They were on an almost equal footing; whoever had served his apprenticeship could, at least in many of the occupations, set himself up independently if he had the means."[10] Hence, conflicts were wholly unusual. Beginning with the fifteenth century things began to change. "The occupational circle is no longer a common organization; it is an exclusive possession of the masters, who alone decided all matters. . . . From that time, a sharp line is drawn between masters and workers. The latter formed, so to speak, an order apart; they had their customs, their rules, their independent associations."[11] Once this separation was effected, quarrels became numerous. "When the workers thought they had a just complaint, they struck or boycotted a village, an employer, and all of them were compelled to obey the letter of the order. . . . The power of association gave the workers the means of combating their employers with equal force."[12] But things were then far from reaching "the point at which we now see them. Workers rebelled in order to secure higher wages or some other change in the condition of labor, but they did not consider the employer as a permanent enemy whom one obeyed because of his force. They wished to make him concede a point, and they worked energetically toward that end, but the conflict was not everlasting. The workshops did not contain two opposing classes. Our socialist doctrines were unknown."[13] Finally, in the seventeenth century, the third phase of this history of the working classes begins: the birth of large-scale industry. The worker is more completely separated from the employer. "He becomes somewhat regimented. Each has his function, and the system of the division of labor makes some progress. In the factory of Van-Robais, which employed 1692 workers, there were particular shops for wheelwrighting, for cutlery, for washing, for dyeing, for warping, and the shops for weaving, themselves contained several types of workers whose labor was entirely distinct."[14]

[9] Levasseur, *Les Classes ouvrières en France jusqu'à la Révolution*, II, 315.

[10] *Ibid.*, I, 496.

[11] Levasseur, I, 496.

[12] *Ibid.*, I, 504.

[13] Hubert Valleroux, *Les Corporations d'arts et de métiers*, p. 49.

[14] Levasseur, II, 315.

At the same time that specialization becomes greater, revolts become more frequent. "The smallest cause for discontent was enough to upset an establishment, and cause a worker unhappiness who did not respect the decision of the community."[15] We well know that, since then, the warfare has become ever more violent.

To be sure, we shall see in the following chapter that this tension in social relations is due, in part, to the fact that the working classes are not really satisfied with the conditions under which they live, but very often accept them only as constrained and forced, since they have not the means to change them. This constraint alone, however, would not account for the phenomenon. In effect, it does not weigh less heavily upon all those generally bereft of fortune, and yet this state of permanent hostility is wholly special to the industrial world. Then, in the interior of this world, it is the same for all workers indiscriminately. But small-scale industry, where work is less divided, displays a relative harmony between worker and employer.[16] It is only in large-scale industry that these relations are in a sickly state. That is because they depend in part upon a different cause.

Another illustration of the same phenomenon has often been observed in the history of sciences. Until very recent times, science, not being very divided, could be cultivated almost entirely by one and the same person. Thus was had a very lively sense of its unity. The particular truths which composed it were neither so numerous nor so heterogeneous that one could not easily see the tie which bound them in one and the same system. Methods, being themselves very general, were little different from one another, and one could perceive the common trunk from which they imperceptibly diverged. But, as specialization is introduced into scientific work, each scholar becomes more and more enclosed, not only in a particular science, but in a special order of problems. Auguste Comte had already complained that, in his time, there were in the scientific world "very few minds embracing in their conception the total scope of even a single science, which is, however, in turn, only a part of a greater whole. The greater part were already occupied with some isolated consideration of a more or less extensive section of one certain science, without being very much concerned with the relation of the

---

[15] *Ibid.*, 319.
[16] See Cauwes, *Précis d'économie politique*, II, 39.

particular labors to the general system of positive knowledge."[17] But then, science, parceled out into a multitude of detailed studies which are not joined together, no longer forms a solidary whole. What best manifests, perhaps, this absence of concert and unity is the theory, so prevalent, that each particular science has an absolute value, and that the scholar ought to devote himself to his special researches without bothering to inquire whether they serve some purpose and lead anywhere. "This division of intellectual labor," says Schaeffle, "offers good reason for fearing that this return to a new Alexandrianism will lead once again to the ruin of all science."[18]

What makes these facts serious is that they have sometimes been considered a necessary effect of the division of labor after it has passed beyond a certain stage of development. In this case, it is said, the individual, hemmed in by his task, becomes isolated in a special activity. He no longer feels the idea of a common work being done by those who work side by side with him. Thus, the division of labor could not be pushed farther without becoming a source of disintegration. "Since all such decomposition," says Auguste Comte, "necessarily has the tendency to determine a corresponding dispersion, the fundamental partition of human labors cannot avoid evoking, in a proportionate degree, individual divergences, both intellectual and moral, whose combined influence must, in the same measure, demand a permanent discipline able to prevent or unceasingly contain their discordant flight. If, on the one hand, indeed, the separation of social functions permits a felicitous development of the spirit of detail otherwise impossible, it spontaneously tends, on the other hand, to snuff out the spirit of togetherness or, at least, to undermine it profoundly. Likewise, from the moral point of view, at the same time that each is thus placed in strict dependence upon the mass, he is naturally deterred by the peculiar scope of his special activity which constantly links him to his own private interest whose true relation with the public interest he perceives but very vaguely. . . . Thus it is that the same principle which has alone permitted the development and the extension of general society threatens, in a different aspect, to decompose it into a multitude of incoherent corporations which

[17] *Cours de philosophie positive,* I, 27.
[18] *Bau und Leben des sozialen Körpers,* IV, 113.

almost seem not to be of the same species."[19] Espinas has expressed himself almost in the same terms: "Division," he says, "is dispersion."[20]

The division of labor would thus exercise, because of its very nature, a dissolving influence which would be particularly obvious where functions are very specialized. Comte, however, does not conclude from his principle that societies must be led to what he himself calls the age of generality, that is, to that state of indistinctness and homogeneity which was their point of departure. The diversity of functions is useful and necessary, but as unity, which is no less indispensable, does not spontaneously spring up, the care of realizing it and of maintaining it would constitute a special function in the social organism, represented by an independent organ. This organ is the state or government. "The social destiny of government," says Comte, "appears to me to consist particularly in sufficiently containing, and preventing, as far as possible, this fatal disposition toward a fundamental dispersion of ideas, sentiments, and interests, the inevitable result of the very principle of human development, and which, if it could follow its natural course without interruption, would inevitably end by arresting social progress in all important respects. This conception, in my eyes, constitutes the first positive and rational basis of an elementary and abstract theory of government properly so called, seen in its noblest and greatest scientific extension, as characterized in general by a universal and necessary reaction, at first spontaneous and then regulated, of the totality of the parts that go to make it up. It is clear, in effect, that the only real means of preventing such a dispersion consists in this indispensable reaction in a new and special function, susceptible of fittingly intervening in the habitual accomplishment of all the diverse functions of social economy, so as to recall to them unceasingly the feeling of unity and the sentiment of common solidarity."[21]

What government is to society in its totality philosophy ought to be to the sciences. Since the diversity of science tends to disrupt the unity of science, a new science must be set up to reestablish it. Since detailed studies make us lose sight of the whole vista of human knowledge, we must institute a particular system of researches to retrieve it and set it

[19] *Cours*, IV, 429.
[20] *Sociétés animales*, Conclusion, IV.
[21] *Cours de philosophie positive*, IV, 430-431.

off. In other words: "We must make an even greater specialty of the study of scientific generalities. A new class of scholars, prepared by suitable education, without devoting themselves to a special culture of any particular branch of natural philosophy, will busy themselves with considering the various positive sciences in their present state, with exactly determining the spirit of each of them, with discovering their relations and their continuity, with summing up, if possible, all their principles in a very small number of principles common to all, and the division of labor in the sciences will be pushed, without any danger, as far as the development of the various orders of knowledge demand."[22]

Of course, we have ourselves shown[23] that the governmental organ develops with the division of labor, not as a repercussion of it, but because of mechanical necessity. As organs are rigorously solidary where functions are very divided, what affects one affects the others, and social events take on a more general interest. At the same time, with the effacement of the segmental type, they penetrate more easily throughout the extent of the same tissue or the same system. For these two reasons, there are more of them which are retained in the directive organ whose functional activity, more often exercised, grows with the volume. But its sphere of action does not extend further.

But beneath this general, superficial life there is an intestine, a world of organs which, without being completely independent of the first, nevertheless function without its intervention, without its even being conscious of them, at least normally. They are freed from its action because it is too remote for them. The government cannot, at every instant, regulate the conditions of the different economic markets, fixing the prices of their commodities and services, or keeping production within the bounds of consumptionary needs, and so on. All these practical problems arise from a multitude of detail, coming from thousands of particular circumstances which only those very close to the problems know about. Thus, we cannot adjust these functions to one another and make them concur harmoniously if they do not concur of themselves. If, then, the division of labor has the dispersive

[22] This bringing together of government and philosophy ought not to surprise us, for, in Comte's eyes, the two institutions are inseparable. Government, as he conceives it, is possible only upon the institution of the positive philosophy.

[23] See above, Book I, Chap. vii, §3.

effects that are attributed to it, they ought to develop without
resistance in this region of society, since there is nothing to
hold them together. What gives unity to organized societies,
however, as to all organisms, is the spontaneous consensus of
parts. Such is the internal solidarity which not only is as
indispensable as the regulative action of higher centers, but
which also is their necessary condition, for they do no more
than translate it into another language and, so to speak, con-
secrate it. Thus, the brain does not make the unity of the
organism, but expresses and completes it. Some speak of the
necessity of a reaction of the totality of parts, but it still is
necessary for this totality to exist; that is to say, the parts
must be already solidary with one another for the whole to
take conscience of itself and react in this way. Else, as work
is divided, one would see a sort of progressive decomposition
produced, not only at certain points but throughout society,
instead of the ever stronger concentration that we really
observe.

But, it is said, there is no need for going into detail. It is
sufficient to call to mind whenever necessary "the spirit of the
whole and the sentiment of common solidarity," and this
action the government alone can execute. This is true, but it
is much too general to assure the concourse of social functions, if that has not been realized by itself. In effect, what is
the point at issue? Is it to make each individual feel that he
is not self-sufficient, but is a part of a whole on which he
depends? But such an abstract, vague, and, withal, intermittent representation, just as all complex representations, can
avail nothing against lively, concrete impressions which occupational activity at every instant evokes in each one of us. If,
then, occupational activity has the effects that are adduced,
if the occupations which fill our daily life tend to detach us
from the social group to which we belong, such a conception,
which is quite dormant and never occupies more than a small
part of the field of conscience, will not be sufficient to hold
us to it. In order that the sentiment of our state of dependence
be effective, it would be necessary for it also to be continuous,
and it can be that only if it is linked to the very practice of
each special function. But then specialization would no longer
have the consequences which it is said to produce. Or else
governmental action would have as its object the maintenance
of a certain moral uniformity among occupations, the preventing of "social affections gradually concentrated in individuals
of the same occupation from becoming more and more foreign

to other classes, for want of sufficient likeness in customs and thoughts."[24] But this uniformity cannot be maintained by force and against the nature of things. Functional diversity induces a moral diversity that nothing can prevent, and it is inevitable that one should grow as the other does. We know, moreover, why these two phenomena develop in parallel fashion. Collective sentiments become more and more impotent in holding together the centrifugal tendencies that the division of labor is said to engender, for these tendencies increase as labor is more divided, and, at the same time, collective sentiments are weakened.

For the same reason, philosophy becomes more and more incapable of assuring the unity of science. As long as the same mind could, at once, cultivate different sciences, it was possible to acquire the competency necessary for their unification. But, as they become specialized, these grand syntheses can no longer be anything more than premature generalizations, for it becomes more and more impossible for one human intelligence to gain a sufficiently exact knowledge of this great multitude of phenomena, of laws, of hypotheses which must be summed up. "It would be interesting to speculate," Ribot justly says, "what philosophy, as the general conception of the universe, will be when particular sciences, because of their growing complexity, become overwhelming in their detail and philosophers are reduced to knowledge of the most general results, which are necessarily superficial."[25]

To be sure, there is some reason for judging as excessive this pride of the scholar, who, hemmed in by his special researches, refuses to recognize any other control. It is certain, however, that to gain an exact idea of a science one must practice it, and, so to speak, live with it. That is because it does not entirely consist of some propositions which have been definitively proved. Along side of this actual, realized science, there is another, concrete and living, which is in part ignorant of itself, and yet seeks itself; besides acquired results, there are hopes, habits, instincts, needs, presentiments so obscure that they cannot be expressed in words, yet so powerful that they sometimes dominate the whole life of the scholar. All this is still science; it is even its best and largest part, for the discovered truths are a little thing in comparison with those which remain to be discovered. More-

[24] *Cours de philosophie positive*, IV, 42.
[25] *Psychologie allemande*, Introduction, p. xxvii.

over, in order to possess a good idea of the first, and understand what is found condensed therein, one must have been close to scientific life while it was still in a free state; that is to say, before it became fixed in the form of definite propositions. Otherwise, one will have the letter, but not the spirit. Each science has, so to speak, a soul which lives in the conscience of scholars. Only a part of this soul assumes sensible bodily form. The formulas which express it, being general, are easily transmitted. But such is not the case with this other part of science which no symbol translates without. Here, all is personal and must be acquired through personal experience. To take part in it, one must put oneself to work and place oneself before the facts. According to Comte, to assure the unity of science, it would be enough to have methods reduced to unity;[26] but it is just the methods which are most difficult to unify, for, as they are immanent in the very sciences, as it is impossible to disengage them completely from the body of established truths in order to codify them separately, we can know them only if we have ourselves practiced them. But it is now impossible for the same man to practice a large number of sciences. These grand generalizations can rest only on a very summary view of things. If, moreover, we remember how slowly and with what patient precautions scholars ordinarily proceed in the discovery of even their most particular truths, we see that improvised disciplines no longer have anything more than a very feeble authority over them.

But, whatever may be the value of these philosophic generalities, science would not find therein the unity it needs. They well express what there is in common among the sciences—laws, specific method—but, besides these resemblances, there are differences which have to be integrated. We often say that the general holds in its power particulars that it sums up, but the expression is not exact. It contains only what is common to them. Now, there are no two phenomena in the world which resemble each other, simple as they may be. That is why every general proposition lets a part of the material it tries to master escape. It is impossible to establish the concrete characters and distinctive properties of things in the same impersonal and homogeneous formula. But, as long as resemblances exceed differences, they are

26 *Op. cit.*, I, 45.

sufficient to integrate the representations thus brought together. The dissonances of detail disappear in the total harmony. On the contrary, as the differences become more numerous, cohesion becomes more unstable and must be consolidated by other means. If we picture the growing multiplicity of special sciences, with their theorems, their laws, their axioms, their conjectures, their methods of procedure, we shall see that a short and simple formula, as the principle of evolution, for example, is not enough to integrate such a prodigious complexity of phenomena. Even when these total views exactly correspond to reality, the part they explain is too small a thing beside what they leave unexplained. It is not, then, by this means that we shall ever be able to take the positive sciences out of their isolation. There is too great a chasm between detailed researches which are their backbone and such syntheses. The tie which binds these two orders of knowledge together is too slight and too loose, and, consequently, if particular sciences can take cognizance of their mutual dependence only through a philosophy which embraces all of them, the sentiment of unity they will have will always be too vague to be efficacious.

Philosophy is the collective conscience of science, and, here as elsewhere, the role of the collective conscience becomes smaller as labor is divided.

Although Comte recognized that the division of labor is a source of solidarity, it seems that he did not perceive that this solidarity is *sui generis* and is little by little substituted for that which social likenesses give rise to. That is why, in remarking that the latter were very much obliterated where functions are very specialized, he considered this obliteration a morbid phenomenon, a menace to social cohesion due to the excess of specialization, and by that he explained the facts of lack of coordination which sometimes accompany the development of the division of labor. But since we have shown that the enfeeblement of the collective conscience is a normal phenomenon, we cannot consider it as the cause of the abnormal phenomena that we are studying. If, in certain cases, organic solidarity is not all it should be, it is certainly not because mechanical solidarity has lost ground, but because all the conditions for the existence of organic solidarity have not been realized.

We know, in effect, that, wherever organic solidarity is

found, we come upon an adequately developed regulation determining the mutual relations of functions.[27] For organic solidarity to exist, it is not enough that there be a system of organs necessary to one another, which in a general way feel solidary, but it is also necessary that the way in which they should come together, if not in every kind of meeting, at least in circumstances which most frequently occur, be predetermined. Otherwise, at every moment new conflicts would have to be equilibrated, for the conditions of equilibrium can be discovered only through gropings in the course of which one part treats the other as an adversary as much as an auxiliary. These conflicts would incessantly crop out anew, and, consequently, solidarity would be scarcely more than potential, if mutual obligations had to be fought over entirely anew in each particular instance. It will be said that there are contracts. But, first of all, all social relations are not capable of assuming this juridical form. We know, moreover, that a contract is not self-sufficient, but supposes a regulation which is as extensive and complicated as contractual life itself. Besides, the links which have this origin are always of short duration. A contract is only a truce, and very precarious; it suspends hostilities for a time only. Of course, as precise as this regulation may be, it will always leave a place for many disturbances. But it is neither necessary nor even possible for social life to be without conflicts. The role of solidarity is not to suppress competition, but to moderate it.

Moreover, in the normal state, these rules disengage themselves from the division of labor. They are a prolongation of it. Assuredly, if it only brought together individuals who united for some few moments to exchange personal services, it could not give rise to any regulative action. But what it brings face to face are functions, that is to say, ways of definite action, which are identically repeated in given circumstances, since they cling to general, constant conditions of social life. The relations which are formed among these functions cannot fail to partake of the same degree of fixity and regularity. There are certain ways of mutual reaction which, finding themselves very conformable to the nature of things, are repeated very often and become habits. Then these habits, becoming forceful, are transformed into rules of conduct. The past determines the future. In other words, there is a certain sorting of rights and duties which is established by

[27] See Book I, Chap. vii.

usage and becomes obligatory. The rule does not, then, create
the state of mutual dependence in which solidary organs find
themselves, but only expresses in clear-cut fashion the result
of a given situation. In the same way, the nervous system, far
from dominating the evolution of the organism, as we have
already said, results from it.[28] The nerve cords are probably
only the lines of passage which the streams of movements and
excitations exchanged between different organs have followed. They are the canals life has hewed for itself while
steadily flowing in the same direction, and the ganglia would
only be the place of intersection of several of these lines.[29]
Because they misunderstood this aspect of the phenomena,
certain moralists have claimed that the division of labor does
not produce true solidarity. They have seen in it only particular exchanges, ephemeral combinations, without past or
future, in which the individual is thrown on his own resources. They have not perceived the slow work of consolidation, the network of links which little by little have been
woven and which makes something permanent of organic
solidarity.

But, in all the cases that we have described above, this regulation either does not exist or is not in accord with the degree
of development of the division of labor. Today, there are no
longer any rules which fix the number of economic enterprises, and, in each branch of industry production is not
exactly regulated on a level with consumption. We do not
wish to draw any practical conclusion from this fact; we are
not contending that restrictive legislation is necessary; we do
not here have to weigh its advantages and disadvantages.
What is certain is that this lack of regulation does not permit
a regular harmony of functions. The economists claim, it is
true, that this harmony is self-established when necessary,
thanks to rises or declines in prices which, according to needs,
stimulate or slacken production. But in every case this is
established only after ruptures of equilibrium and more or less
prolonged disturbances. Moreover, these disturbances are
naturally as much more frequent as functions are more specialized, for the more complex an organization is, the more is
the need of extensive regulation felt.

The relations of capital and labor have, up to the present,
remained in the same state of juridical indetermination. A

[28] Perrier, *Colonies animales*, p. 746.
[29] See Spencer, *Principles of Biology*, II, 438 ff.

contract for the hire of services occupies a very small place in our codes, particularly when one thinks of the diversity and complexity of the relations which it is called upon to regulate. But it is not necessary to insist upon a gap whose presence is keenly felt by all, and which everybody seeks to fill.[30]

Methodological rules are for science what rules of law and custom are for conduct; they direct the thought of the scholar just as the others govern the actions of men. But if each science has its method, the order that it realizes is wholly internal. It coordinates the findings of scholars who cultivate the same science, not their relations with the outside world. There are hardly any disciplines which bring together the work of the different sciences in the light of a common end. This is particularly true of the moral and social sciences, for the sciences of mathematics, physics, chemistry, and even biology, do not seem to be strangers to one another in this respect. But the jurist, the psychologist, the anthropologist, the economist, the statistician, the linguist, the historian, proceed with their investigations as if the different orders of fact they study constituted so many independent worlds. In reality, however, they penetrate one another from all sides; consequently, the case must be the same with their corresponding sciences. This is where the anarchical state of science in general comes from, a state that has been noted not without exaggeration, but which is particularly true of these specific sciences. They offer the spectacle of an aggregate of disjointed parts which do not concur. If they form a whole without unity, this is not because they do not have a sentiment of their likenesses; it is because they are not organized.

These different examples are, then, varieties of the same species. If the division of labor does not produce solidarity in all these cases, it is because the relations of the organs are not regulated, because they are in a state of *anomie*.

But whence comes this state?

Since a body of rules is the definite form which spontaneously established relations between social functions take in the course of time, we can say, a priori, that the state of *anomie* is impossible wherever solidary organs are sufficiently in contact or sufficiently prolonged. In effect, being contigu-

---

[30] This was written in 1893. Since then, industrial legislation has taken a more important place in our law. This is proof of how serious the gap was and that there was need of its being filled.

ous, they are quickly warned, in each circumstance, of the need which they have of one another, and, consequently, they have a lively and continuous sentiment of their mutual dependence. For the same reason that exchanges take place among them easily, they take place frequently; being regular, they regularize themselves accordingly, and in time the work of consolidation is achieved. Finally, because the smallest reaction can be felt from one part to another, the rules which are thus formulated carry this imprint; that is to say, they foresee and fix, in detail, the conditions of equilibrium. But, on the contrary, if some opaque environment is interposed, then only stimuli of a certain intensity can be communicated from one organ to another. Relations, being rare, are not repeated enough to be determined; each time there ensues new groping. The lines of passage taken by the streams of movement cannot deepen because the streams themselves are too intermittent. If some rules do come to constitute them, they are, however, general and vague, for under these conditions it is only the most general contours of phenomena that can be fixed. The case will be the same if the contiguity, though sufficient, is too recent or has not endured long enough.[31]

Generally, this condition is found to be realized in the nature of things. A function can be apportioned between two or several parts of an organism only if these parts are more or less contiguous. Moreover, once labor is divided, since they need one another, they naturally tend to lessen the distance separating them. That is why as one goes up in the animal scale, one sees organs coming together, and, as Spencer says, being introduced in the interstices of one another. But a set of exceptional circumstances can bring this about differently.

This is what happens in the cases we are discussing. In so far as the segmental type is strongly marked, there are nearly as many economic markets as there are different segments. Consequently, each of them is very limited. Producers, being near consumers, can easily reckon the extent of the needs to be satisfied. Equilibrium is established without any trouble and production regulates itself. On the contrary, as the organ-

---

[31] There is, however, a case where *anomie* can be produced, although the contiguity is sufficient. This occurs when the necessary regulation can be established only by submitting to transformations of which the social structure is incapable. The plasticity of societies is not indefinite. When it reaches its limit, even necessary changes are impossible.

ized type develops, the fusion of different segments draws the markets together into one which embraces almost all society. This even extends beyond, and tends to become universal, for the frontiers which separate peoples break down at the same time as those which separate the segments of each of them. The result is that each industry produces for consumers spread over the whole surface of the country or even of the entire world. Contact is then no longer sufficient. The producer can no longer embrace the market in a glance, nor even in thought. He can no longer see its limits, since it is, so to speak, limitless. Accordingly, production becomes unbridled and unregulated. It can only trust to chance, and in the course of these gropings it is inevitable that proportions will be abused, as much in one direction as in another. From this come the crises which periodically disturb economic functions. The growth of local, restricted crises which result in failures is in all likelihood an effect of the same cause.

As the market extends, great industry appears. But it results in changing the relations of employers and employees. The great strain upon the nervous system and the contagious influence of great agglomerations increase the needs of the latter. Machines replace men; manufacturing replaces handwork. The worker is regimented, separated from his family throughout the day. He always lives apart from his employer, and so on. These new conditions of industrial life naturally demand a new organization, but as these changes have been accomplished with extreme rapidity, the interests in conflict have not yet had the time to be equilibrated.[32]

Finally, the explanation of the fact that the moral and social sciences are in the state we have suggested is that they were the last to come into the circle of positive sciences. It is hardly a century since this new field of phenomena has been opened to scientific investigation. Scholars have installed themselves in them, some here, some there, according to their tastes. Scattered over this wide surface, they have remained until the present too remote from one another to feel all the ties which unite them. But, solely because they will push their researches further from their points of departure, they will necessarily end by reaching and, consequently, taking con-

---

[32] Let us remember, however, that, as we shall see in the following chapter, this antagonism is not entirely due to the rapidity of these changes, but, in good part, to the still very great inequality of the external conditions of the struggle. On this factor, time has no influence.

science of their solidarity. The unity of science will thus form of itself, not through the abstract unity of a formula, far too scanty for the multitude of things that it must embrace, but through the living unity of an organic whole. For science to be unitary, it is not necessary for it to be contained within the field of one and the same conscience—an impossible feat anyhow—but it is sufficient that all those who cultivate it feel that they are collaborating in the same work.

The preceding has removed one of the most serious charges brought against the division of labor.

It has often been accused of degrading the individual by making him a machine. And truly, if he does not know whither the operations he performs are tending, if he relates them to no end, he can continue to work only through routine. Every day he repeats the same movements with monotonous regularity, but without being interested in them and without understanding them. He is no longer a living cell of a living organism which unceasingly vibrates with neighboring cells, which acts upon them, and to whose action it responds and with whose needs and circumstances it changes. He is no longer anything but an inert piece of machinery, only an external force set going which always moves in the same direction and in the same way. Surely, no matter how one may represent the moral ideal, one cannot remain indifferent to such debasement of human nature. If morality has individual perfection as its goal, it cannot thus permit the ruin of the individual, and if it has society as its goal it cannot let the very source of social life be drained, for the peril does not threaten only economic functions, but all social functions, as elevated as they may be. "If," says Comte, "we have often justly deplored, in the material world, the workman being exclusively occupied during his whole life with the manufacture of knife handles or pinheads, healthy philosophy ought not less bemoan, in the intellectual order, the exclusive and continuous employment of the human brain in the resolution of some equations or in the classification of some insects. The moral effect, in one case, as in the other, is unfortunately very much the same."[33]

As a remedy, it has sometimes been proposed that, in addition to their technical and special instruction, workers be given a general education. But, suppose that we can thus relieve some of the bad effects attributed to the division of labor; that is not a means of preventing them. The division does

[33] *Cours,* IV, 430.

not change its nature because it has been preceded by general culture. No doubt, it is good for the worker to be interested in art, literature, and so on, but it is nonetheless bad that he should be treated as a machine all day long. Who cannot see, moreover, that two such existences are too opposed to be reconciled, and cannot be led by the same man! If a person has grown accustomed to vast horizons, total views, broad generalities, he cannot be confined, without impatience, within the strict limits of a special task. Such a remedy would make specialization inoffensive by making it intolerable, and, consequently, more or less impossible.

What solves the contradiction is that, contrary to what has been said, the division of labor does not produce these consequences because of a necessity of its own nature, but only in exceptional and abnormal circumstances. In order for it to develop without having such a disastrous influence on the human conscience, it is not necessary to temper it with its opposite. It is necessary and it is sufficient for it to be itself, for nothing to come from without to denature it. For, normally, the role of each special function does not require that the individual close himself in but that he keep himself in constant relations with neighboring functions, take conscience of their needs, of the changes which they undergo, and so on. The division of labor presumes that the worker, far from being hemmed in by his task, does not lose sight of his collaborators, that he acts upon them, and reacts to them. He is, then, not a machine who repeats his movements without knowing their meaning, but he knows that they tend, in some way, toward an end that he conceives more or less distinctly. He feels that he is serving something. For that, he need not embrace vast portions of the social horizon; it is sufficient that he perceive enough of it to understand that his actions have an aim beyond themselves. From that time, as special and uniform as his activity may be, it is that of an intelligent being, for it has direction, and he knows it. The economists would not have left this essential character of the division of labor in the shade and, accordingly, would not have exposed it to this unmerited reproach, if they had not reduced it to being merely a means of increasing the produce of social forces, if they had seen that it is above all a source of solidarity.

CONCLUSION

WE are now in a position to solve the practical problem that we posed for ourselves at the beginning of this work.

If there is one rule of conduct which is incontestable, it is that which orders us to realize in ourselves the essential traits of the collective type. Among lower peoples, this reaches its greatest rigor. There, one's first duty is to resemble everybody else, not to have anything personal about one's beliefs or actions. In more advanced societies, required likenesses are less numerous; the absences of some likenesses, however, is still a sign of moral failure. Of course, crime falls into fewer different categories; but today, as heretofore, if a criminal is the object of reprobation, it is because he is unlike us. Likewise, in lesser degree, acts simply immoral and prohibited acts such as those which evince dissemblances less profound but nevertheless considered serious. Is this not the case with the rule which common morality expresses when it orders a man to be a man in every sense of the word, which is to say, to have all the ideas and sentiments which go to make up a human conscience? No doubt, if this formula is taken literally, the man prescribed would be man in general and not one of some particular social species. But, in reality, this human conscience that we must integrally realize is nothing else than the collective conscience of the group of which we are a part. For what can it be composed of, if not the ideas and sentiments to which we are most attached? Where can we find the traits of our model, if not within us and around us? If we believe that this collective ideal is that of all humanity, that is because it has become so abstract and general that it appears fitting for all men indiscriminately. But, really, every people makes for itself some particular conception of this type which pertains to its personal temperament. Each represents it in its own image. Even the moralist who thinks he can, through thought, overcome the influence of transient ideas, cannot do so, for he is impregnated with them, and no matter what he does, he finds these precepts in the body of his deductions. That is why each nation has its own school of moral philosophy conforming to its character.

On the other hand, we have shown that this rule had as its function the prevention of all agitation of the common conscience, and, consequently, of social solidarity, and that it could accomplish this role only by having a moral character. It is impossible for offenses against the most fundamental collective sentiments to be tolerated without the disintegration of society, and it is necessary to combat them with the aid of the particularly energetic reaction which attaches to moral rules.

But the contrary rule, which orders us to specialize, has exactly the same function. It also is necessary for the cohesion of societies, at least at a certain period in their evolution. Of course, its solidarity is different from the preceding, but though it is different it is no less indispensable. Higher societies can maintain themselves in equilibrium only if labor is divided; the attraction of like for like less and less suffices to produce this result. If, then, the moral character of the first of these rules is necessary to the playing of its role, it is no less necessary to the second. They both correspond to the same social need, but satisfy the need differently, because the conditions of existence in the societies themselves differ. Consequently, without speculating concerning the first principle of ethics, we can induce the moral value of one from the moral value of the other. If, from certain points of view, there is a real antagonism between them, that is not because they serve different ends. On the contrary, it is because they lead to the same end, but through opposed means. Accordingly, there is no necessity for choosing between them once for all nor of condemning one in the name of the other. What is necessary is to give each, at each moment in history, the place that is fitting to it.

Perhaps we can even generalize further in this matter.

The requirements of our subject have obliged us to classify moral rules and to review the principal types. We are thus in a better position than we were in the beginning to see, or at least to conjecture, not only upon the external sign but also upon the internal character which is common to all of them and which can serve to define them. We have put them into two groups: rules with repressive sanctions, which may be diffuse or organized, and rules with restitutive sanctions. We have seen that the first of these express the conditions of the solidarity, *sui generis*, which comes from resemblances, and to which we have given the name mechanical; the second, the conditions of negative solidarity[34] and organic solidarity. We can thus say that, in general, the characteristic of moral rules is that they enunciate the fundamental conditions of social solidarity. Law and morality are the totality of ties which bind each of us to society, which make a unitary, coherent aggregate of the mass of individuals. Everything which is a source of solidarity is moral; everything which forces man to take account of other men is moral; everything which forces him

[34] See Book I, Chap. iii, §2.

to regulate his conduct through something other than the striving of his ego is moral; and morality is as solid as these ties are numerous and strong. We can see how inexact it is to define it, as is often done, through liberty. It rather consists in a state of dependence. Far from serving to emancipate the individual, or disengaging him from the environment which surrounds him, it has, on the contrary, the function of making him an integral part of a whole, and, consequently, of depriving him of some liberty of movement. We sometimes, it is true, come across people not without nobility who find the idea of such dependence intolerable. But that is because they do not perceive the source from which their own morality flows, since these sources are very deep. Conscience is a bad judge of what goes on in the depths of a person, because it does not penetrate to them.

Society is not, then, as has often been thought, a stranger to the moral world, or something which has only secondary repercussions upon it. It is, on the contrary, the necessary condition of its existence. It is not a simple juxtaposition of individuals who bring an intrinsic morality with them, but rather man is a moral being only because he lives in society, since morality consists in being solidary with a group and varying with this solidarity. Let all social life disappear, and moral life will disappear with it, since it would no longer have any objective. The state of nature of the philosophers of the eighteenth century, if not immoral, is, at least, *amoral*. Rousseau himself recognized this. Through this, however, we do not come upon the formula which expresses morality as a function of social interest. To be sure, society cannot exist if its parts are not solidary, but solidarity is only one of its conditions of existence. There are many others which are no less necessary and which are not moral. Moreover, it can happen that, in the system of ties which make up morality, there are some which are not useful in themselves or which have power without any relation to their degree of utility. The idea of utility does not enter as an essential element in our definition.

As for what is called individual morality, if we understand by that a totality of duties of which the individual would, at the same time, be subject and object, and which would link him only to himself, and which would, consequently, exist even if he were solitary—that is an abstract conception which has no relation to reality. Morality, in all its forms, is never met with except in society. It never varies except in relation to social conditions. To ask what it would be if societies did not exist is thus to depart from facts and enter the domain of gratuitous hypotheses and unverifiable flights of the imagination. The duties of the individual toward himself are, in reality, duties toward society. They correspond to certain collective sentiments which he cannot offend, whether the offended and the offender are one and the same person, or whether they are distinct. Today, for example, there is in all healthy consciences a very lively sense of respect for human dignity, to which we are supposed to conform as much in our relations with ourselves as in our relations with others, and this constitutes the essential quality of what is called individual morality. Every act which contravenes this is censured, even when the agent and the sufferer are the same person. That is why, according to the Kantian formula, we ought to respect human personality wherever we find it, which is to say, in ourselves as in those like us. The sentiment of which it is the object is not less offended in one case than in the other.

But not only does the division of labor present the character by which we have defined morality; it more and more tends to become the essential condition of social solidarity. As we advance in the evolutionary scale, the ties which bind the individual to his family, to his native soil, to traditions which the past has given to him, to collective group usages, become loose. More mobile, he changes his environment more easily, leaves his people to go elsewhere to live a more autonomous existence, to a greater extent forms his own ideas and sentiments. Of course, the whole common conscience does not, on this account, pass out of existence. At least there will always remain this cult of personality, of individual dignity of which we have just been speaking, and which, today, is the rallying point of so many people. But how little a thing it is when one contemplates the ever increasing extent of social life, and, consequently, of individual consciences! For, as they become more voluminous, as intelligence becomes richer, activity more varied, in order for morality to remain constant, that is to say, in order for the individual to remain attached to the group with a force equal to that of yesterday, the ties which bind him to it must become stronger and more numerous. If, then, he formed no others than those which come from resemblances, the effacement of the segmental type would be accompanied by a systematic debasement of morality. Man would no longer be sufficiently obligated; he would no longer feel about and above him this salutary pressure of society which moderates his egoism and makes him a moral being. This is what gives moral value to the division of labor. Through it, the individual becomes cognizant of his dependence upon society; from it come the forces which keep him in check and restrain him. In short, since the division of labor becomes the chief source of social solidarity, it becomes, at the same time, the foundation of the moral order.

We can then say that, in higher societies, our duty is not to spread our activity over a large surface, but to concentrate and specialize it. We must contract our horizon, choose a definite task, and immerse ourselves in it completely, instead of trying to make ourselves a sort of creative masterpiece, quite complete, which contains its worth in itself and not in the services that it renders. Finally, this specialization ought to be pushed as far as the elevation of the social type, without assigning any other limit to it.[35] No doubt, we ought so to work as to realize in ourselves the collective type as it exists. There are common sentiments, common ideas, without which, as has been said, one is not a man. The rule which orders us to specialize remains limited by the contrary rule. Our conclusion is not that it is good to press specialization as far as possible, but as far as necessary. As for the part that is to be played by these two opposing necessities, that is determined by experience and cannot be calculated a priori. It is enough for us to have shown that the second is not of a different nature from the first, but that it also is moral and that, moreover, this duty becomes ever more important and pressing, because the general qualities which are in question suffice less and less to socialize the individual.

It is not without reason that public sentiment reproves an

[35] There is, however, probably another limit which we do not have to speak of since it concerns individual hygiene. It may be held that, in the light of our organicopsychic constitution, the division of labor cannot go beyond a certain limit without disorders resulting. Without entering upon the question, let us straightway say that the extreme specialization at which biological functions have arrived does not seem favorable to this hypothesis. Moreover, in the very order of psychic and social functions, has not the division of labor, in its historical development, been carried to the last stage in the relations of men and women? Have not there been faculties completely lost by both? Why cannot the same phenomenon occur between individuals of the same sex? Of course, it takes time for the organism to adapt itself to these changes, but we do not see why a day should come when this adaptation would become impossible.

ever more pronounced tendency on the part of dilettantes and even others to be taken up with an exclusively general culture and refuse to take any part in occupational organization. That is because they are not sufficiently attached to society, or, if one wishes, society is not sufficiently attached to them, and they escape it. Precisely because they feel its effect neither with vivacity nor with the continuity that is necessary, they have no cognizance of all the obligations their positions as social beings demand of them. The general ideal to which they are attached being, for the reasons we have spoken of, formal and shifting, it cannot take them out of themselves. We do not cling to very much when we have no very determined objective, and, consequently, we cannot very well elevate ourselves beyond a more or less refined egotism. On the contrary, he who gives himself over to a definite task is, at every moment, struck by the sentiment of common solidarity in the thousand duties of occupational morality.[36]

But does not the division of labor by making each of us an incomplete being bring on a diminution of individual personality? That is a reproach which has often been leveled at it.

Let us first of all remark that it is difficult to see why it would be more in keeping with the logic of human nature to develop superficially rather than profoundly. Why would a more extensive activity, but more dispersed, be superior to a more concentrated, but circumscribed, activity? Why would there be more dignity in being complete and mediocre, rather than in living a more specialized but more intense life, particularly if it is thus possible for us to find what we have lost in this specialization, through our association with other beings who have what we lack and who complete us? We take off from the principle that man ought to realize his

[36] Among the practical consequences that might be deduced from the proposition that we have just established, there is one of interest to education. We always reason, in educational affairs, as if the moral basis of man was made up of generalities. We have just seen that such is not the case at all. Man is destined to fill a special function in the social organism, and, consequently, he must learn, in advance, how to play this role. For that an education is necessary, quite as much as that he should learn his role as a man. We do not, however, wish to imply, that it is necessary to rear a child prematurely for some certain profession, but that it is necessary to get him to like the idea of circumscribed tasks and limited horizons. But this taste is quite different from that for general things, and cannot be aroused by the same means.

nature as man, to accomplish his ὀικεῖον ἔργον, as Aristotle said. But this nature does not remain constant throughout history; it is modified with societies. Among lower peoples, the proper duty of man is to resemble his companions, to realize in himself all the traits of the collective type which are then confounded, much more than today, with the human type. But, in more advanced societies, his nature is, in large part, to be an organ of society, and his proper duty, consequently, is to play his role as an organ.

Moreover, far from being trammeled by the progress of specialization, individual personality develops with the division of labor.

To be a person is to be an autonomous source of action. Man acquires this quality only insofar as there is something in him which is his alone and which individualizes him, as he is something more than a simple incarnation of the generic type of his race and his group. It will be said that he is endowed with free will and that is enough to establish his personality. But although there may be some of this liberty in him, an object of so many discussions, it is not this metaphysical, impersonal, invariable attribute which can serve as the unique basis for concrete personality, which is empirical and variable with individuals. That could not be constituted by the wholly abstract power of choice between two opposites, but it is still necessary for this faculty to be exercised toward ends and aims which are proper to the agent. In other words, the very materials of conscience must have a personal character. But we have seen in the second book of this work that this result is progressively produced as the division of labor progresses. This effacement of the segmental type, at the same time that it necessitates a very great specialization, partially lifts the individual conscience from the organic environment which supports it, as from the social environment which envelops it, and, accordingly, because of this double emancipation, the individual becomes more of an independent factor in his own conduct. The division of labor itself contributes to this enfranchisement, for individual natures, while specializing, become more complex, and by that are in part freed from collective action and hereditary influences which can only enforce themselves upon simple, general things.

It is, accordingly, a real illusion which makes us believe that personality was so much more complete when the division of labor had penetrated less. No doubt, in looking from without at the diversity of occupations which the individual then embraces, it may seem that he is developing in a very free and complete manner. But, in reality, this activity which he manifests is not really his. It is society, it is the race acting in and through him; he is only the intermediary through which they realize themselves. His liberty is only apparent and his personality borrowed. Because the life of these societies is, in certain respects, less regular, we imagine that original talents have more opportunity for free play, that it is easier for each one to pursue his own tastes, that a very large place is left to free fantasy. But this is to forget that personal sentiments are then very rare. If the motives which govern conduct do not appear as periodically as they do today, they do not leave off being collective, and, consequently, impersonal, and it is the same with the actions that they inspire. Moreover, we have shown above how activity becomes richer and more intense as it becomes more specialized.

Thus, the progress of individual personality and that of the division of labor depend upon one and the same cause. It is thus impossible to desire one without desiring the other. But no one today contests the obligatory character of the rule which orders us to be more and more of a person.

One last consideration will make us see to what extent the division of labor is linked with our whole moral life.

Men have long dreamed of finally realizing in fact the ideal of human fraternity. People pray for a state where war will no longer be the law of international relations, where relations between societies will be pacifically regulated, as those between individuals already are, where all men will collaborate in the same work and live the same life. Although these aspirations are in part neutralized by those which have as their object the particular society of which we are a part, they have not left off being active and are even gaining in force. But they can be satisfied only if all men form one society, subject to the same laws. For, just as private conflicts can be regulated only by the action of the society in which the individuals live, so intersocial conflicts can be regulated only by a society which comprises in its scope all others. The only power which can serve to moderate individual egotism is the power of the group; the only power which can serve to moderate the egotism of groups is that of some other group which embraces them.

Truly, when the problem has been posed in these terms, we must recognize that this ideal is not on the verge of being integrally realized, for there are too many intellectual and moral diversities between different social types existing together on the earth to admit of fraternalization in the same society. But what is possible is that societies of the same type may come together, and it is, indeed, in this direction that evolution appears to move. We have already seen that among European peoples there is a tendency to form, by spontaneous movement, a European society which has, at present, some idea of itself and the beginning of organization.[37] If the formation of a single human society is forever impossible, a fact which has not been proved, at least the formation of continually larger societies brings us vaguely near the goal. These facts, moreover, in no wise contradict the definition of morality that we have given, for if we cling to humanity and if we ought to cling to it, it is because it is a society which is in process of realizing itself in this way, and with which we are solidary.[38]

But we know that greater societies cannot be formed except through the development of the division of labor, for not only could they not maintain themselves in equilibrium without a greater specialization of functions, but even the increase in the number of those competing would suffice to produce this result mechanically; and that, so much the more, since the growth of volume is generally accompanied by a growth in density. We can then formulate the following proposition: the ideal of human fraternity can be realized only in proportion to the progress of the division of labor. We must choose: either to renounce our dream, if we refuse further to circumscribe our activity, or else to push forward its accomplishment under the condition we have just set forth.

But if the division of labor produces solidarity, it is not only because it makes each individual an *exchangist,* as the

[37] There is nothing that forces the intellectual and moral diversity of societies to be maintained. The ever greater expansion of higher societies, from which there results the absorbtion or elimination of less advanced societies, tends, in any case, to diminish such diversity.

[38] Thus, the duties that we have toward it do not oppress those which link us to our country. For the latter is the only actually realized society of which we are members; the other is only a desideratum whose realization is not even assured.

economists say;[39] it is because it creates among men an entire system of rights and duties which link them together in a durable way. Just as social similitudes give rise to a law and a morality which protect them, so the division of labor gives rise to rules which assure pacific and regular concourse of divided functions. If economists have believed that it would bring forth an abiding solidarity, in some manner of its own making, and if, accordingly, they have held that human societies could and would resolve themselves into purely economic associations, that is because they believed that it affected only individual, temporary interests. Consequently, to estimate the interests in conflict and the way in which they ought to equilibrate, that is to say, to determine the conditions under which exchange ought to take place, is solely a matter of individual competence; and, since these interests are in a perpetual state of becoming, there is no place for any permanent regulation. But such a conception is, in all ways, inadequate for the facts. The division of labor does not present individuals to one another, but social functions. And society is interested in the play of the latter; insofar as they regularly concur, or do not concur, it will be healthy or ill. Its existence thus depends upon them, and the more they are divided the greater its dependence. That is why it cannot leave them in a state of indetermination. In addition to this, they are determined by themselves. Thus are formed those rules whose number grows as labor is divided, and whose absence makes organic solidarity either impossible or imperfect.

But it is not enough that there be rules; they must be just, and for that it is necessary for the external conditions of competition to be equal. If, moreover, we remember that the collective conscience is becoming more and more a cult of the individual, we shall see that what characterizes the morality of organized societies, compared to that of segmental societies, is that there is something more human, therefore more rational, about them. It does not direct our activities to ends which do not immediately concern us; it does not make us servants of ideal powers of a nature other than our own, which follow their directions without occupying themselves with the interests of men. It asks only that we be thoughtful of our fellows and that we be just, that we fulfill our duty, that we work at the function we can best execute, and receive the just

[39] The word is De Molinari's, *La Morale économique*, p. 248.

reward for our services. The rules which constitute it do not have a constraining force which snuffs out free thought; but, because they are rather made for us and, in a certain sense, by us, we are free. We wish to understand them; we do not fear to change them. We must, however, guard against finding such an ideal inadequate on the pretext that it is too earthly and too much to our liking. An ideal is not more elevated because more transcendent, but because it leads us to vaster perspectives. What is important is not that it tower high above us, until it becomes a stranger to our lives, but that it open to our activity a large enough field. This is far from being on the verge of realization. We know only too well what a laborious work it is to erect this society where each individual will have the place he merits, will be rewarded as he deserves, where everybody, accordingly, will spontaneously work for the good of all and of each. Indeed, a moral code is not above another because it commands in a drier and more authoritarian manner, or because it is more sheltered from reflection. Of course, it must attach us to something besides ourselves, but it is not necessary for it to chain us to it with impregnable bonds.

It has been said[40] with justice that morality—and by that must be understood not only moral doctrines but customs—is going through a real crisis. What precedes can help us to understand the nature and causes of this sick condition. Profound changes have been produced in the structure of our societies in a very short time; they have been freed from the segmental type with a rapidity and in proportions such as have never before been seen in history. Accordingly, the morality which corresponds to this social type has regressed, but without another developing quickly enough to fill the ground that the first left vacant in our consciences. Our faith has been troubled; tradition has lost its sway; individual judgment has been freed from collective judgment. But, on the other hand, the functions which have been disrupted in the course of the upheaval have not had the time to adjust themselves to one another; the new life which has emerged so suddenly has not been able to be completely organized, and above all, it has not been organized in a way to satisfy the need for justice which has grown more ardent in our hearts. If this be so, the remedy for the evil is not to seek to resuscitate traditions and practices which, no longer responding to pres-

[40] Beaussire, *Les Principes de la morale,* "Introduction."

ent conditions of society, can live only an artificial, false existence. What we must do to relieve this anomie is to discover the means for making the organs which are still wasting themselves in discordant movements harmoniously concur by introducing into their relations more justice by more and more extenuating the external inequalities which are the source of the evil. Our illness is not, then, as has often been believed, of an intellectual sort; it has more profound causes. We shall not suffer because we no longer know on what theoretical notion to base the morality we have been practicing, but because, in certain of its parts, this morality is irremediably shattered, and because that which is necessary to us is only in process of formation. Our anxiety does not arise because the criticism of scholars has broken down the traditional explanation we use to give to our duties; consequently, it is not a new philosophical system which will relieve the situation. Because certain of our duties are no longer founded in the reality of things, a breakdown has resulted which will be repaired only insofar as a new discipline is established and consolidated. In short, our first duty is to make a moral code for ourselves. Such a work cannot be improvised in the silence of the study; it can arise only through itself, little by little, under the pressure of internal causes which make it necessary. But the service that thought can and must render is in fixing the goal that we must attain. That is what we have tried to do.

Georges Sorel
(1847–1922)

THE ETHICS OF VIOLENCE

In an era in which we are confronted at all times with the growth of large-scale organization and the increasing significance of political élites, the writings of Georges Sorel, radical syndicalist and political analyst, have lost nothing of their importance. His influence on Vilfredo Pareto and Robert Michels is evident, and with them "he argued that large-scale organization necessarily leads to the formation of a group of leaders, who will act only for self-aggrandizement and who will be prey to the enervation and corruption always produced by the exercise of power and opportunities for advantage."[1] Sorel is much more a philosopher of politics than a sociologist or social theorist. His works, however, have sociological overtones and implications. His conception of the "myth," as Shils has remarked, as the value system and picture of the world of the fraternal band, of the charismatic sect, help us to define more closely some of the explosive potentialities in the thought and structure of modern society since the Reformation.[2]

In his writings Sorel is primarily concerned with the development of a human type rather than with the elaboration of a political doctrine. Sorel's conception of socialism was as a radical syndicalist movement which originated in the moral disintegration of the ruling bourgeoisie. He was, however, opposed to a revolutionary transformation of the economic system.

He declared that social change was economically as well as historically determined. Sorel believed strongly in "action directe" against the ruling bourgeoisie. His doctrine of direct action implies a sharp reaction to every attempt at mediation and humanitarian neutralization, which prefers compromise to the obtaining of the workers' just due by the use of militant tactics.

---

[1] Edward A. Shils in the American introduction to *Reflections on Violence*, Glencoe, The Free Press, 1950.
[2] Ibid.

"Militant" is the basic tone and philosophy of his writings. I have selected parts of his most militant essay Reflections on Violence *for reprinting here. His remarks are especially interesting to contemporary social scientists in that Sorel presents us with a penetrating analysis of the origins of violence.*

Georges Sorel was born in Cherbourg in 1847. He attended the Ecole Polytechnique and became an engineer in the Department of Bridges and Highways. He retired from the Department when he was forty-four and devoted the rest of his life to writing. He also played an active part in the Syndicalist movement. He led a modest, almost bourgeois existence in one of the Paris suburbs. He was very happily married, but had no children. His wife died young and it was to her memory that Sorel dedicated his Reflections on Violence.

THE ETHICS OF VIOLENCE

I. OBSERVATIONS OF P. BUREAU AND OF P. DE ROUSIERS— THE ERA OF MARTYRS—POSSIBILITY OF MAINTAINING THE CLEAVAGE WITH VERY LITTLE VIOLENCE, THANKS TO A CATASTROPHIC MYTH

THERE are so many legal precautions against violence, and our upbringing is directed toward so weakening our tendencies toward violence, that we are instinctively inclined to think that any act of violence is a manifestation of a return to barbarism. Peace has always been considered the greatest of blessings and the essential condition of all material progress, and it is for this reason that industrial societies have so often been contrasted favorably with military ones. This last point of view explains why, almost uninterruptedly since the eighteenth century, economists have been in favor of strong central authorities, and have troubled little about political liberties. Condorcet levels this reproach at the followers of Quesnay, and Napoleon III had probably no greater admirer than Michel Chevalier.[3]

[3] "One day Michel Chevalier came beaming into the editorial room of the *Journal des débats*. His first words were: 'I have achieved liberty!' Everybody was all agog; he was asked to explain. He meant the liberty of the slaughterhouses" (Renan, *Feuilles détachées*, p. 149).

It may be questioned whether there is not a little stupidity in the admiration of our contemporaries for gentle methods. I see, in fact, that several authors, remarkable for their perspicacity and their interest in the ethical side of every question, do not seem to have the same fear of violence as our official professors.

P. Bureau was extremely surprised to find in Norway a rural population which had remained profoundly Christian. The peasants, nevertheless, carried a dagger at their belt; when a quarrel ended in a stabbing affray, the police inquiry generally came to nothing for lack of witnesses ready to come forward and give evidence.

The author concludes thus: "In men, a soft and effeminate character is more to be feared than their feeling of independence, however exaggerated and brutal, and a stab given by a man who is virtuous in his morals, but violent, is a social evil less serious and more easily curable than the excessive profligacy of young men reputed to be more civilized."[4]

I borrow a second example from P. de Rousiers, who, like P. Bureau, is a fervent Catholic, and interested especially in the moral side of all questions. He narrates how, toward 1860, the locality of Denver, the great mining center of the Rocky Mountains, was cleared of the bandits who infested it; the American magistracy being impotent, courageous citizens undertook the work. "Lynch law was frequently put into operation; a man accused of murder or of theft might be arrested, condemned, and hanged in less than a quarter of an hour, if an energetic vigilance committee could get hold of him. The American who happens to be honest has one excellent habit—he does not allow himself to be crushed on the pretext that he is virtuous. A law-abiding man is not necessarily a craven, as is often the case with us; on the contrary, he is convinced that his interests ought to be considered before those of a habitual criminal or of a gambler. Moreover, he possesses the necessary energy to resist, and the kind of life he leads makes him capable of resisting effectively, even of taking the initiative and the responsibility of a serious step when circumstances demand it. . . . Such a man, placed in a new country, full of natural resources, wishing to take advantage of the riches it contains and to acquire a superior situation in life by his labor, will not hesitate to suppress, in the

[4] P. Bureau, *Le Paysan des fjords de Norwège*, pp. 114 and 115.

name of the higher interests he represents, the bandits who compromise the future of this country. That is why, twenty-five years ago at Denver, so many corpses were dangling above the little wooden bridge thrown across Cherry Creek."[5]

This is a considered opinion of P. de Rousiers, for he returns elsewhere to this question. "I know," he says, "that lynch law is generally considered in France as a symptom of barbarism . . . ; but if honest, virtuous people in Europe think thus, virtuous people in America think quite otherwise."[6] He highly approved of the vigilance committee of New Orleans which, in 1890, "to the great satisfaction of all virtuous people," hanged *maffiosi* acquitted by the jury.[7]

In Corsica, at the time when the vendetta was the regular means of supplying the deficiencies or correcting the action of a too halting justice, the people do not appear to have been less moral than today. Before the French conquest, Kabylie had no means of punishment other than private vengeance, yet the Kabyles were not a bad people.

It may be conceded to those in favor of mild methods that violence may hamper economic progress, and even, when it goes beyond a certain limit, that it is a danger to morality. This concession cannot be used as an argument against the doctrine set forth here, because I consider violence only from the point of view of its influence on social theories. It is, in fact, certain that a great development of brutality accompanied by much bloodletting is quite unnecessary in order to induce the workers to look upon economic conflicts as the reduced facsimiles of the great battle which will decide the future. If a capitalist class is energetic, it is constantly affirming its determination to defend itself; its frank and consistently reactionary attitude contributes at least as greatly as proletarian violence toward keeping distinct that cleavage between the classes which is the basis of all Socialism.

We may make use here of the great historical example provided by the persecutions which Christians were obliged to suffer during the first centuries. Modern authors have been so struck by the language of the Fathers of the Church, and

[5] De Rousiers, *La Vie américaine*, "Ranches, fermes, et usines," pp. 224-225.

[6] De Rousiers, *La Vie américaine*, "L'education et la société, p. 218.

[7] De Rousiers, *loc. cit.* p. 221.

by the details given in the Acts of the Martyrs, that they have generally imagined the Christians as outlaws whose blood was continually being spilled. The cleavage between the pagan world and the Christian world was extraordinarily well marked; without this cleavage the latter would never have acquired all its characteristic features; but this cleavage was maintained by a combination of circumstances very different from that formerly imagined.

Nobody believes any longer that the Christians took refuge in subterranean quarries in order to escape the searches of the police; the catacombs were dug out at great expense by communities with large resources at their disposal, under land belonging generally to powerful families which protected the new cult. Nobody has any doubt now that before the end of the first century Christianity had its followers among the Roman aristocracy: "In the very ancient catacomb of Priscilla . . . has been found the family vault in which was buried from the first to the fourth century the Christian line of the Acilii."[8] It seems also that the old belief that the number of the martyrdoms was very great must be abandoned.

Renan still asserted that the literature of martyrdom should be taken seriously. "The details of the Acts of the Martyrs," he said, "may be false for the most part; the dreadful picture which they unroll before us was nevertheless a reality. The true nature of this terrible struggle has often been misconceived, but its seriousness has not been exaggerated."[9] The researches of Harnack lead to quite another conclusion: the language of the Christian authors was entirely disproportionate to the actual importance of the persecutions; there were very few martyrs before the middle of the third century. Tertullian is the writer who has most strongly indicated the horror which the new religion felt for its persecutors, and yet here is what Harnack says: "If, with the help of the works of Tertullian, we consider Carthage and northern Africa we shall find that before the year 180 there was in those regions no case of martyrdom and that from that year to the death of Tertullian (after 220), and adding Numidia and the Mauritanias, scarcely more than two dozen could be counted."[10] It must be remembered that at that time there was in Africa a rather large number of Montanists, who extolled the glory of mar-

[8] P. Allard, *Dix leçons sur le martyre,* p. 171.
[9] Renan, *Église chrétienne,* p. 137.
[10] P. Allard, *op. cit.* p. 137.

tyrdom, and denied that anyone had the right to fly from persecution.

P. Allard combats Harnack's proposition with arguments which seem to me somewhat weak.[11] He is unable to understand the enormous difference which probably exists between the reality of the persecutions and the conceptions which the persecuted formed of them. "The Christians," says the German professor, "were able to complain of being persecuted flocks, and yet such persecution was exceptional; they were able to look upon themselves as models of heroism, and yet they were rarely put to the proof"; and I call attention to the end of this sentence: "They were able to place themselves above the grandeurs of the world, and yet at the same time to make themselves more and more at home in it."[12]

There is something paradoxical at first sight in the situation of the Church, which had its followers in the upper classes, who were obliged to make many concessions to custom, and who yet could hold beliefs based on the idea of an absolute cleavage. The inscriptions on the catacomb of Priscilla prove "the continuance of the faith through a series of generations of the Acilii, among whom were to be found not only consuls and magistrates of the highest order, but also priests, priestesses, even children, members of illustrious idolatrous colleges, reserved by privilege for patricians and their sons."[13] If the Christian system of ideas had been rigorously based on actual facts, such a paradox would have been impossible.

The statistics of persecutions therefore play no great part in this question; what was of much greater importance than the frequency of the torments were the remarkable occurrences which took place during the scenes of martyrdom. The Christian ideology was based on these rather rare but very heroic events; there was no necessity for the martyrdoms to be numerous in order to prove, by the test of experience, the absolute truth of the new religion and the absolute error of the old, to establish thus that there were two incompatible ways, and to make it clear that the reign of evil would come to an end. "In spite of the small number of martyrs," says Harnack, "we may estimate at its true value the courage needed to become a Christian and to live as one. Above all else we ought to praise the conviction of the martyr whom a

---

[11] *Revue des questions historiques*, July, 1905.

[12] P. Allard, *op. cit.* p. 142. Cf. what I have said in *Le Système historique de Renan*, pp. 312-315.

[13] P. Allard, *op. cit.* p. 206.

word or a gesture could save, and who preferred death to such freedom."[14] Contemporaries who saw in martyrdom a *judicial proof*, testifying to the honor of Christ,[15] drew from these facts conclusions quite other than those which a modern historian, whose mind runs in modern grooves, might draw from them; no ideology was ever more remote from the facts than that of the early Christians.

The Roman administration dealt very severely with anyone who showed a tendency to disturb the public peace, especially with any accused person who defied its majesty. In striking down from time to time a few Christians who had been denounced to it (for reasons which have generally remained hidden from us) it did not think that it was accomplishing an act which would ever interest posterity; it seems that the general public itself hardly ever took any great notice of these punishments; and this explains why the persecutions left scarcely any trace on pagan literature. The pagans had no reason to attach to martyrdom the extraordinary importance which the faithful and those who already sympathized with them attached to it.

This ideology would certainly not have been formed in so paradoxical a manner had it not been for the firm belief that people had in the catastrophes described by the numerous apocalypses which were composed at the end of the first century and at the beginning of the second; it was the conviction of all that the world was to be delivered up completely to the reign of evil and that Christ would then come and give the final victory to His elect. Any case of persecution borrowed from the mythology of the Antichrist something of its dread dramatic character; instead of being valued on its actual importance as a misfortune which had befallen a few individuals, a lesson for the community, or a temporary check on propaganda, it became an incident of the war carried on by Satan, prince of this world, who was soon to reveal his Antichrist. Thus the cleavage sprang at the same time from the persecutions and from the feverish expectation of a decisive battle. When Christianity had developed sufficiently, the apocalyptic literature ceased to be cultivated to any extent; although the root idea contained therein still continued to exercise its influence, the Acts of the Martyrs were drawn up in such a way that they might excite the same feelings that

[14] P. Allard, *op. cit.* p. 142.
[15] G. Sorel, *Le Système historique de Renan,* pp. 335-336.

the apocalypses excited; it may be said that they replaced these:[16] we sometimes find in the literature of the persecutions, set down as clearly as in the apocalypses, the horror which the faithful felt for the ministers of Satan who persecuted them.[17]

It is possible, therefore, to conceive of Socialism as being perfectly revolutionary, although there may only be a few short conflicts, provided that these have strength enough to evoke the idea of the general strike: all the events of the conflict will then appear under a magnified form, and the idea of catastrophe being maintained, the cleavage will be perfect. Thus one objection often urged against revolutionary Socialism may be set aside—there is no danger of civilization succumbing under the consequences of a development of brutality, since the idea of the class war by means of incidents which would appear to middle-class historians as of small importance.

When the governing classes, no longer daring to govern, are ashamed of their privileged situation, are eager to make advances to their enemies, and proclaim their horror of all cleavage in society, it becomes much more difficult to maintain in the minds of the proletariat this idea of cleavage which without Socialism cannot fulfill its historical role. So much the better, declare the worthy progressives; we may then hope that the future of the world will not be left in the hands of brutes who do not even respect the state, who laugh at the lofty ideas of the middle class, and who have no more admiration for the professional expounders of lofty thought than for priests. Let us therefore do more and more every day for the disinherited, say these gentlemen; let us show ourselves more Christian, more philanthropic, or more democratic (according to the temperament of each); let us unite for the accomplishment of *social duty*. We shall thus get the better of these dreadful Socialists, who think it possible to destroy the prestige of the intellectuals now that the intellectuals have destroyed that of the Church. As a matter of fact, these

---

[16] It is probable that the first Christian generation had no clear idea of the possibility of replacing the apocalypses imitated from Jewish literature by the Acts of the Martyrs; this would explain why we possess no accounts prior to the year 155 (letter of Smyrniotes telling of the death of St. Polycarpe), and why all memory of a certain number of very ancient Roman martyrs has been lost.

[17] *Marc Aurèle*, p. 500.

cunning moral combinations have failed; it is not difficult to see why.

The specious reasoning of these gentlemen—the pontiffs of "social duty"—supposes that violence cannot increase, and may even diminish in proportion as the intellectuals unbend to the masses and make platitudes and grimaces in honor of the union of the classes. Unfortunately for these great thinkers, things do not happen in this way; violence does not diminish in the proportion that it should diminish according to the principles of advanced sociology. There are, in fact, Socialist scoundrels, who, profiting by middle-class cowardice, entice the masses into a movement which every day becomes less like that which ought to result from the sacrifices consented to by the middle class in order to obtain peace. If they dared, the sociologists would declare that the Socialists cheat and use unfair methods, so little do the facts come up to their expectations.

However, it was only to be expected that the Socialists would not allow themselves to be beaten without having used all the resources which the situation offered them. People who have devoted their life to a cause which they identify with the regeneration of the world could not hesitate to make use of any weapon which might serve to develop to a greater degree the spirit of the class war, seeing that greater efforts were being made to suppress it. Existing social conditions favor the production of an infinite number of acts of violence, and there has been no hesitation in urging the workers not to refrain from brutality when this might do them service. Philanthropic members of the middle class having given a kindly reception to members of the syndicates who were willing to come and discuss matters with them, in the hope that these workmen, proud of their aristocratic acquaintances, would give peaceful advice to their comrades, it is not to be wondered their fellow workmen soon suspected them of treachery when they became upholders of "social reform." Finally, and this is the most remarkable fact in the whole business, antipatriotism becomes an essential element of the Syndicalist program.[18]

---

[18] As we consider everything from the historical point of view, it is of small importance to know what reasons were actually in the mind of the first apostles of antipatriotism; reasons of this kind are almost never the right ones; the essential thing is that for the revolutionary workers antipatriotism appears an inseparable part of Socialism.

The introduction of antipatriotism into the working-class movement is all the more remarkable because it came just when the government was about to put its theories about the solidarity of the classes into practice. It was in vain that Léon Bourgeois approached the proletariat with particularly amiable airs and graces; in vain that he assured the workers that capitalist society was one great family, and that the poor had a right to share in the general riches; he maintained that the whole of contemporary legislation was directed toward the application of the principles of solidarity; the proletariat replied to him by denying the social compact in the most brutal fashion—by denying the duty of patriotism. At the moment when it seemed that a means of suppressing the class war had been found, behold, it springs up again in a particularly displeasing form.[19]

Thus all the efforts of the worthy progressives only brought about results in flat contradiction with their aims; it is enough to make one despair of sociology! If they had any common sense, and if they really desired to protect society against an increase of brutality, they would not drive the Socialists into the necessity of adopting the tactics which are forced on them today; they would remain quiet instead of devoting themselves to "social duty"; they would bless the propagandists of the general strike, who, as a matter of fact, endeavor to *render the maintenance of Socialism compatible with the minimum of brutality*. But these *well-intentioned* people are not blessed with common sense; and they have yet to suffer many blows, many humiliations, and many losses of money, before they decide to allow Socialism to follow its own course.

II. Old habits of brutality in schools and workshops— The dangerous classes—Indulgence for crimes of cunning—Informers

We must now carry our investigations farther, and inquire what are the motives behind the great aversion felt by moralists for acts of violence; a very brief summary of a few very curious changes which have taken place in the manners of the working classes is first of all indispensable.

[19] This propaganda produced results which went far beyond the expectations of its promoters and which would be inexplicable without the revolutionary idea.

A. I observe, in the first place, that nothing is more re-markable than the change which has taken place in the methods of bringing up children; formerly it was believed that the rod was the most necessary instrument of the school-master; nowadays corporal punishments have disappeared from our public elementary schools. I believe that the compe-tition which the latter had to maintain against the Church schools played a very great part in this progress; the brothers applied the old principles of clerical pedagogy with extreme severity; and these, as is well known, involve an excessive amount of corporal punishment inflicted for the purpose of taming the demon who prompted so many of the child's bad habits.[20] The government was intelligent enough to set up in opposition to this barbarous system a milder form of educa-tion which brought it a great deal of sympathy; it is not at all improbable that the severity of clerical punishments is largely responsible for the present tumult of hatred against which the Church is struggling with such difficulty. In 1901 I wrote: "If [the Church] were well advised, it would suppress entirely that part of its activities which is devoted to children; it would do away with its schools and workshops; it would thus do away with the principal sources of anticlericalism: far from showing any desire to adopt this course, it seems to be its intention to develop these establishments still further, and thus it is laying up for itself still further opportunities for dis-plays of popular hatred for the clergy."[21] What has happened since 1901 surpasses my forecast.

In factories and workshops customs of great brutality for-merly existed, especially in those where it was necessary to employ men of superior strength, to whom was given the name of *grosses culottes* [big breeches]; in the end these men managed to get entrusted with the task of engaging other men, because "any individual taken on by others was sub-jected to an infinite number of humiliations and insults"; the man who wished to enter *their* workshop had to buy them drink, and on the following day to treat all his fellow work-ers. "The notorious *When's it to be?* [*Quand est-ce?*][22] would

---

[20] Cf. Renan, *Histoire du peuple d'Israël*, IV, 289 and 296; Y. Guyot, *La Morale*, pp. 212-215; Alphonse Daudet, *Numa Rou-mestan*, Chap. iv.

[21] G. Sorel, *Essai sur l'église et l'état*, p. 63.

[22] *Quand est-ce?* This was the question addressed to the new-comer in a workshop, to remind him that according to custom he must pay for drinks all round—"Pay your footing."

be started; everybody gets tipsy. . . . *When's it to be?* is the devourer of savings; in a workshop where *When's it to be?* is the custom, you must stand your turn, or beware." Denis Poulot, from whom I borrow these details, observes that machinery did away with the prestige of the *grosses culottes*, who were scarcely more than a memory when he wrote in 1870.[23]

The manners of the *compagnonnages*[24] [a kind of trade union] were for a long time remarkable for their brutality. Before 1840 there were constant brawls, often ending in bloodshed, between groups with different rites. Martin Saint-Léon, in his book on the *compagnonnage*, gives extracts from really barbarous songs.[25] Initiation into the lodge was accompanied by the severest tests; young men were treated as if they were pariahs in the *"Devoirs de Jacques et de Subise"*:[26] *"Compagnons* [carpenters] have been known," says Perdiguier, "to call themselves the Scourge of the Foxes [the candidates for admission], the Terror of the Foxes. . . . In the provinces, a 'fox' rarely works in the towns; he is hunted back, as they say, into the brushwood."[27] There were many secessions when the tyranny of the companions came into opposition with the more liberal habits which prevailed in society. When the workers were no longer in need of protection, especially for the purpose of finding work, they were no longer so willing to submit to the demands which had formerly seemed to be of little consequence in comparison with

[23] Denis Poulot, *Le Sublime,* pp. 150-153. I quote from the edition of 1887. This author says that the *grosses culottes* very much hampered progress in the forges.

[24] The *compagnonnages* were very ancient workmen's associations, whose principal purpose was to enable carpenters, joiners, locksmiths, farriers, and others, to make a circular tour round France, in order to learn their trades thoroughly. In the towns on this circuit there was a hotel kept by the *Mère des compagnons;* the newly arrived workman was received there and the older men found him work. The *compagnonnages* are now in the state of decay.

[25] Martin Saint-Léon, *Le Compagnonnage,* pp. 115, 125, 270-273, 277-278.

[26] Each trade possessed often several rival associations of workmen, which often engaged each other in bloody combats. Each association was called a *Devoir.* What was intended by *de Jacques* and *de Subise* has long been forgotten. They are traditional words indicating the rules, and so, by extension, the associations which follow these rules.

[27] Martin Saint-Léon, *op. cit.* p. 97. Cf. pp. 91-92, p. 107.

the advantages of the *compagnonnage*. The struggle for work more than once brought candidates into opposition with companions who wished to reserve certain privileges.[28] We might find still other reasons to explain the decline of an institution which, while rendering many important services, had contributed very much to maintaining the idea of brutality.

Everybody agrees that the disappearance of these old brutalities is an excellent thing. From this opinion it was so easy to pass to the idea that all violence is an evil, that this step was bound to have been taken; and, in fact, the great mass of the people, who are not accustomed to thinking, have come to this conclusion, which is accepted nowadays as a dogma by the bleating herd of moralists. They have not asked themselves what there is in brutality which is reprehensible.

When we no longer remain content with current stupidity, we discover that our ideas about the disappearance of violence depend much more on a very important transformation which has taken place in the criminal world than on ethical principles. I shall endeavor to prove this.

B. Middle-class scientists are very chary of touching on anything relating to the dangerous classes;[29] that is one of the reasons why their observations on the history of morals always remain superficial; it is not very difficult to see that it is a knowledge of these classes which alone enables us to penetrate the mysteries of the moral thought of peoples.

The dangerous classes of past times practiced the simplest form of offense, that which was nearest to hand, that which is nowadays left to groups of young scoundrels without experience and without judgment. Offenses of brutality seem to us nowadays something abnormal; so much so, that when the brutality has been great we often ask ourselves whether the culprit is in possession of all his senses. This transformation

---

[28] In 1823 the companion joiners claimed La Rochelle as theirs, a town which they had for a long time neglected as being of too little importance; they had previously stopped only at Nantes and Bordeaux (Martin Saint-Léon, *op. cit.* p. 103). *L'Union des travailleurs du tour de France* was formed in 1830 to 1832 as a rival organization to the *compagnonnage*, following the refusals with which the latter had met a few rather modest demands for reforms presented by the candidates for election (pp. 108-116, 126, 131).

[29] On March 30, 1906, Monis said in the Senate, "We cannot write in a legal text that prostitution *exists* in France for both sexes."

has evidently not come about because criminals have become moral but because they have changed their method of procedure to suit the new economic conditions, as we shall see further on. This change has had the greatest influence on popular thought.

We all know that by using brutality, associations of criminals manage to maintain excellent discipline among themselves. When we see a child ill-treated we instinctively suppose that its parents have criminal habits. The methods used by the old schoolmasters, which the ecclesiastical houses persist in preserving, are those of vagabonds who steal children to make clever acrobats or interesting beggars out of them. Everything which reminds us of the habits of dangerous classes of former times is extremely odious to us.

There is a tendency for the old ferocity to be replaced by cunning, and many sociologists believe that this is a real progress. Some philosophers who are not in the habit of following the opinions of the herd do not see exactly how this constitutes progress, from the point of view of morals: "If we are revolted by the cruelty, by the brutality of past times," says Hartmann, "it must not be forgotten that uprightness, sincerity, a lively sentiment of justice, pious before holiness of morals characterized the ancient peoples; while nowadays we see predominant lies, duplicity, treachery, the spirit of chicanery, the contempt for property, disdain for instinctive probity and legitimate customs—the value of which is not even understood.[30] Robbery, deceit, and fraud increase in spite of legal repression more rapidly than brutal and violent crimes, like pillage, murder, rape, and so on, decrease. Egoism of the basest kind shamelessly breaks the sacred bonds of the family and friendship in every case in which these oppose its desires."[31]

At the present time money losses are generally looked upon as accidents to which we are constantly exposed and which are easily made good again, while bodily accidents are not so

[30] Hartmann here bases his statements on the authority of the English naturalist Wallace, who has greatly praised the simplicity of life among the Malays; there must surely be a considerable element of exaggeration in this praise, although other travelers have made similar observations about some of the tribes of Sumatra. Hartmann wishes to show that there is no progress toward happiness, and this preoccupation leads him to exaggerate the happiness of the ancients.

[31] Hartmann, *Philosophy of the Unconscious,* French trans., pp. 464-465.

easily reparable. Fraud is therefore regarded as infinitely less serious than brutality; criminals benefit from this change which has come about in legal sentences.

Our penal code was drawn up at a time when the citizen was pictured as a rural proprietor occupied solely with the administration of his property, as a good family man, saving to secure an honorable position for his children; large fortunes made in business, in politics, or by speculation were rare and were looked on as real monstrosities; the defense of the savings of the middle classes was one of the first concerns of the legislator. The previous judicial system had been still more severe in the punishment of fraud, for a royal declaration of August 5, 1725, punished a fraudulent bankrupt with death; it would be difficult to imagine anything further removed from our customs. We are now inclined to consider that offenses of this sort can, as a rule, only be committed as the result of the imprudence of the victims and that it is only exceptionally that they deserve severe penalties; we, on the contrary, content ourselves with light punishment.

In a rich community where business is on a very large scale, and in which everybody is wide awake in defense of his own interests, as in America, crimes of fraud never have the same consequences as in a community which is forced to practice rigid economy; as a matter of fact, these crimes seldom cause a serious and lasting disturbance in the economic system; it is for this reason that Americans put up with the excesses of their politicians and financiers with so little complaint. P. de Rousiers compares the American to the captain of a ship who, during a dangerous voyage, has no time to look after his thieving cook. "When you point out to Americans that they are being robbed by their politicians, they usually reply, 'Of course we are quite aware of that! But as long as business is good and politicians do not get in the way, it will not be very difficult for them to escape the punishment they deserve.' "[32]

In Europe also, since it has become easy to gain money, ideas, analogous to those current in America, have spread among us. Great company promoters have been able to escape punishment because in their hour of success they were clever enough to make friends in all circles. We have finally come to believe that it would be extremely unjust to condemn bank-

[32] De Rousiers, *La Vie américaine: L'education et la société*, p. 217.

rupt merchants and lawyers who retire ruined after moderate catastrophes, while the princes of financial swindling continue to lead gay lives. Gradually the new industrial system has created a new and extraordinary indulgence for all crimes of fraud in the great capitalist countries.[33]

In those countries where the old parsimonious and non-speculative family economy still prevails, the relative estimation of acts of fraud and acts of brutality has not followed the same evolution as in America, England, and France; this is why Germany has preserved so many of the customs of former times,[34] and does not feel the same horror that we do for brutal punishments; these never seem to them, as they do to us, suitable only to the most dangerous classes.

Many philosophers have protested against this mitigation of sentences; after what we have related earlier about Hartmann, we shall expect to meet him among those who protest. "We are already," he says, "approaching the time when theft and lying condemned by law will be despised as vulgar errors, as gross clumsiness, by the clever cheats who know how to preserve the letter of the law while infringing the rights of other people. For my part, I would much rather live among the ancient Germans, at the risk of being killed on occasion, than be obliged, as I am in modern cities, to look on every man as a swindler or a rogue unless I have evident proofs of his honesty."[35] Hartmann takes no account of economic conditions; he argues from an entirely personal point of view, and never looks at what goes on round him. Nobody today wants to run the risk of being slain by ancient Germans; fraud or a theft are very easily reparable.

C. Finally, in order to get to the heart of contemporary thought on this matter, it is necessary to examine the way in which the public judges the relations existing between the state and the criminal associations. Such relations have always existed; these associations, after having practiced violence, have ended by employing craft alone, or at least their acts of violence have become somewhat exceptional.

---

[33] Several small countries have adopted these ideas, thinking by such imitation to reach the greatness of the large countries.

[34] It must be noticed that in Germany there are so many Jews in the world of speculation that American ideas do not spread very easily. The majority look upon the speculator as a *foreigner who is robbing the nation.*

[35] Hartmann, *loc. cit.,* p. 465.

Nowadays we should think it very strange if the magistrates were to put themselves at the head of armed bands, as they did in Rome during the last years of the Republic. In the course of the Zola trial, the anti-Semites recruited bands of paid demonstrators, who were commissioned to manifest patriotic indignation; the government of Méline protected these antics, which for some months had considerable success and helped considerably in hindering a fair revision of the sentence on Dreyfus.

I believe that I am not mistaken in saying that these tactics of the partisans of the Church have been the principal cause of all the measures directed against Catholicism since 1901; the middle-class liberals would never have accepted these measures if they had not still been under the influence of the fear they had felt during the Dreyfus affair. The chief argument which Clemenceau used to stir up his followers to fight against the Church was that of fear; he never ceased to denounce the danger which the Republic ran in the continued existence of the Romish faction; the laws about the congregations, about education and the administration of the churches were made with the object of preventing the Catholic party again taking up its former warlike attitude, which Anatol France so often compared to that of the League;[36] they were *laws inspired by fear*. Many Conservatives felt this so strongly that they regarded with displeasure the resistance recently opposed to the inventories of churches; they considered that the employment of bands of pious apaches would make the middle classes still more hostile to their cause.[37] It was not a little surprising to see Brunetière, who had been one of the admirers of the anti-Dreyfus apaches, advise submission; this was because experience had enlightened him as to the consequences of violence.

Associations which work by craft provoke no such reactions

[36] [The League was a political organization directed by the partisans of the Duc de Guise against the Protestants; it resisted Henri IV for a considerable time.—*Trans. Note.*]

[37] At a meeting of the Municipal Council of Paris on March 26, 1906, the Prefect of Police said that the resistance was organized by a committee sitting at 86 rue de Richelieu, which hired *pious apaches* at between three and four francs a day. He asserted that fifty-two Parisian curés had promised him either to facilitate the inventories or to be content with a merely passive resistance. He accused the Catholic politicians of having forced the hands of the clergy.

in the public; in the time of the "clerical republic,"[38] the society of St. Vincent de Paul was an excellent center of surveillance over officials of every order and grade; it is not surprising, then, that Freemasonry has been able to render services to the Radical government of exactly the same kind as those which Catholic philanthropy was able to render to former governments. The history of recent spying scandals has shown very plainly what the point of view of the country actually was.

When the nationalists obtained possession of the documents containing information about officers of the army, which had been compiled by the dignitaries of the Masonic lodges, they believed that their opponents were lost; the panic which prevailed in the Radical camp for some time seemed to justify their hopes, but before long the democracy showed only derision for what they called the "petty virtue" of those who publicly denounced the methods of General André and his accomplices. In those difficult days Henry Bérenger showed that he understood admirably the ethical standards of his contemporaries; he did not hesitate to approve of what he called the "legitimate supervision of the governing classes exercised by the organizations of the vanguard"; he denounced the cowardice of the government which had "allowed those who had undertaken the difficult task of opposing the military caste and the Roman Church, of examining and denouncing them, to be branded as informers" (*Action*, October 31, 1904); he loaded with insults the few Dreyfusards who dared to show their indignation; the attitude of Joseph Reinach appeared particularly scandalous to him; in his opinion the latter should have felt himself extremely honored by being tolerated in the "League of the Rights of Man," which had decided at last to lead "the good fight for the defense of rights of the citizen, sacrificed too long to those of one man" (*Action*, December 12, 1904). Finally, a law of amnesty was voted declaring that no one wanted to hear anything more of these trifles.

There was some opposition in the provinces,[39] but was it very serious? I am inclined to think not, when I read the documents published by Péguy in the ninth number of the

---

[38] [I.e. in the time when Mac-Mahon was President.—*Trans. Note.*]

[39] The people in the provinces are not, as a matter of fact, so accustomed as the Parisians are to indulgence toward nonviolent trickery and brigandage.

sixth series of his *Cahiers de la quinzaine*. Several people, accustomed to speaking a verbose, sonorous, and nonsensical language, doubtless found themselves a little uncomfortable under the smiles of the leading grocers and eminent chemists who constituted the élite of the learned and musical societies before which they had been accustomed to hold forth on Justice, Truth, and Light. They found it necessary to adopt a stoical attitude.

Could anything be finer than this passage from a letter of Professor Bougle, an eminent doctor of social science, which I find on page 13: "I am very happy to learn that at last the League is going to speak. *Its silence astonishes and frightens us.*" He must be a man who is easily astonished and frightened! Francis de Pressensé also suffered some anxiety of mind—he is a specialist in that kind of thing—but his feelings were of a very distinguished kind, as is only proper for an aristocratic Socialist; he was afraid that democracy was threatened with a new *guillotine sèche*,[40] resembling that which had done so much harm to virtuous democrats during the Panama scandal.[41] When he saw that the public quietly accepted the complicity of the government with a philanthropic association which had turned into a criminal association, he hurled his avenging thunders against the protestors. Among the most comical of these protestors I pick out a political pastor of Saint-Étienne called L. Comte. He wrote in the extraordinary language employed by the members of the League of the Rights of Man: "I had hoped that the [Dreyfus] affair would have definitely cured us of the moral malaria from which we suffer, and that it would have cleansed the republican conscience of the clerical virus with which it was impregnated. It has done nothing. We are more clerical than ever."[42] Accordingly this austere man remained in the League! Protestant and middle-class logic! It is always possible, you see, that the League might one of these days be able

[40] ["Dry guillotine," a popular expression meaning persecution. —*Trans.*]

[41] *Cahiers de la quinzaine* 9th of the VIth series, p. 9. F. de Pressensé was at the time of the Panama affair Hébrard's principal clerk; we know that the latter was one of the principal beneficiaries from the Panama booty, but that has not injured his position in the eyes of the austere Huguenots; the *Temps* continues to be the organ of moderate democracy and of the ministers of the Gospel.

[42] *Cahiers de la quinzaine, loc. cit.* p. 13.

to render some small service to the deserving ministers of the Gospel.

I have insisted rather lengthily on these grotesque incidents because they seem to me to characterize very aptly the moral ideas of the people who claim to lead us. Henceforth it must be taken for granted that politico-criminal associations which work by craft have a recognized place in any democracy that has attained its maturity. P. de Rousiers believes that America will one day cure itself of the evils which result from the guilty maneuvers of its politicians. Ostrogorski, after making a long and minute inquiry into "Democracy, and the organization of political parties," believes that he has found remedies which will enable modern states to free themselves from exploitation by political parties. These are platonic vows; no historical experience justifies the hope that a democracy can be made to work in a capitalist country, without the criminal abuses experienced everywhere nowadays. When Rousseau demanded that the democracy should not tolerate the existence in its midst of any private association, he reasoned from his knowledge of the republics of the Middle Ages; he knew that part of history better than his contemporaries did, and was struck with the enormous part played at that time by the politico-criminal associations; he asserted the impossibility of reconciling a rational democracy with the existence of such forces, but we ought to learn from experience that there is no way of bringing about their disappearance.[43]

[43] Rousseau, stating the question in an abstract way, appeared to condemn every kind of association, and our governments for a long time used his authority to subject every association to authority.

Max Scheler
(1874–1928)

MAN IN AN AGE OF ADJUSTMENT

Max Scheler, distinguished German philosopher and sociologist, has been neglected too long in anthologies of social theory.

He attended the University of Berlin and was a student of the noted philosopher Dilthey and the sociologist Simmel. He became professor of sociology and philosophy at the University of Köln and was a colleague of the outstanding sociologist Leopold von Wiese. Scheler's philosophical system went through many changes during his fruitful but regrettedly short life. Once a devout Catholic, he became an almost belligerent anti-Catholic bordering on atheism. "Scheler was a curious combination of the man of the world and ecstatic mystic, of roué and saint"[1] as Howard Becker remarks, and he recalls that when he once attended one of Scheler's lectures he witnessed a "display of histrionic virtuosity that the greatest of actors might have envied."[2]

Beside his significant work in phenomenological ethics, Scheler is also considered one of the founders of the "sociology of knowledge." He was the first to introduce the term Soziologie des Wissens, and in 1924 he formulated his ideas on this subject in his book Versuche zu einer Soziologie des Wissens. The main argument of this book is that there are a number of forms of knowledge, and the basic forms are the fundamental cultural axioms of the group, which form the climate of opinion. The fundamental task of the sociology of knowledge is to isolate these basic suppositions and their transformations.[3]

Scheler also wrote a profound study of the nature of sympathy and emotional understanding. The book was first published in 1913, but was revised by Scheler in 1922 and

[1] P. 908, Howard Becker and Harry Elmer Barnes, *Social Thought from Lore to Science*, Vol. III, New York, Dover Publications, 1961.

[2] Ibid.

[3] P. 275, Don Martindale, *The Nature and Types of Sociological Theory*, Boston, Houghton Mifflin, 1960.

published as Wesen und Formen der Sympathie. *It was translated into English as* Nature and Form of Sympathy.

In the essay "Man in an Age of Adjustment" Scheler interprets Man in a definite sociological-historical context, and his remarks, though made in 1927, have lost nothing of their applicability for today.

MAN IN AN AGE OF ADJUSTMENT[4]

THE German Institute for Politics does not limit itself to those objectives which characterize such institutions in all lands, to teach scientifically accurate and sober knowledge of all the realities in our society of nations which are pertinent to the policy of state. It has *two* further objectives and justifications for existence, which are rooted in the historic nature and the historic position of our nation: First, it must contribute with all it has and can offer toward overcoming the ancient and tragic German *opposition between power and spirit* which our new and democratic republic has intensified rather than diminished. Second, it must and can help to bring to light the institution which, by its presence or absence, will, I am firmly convinced, decide the fate of this state, a growing German *elite* that can, through its spirit and will derived from the profundities of German history, slowly penetrate and unobtrusively direct our political leadership in all areas. Not a copy, but the *rebirth* of the German spirit, this elite will be wide awake to the contemporary world and to the requirements of the hour.

One can commit no greater error than to consider *democracy and elite* as mutually exclusive concepts. Unfortunately, partisans of this form of government, who are friendly to elites, do so just as frequently as their opponents, whether monarchists or adherents of some form of dictatorship. Pareto, one of the outstanding experts in the matter of elites, said quite correctly not only that history is a "circulation of elites," but that this is true regardless of the form of government under which men live. We know that democracy more ruth-

[4] Address given on the anniversary of the Deutsche Hochschule für Politik [German Institute for Politics] in Berlin on Nov. 5, 1927.

lessly *reveals* the existence of historical contrasts between population groups, confessions, classes, and parties in a nation but that it does not produce them; and by revealing them, it sharply and clearly outlines the future *problems* which the elite has to solve. For very profound reasons which we cannot discuss here, it is, of course, also true that parliamentary democracy in almost the entire world today faces a dangerous crisis. It has a difficult struggle, not, as formerly, against conservative legitimists of some sort (today this opposition is almost dead), but against tendencies toward dictatorship on the right and on the left. Democracy will be able to survive only if it can, so to speak, seize the weapons from its opponents and produce and tolerate a well-chosen, mobile, effective elite which provides the nation with a *unity of culture and power*. Whether we Germans will succeed in this task or not will determine not only the fate of our national culture and the dignity of our human form, but also the historical destiny of our state.

I could not begin to discuss the general, great, sociological problem of historical elites, their types, formation, maintenance, spread, and collapse, not even if I limited myself to our country. It is a sociological problem of the greatest importance and, perhaps, particularly worthy of being considered by this Institute. One thing is certain: The elite will *not* be an elite of mere blood and tradition like the old Prussian aristocracy and the caste of state employees which it sponsored. The tasks of our epoch call for human qualities and abilities unlikely to be transmitted from father to son by the principles of psychic inheritance. Nor will the elite arise from one of our all too numerous political parties which have such strong ideological orientations and are so inclined to saw off the limb on which they sit, that is, by ignoring the measure of *unity* in our national culture and in our conception of German history, without which free democratic discussion and formulation of opinions are impossible in a parliament (we see these difficulties again in the still-unfinished fight for the law on public schools). If for no other reason, this will not occur because even specifically political elites—think of that noble elite which arose under the impulse of the War of Liberation [in 1813]—hardly ever grow directly out of the political sphere, but are born in movements which are *spiritually* new and, at the same time, are impelled by a new feeling of *vitality*, and because only then do they slowly enter the political domain. Thus, the Fascist movement grew out of a movement for national rebirth among war veterans and Italian youth. Elites arise no more easily from particular classes nor from definite professions.

At times, some elites have the important function of maintaining and administering particular cultural attainments. However, those elites which time itself exhorts with the word "create" must ripen in the mysterious depths of the nation and come to light slowly. Above all, they must not be premature in manifesting themselves. They can hardly arise except through the gradual amalgamation of "cultural groups" which have formed around leading personalities. It is my firm belief, derived from years of experience and observation, that such elites are in the early stages of development today, under our new form of government which, in the beginning, was so little adapted to the German people. It may be years yet, perhaps decades, before this growing elite, which today is still too *critical* of our culture, will be prepared for reality and life, able to become effective in our political arena also, and able to replace the present interim leadership in Germany. This rebirth will, however, come not to destroy what our fathers have built at Weimar, but to instill into this emergency framework the ideal of *arete* [virtue] and a *live, spiritual content.*

One condition of forming such an elite, a condition that can be considered even today, is that we should, inasfar as possible, acquire a common *conception* of the *structure of the era* we have entered and, at the same time, of the manner in which to refashion the *type* of leader appropriate to this era. I say "era," and not merely "age," purposely, for the import of this profound transformation of environment and man, which is beginning today, can hardly be overestimated. Compared with the divisions which historians establish in the life and times of what they call the "modern European period," this change seems even more infinitely profound and varied than the fundamental transformation which leads from the so-called European Middle Ages to modern times. We must go back to the origins of Christianity and to the rise of the Germanic-Romanic society of nations to find an approximate equivalent of such a profound change. It is not only a transformation of things, circumstances, institutions, of the basic concepts and forms of art, and of almost all other disciplines; it is a *transformation of man himself,* of the nature of his internal constitution in body, drives, soul, and spirit. It is not only a change in his actual being, but in his standards of judgment. The following comment of one of the leaders of German youth is touching in its awkwardness: "We carry in us an [ideal] image of man, but it is such that it cannot serve as our model. However, since we carry it in us, it becomes ever more visible in that the individual reveals it in the freedom of his inner growth."

Especially in times of profound change, all deeper human aspirations, all politics also, are supported, consciously or unconsciously, by such a mysterious, I should say, eschatological, image or ideal of man. Friedrich Nietzsche, the last German genius to try consciously to create such an image and to tie it closely to the idea of a new European elite, called this image of his longing "*superman.*" Even if this image has, in a way, powerfully affected all Europe and countries beyond— I call to mind only Mussolini and Fascism—it suffers not only from the unworldly and unreal vagueness of almost all the statements of this great and lonely poet and thinker, but it traversed, in its own development, a number of profoundly different phases which I cannot describe here. Its first and altogether eschatological form was the idea of a new *kind* of man in the biological sense. Its last form was the conception of consciously raising and educating a new historical *elite* within existing species. Nietzsche cites many examples of this from past history, but adds that these represented "only chance and fortunate accident." In this last phase, in which Nietzsche's critique of Darwin and of the general theory of evolution (in many ways, this critique is valuable even today) becomes most pointed, superman is only the conceptualized symbol for establishing the "new tables of value" which resulted from his powerful critique of traditional historical "codes of ethics." I cannot begin to criticize the content of this image. I should like to say only this: As startling as this image may have been, it does *not* seem one which the growing elite of our times can accept as its eschatology of man.

We must completely abandon all thought of an essential transformation of man in the *biological,* especially in the morphological, sense. The entire teaching of scientific biology contradicts the possibility of such a transformation, and supports the idea (which I cannot elucidate here) that man is definitively *fixed* in his morphology. The fact that the possibility of evolving decreases as species attain a more perfect organization and differentiate themselves (Weismann) prevents us from expecting any further biological evolution of man. In historical times, man has certainly not undergone any essential change in his organization. The differentiation of races is probably an early consequence of self-domestication and culture. The evolution of a specifically human "spirit" and of "intelligence," which man shares with the primates, has so basically and methodically replaced the morphological development of man's physical organs, that even the strongest resublimation [see below], and even centuries of it could, at best, maintain the present form of his species, but could not produce forces for a continued organic evolution.

The belief that man can change organically by inheriting functionally acquired characteristics, as Herbert Spencer assumed and considered along with spiritual development, seems erroneous to me. Modern scientific research in heredity rejects this theory. Scientists can still investigate whether acquired "propensities" to develop certain characteristics can be inherited, not, however, as directly and somatically induced in the inheritance-carrying genes of the germ plasm, but only in its protoplasmic structure. The process is, therefore, much more indirect and works over much more extensive periods of time than Spencer assumed. Furthermore, not only the accumulation of actions but also the development of the spirit and of its forms of activity in man have become *autonomous* and *independent of his physical organization* and are, therefore, to be studied by "intellectual disciplines" independent of biology. Therefore, when Spencer wants to give biological reasons for growth in psychic and social harmony, in the a priori assets of the human mind, and in the moral sentiments of man; when, to express it in pictorial language, he sees a movement of the species toward the increasingly tame and intellectual herd animal and toward a so-called "social equilibrium," his expectation of things to come lacks all scientific foundation.

If such a progressive biological evolution of the species and growth of man on earth seem quite improbable, his biological *decadence* is no less so. While the picture of the future drawn by Spencer, Darwin, and Nietzsche was too brilliant, today an image which is equally exaggerated in its gloom appeals to large segments of youth, especially German youth. I am thinking particularly of the picture of the future, also biologically conceived, which Ludwig Klages displays with much imagination and skill. Klages' judgment is characteristic of German late romanticism. His theory of the nature of man sees the "spirit," consciousness, the will, and the ego in history gnawing more and more at "life" and "soul," which contain all the high values of existence. Consequently, to the extent that man "thinks," he *must* think "mechanically," and to the extent that he "wills," he must produce an increasing number of mechanisms and place them between himself and virginal nature, to a point where he can no longer dominate and rule these mechanisms and where they, so to speak, bury him. I named Ludwig Klages as the outstanding exponent of such panromanticism. (I could equally well have mentioned Leo Frobenius, Edgar Dacqué, Oswald Spengler, Theodor Lessing.) According to their doctrine, inasfar as it is man who technologically dominates organic nature, the road of the spirit is the *road of death* for the life and soul of man as well as for living nature, since the individual being itself psychologically and physiologically produces the mechanisms which cause its death.

How understandable psychologically, at the same time how suggestive for our hearts, is this somber picture of the future of man which seems to indicate only one solution, to take refuge in a remote corner of nature and there mourn for man and his history, admire his distant past and its last remnants in myth, legend, tale, and usage, and to intoxicate oneself, shun all "action," and thus immerse oneself pathologically in the lost days of the original soul! During the World War we used to read in the reports, "for technical reasons it was impossible . . . ," for instance, to cancel the submarine warfare at the decisive moment or, at the outset of the war, for the Czars to revoke the Russian mobilization, and so on. Those of us who lived through this, who experienced all the recent developments of the Occident in the twentieth century in their small and large aspects, the increasing difficulty of controlling the masses, the impossibility of directing capital which has become autonomous—did we not, every one of us, in our own bosoms, experience feelings akin to this somber theory of decadence? But what significance has this late Occidental intermezzo for the whole of *humanity?* It is minor or nonexistent! This pessimistic theory is just as narrowly European as positivism which believes in progress, only with inverse values. After all, a European crisis is neither the signal for the death of humanity nor for the "decline of the West"! This pessimistic attitude may be important as a call to arms, but it does *not* foretell our future. The "spirit" is no enemy of life or of the soul! Of course, it causes wounds, but it also heals them. For instance: Capitalism brought about the devastation of organic nature when man, until the eighteenth century, used wood for heating purposes; in the subsequent period, when heating was done with coke and coal, the same

capitalism placed inorganic energy in the service of the economy and thus left organic life protected and safe; and capitalism will, in the future, know how to use sources of energy
which transfer the same socially useful tasks to more inferior
forces (like waterpower, radioactive energy) in order thus to
liberate higher ones. Not the spirit, only the oversublimated
"intellect," which Klages confuses with "spirit," the "intellect
which lacks wisdom," devoid of elevated *ideas* and values of
reason—*it* is, in some measure, the enemy of life! Is *re*sublimation—I shall explain later what I mean by this—not possible
here, using systematic eugenics following the system so meri-
toriously propagated, in Germany, by Eugen Fischer of the
Kaiser Wilhelm Institute, and in many other ways? One more
thing: I admit that our limited cultural sphere is in danger of
perishing through mechanization; that means not of dying
out, but of becoming politically and culturally impotent, but
only if no new art of *self*-control comes to the aid of the control *over nature* which the Occident has, up to now, developed
so exclusively. We shall consider this later.

Speaking of the future and of a new image of man, I cannot conceive any future image which envisages an automatic
transformation, whether positive or negative, of man's organic,
natural aptitude, but only one which represents an "ideal"
that admits man's *freedom to develop himself*, an ideal implying that man himself will shape that infinitely plastic segment
of his nature which can be influenced directly or indirectly
by the spirit and the will. What comes from the spirit does
not come automatically, nor does it come of itself. It must be
guided! In this sense, we accept the word of the Frenchman
Gratry: "Not only the individual, but also humanity can end
as saint or criminal, depending on how it directs its *will.*"
Man is a creature whose very essence is the open discussion.
What does he want to *be* and to *become*?

However, this ideal for man is, if it must have a name, the
"total man," not the "superman" conceived separately from
the masses and from all democracy. Through the ideal of total
man, superman and subman are to become *human*.

In his known history, man has proved himself a being of
tremendous *plasticity*. Therefore, the greatest danger for all
philosophical attitudes is to conceive the idea of man too
narrowly, to derive it unintentionally from *one* natural or even
historical form, or to see it contained in any such narrow conception. The idea of the *"animal rationale"* in the classic sense
was much too restricted. *"Homo faber"* of the positivists,

"Dionysian man" of Nietzsche, man as a "disease of life" of the new panromantic doctrines, "superman," "*homo sapiens*" of Linné, "*l'homme machine*" of La Mettrie, man solely as "power," "*libido*," and "economic" being, in Machiavelli, Freud, and Marx, fallen, God-created Adam—*all* these conceptions are much too narrow to encompass the *whole* of man. Furthermore, all these concepts are like ideas of *things*. But man is not a thing. He is a direction of the *movement of the universe* itself, even of its source. Man is "microcosm and a being filled with spirit." I hope that these definitions are not already too narrow to include his many possibilities and forms. *Allow us, therefore, room for man and for his movement which is infinite by nature, and do not tie man to a "model," to a pattern, whether in natural or in world history!* "Mankind bears in itself an infinite number of developments, more mysterious and larger than one might imagine" (Leopold von Ranke).

Total man, in the absolute sense, is hardly close to us. It is the idea of a man who contains and has realized *all* his essential capabilities. Indeed, he is as far from us as God who, insofar as we grasp his essence in spirit and life, is nothing but the *essentia* [essence] of man, only in infinite form and fullness. However, every age of human history knows a *relatively total man*, a *maximum* of total humanity which is accessible to it, a relative maximum of participation in the highest forms of human existence. This is also true for us.

In order to qualify this relatively total man, accessible today, as our guiding ideal, permit me to start from the idea of the *task for the coming era*.

If I had to inscribe a name on the gate of the incipient era, a name which was to render the inclusive trend of this era, only one would seem appropriate to me, that of "*adjustment*"; adjustment of almost all characteristic and specifically *natural* traits, physical and psychic, which distinguish the social groups into which we can divide humanity, and, at the same time, a tremendous *increase* in *spiritual*, individual, and relatively individual, for example, national differences; adjustment of *racial* tensions; adjustment between mentalities, conceptions of self, world, and God, in the great *cultural groupings* especially in Asia and Europe; adjustment between the specifically *male* and *female* ways of thinking in their rule over human society; adjustment between *capitalism* and *Socialism* and, thereby, of class arguments and class conditions and rights between *upper* and *lower classes;* adjustment in the share of political power of so-called *civilized, half-civilized,* and *primitive peoples;* adjustment also between relatively primitive and highly civilized mentalities; relative adjustment between *youth* and *old age* in the evaluation of their mental attitudes; adjustment between *technical knowledge* and *cultural growth,* between physical and spiritual labor; adjustment between the spheres of *national economic* interests and the contributions which the *nations* make, in the realm of the *spirit* and civilization, to the total culture and civilization of humanity; finally, adjustment between the one-sided *ideas about the nature of man* of which I have just named several types.

Let us note: This tendency toward adjustment which is accompanied by an ever increasing differentiation of the spiritual individuality of man, this adjustment is not something we "choose"; it is inescapable *fate.* Whoever resists, whoever wishes to cultivate some so-called "characteristic," "specific" ideal of man, one already concretely formed in history, will work in thin air. The modern world is full of attempts to revive all possible forms of the species "man," as if the world were a secondhand shop full of discarded relics, "pagan" man, "early Christian" man, "Gothic" man, "Renaissance" man, "Latin-Catholic" man (France), "mushik" man [Russia], and so on. Humanity will silently pass by such artificial romantic aspirations!

As I said, adjustment itself is the *inescapable fate* of mankind which found its first truly common experience in the World War, for it is the beginning of the *one* common history of so-called humanity. Even so, it is the *task of the spirit* to *guide* and *direct* this adjustment of group qualities and forces in such a way that the species will *gain in value* while the adjustment takes place. This is the task of all *politics,* indeed, its primary task.

The last epoch was essentially one of growing tensions which kept becoming more particularized, the epoch of the "growth of forces," as Rudolf Eucken called it. This trend was relatively seldom interrupted by violent revolutionary processes which released tension, such as the Peasant Wars, the English and French revolutions, the little German and the great Russian revolution. However, the most general formula applicable to the incipient era, the era of a *universal relaxation of tensions* in human relations, is, it seems to me, that of the *adjustment* of forces. It is, at the same time, an era in which man once again relies on his living spirit and heart and tries to become the *master* of demonic powers which had become *centers of attention* after being unleashed by the last epoch. His purpose is to make these powers serve the salvation of humanity and the meaningful realization of spiritual values. Every policy intended merely to prevent or hinder this fated adjustment or a portion thereof will be swept away by the powerful, irresistible current toward adjustment, and, today, every *political objective,* conceived in formally correct terms, is, in fact, a task of guiding and directing some phase of this adjustment, so that it may proceed with a minimum of destruction, explosion, blood, and tears.

As I said, this seems to me the most universal formula for any policy in the new era, for we must clearly understand one thing: Not the periods of increasing tension and particularization of forces, but the *periods of adjustment* are the *most dangerous* for humanity, the most filled with death and tears. Every process which we call explosion, catastrophe, in nature and history, is a process of adjustment which is *not* meaningfully led by the spirit and will, or is not amenable to their leadership.

Let us sketch a few *types* of this coming adjustment.

The racial adjustment, the mixing of blood, will progress irresistibly. Immanuel Kant had already predicted that adjustment of racial tension was inevitable. Whoever sees the salvation of the world in the maintenance of a "pure" race, in his opinion a "noble race," can do nothing but imitate the "seven faithful friends" of Count Gobineau; let him withdraw to an island with his pure race, and despair! The rise of independent colored peoples has already made striking progress. An adjustment between white and colored peoples has to come, *but* it can be carried out well or badly, either so that the right kind of blood is mixed, producing higher values according to scientific experience, or so that an inadequate mixture leads to the depreciation of values in the species. Whether one interprets the great racial groups that make up humanity polygenetically and does not believe humanity is racially related, or whether one thinks monophyletically, in any event, the distinction of races was part of the process of *becoming* man. A *united* humanity was not a starting point of history, racially or culturally, but remains its *objective*. In its most formal structure, world history consists neither of a rhythmic unfolding of a plurality of elements, whether the fate of races, or so-called "cultures" which flourish, ripen, and decline near and independently from each other, as Oswald Spengler so suggestively presented it while neglecting all mixtures of race, all reception of foreign ideas and renaissance movements; nor is history one *single* movement, continuous since the beginning and only later separated into different streams through differences in milieu or in historically acquired talent, as is assumed by all specifically Christian and positivistic conceptions of history, both limited in their European view. Instead, the structure of history resembles a river system in which a great number of rivers continue their particular courses for centuries but, nourished by innumerable affluents, finally tend to converge ever more directly and to unite in *one* great stream. The historical currents, which decrease in number, give birth to the historical organisms we call civilizations and cultures. Insofar as these stem from the rational *spirit* of the unity of a people, a spirit that, in its structure, is always concretely unique, they are immortal on earth and *outlive* the ethnic unities and their political and economic institutions. Their objective content of meaning and value, which forms the spirit, can, at any time, rise again in renaissance movements and in mixed cultures and form men. Thus, for instance, antiquity was able to fertilize the Occidental world in ever renewed form and manner. However, to the extent that historical organisms are merely "expressions," merely physiognomies of the *soul* and *life* of groups (like legend, fairy tale, myth, usage, custom, and so on), their significance as living values is definitely destroyed and lost when the ethnic unit dies; they are *mortal*. In strong contrast to purely "spiritual culture" and also to "patterns of expression and life of the soul," the collective products of spirit, drive to power, and intelligence, especially experimental science, technology, forms of government and administration, rules of law, in short, the civilizing, not cultural, organisms are the only ones that simultaneously manifest a "progress" continuing beyond national existence, cutting across forms of culture, and also a rectilinear "cumulative effect" that becomes more and more "international." However, "cosmopolitan" adjustment which is the adjustment of purely spiritual forms of culture, not only contemporary ones but those which arose in the past, survive, and are capable of surviving, is incomparably slower and proceeds by very different means than the "international" adjustment of civilization and technology which is linked particularly to world trade and which is, true enough, a prior condition for "cosmopolitan" adjustment.[5]

Among the various kinds of adjustment, a very important one is the cultural adjustment appropriate to the *man himself* of our era, to man who produces and creates all history.

An adjustment which, even today, strikes our attention wherever man, growing into total man, begins to form elites is that between *"Apollonian"* and *"Dionysian"* man, taken as ideas, as species. In the form of "rationalism" and "anti-rationalism," as "philosophy of ideas" and "philosophy of life," this opposition has, up to now, introduced a dichotomy into the philosophical thought of all nations.[6] This adjustment appears not only in the Occident, but no less in America, as a strange process which is already well under way and scares and even terrifies too many among us who measure only by the standards of the past era. In order to encompass this process with *all* the wealth of the symptoms that we can observe today, I should like to call it a *process of resublimation.* By resublimation I mean the spiritually conscious act of reducing the amount of accumulated energy which the organism transfers to the brain or to the intellect, the apparent locus of all purely spiritual activity, that is, of all acts of ideation.

This process of resublimation first manifests itself only in a *diminished appreciation of the spirit,* especially of intellectuality, of the works of the spirit and its specific social agents. Today, all great modern mass movements in Europe and in America are strangely united in their conscious *antirational, anti-intellectual* attitude which frequently even makes a show of despising the spirit and all spiritual values. The nature and politics of the Soviet Union rest on two elements. They are fed by the fire of anti-intellectual, anti-Western, romantic Pan-Slavism, and supported by the doctrine of western European "Marxism" that spurns ideas. Fascism is specifically vitalistic. Its activist representatives despise scholars and intellectuals. Some time ago, Mussolini said to someone I know, "Here, in Italy, they teach the practical application of the birth of tragedy," that is, of "Dionysian" man. We need only look at the *athletic* movement, growing monstrously in all

---

[5] Cf. the comments on the dynamics of knowledge in "Probleme einer Soziologie des Wissens," in the book *Die Wissensformen und die Gesellschaft* (1926), pp. 25 f.

[6] Cf. "Das Nationale im Denken Frankreichs," in *Nation und Weltanschauung: Schriften zur Soziologie und Weltanschauungslehre II* (Leipzig, 1923).

countries; the *youth* movements with their modern "body consciousness" and appreciation of the body, not only as a source of work and enjoyment, but, in itself, as beauty and form. We see the mighty *eugenic* movement in America; the disappearance of the Puritan ideal of morals, as Ben Lindsey, judge of a juvenile court, describes it in his book *The Revolt of Modern Youth;* the new *erotic* customs of youth in all countries; the great movement of *psychoanalysis* and the *modern psychology of drives;* the rage of dancing all around the world; the *panvitalistic* doctrines, newly formed since Nietzsche and Bergson; the strange contemporary propensity toward dark *mysticism*[7] and the very childish despising of science in favor of fraternal or group ideologies; the rapidly decreasing appreciation of the man who is exclusively a scholar, of the intellectual artist, of the intellectual theater; the "heroic types" in contemporary sport or cinema, who have already become almost mythological; the feverish desire for "strength," "beauty," and "youth"; the new appraisal of *infant* existence and of youth as something of intrinsic value; the enjoyment of *primitive,* mystical mentality, art, and spirit; the whole trend to reintroduce into Europe the customs of peoples who were once civilized by Europe, the "countercolonization" of Europe (Moritz Julius Bonn). *All* these circumstances and thousands of others point toward what I would call *a systematic revolt of man's drives in the new era against one-sided sublimation,* against the exaggerated intellectualism of our fathers, their century-old ascetic practices, and their techniques of sublimation (already subconscious) which, up to the present, have fashioned Occidental man. For the time being, the gods of so-called "life" seem to have replaced the rule of the gods of the "spirit"; for I do not consider this movement as a very transitory "postwar phenomenon." It had begun before the war, as the figure of Nietzsche suffices to show; he gave the word "life" its magic sound. In fact, I see a collective movement, deeply rooted in the history of the Occident, aiming at a *redistribution* of man's *total energy* between the cortex and the rest of his organism.

Are these movements so surprising after all? Do they not constitute necessary ways to *health* for modern mankind, even if they first far transgress all boundaries of truth and justice, especially in their ideological expression, as does every typical movement of reaction? Man finds his way to God, as Luther

---

[7] Cf. "Probleme einer Soziologie des Wissens," pp. 63, 125.

says, only like a drunken peasant, reeling to the right and left. Ever since late antiquity and the appearance of Jesus, ever since the Judaic theistic view began to rule the Occident, the ascetic ideal has developed a most *one-sided* species of man, in ever renewed forms and with completely different causal explanations. Finally, this species began seriously to endanger the equilibrium of human powers. First came the early Christian and patristic asceticism as an antithesis to the paganism of antiquity; then the asceticism of medieval monks and monasteries, relatively harmless since it affected only a small minority; then the progress of this ascetic ideal among the masses and "laymen," not least of all through Protestant asceticism, the "advocates of the inner world," as Max Weber and Ernst Troeltsch called them; and, finally and increasingly, the tremendous capitalistic "asceticism of the golden idol" (Karl Marx), the asceticism of work and industry aiming for unlimited accumulation of products. These forms have, in our culture, led men to a degree of "intellectualization" in their functions or, psychologically speaking, to a "sublimation" which, in the present era, had to turn into a revolution of life and drives if the human equilibrium was to be reestablished. The *revolt of nature in man had to* come someday, the revolt of all that is dark, impulsive, and instinctive, of the child against the grown-up, the wife against her husband, the masses against the established elites, of the colored against the whites, of what is unconscious against the conscious, of circumstances themselves against man and his intellect! Not in its purely political causes, of course, but in the attitudes of the masses toward it, the World War itself was a *result* rather than a cause of this repression of drives and of this incipient revolt of the drives against the highly intensified, *over*intensified "Apollonian" and ascetic "rationalism" of the past. The movement, insofar as it concerns the psychophysiological process of *re*sublimation, is, therefore, neither to be praised nor reprimanded! It represents almost an organic need, although it is, of course, being pursued most onesidedly, but no more so than the unlimited asceticism and spiritualization of the preceding epoch of sublimation.

This is not true for the ideological bubbles produced by the movement, the one-sided philosophies and "religions of life" which are, of course, not justified in pretending to reveal lasting truth. These ideologies forget *two* circumstances: *young,* forceful peoples and men, thirsting for life and still unaccustomed to higher intellectual activity, arrive themselves at *ascetic* ideals and at a higher appreciation of *spiritual* life, and have the urge to sublimate. Thus, the young, forceful, Germanic nations enthusiastically accepted the spiritual Christianity of late antiquity. The *re*sublimation, however, wherever it appears and in whatever ideas and forms of value it is clothed, is itself a sign of *old age*, of tiring vital functions, just like rereflection, the yearning, produced by reflection, for the primitive and childlike, for a "second" childhood. It is, of course, also a first systematic attempt to *counteract* and overcome the sublimation in the direction of intellect! Anyone who takes the cry for "life," the whole theoretical and practical "vitalism" of our times, to be the expression of a particular unusual fullness of *life* is being childish. The vitalism of our times is a *counterideal*, a *"medicina mentis"* [mental antidote], not an immediate expression of excess strength. Children want to grow, not to remain children. The high value attached to childhood is a product of adults who yearn to be children again!

Quite aside from this, the Occident has for so long sublimated its vital force in a one-sided manner, has tried to banish all expressions of "nature" from man with such insistence, and has cultivated such one-sided, spirit-centered consciousness of self and a feeling for life so infinitely *dualistic*, that even a century of systematic resublimation can do no harm. In any event, man is entitled to curtail the asceticism and sublimation of his historical evolution, since he has already spiritualized himself automatically and ontologically. The history of ethics is a story of *loosening* external restrictions as appropriate levels of sublimation and an appropriate force of inner commitment are attained.

Of course, what we see today does not as yet approach even a relative realization of total man. It is only an introduction, the overture to such an evolution. If resublimation has succeeded, up to a point, if we again take the vital values to be *self-evident*, those values which modern times, especially the trend of thought since Descartes, have buried under intellectuality and mechanistic attitudes, we have yet to reestablish a new *equilibrium*, so that the spirit and spiritual values will regain the importance befitting the *nature* of man. Only then will we have made a step ahead toward total man, that is, toward the man of *highest tension between spirit and drive*, idea and sensuality, who is *also* the man with an organized, *harmonious integration* of these two forces into *one* form of existence and one kind of action. Only then shall we have overcome that fatal and even infamous romantic decomposition, that disunity of idea and reality, of thought and action, which is the disease of all intellectual life in Europe and, unfortunately not least of all in our Germany.

The man who is most deeply rooted in the darkness of earth and nature, and of the *"natura naturans"* which produces all natural phenomena, *"natura naturata,"* the man who, *simultaneously,* as a spiritual person, in his consciousness of self, reaches the utmost heights of the luminous world of ideas, that man is approaching the idea of total man, and, therewith, the idea of the substance of the very source of the world, through a constantly *growing interpenetration of spirit and drive.* "The person who has had the deepest thoughts, loves what is most alive" (Hölderlin).

This movement toward adjustment between spiritual and vital principles in man is paralleled by another, no less significant, the analogous adjustment between *male and female principles* in mankind. The thoroughly terrestrial, earthly, Dionysian phase of our era has a clear tendency toward a new *rise in the value* and *power* of *women.* Today we sense it deeply and it will, no doubt, further affect our deepest and ultimate concepts. Since the disappearance of the cult of mother earth, the Occidental concept of God has been influenced ever more one-sidedly by the masculine and logical element. In the framework of the Christian Church, Protestantism destroyed the last vestige of the ancient cult of the mother goddess, the cult of Mary as *Theotokos,* as well as the cult of the "mother church." Up to now, the idea of God has been entirely *virile* in conception and feeling. This has been well expressed by H. G. Wells in his book *God: The Invisible King.* (Bismarck, that virile spirit, felt and judged in a similar way, and Soloviev also makes pronouncements to this effect.) As a dogmatic concept, our idea of God seems not to have developed in this direction. I say, it only *seems* that way because, as long as the source of all being is just "pure spirit" and "light," and as long as only a *spiritual* principle is attributed to it, without the attributes of "life" and "drive," this source is *de facto* conceived and expressed, as being and idea, in just as one-sided a virile, logical way as the classical idea of man as *"homo sapiens."*[8] Etymologically, in many languages, the term for "human being" goes back to the word

---

[8] Cf. *Die Stellung des Menschen im Kosmos* (5th ed.; Munich, 1949); also, "Man and History" in this collection.

"man." The recent movement toward a new significance and adoration of woman, a hetaerism rather than a cult of Demeter [of physical enjoyment rather than of fruitfulness], toward adjustment between the value of the sexes, though not quite toward a "matriarchal" law, can be accompanied by excesses of all kinds. Still, this development is a link in the total process which I designate as resublimation. It will also serve to show the way toward total man to persons who are exclusively and excessively spiritual and *over*sublimated, and who measure everything according to male standards of value.

A further adjustment of major importance, affecting the formation of man, is that between *Europe* and the three great *Asiatic* centers, India, China, and Japan, with Islam as an intermediary. It started long ago and will progress considerably in the future. Here also, Europe has long ceased to be the only active contributor. Since Europe has transmitted and continues to transmit the methods of its technical and economic production, and the sciences on which they are based, to these Asiatic nations, they become increasingly independent of Europe by developing their own industries. Europe, on the other hand, and Germany, since Wilhelm von Humboldt, Schelling, and Schopenhauer, absorbs more and more deeply into its spiritual body the old wisdom of the East, for example, the ancient Asiatic technique of living and suffering. This knowledge comes to it through innumerable channels and, recently, in much greater proportions. Thus, Europe may succeed in making it its own *living* possession. A truly cosmopolitan world philosophy is in the making or is, at least, the basis of a current movement. It not only records for history the highest axioms of existence and life in Indian philosophy, Buddhist religion, Chinese and Japanese wisdom, which for so long were completely unknown to us; it also tests them *objectively* and makes them into a *vital* element of its own thought. The spiritual modes established by antiquity, Christianity, and modern science are not being abandoned. Such an attempt would lead in the wrong direction. However, the picture of modern man is being essentially and considerably modified.

Another result is an adjustment of the *ideas* about man and the *models* he emulates. Such an adjustment will have to reconcile, above all, the basic Occidental ideal of the extroverted, *active "hero,"* and the ideal, most widespread in Asia, particularly in early southern Buddhism, of the *suffering "sage"* who meets the pain and evils of existence by his art of suffering, of "nonresistance," or rather by spiritual resistance to the extroverted and automatic reactions to evil. It is characteristic of human nature to annul every pain and evil, from the simplest physical pain to the most profound suffering of the spiritual person, in one of two ways: from *without,* by transforming external irritations that cause it; from *within,* by removing our instinctive resistance to the irritation, in short, by the art of endurance.[9]

We Occidentals lack any *systematic technique for overcoming suffering from within.* We do not believe in such a technique, nor in our ability to keep developing it. This, I firmly believe, is the principal reason for our centuries of fixation on the Judeo-Christian doctrine of the Fall of Man, of original sin, of suffering imposed as punishment for this, and of the closely related need to save *others* (and of the consequent doctrines of grace and revelation), unknown to the elites of classical antiquity. Until recently, we also lacked psychological techniques, in the sense of systematic psychotherapy and of the art of guiding the inner life and soul. The past century of essentially naturalistic medicine, intent on treating individual organs and cell groups, paid no attention to such methods. But, since the living body and soul are structurally *one,* the entire life process must theoretically be subject to *two* types of influences, to physical, chemical stimuli *and* to those exerted through the corridor of consciousness. Whether and to what extent this is true must be ascertained by experimental science and techniques. These effects can be observed not only in nervous diseases, but in organic and internal diseases of the organism.

Up to the present, there is one thing we have not seriously asked ourselves, the question of whether our whole Western civilization, this one-sided and overactive, *extroverted* process, might not, in the final analysis, be an *attempt to proceed with inadequate means,* judging from the experience of history as a whole, unless this process is accompanied by the contrasting art of winning *inner* power over our whole inferior, nonspiritual, psychophysical "life," which normally operates automatically, an art of meditation, introspection, endurance, and contemplation of being. Might it not be—I propose the extreme case—that the man intent *only* on external

[9] Here and for what follows, cf. the essay "Vom Sinn des Leidens," in *Moralia: Schriften zur Soziologie und Weltanschauungslehre, I* (1922).

power over other men and objects, over nature and body, *without* the above mentioned action and counterbalance of a technique of self-control, would accomplish the *opposite* objective from the one he has in mind, that he might sink into an ever increasing, *slavish dependence* on that mechanism of nature which he himself has read into and placed into nature as the ideal area for his active interference? Bacon said, *"Naturam nisi parendo vincimus"* [We defeat nature only by obeying it]. Is it, however, not equally true that *"naturam paremus, si nil volumus quam naturam vincere"* [We obey nature if we want to do nothing but defeat nature]? An Indian myth tells us of the young God Krishna who, for a long time, had vainly fought in a river with the world snake that was coiled around him. The snake is the symbol of causal relationship in the world. When Krishna's divine father called on him to remember his celestial nature, he escaped the hostile embrace of the snake by adapting his entire body to the coils of the snake, by *giving in* to them completely! The Indian myth adds that he escaped as easily as a lady takes her hand out of a glove. The Judeo-Christian concept of man is altogether *one-sided* and essentially inadequate as compared, for instance, to the Chinese, Indian, and classical Greek ideas of man. In accord with its conception of a creative and working God, unknown to the Greeks, to Plato, and to Aristotle, the Judeo-Christian idea fixedly opposes man, particularly as lord of creation and creature of power and purpose, to nature. Thus, it *lifts* him *out* of the total structure of life and out of the natural cosmos in a way no other historical idea of man has done. This idea does not become more adequate by being associated with the errors of the "classical" conception of "spontaneous reason" and the "spontaneous power of ideas"!

Man must again learn to grasp the great, invisible, mutual *solidarity of all beings* in total life, of all spirits in the eternal spirit, and, simultaneously, the *solidarity of the world process with the evolution of its first cause* and the solidarity of this cause with the world process. Man must accept this relatedness of the world not only as a theory; he must also live it and practice and activate it externally and internally. God's essence is no more "lord" of the world than man is "lord and king" of creation, but both are, above all, companions of each other's fate, enduring, overcoming, some day perhaps victorious.

The contrast between Eastern and Western approaches to the world, which I have just indicated, also finds special expression in *politics* and political methods. The significance of this effect is generally far underestimated. I mean that profound contrast between "politics of the hunter," positive power politics, and "politics of the victim," negative politics of nonresistance, which is the art of enticing the "hunter" into chaotic spaces, into large areas where the hunter will tend to err and stumble and fail to find a center of force from which he can control the entire area. The terrifying moment in Napoleon's life when Moscow had been set afire by the Russians themselves, as Leopold von Ranke so strikingly described it in his *Erhebung Preussens*, was perhaps the first example of a *kind* of situation which may recur frequently in future conflicts between the positive power politics of European states and the negative political methods of Asiatic countries. This also applies to British politics and capabilities in China, and to the policy of "nonresistance" in which Mahatma Gandhi unites Hindus and Mohammedans against British despotism in India.

If we acquire and perfect special techniques of endurance and suffering and integrate them with the technique of exerting external power, so thoroughly developed in the Occident, we shall be able to effect a *transformation of all knowledge of culture;* I mean, we shall be able to subordinate technical and experimental knowledge of achievement, as well as knowledge of culture, to metaphysical knowledge of grace and salvation.[10] Contemplation of essence, the fundamental approach to being, peculiar to metaphysical knowledge, is principally and necessarily tied to a "passive" and submissive attitude which, at times, *stops* the center of vital drive and its activity. True *"experience"* of nature, as opposed to natural *"science,"* with its objective of controlling nature, also demands an attitude of *loving* devotion. We must again acquire a deep understanding of the "language" of nature, as Francis of Assisi once understood it, or Fabre in his *Souvenirs entomologiques.* We must unlearn the foolish theory that mathematical natural science. admirable as it may be, is the only possible way for us to participate in nature. Goethe's profound insight—"Is not the nucleus of nature in the heart of man?"—self-immersion in *"natura naturans"* itself, that inner dynamic cooperation with the great, inclusive process of growth from which every natural organism stems, as it springs

[10] Cf. "The Forms of Knowledge and Culture" in this collection.

from the spirit and drive of eternal substance—all this is something quite different from mathematical science! As Fabre shows, such knowledge from within can produce in individual living creatures not only a general Dionysian participation in vital cosmic being, but also a great Apollonian experience of culture. This knowledge makes man *noble* and happy, while natural science educates him and empowers him to organize and *control* nature. Had man *not* undertaken an inner return to nature, had he *not* acquired a new feeling of oneness with nature, this new love for nature, which manifested itself so powerfully a few years ago in the German and Italian youth movements, then, indeed, the time might have come when man would no longer have cared to control even what, before, he had so exclusively wanted to control and when he would not have considered life worth enough to pursue the specific vitalistic value of having "power over nature"!

Analogous considerations apply to *metaphysics* which has true meaning only if it really penetrates man by constant ideation and by reducing individual fortuitous experiences to their essential aspects. Only in this manner is the self liberated and redeemed from fear, from the pressure of mere "existence," from the fortuitousness of fate; only thus does it become what it was for Plato, Aristotle, Spinoza, and Kant, the *free breath of man* in danger of being stifled by the specific, concrete nature of his "environment." The Occident has almost completely lost the idea of metaphysics and, even more, its technique and method of attaining knowledge. Metaphysics is completely stifled, on the one hand, by the rough dogmatism of the churches and, on the other hand, by experimental and technical knowledge of achievement. To isolate and separate man from his immediate existential environment and contact with life, from the source of all things, means to restrict his horizon terribly, indeed, to choke his inner life; this is just as bad as to cut him off from nature. As Goethe said, man needs *three* objects of veneration, veneration of what is above him, under him, and beside him.

An adjustment must and will take place in this sphere. It is one of the most important *tasks of cultural policy* to guide it in the right direction. Above all, the *cultural task* of our German schools, especially of the advanced institutes, must not be looked upon, as it was in the past, as a merely secondary concern, as something incidental compared with *technological* education. This increasing adjustment between *physical and mental labor* (Rathenau), a generous movement of popular education that fills the soul of the proletariat which had been almost excluded from the spiritual values of the nation—all this is possible only if the higher classes of society understand the cultural task as a special, separate concern.[11] Mere technical knowledge and methods divide men, but true cultural knowledge permits them to breathe together in *one* spiritual, national realm. A minority of uneducated technicians, superimposed on an unformed mass of laborers, would be civilized barbarism.

These critical forms of future adjustment, which affect the human qualities of new elites, lead us to the adjustment affecting *classes* and *nations*.

The adjustment of *political* and *economic* tensions in Europe is a *fate* imposed by the results of the World War and the changed power structure of the whole continent. The increasing adjustment of tensions in the spheres of political power and economic interests will not in the least threaten the great historic and national cultural entities; it will further stimulate and establish their spiritual and cultural autonomy. Of course, the great historical idea of the nineteenth century, that of the national state, absolutely sovereign and centralized, with an expansive economy and colonial policy, will have to retreat considerably in the coming era. For this reason alone, we Germans have little cause for acquiring new colonies. A certain measure of federalism will be realized in various forms. England has already proceeded most generously with its dominions. One circumstance has been insufficiently noted so far: The *bourgeoisie* and, above all, independent bourgeois entrepreneurs have suffered increasing losses in power and importance, even though the bourgeoisie consisted of *those* classes and groups which were truly responsible for the "nation," for that form of group life which was originally most revolutionary, and for its progress throughout historical development toward the modern national state, even though it consisted of those classes that overcame the obstacles to this evolution, the power of church, nobility, peasantry, feudal interests, hereditary principalities and their cadres of state officials. Not only the *proletariat*, insofar as it is internationally minded, but also entirely *new classes* have separated themselves from the bourgeoisie proper and have tended either to

[11] Cf. my fundamental explanations in "Universität und Volkshochschulen," in *Die Wissensformen und die Gesellschaft.*

rise above it or to sink beneath it. The group that fell is the growing class of employees in large private enterprises which have continually become more bureaucratic; the group that rose represents the magnates of finance and the energizing industries. The independent middle classes which, in recent times, were the support of French national power politics (Poincaré), have, in all countries, been hit, more or less severely, by the war. All these *new* groups tend, however, more or less vigorously, to form *international* groups which cut *across* nations. This will forcibly bring about more and more tolerance for other countries, an attitude which resembles the tolerance for other confessions that resulted from the Thirty Years' War. When I visited the last convention of the League for Cultural Cooperation, founded by Prince Rohan, held in Heidelberg and Frankfurt, I was considerably surprised, in spite of my close acquaintance with this movement over several years, that the tendencies there expressed resembled so closely the spirit and policies of the "Holy Alliance." If they were somewhat less "holy," they were so much the more impelled by a growing fear, shared by the great bourgeois classes in Europe, that their power as a class would be endangered by any future war between nations. We can, in the future, count on the growth of pacifism in the capitalistic upper bourgeoisie. Europeanism, advanced by the lower as well as by the upper classes of society, is indeed our *destiny*, not our choice. And here again, it is our task to guide the adjustment politically and economically into the proper channels and forms.

Even the opposition between *capitalistic* and *socialistic* societies, which so exclusively preoccupies our epoch, will find its adjustment. Again we ask whether the political ability of future elites will suffice to effect it *peacefully* or whether it will come about not only through bloody class struggle but also through class wars. The difficult problems indicated by the two slogans have changed their meaning in two ways since the prewar period. The old, once essentially *internal*, problem of Socialism versus capitalism is beginning to find a parallel of almost equal importance in the conflict between the national welfare state, concerned with the welfare of its total community, and the powerful commercial alliances which follow North American patterns and also work for international association. And it is even more significant that, today, powerful states and entire national entities (England, Russia) like to see themselves identified with the opposition between bourgeoisie and proletariat, whereas only class distinction within a *single* state had previously existed. As a consequence, the imminent class struggle takes on the much more threatening and somber character of a class *war*. Thus, a problem of internal politics has, increasingly, become one of foreign policy. There is no darker cloud on the political horizon of Europe and, above all, in Germany, than the tensions between London and Moscow. There is no greater danger for our nation than that one or another power of the European continent might let itself be engulfed in a power conflict between England and Russia, or that they might, by favoring such a policy, encourage England, today still hesitant, to draw the sword against Russia. The very *question* of how to act in such a case, if put to our people, would drive a terrifying *wedge* into our German nation and would cause something of a spiritual civil war. Even the well-justified promise of our statesmen to maintain "strict neutrality" can hardly save us in such a case, for the very maintenance of neutrality demands power, and primarily military power. A weak German state, in its particular geographic location, will hardly be able to maintain this postulate of neutrality. If, however, the nations of the continent remain united in every respect, at Geneva too, this international adjustment between capitalistic and Communistic orders *can* very well occur peacefully. Russia has had to adopt more and more from capitalism since the Soviet Republic and the new economic order were established, and, even as a state, it regains more and more of its typical *national* pattern with the rising predominance of the peasantry. On the other hand, the so-called "capitalistic" nations, in spite of maintaining the principle of private property, increasingly absorb so much so-called Socialism of all kinds, of fully or partially collectivized economic policy, that the *actual conditions* on both sides bridge more and more the contradictions between names and concepts.[12]

Whoever and wherever he may be, the person who works for the new elite and for this adjustment between classes will have to encompass the different *kinds of thought, moral codes,* and *religious* modes of life which he finds in the upper and lower classes; he will have to reconcile them through an *inner* adjustment in spirit and heart. I have elsewhere devel-

---

[12] I am here in complete agreement with the conclusions of W. Sombart, concerning the "Zukunft des Kapitalismus," in *Der moderne Kapitalismus,* II, 1016.

oped this problem in detail, as it affects the different ideologies.[13] We are faced with two basic philosophies of history:
the conception of the past as predominantly collective experience *or* as primarily the work of great personalities; history
as dialectical process *or* as the sum of happenings within the
"limits" of a stable, teleological "divine order"; praise of the
"good old days" for fear of the future *or* eschatological hope
and an enduring expectation of some utopian ideal which implies a stern rejection of the past; a rather materialistic *or* a
rather ideological philosophy of history. *Neither* of the two
philosophies results from the nature of things, but both are
logical categories, *ideologies,* exclusively dependent on class
myth. They testify that interests are more powerful than
reason. Everyone who wants to see clearly in politics must
abandon them *both.*

Therefore, only the person who knows how to take the
sources of *deception* into account, the effect of his belonging
to a class and of his participation in the *mythos* of national
history, only the person who knows how to ban these webs
from his mental eye can see realities with sober clarity and
discern possible ways of bridging the contradictions they en-
tail. For this reason, a thorough reform in the teaching of
history is of highest importance. As long as "classical" ideology
with its conception of man and history and the related, one-
sided theism rules our upper classes, just that long will the
lower classes, and the states which have risen to defend their
interests, adhere to their naturalism which profanes the spirit
and, reduced to a blunt formula, signifies, "Man is what he
eats," or will adhere to some similar but more refined ideology, and mock all man's metaphysical ties.

One should not delude oneself into thinking that the mass
of the proletariat can ever be won back to any kind of
organized religion or be recaptured by *any* kind of creed, even
though the church, today, has gained in power through the
confusion and despair of the bourgeoisie and through the consequent decrease in the authority of the state. The Christian
idea of a purely spiritual, creative God, of the Fall of Man,
and of the hereditary, irremediably sinful constitution of man,
through which Christianity explains a great number of natural and social evils, such as war, the use of force by states,
prostitution, and so on, as if they were in some measure inevitable and not subject to reform—all these concepts, just like

[13] Cf. "Probleme einer Soziologie des Wissens," pp. 203 f.

the classical idea of man with all its variants, are exclusively *ideologies of the upper class.* Furthermore, the fact that personalized theism had its ethnic origin exclusively in the great Eastern monarchies proves that it is a monarchic ideology with a strongly paternalistic culture and mentality. *Pantheistic* conceptions of God as "pure spirit" (Hegel) are also basically upper-class ideologies. The lower class will, as we have said, maintain its *purely* naturalistic conception of man, associated with an exclusively social and economic explanation of religion and of its authorities, as long as the upper class believes only in the *spontaneous* power of pure spirit, the active, positive force of pure will, and is not satisfied with a *"guiding and directing"* role of spiritual will in man and in human history, and just as long as the upper class makes its belief into the basis for its political and social efforts, especially in the field of education.

A completely *metaphysical and religious* and, therefore, also political and social *integration and reconciliation of classes* will be possible only on the basis of a metaphysics, a conception of self, world, and God, which comprises light and darkness, the spirit and the fate-determining, demonic drive for existence and life. This conception roots man, both as a creature of *spirit* and of *drive*, in the divine source of all things; it accepts the general and total *dependence* of life or nature on spirit, along with the dependence of spirit on life and nature; and it integrates this interdependence into the idea of the source of the world which, as substance, stands above both poles of this contrast, and in which the *reconciliation of spirit and life*, of *idea and power*, takes place, although only in the course of world history and not independently of human action.

The sociology of religions and metaphysical systems, a field in which Max Weber, Ernst Troeltsch, Carl Schmitt, and some ethnologists have made very important contributions, has as its objective to relate the ideas of God and salvation to *social patterns* and forms of political rule.[14] It is not true, as Karl Marx thought, that the world of religious ideas can be derived directly from historical patterns or even from conditions of economic production. However, both are related by an inner bond, a common, ultimate conception and attitude toward being, as hard as it may be to recognize and identify. If this

---

[14] I have made several comments concerning this point in my essay "Probleme einer Soziologie des Wissens."

common bond does not exist, if the total life of man is no longer alive and permeated by inner religious perception, religion becomes a dead tradition. In such a case, it no longer unifies men, as does the true essence of all living conceptions of transcendental and holy values, but it separates and divides men. Only then does religion assume what Marx erroneously considered its ultimate nature, the expression of nonspiritual interests of all kinds and the expression of an ideology that wishes to render outdated social conditions permanent in order to benefit a certain class. Contemporary ideas of man and divinity, which can change only *simultaneously*, are indeed such that they *no longer correspond to the historical stage* of being, nor to the present social structure of mankind. They place man into a relationship to the source of the world characteristic of periods of immaturity, when humanity is staunchly segregated into separate cultural groups and has little impetus toward adjustment. This is why we must considerably revise our view of the metaphysical place of man in the cosmos and do our utmost to integrate it into historical reality.

Thus, we have indicated the metapyhsical ideas within the limits of which the new elite, including the political elite, will move in its *relations to religion and metaphysics*. I should like to add a few comments about the fundamental attitude of the elite toward church *creeds*.

I believe that there are *four* possible attitudes of a political *elite* with respect to religion and metaphysics. The first is credal faith in church dogma with *all* its consequences, complete self-integration into the church, whether in simple faith or through willful submission to church ethics and canon law. The second attitude is denoted by the words *"écrasez l'infâme"* [crush the beast], for example, the policy of the Soviet Republic and of orthodox Marxism in general. The third attitude is that of Machiavelli, widely practiced today by the *Action française* and by Fascism. The politician himself is here a complete skeptic with respect to religion, and operates on principles of power. Externally, he favors religion and the church as a means of taming the masses or as a "mythos of the nation," but in reality he is quite indifferent to it, if he does not despise it. The fourth attitude is that of *all* great ancient and modern philosophers toward organized religion and metaphysics, since Plato and Aristotle, via Spinoza to Goethe, Hegel, Schopenhauer, and Eduard von Hartmann. The keenest expression of this attitude was furnished by

Spinoza: "Religion is the metaphysics of the masses, metaphysics the religion of thinkers." While the masses invoke and honor what is veiled by pictures and symbols, the thinker selects their pure and valid components and raises them reverently into the sphere of thought. A profound *identity of meaning* unites the two in their different approaches to the absolute, as long and insofar as both are involved in *living* movements of spirit.

As for the four attitudes, the second is completely senseless, since *some* kind of religious mythos belongs to the existence of every nation and since "the masses will never be philosophers" (Plato). The third position is a repulsive sham which falsely isolates the political element from the whole of man and brings with it the decomposition of religion and of the church itself. With respect to the first position, I must say this: It is most unlikely that an elite, today, can stand in such complete agreement with the doctrines of any organized church and, at the same time, do justice to the demands of the historical moment, without having to bend and twist these doctrines so much that only the *semblance* of agreement remains. Catholic circles, for instance, have seriously discussed whether the terms of the Weimar Constitution concerning the sovereignty of the German people are not in direct opposition to the strong condemnation of this principle by the highest church authority.

My conviction leads me to believe that the elite, as a group that must guide the coming adjustment into the right paths, may *not* give allegiance to *any* organized church. Such an elite will look reverently upon the great religious traditions and ecclesiastical institutions, fight to prevent confessional disputes, and demand free exchange of opinions, on the highest spiritual and moral plane, concerning the worth and truth of organized religion. It will not base its own metaphysical view of the ultimate as exclusively on the tradition of Luther, Kant, and German idealism, as the elites in the recent German past have done. Neither will it base itself exclusively on any other tradition, but will make room for the *fullness and variety of insight* which the history of religion and metaphysics offers. Essentially, the elite will derive its picture of God and world, to which its life and deed are committed from the *spontaneous* forces of its own spirit, from its own experience in the world and history, observing the example and teaching of all great thinkers of the past. And from this firm position, it will, first of all, try to *decide* which elements of the established dogma of a church, of its idea of justice, and its ethics are or are not *relevant* to the conceptions acquired in its own debate with the fullness of reality. In doing so, it will keep in mind that, in the sphere of meaning and of spiritual values, pictorial symbols and historical accounts, which are characteristic of all organized religions, may, in many respects, coincide with rational views and conceptions and with specific moral philosophies. As Hegel very appropriately remarked, the same "meaning" may appear in the imagery of religious faith and in the form of a philosophic concept.

I will say nothing about the ultimate and highest object of adjustment in the coming era, adjustment between the content of our various metaphysical ideas of God, world, and man. Still, I venture to affirm that, even in this highest objective sphere, we can observe an increasing, almost strange, *convergence* of all fundamental opinions among the spiritual elites of thinkers in all nations, and that, here as well, an adjustment of tremendous proportions is in full progress although, so far, very few persons have apprehended it.

Sigmund Freud
(1856–1939)

THE RESISTANCES TO PSYCHOANALYSIS

It would be hopeless to delineate successfully in a few words the immense significance of the life and work of Sigmund Freud. For the reader who wishes to know more about the man and his impact on the modern world, the three magnificent volumes written by Ernest Jones are essential.[1]

Freud is known chiefly for his innovations in psychology and for his work as the founder of psychoanalysis. However, he has also made important contributions to the social sciences. He wrote five books in this field: Totem and Taboo *(1913),* Group Psychology and the Analysis of the Ego *(1921),* The Future of an Illusion *(1928),* Civilization and Its Discontents *(1930), and* Moses and Monotheism *(1939).*

In addition to these works, contemporary social scientists owe to Freud the discovery, isolation, and definition of certain basic mechanisms,[2] and the general usage of terms like anxiety, repression, insecurity, guilt, *and so on, are directly derived from Freud's profound influence.*

As Kardiner and Preble have remarked: "Freud is a force to be reckoned with in the social sciences because he provided access to a dimension long known to social science, but ignored for want of an adequate approach. This new dimension was man—the effective unit of society, and its creator."[3]

Sigmund Freud was born in 1856 in Freiberg, Moravia, which at that time formed a part of the Austro-Hungarian Empire. His parents came to Vienna when Freud was four years old and he remained in Vienna for almost the entire rest of his life. From 1876 to 1882 he worked in the Physiological Institute and in a hospital in Vienna, where he received

---

[1] Ernest Jones, *The Life and Work of Sigmund Freud*, 3 vols., New York, Basic Books, 1953-1958.

[2] Will Herberg, "Freud, The Revisionists, and Social Reality," in *Freud and the 20th Century*, ed. Benjamin Nelson, New York, Meridian Books, 1957, p. 144.

[3] Abram Kardiner and Edward Preble, *They Studied Man*, New York, World Publishing Co., 1961, p. 232.

his M.D. in 1881. One of the most important preparations for his later discovery of psychoanalysis was his year of study with the neurologist Charcot in Paris. His early research with his friend and colleague Joseph Breuer in the use of hypnosis in the treatment of hysteria was most significant for the development of his psychoanalytic hypotheses.

Freud's concepts were slowly accepted in the medical world, and resistance to his ideas was especially strong in Vienna. The University of Vienna denied him a full professorship for many years; it was only during the last years in Vienna that he was finally awarded a professorship. In America the reception given his writings was far different. In 1909 Freud, accompanied by Ernest Jones, Sandor Ferenczi, and Carl Jung (at that time still in good standing!) left for the United States at the invitation of Stanley Hall, president of Clark University in Worcester, Massachusetts. Freud delivered five lectures at the university and also received an honorary degree. He also met William James, who attended his lectures, and who made the classic statement: "The future of psychology belongs to your work."[4]

Freud remained in Vienna until the Nazis occupied Austria. With the help of the American ambassador in Paris, the personal intervention of President Roosevelt, and the unfailing support of his friends Princess Marie Bonaparte and Ernest Jones, Freud was able to go to London, where he died in 1939.

The following essay on *The Resistances to Psychoanalysis* has been selected for its clear and eloquent defense of psychoanalysis and its broad ramifications for our whole society.

THE RESISTANCES TO PSYCHOANALYSIS[5]

A CHILD in his nurse's arms will turn away screaming at the sight of a strange face; a pious man will begin the new season with a prayer and he will also greet the firstfruits of the year with a blessing; a peasant will refuse to buy a scythe unless

[4] Ernest Jones, *The Life and Work of Sigmund Freud*, vol. 2, p. 57.
[5] "Die Widerstände gegen die Psychoanalyse" was first published in French in *La Revue juive*, 1925. The original German appeared in *Imago*, 11 (1925), 1; reprinted *Ges. Schr.*, 11, 224, and *Ges. W.*, 14, 99. Translation by James Strachey.

it bears the trademark that was familiar to his parents. The distinction between these situations is obvious and would seem to justify one in looking for a different motive in each of them.

Nevertheless, it would be a mistake to overlook what they have in common. In each case we are dealing with unpleasure of the same kind. The child expresses it in an elementary fashion, the pious man lulls it by an artifice, while the peasant uses it as the motive for a decision. The source of this unpleasure is the demand made upon the mind by anything that is *new*, the psychical expenditure that it requires, the uncertainty, mounting up to anxious expectancy, which it brings along with it. It would be interesting to devote a whole study to mental reactions to novelty; for under certain, no longer primary, conditions we can observe behavior of the contrary kind—a thirst for stimulation which flings itself upon anything that is new merely because it *is* new.

In scientific affairs there should be no place for recoiling from novelty. Science, in her perpetual incompleteness and insufficiency, is driven to hope for her salvation in new discoveries and new ways of regarding things. She does well, in order not to be deceived, to arm herself with skepticism, and to accept nothing new unless it has withstood the strictest examination. Sometimes, however, this skepticism shows two unexpected features: it may be sharply directed against what is new while it spares what is familiar and accepted, and it may be content to reject things before it has examined them. But in behaving thus it reveals itself as a prolongation of the primitive reaction against novelties and as a cloak for the retention of that reaction. It is a matter of common knowledge how often in the history of scientific research it has happened that innovations have met with intense and stubborn resistance, while subsequent events have shown that the resistance was unjustified and that the novelty was valuable and important. What provoked the resistance was, as a rule, certain factors in the subject matter of the novelty, while, on the other side, several factors must have combined to make the irruption of the primitive reaction possible.

A particularly bad reception was accorded to psychoanalysis, which the present writer began to develop nearly thirty years ago from the discoveries of Josef Breuer (of Vienna) on the origin of neurotic symptoms. It cannot be disputed that it possessed the quality of novelty, even though it made use of plenty of material which was well known from other sources (quite apart from Breuer's discoveries), such as the lessons from the teachings of Charcot, the great neuropathologist, and impressions derived from the sphere of hypnotic phenomena. Its original significance was purely therapeutic: it aimed at creating a new and efficient method for treating neurotic illnesses. But connections which could not be foreseen in the beginning caused psychoanalysis to reach out far beyond its original aim. It ended by claiming to have set our whole view of mental life upon a new basis and therefore to be of importance for every field of knowledge that is founded on psychology. After the years of complete neglect, it suddenly became a subject of general interest—and let loose a storm of indignant opposition.

The *forms* in which the resistance to psychoanalysis found expression need not now be considered. It is enough to say that the struggle over this innovation is by no means at an end, though it is already possible to see what direction it will take. Its opponents have not succeeded in suppressing the movement. Psychoanalysis, of which twenty years ago I was the only spokesman, has since attracted the support of numerous valuable and active workers, medical and nonmedical, who make use of it as a procedure for the treatment of nervous diseases, as a method of psychological research, and as an auxiliary instrument for scientific work in the most various departments of intellectual life. In the following pages our interest will be directed only to the *motives* of the resistance to psychoanalysis, with particular stress upon the composite character of that resistance and upon the differing amount of weight carried by its components.

From a clinical standpoint the neuroses must necessarily be put alongside the intoxications and such disorders as Graves' disease. These are conditions arising from an excess or a relative lack of certain highly active substances, whether produced inside the body or introduced into it from outside—in short, they are disturbances of the chemistry of the body, toxic conditions. If someone succeeded in isolating and demonstrating the hypothetical substance or substances concerned in neuroses, he would have no need to worry about opposition from the medical profession. For the present, however, no such avenue of approach to the problem is open. At the moment we can start only from the symptoms presented by a neurosis—symptoms which in the case of hysteria, for instance, consist of a combination of somatic and mental disturbances. Now Charcot's experiments as well as Breuer's clinical observations taught us that the *somatic* symptoms of hysteria are psychogenic too, that is, that they are precipitates of expired mental processes. By putting a subject into a state of hypnosis it was possible at will to produce the somatic symptoms of hysteria artificially.

Psychoanalysis took hold of this new realization and began to consider the problem of the nature of the psychical processes which led to these unusual consequences. But the direction taken by this inquiry was not to the liking of the contemporary generation of doctors. They had been brought up to respect only anatomical, physical, and chemical factors. They were not prepared for taking psychical ones into account and therefore met them with indifference or antipathy. They obviously had doubts whether mental events allowed of any exact scientific treatment whatever. As an excessive reaction against an earlier phase during which medicine had been dominated by what was known as the "philosophy of Nature,"[6] they regarded abstractions, such as those with which psychology is obliged to work, as nebulous, fantastic, and mystical; while they simply refused to believe in remarkable phenomena which might have been the starting point of research. The symptoms of hysterical neuroses were looked upon as shamming and the phenomena of hypnotism as a hoax. Even the psychiatrists, upon whose attention the most unusual and astonishing mental phenomena were constantly being forced, showed no inclination to examine their details or inquire into their connections. They were content to classify the variegated array of symptoms and trace them back, so far as they could manage, to somatic, anatomical, or chemical etiological disturbances. During this materialistic or, rather, mechanistic period, medicine made splendid advances, but it also showed a shortsighted misunderstanding of the most prominent and most difficult problems of life.

It is easy to understand why doctors, with an attitude of this kind toward the mind, should have had no liking for psychoanalysis and should have demurred to its demand for learning many things afresh and for seeing many things in a different light. But as a compensation it might be supposed that the new theory would be all the more likely to meet with applause from philosophers. For philosophers were accustomed

---

[6] A pantheistic attitude, chiefly associated with the name of Schelling, which was very prevalent in Germany during the first part of the nineteenth century. Some details will be found in Bernfeld (1944).

to putting abstract concepts (or, as unkind tongues would say, hazy words) in the forefront of their explanations of the universe, and it would be impossible that they should object to the extension of the sphere of psychology proposed by psychoanalysis. But here another obstacle arose. The philosophers' idea of what is mental was not that of psychoanalysis. The overwhelming majority of philosophers regard as mental only the phenomena of consciousness. For them the world of consciousness coincides with the sphere of what is mental. Everything else that may take place in the "mind"—an entity so hard to grasp—is relegated by them to the organic determinants of mental processes or to processes parallel to mental ones. Or, more strictly speaking, the mind has no contents other than the phenomena of consciousness, and consequently psychology, the science of the mind, has no other subject matter. And on this point the layman's view is the same.

What, then, can a philosopher say to a theory which, like psychoanalysis, asserts that on the contrary what is mental is in itself *unconscious* and that being conscious is only a *quality*, which may or may not accrue to a particular mental act and the withholding of which may perhaps alter that act in no other respect? He will naturally say that anything both unconscious and mental would be a monstrosity, a *contradictio in adjecto*, and he will fail to observe that in making this judgment he is merely repeating his own definition of what is mental, a definition which may perhaps be too narrow. It is easy for philosophers to feel this certainty, since they have no acquaintance with the material whose investigation has compelled analysts to believe in unconscious mental acts. Philosophers have never taken account of hypnosis; they have not concerned themselves with the interpreting of dreams— on the contrary, like doctors, they regard dreams as the meaningless products of reduced mental activity during sleep— they are scarcely aware that there are such things as obsessions and delusions and they would find themselves in a most embarrassing situation if they were asked to explain them on the basis of their own psychological premises. Analysts, likewise, refuse to say what the unconscious is, but they can indicate the domain of phenomena whose observation has obliged them to assume its existence. Philosophers, who know no kind of observation other than self-observation, cannot follow them into that domain.

So it comes about that psychoanalysis derives nothing but disadvantages from its middle position between medicine and philosophy. Doctors regard it as a speculative system, and refuse to believe that, like every other natural science, it is based upon a patient and tireless elaboration of facts from the world of perception; philosophers, measuring it by the standard of their own artificially constructed systems, find that it starts from impossible premises and reproach it because its most general concepts (which are only now in process of evolution) lack clarity and precision.

This state of affairs is enough to account for the reluctant and heistant reception of analysis in scientific quarters. But it does not explain the outbursts of indignation, derision, and scorn which, in disregard of every standard of logic and good taste, have characterized the controversial methods of its opponents. A reaction of such kind suggests that resistances other than purely intellectual ones were stirred up and that powerful emotional forces were aroused. And there are indeed plenty of things to be found in the theory of psychoanalysis calculated to produce such an effect as this upon the passions of men of every kind and not upon scientists alone. Above all, there is the very important place in the mental life of human beings which psychoanalysis assigns to what are known as the sexual instincts. According to psychoanalytic theory the symptoms of the neuroses are distorted substitutive satisfactions of sexual instinctual forces, the direct satisfaction of which has been frustrated by internal resistances. Later on, when analysis had extended beyond its original field of work and began to be applied to normal mental life, it sought to show that these same sexual components, which could be diverted from their immediate aims and directed to other things, made the most important contributions to the cultural achievements of the individual and of society. These views were not entirely new. The incomparable significance of sexual life had been proclaimed by the philosopher Schopenhauer in an intensely impressive passage. Moreover, what psychoanalysis called sexuality was by no means identical with the impulsion toward a union of the two sexes or toward producing a pleasurable sensation in the genitals; it had far more resemblance to the all-inclusive and all-preserving Eros of Plato's *Symposium*.

But the opponents of psychoanalysis forgot its illustrious forerunners; they fell upon it as though it had made an assault upon the dignity of the human race. They accused it of "pansexualism," though the psychoanalytic theory of the instincts had always been strictly dualistic and had at no time failed to recognize, alongside the sexual instincts, others to which it actually ascribed force enough to suppress the sexual instincts. (These mutually opposing forces were described to begin with as the sexual instincts and the ego instincts. A later theoretical development changed them into Eros and the instinct of death or destruction.) The suggestion that art, religion, and social order originated in part in a contribution from the sexual instincts was represented by the opponents of analysis as a humiliation of the highest possessions of civilization. They emphatically declared that men have other interests besides this eternal one of sex, overlooking in their zeal the fact that animals too have other interests—indeed, they are subject to sexuality, not permanently like men, but only in bouts occurring at specific periods—overlooking, too, the fact that the existence of these other interests in men had never been disputed and that nothing can be altered in the value of a cultural achievement by its being shown to have been derived from elementary animal instinctual sources.

Such a display of unfairness and lack of logic cries out for an explanation. Its origin is not hard to find. Human civilization rests upon two pillars, of which one is the control of natural forces and the other the restriction of our instincts. The ruler's throne rests upon fettered slaves. Among the instinctual components which are thus brought into service, the sexual instincts, in the narrower sense of the word, are conspicuous for their strength and savagery. Woe, if they should be set loose! The throne would be overturned and the ruler trampled underfoot. Society is aware of this—and will not allow the subject to be mentioned.

But why not? What harm could the discussion do? Psychoanalysis has never said a word in favor of unfettering instincts that would injure our community; on the contrary it has issued a warning and an exhortation to us to mend our ways. But society refuses to consent to the ventilation of the question because it has a bad conscience in more than one respect. In the first place it has set up a high ideal of morality—morality being restriction of the instincts—and insists that all its members shall fulfill that ideal without troubling itself with the possibility that obedience may bear heavily upon the individual. Nor is it sufficiently wealthy or well organized to be able to compensate the individual for his expenditure in instinctual renunciation. It is consequently left to the individual to decide how he can obtain enough compensation for the sacrifice he has made to enable him to retain his mental balance. On the whole, however, he is obliged to live psychologically beyond his income, while the unsatisfied claims of his instincts make him feel the demands of civilization as a constant pressure upon him. Thus society maintains a condition of cultural hypocrisy, which is bound to be accompanied by a sense of insecurity and a necessity for guarding what is an undeniably precarious situation by forbidding criticism and discussion. This line of thought holds good for all the instinctual impulses, including therefore, the egoistic ones. The question whether it applies to all possible forms of civilization, and not merely to those which have evolved hitherto, cannot be discussed here. As regards the sexual instincts in the narrower sense, there is the further point that in most people they are tamed insufficiently and in a manner which is psychologically wrong and are therefore readier than the rest to break loose.

Psychoanalysis has revealed the weaknesses of this system and has recommended that it should be altered. It proposes that there should be a reduction in the strictness with which instincts are repressed and that correspondingly more play should be given to truthfulness. Certain instinctual impulses, with whose suppression society has gone too far, should be permitted a greater amount of satisfaction; in the case of certain others the inefficient method of suppressing them by means of repression should be replaced by a better and more secure procedure. As a result of these criticisms psychoanalysis is regarded as "inimical to culture" and has been put under a ban as a "social danger." This resistance cannot last for ever. No human institution can in the long run escape the influence of fair criticism; but men's attitude to psychoanalysis is still dominated by this fear, which gives rein to their passions and diminishes their power of logical argument.

By its theory of the instincts psychoanalysis offended the feelings of individuals insofar as they regarded themselves as members of the social community; another branch of its theory was calculated to hurt every single person at the tenderest point of his own psychical development. Psychoanalysis disposed once for all of the fairy tale of an asexual childhood. It demonstrated the fact that sexual interests and activities occur in small children from the beginning of their lives. It showed what transformations those activities pass through, how at about the age of five they succumb to inhibition, and how from puberty onward they enter the service of the reproductive function. It recognized that early infantile sexual life reaches its peak in what is known as the Oedipus complex (an emotional attachment by the child to the parent of the opposite sex accompanied by an attitude of rivalry to the parent of the same sex) and that at that period of life these impulses still continue uninhibited as straightforward sexual desires. This can be confirmed so easily that only the greatest efforts could make it possible to overlook it. Every individual has in fact gone through this phase but has afterward energetically repressed it and succeeded in forgetting it. A horror of incest and an enormous sense of guilt are left over from this prehistoric epoch of the individual's existence. It may be that something quite similar occurred in the prehistoric epoch of the human species as a whole and that the beginnings of morality, religion, and social order were intimately connected with the surmounting of that primeval age. To adults their prehistory seems so inglorious that they refuse to allow themselves to be reminded of it: they were infuriated when psychoanalysis tried to lift the veil of amnesia from their years of childhood. There was only one way out: what psychoanalysis asserted must be false and what posed as a new science must be a tissue of fancies and distortions.

Thus the strongest resistances to psychoanalysis were not of an intellectual kind but arose from emotional sources. This explained their passionate character as well as their poverty in logic. The situation obeyed a simple formula: men in the mass behaved to psychoanalysis in precisely the same way as individual neurotics under treatment for their disorders. It is possible, however, by patient work to convince these latter individuals that everything happened as we maintained it did: we had not invented in ourselves but had arrived at it from a study of other neurotics covering a period of twenty or thirty years. The position was at once alarming and consoling: alarming because it was no small thing to have the whole human race as one's patient, and consoling because after all everything was taking place as the premises laid down by psychoanalysis declared that it was bound to.

If we cast our eyes once again over the various resistances to psychoanalysis that have been enumerated, it is evident that only a minority of them are of the kind which habitually arise against most scientific innovations of any considerable importance. The majority of them are due to the fact that powerful human feelings are hurt by the subject matter of the theory. Darwin's theory of descent met with the same fate, since it tore down the barrier that had been arrogantly set up between men and beasts. I drew attention to this analogy in an earlier paper (1917), in which I showed how the psychoanalytic view of the relation of the conscious ego to an overpowering unconscious was a severe blow to human self-love. I described this as the *psychological* blow to men's narcissism, and compared it with the *biological* blow delivered by the theory of descent and the earlier *cosmological* blow aimed at it by the discovery of Copernicus.

Purely external difficulties have also contributed to the resistance to psychoanalysis. It is not easy to arrive at an independent judgment upon matters to do with analysis without having experienced it oneself or practiced it on someone else. Nor can one do the latter without having acquired a specific and decidedly delicate technique, while until recently there was no easily accessible means of learning psychoanalysis and its technique. This position has now been improved by the foundation (in 1920) of the Berlin Psychoanalytic Clinic and Training Institute, and soon afterward (in 1922) of an exactly similar institute in Vienna.

Finally, with all reserve, the question may be raised whether the personality of the present writer as a Jew who has never sought to disguise the fact that he is a Jew may not have had a share in provoking the antipathy of his environment to psychoanalysis. An argument of this kind is not often uttered aloud. But we have unfortunately grown so suspicious that we cannot avoid thinking that this factor may not have been quite without its effect. Nor is it perhaps entirely a matter of chance that the first advocate of psychoanalysis was a Jew. To profess belief in this new theory called for a certain degree of readiness to accept a position of solitary opposition —a position with which no one is more familiar than a Jew.

Alfred Weber
(1868–1957)

FUNDAMENTALS OF CULTURE SOCIOLOGY

Alfred Weber was born in 1868 in Erfurt, Germany. He studied law and economics at the universities of Bonn, Tübingen, and Berlin. In 1899 he was appointed as Privat-dozent *at the University of Berlin, and in 1904 he went to the University of Prague, where he came into close contact with Thomas Masaryk, who at that time served as a professor of sociology. He was called to the University of Heidelberg in 1907 and taught there until 1933, when he resigned because of the Nazi takeover. In 1945 he resumed his teaching position at the University of Heidelberg. The University of Hamburg awarded him the Goethe prize in 1957 in recognition of his contributions to modern culture sociology. He died that same year.*

To Alfred Weber sociology is a cultural, not a natural, science. Sociology should show a respect for history; in a sense cultural sociology, as Weber saw it, should accept the maxims which Leopold von Ranke set for historical science: the task of revealing the past as it actually happened (wie es eigentlich gewesen ist).

Weber did not consider sociology to be a rigid system. On the contrary, he rejects outright a sociology which is alien (lebensfremd) *and also a "formal" sociology which satisfies nobody* (die niemand satt macht). *In his writings one discovers a firm social responsibility.*

Alfred Weber was the brother of Max Weber, and although he has great respect for the studies and teachings of his brother, he preferred to go on his own way. It is unfortunate that his writings are sometimes overshadowed by those of Max Weber, because Alfred Weber is certainly one of the most outstanding social scientists of the twentieth century and deserves full recognition as such.

His most important work is Kulturgeschichte als Kultur-soziologie, *which was published in 1935 in Holland, because by that time Weber was unwelcome in Germany. His rejection of the National-Socialistic philosophy is best illustrated in his* Abschied von der bisherigen Geschichte *(1946). During*

the war he published Das Tragische und die Geschichte
(1943), followed in 1953 by Der dritte oder der vierte Mensch
and by his well-known Einführung in die Soziologie *in 1955.*[1]

FUNDAMENTALS OF CULTURE SOCIOLOGY

I

IT seems expedient for all culture sociology to distinguish
between three different spheres of historical events, namely:
social process, civilizational process, and culture movement.

It is the nature of political as well as economic and social
history to examine the destiny of great historical organisms,
those great geographic, cultural, and dramatic units of mankind, to examine them with the purpose of clarifying their
peculiar destinies by establishing the concrete facts essential
to the total process. These disciplines regard the Chinese,
Hindu, West-Asiatic-Egyptian, Classical, Arabian, Germano-
Roman, and other historical spheres each as a partly "corporeal unit" containing a course of events that gives it temporal
and spatial identity; and for the collective destiny of each they
assume the task of collecting the principal data. Accordingly
they seek to base their version and, in part, their explanation
of the major historical events, the portraits of great men and
the fate of the masses, upon the body economic, the structural
development of political patterns, the social metamorphoses,
and upon other corporeal formations and transformations.
Their task is concrete historical morphology.[2] The introduction of so-called mental factors and currents does not disturb
their essential preoccupation with corporeal destiny. At the
same time the histories of art, literature, music, religion,
philosophy, and science, in a word, all the parts of culture
history which are today separate disciplines (cultural history

---

[1] For the preceding notes on Alfred Weber I owe much to the
essay by Sigmund Neumann "Alfred Weber's Conception of Historicocultural Sociology" in Harry Elmer Barnes' *An Introduction
to the History of Sociology,* University of Chicago Press, Chicago,
1948.

[2] It should be noted that this concept did not originate with
Spengler but lies implicitly or explicitly at the bottom of all the
more recent historiography. Likewise, the "adolescence" and "maturity" of historical organisms have long been ingredients in this
point of view.

does not exist as a unified discipline)[3] operate in a profoundly different manner and fairly independently of one another.

For them, corporeal formations of history do not exist as essential objects of examination or data of development. The interpretation of the great cultural emanations and movements with which they are concerned, the mental currents and systems of thought which they seek to expound in principle and bring home to us, proceeds (insofar as they consider it incorrect to restrict themselves to the mere portrayal of form and content) from the disclosure of coherences—coherences, generally speaking, between "problems" to be solved in the cultural field on the one hand (problems in history of philosophy, and so on) and, on the other hand, chiefly the working methods of the various fields, their development and expressive value (development of painting and plastic technique, laws of harmony in music, laws of language development, of literary styles and forms of expression, and so on). The result is a substantiation of a sequence and rhythm of events usually left open for more methodical investigation, substantiation of a conflict of "mental currents," styles, forms, and sundry—always a substantiation of an even progression which, according to its nature, seems to lie either technically or intrinsically within the principles of the cultural field proper. These disciplines, according to the principles of their operation, view cultural history largely as an autonomous historic sphere whose movement and development they seek to explain from within.[4] The political historian thereupon assumes the right to weave somehow the products of all these cultural-historical disciplines into his view of historical events; to place the "mental currents and facts" illuminated by the other disciplines into the setting of "corporeal" events which he in his turn illuminates; to assemble his versions of the destiny of the great historical organisms *(Geschichtskörper)* into a general view, and when he has combined all these general views, to write universal history.

For reasons pertaining not only to the history of science but also necessarily to working technique and methods, it is really

---

[3] Despite the brilliant personal contribution of Jacob Burckhardt and others.

[4] We are not overlooking such comprehensive treatments as those of Max Weber and Troeltsch in the history of religion, nor the partly "impromptu" attempts to be found in the numerous recent treatises on the different cultural fields.

a fairly motley, incoherent, at best, a loosely and superficially matched collection of building stones that confronts the sociologist when, in his turn, he finally undertakes to view things uniformly. For example, let him but try to comprehend as a whole any part of historical fact, like cultural process; let him try to comprehend the necessity by which it grows out of the general movement of history and undertake to establish its typical and lawful connection with this general movement. The same is true if, as sociologist, he tries logically to bind the cultural emanations of the Occident—their essential import—the recurrence or nonrecurrence of their typical forms and aspects to the larger collective destiny of the Occident. If he tries to place these emanations in distinct and intelligible relationship with the factual sequences (corporeal sequences) which the various historical disciplines unearth and which mark history's general course, he is confronted at the outset, as we have said, by event-series, factually discrete and, in the general version of history, only superficially connected. Should he wish to connect these series, the difference in objective between himself and the various special disciplines will force him to organize his material accordingly. For his purpose he must attempt a conceptual regrouping of the synthesis. Thus, whatever facts the political, economic, and social historians have established concerning the external form of history will necessarily fall into a new perspective. And there will be disclosed to him a great unified social process which, despite the widest variations in the different collective destinies, will reveal typical forms and stages of development. The major events (wars, revolutions, reformations, and the like) will in some typical fashion become incorporated in these forms and stages, and great men will arise not accidentally but necessarily in certain places. Furthermore, he will find that this social process is influenced by the mental sphere, that is, by those facts and processes presented by the cultural disciplines. When he now examines its kernel, he will see it as the form which gives some necessary pattern to the totality of natural human forces of impulse and will (operating as "population" in the various communal destinies), a pattern limited, of course, by certain natural (geographic, climatic, and other) conditions. The impressed pattern, or patterns, will undergo developmental alteration, will oppose and replace one another, and in their struggle produce the great *peripeteiai*, the secular historic events. At the same time he will notice how this process in the larger collective destinies, which he likewise views as corporeally closed systems, arises from primitive relationships, residues of gentilic forms, in which they first appear on the historical stage, and passes through similar forms everywhere, though, to be sure, in totally different groupings. He will observe how it seems to lead over spaces of social movement to different final outlets, to a lasting paralysis of form, to senile decay, or to a world expansion of forces, passing through like phases to various outlets which empty into the universal stream of human history. He will see the Chinese and Hindu historical cycles—once their natural conditions and direction of development are given—pursue a necessary social course through the millenniums and finally yield to that senile torpor in which they remain through the centuries, and in which they still remain today, washed by the tide of Occidental world expansion. Likewise, by considering the natural conditions of existence (chiefly the systems of canals and irrigation), he will distinctly recognize the type and direction of social development in the West-Asiatic and Egyptian culture cycle, whose early millenniums B.C. he can today reinvestigate by means of unearthed documents. And in terms of these natural conditions of development will he understand the senile torpor in which both were caught during the last millennium B.C. by that new wave of development, the Classical-Mediterranean cycle. He will observe how the conditions of existence, notably the sea, its commerce and "freedom" similarly propel the latter through a given social development—social development in the widest sense, comprising, as suggested, the total corporeal event of the historic cycle—and he will follow its lead to a type of world expansion wherein must ensue the senile decay of the forms and corporeal identity of the cycle. The historic lapse of the late Classical period in the time of the Caesars is exactly this kind of senile decay. And likewise with reference to the conditions which ushered it in, he will observe the Occidental cycle which followed the Classical and, after the migration of races, carried the scene of history northward; he will observe how it passes through an entirely different yet equally necessary development, one that retains its corporeal identity through many revolutionary stages and convulsions to reach the greatest world expansion known, embracing the entire globe. And now its inherent forms seem to be dissolving, and the cycle itself it probably passing over into something new: utter decline or the emergence of another historical organism.

In brief, the concrete event-process of the various great historical organisms, their more or less corporeal destiny which the political, economic, and social historians present, will always be viewed by the sociologist as a social evolution, specific but nevertheless fundamentally determined by natural necessity, which undergoes regroupings and realignments of general forms, runs through a predetermined number of stages and reaches a predetermined result. In this evolution the universally given social forces always assume specificity, universally given social forms present a definite and specific character and urgency, universally given processes occur in different groupings and with different results—all of which means that a general social principle of development functions in different guise. The major events and upheavals substantiated by the historian thus become landmarks indicating stages of development, or the expression of the vicissitudes bound up with evolutions, and the great men seem to rise as shield bearers and exponents of new periods.

This is the way the sociologist transforms the concretely individuated material supplied by the historian, the "corporeal" development of the different historic cycles, into a new conceptual form adequate for his mode of thinking—the way he transforms the mass of historic events pertaining to these cycles into his view of that sphere, which I intend to call the "social process."

II

IN this process, primarily moved, in his view, by the natural impulse and will of mankind and primarily determined in form and direction by the natural conditions peculiar to each historical organism, he will recognize secondary factors which the other group of historians substantiate: ideas, "mental currents," artistic views, religious convictions, and so on. He must at first be indifferent to their closer dynamic relation to the stages, vicissitudes, social formation, and all else pertaining to "corporeal" development, their causal influence on this development, or the *prius* and *post* of the form and content of the "mental" and "corporeal" spheres.[5] What he does see is a mental-cultural sphere existing as a totality in each

---

[5] Clearly, we are now dealing with marginal questions of the materialistic interpretation of history. This school's inquiry into "interest" does not lead to the clarification of the final categories of cognition.

historical organism along with the "corporeal." And no matter what he may think of their mutual interaction, he notes in this mental-cultural entity, just as in the social process, certain regularities whose connection with the corporeal social process is still obscure. He discerns in it a surge and a decline; he sees parallels between the destinies of the "cultures" of the various historical organisms, a somehow predetermined appearance of successive developmental stages, a characteristically recurring rhythm of productivity, an emergence, variegated yet exhibiting certain regularities, of the different cultural expressions (religion, philosophy, art, and within art: music, epic, lyric, drama, painting, and so on) and modes (classic, romantic, and so on), a characteristic recurrence of great religious movements and related currents of ideas under similar conditions, in the social process of the various "organisms." In short, he notes a mental-cultural development in the various historical organisms that is related in some fashion, or at least is somehow parallel to their social process. He is compelled as a sociologist to view this mental-cultural development also as a unit, a second sphere of historic events. For this purpose he has to order the disconnected facts presented to him by the different branches of knowledge into a whole historical movement which he sets as a total process occurring in the various historical organisms side by side with their social process. He is thereby tempted—in fact, he now feels it his duty—to clarify the actual dynamic relationships between these spheres in the various historical organisms.

But the attempt to fulfill this duty, to scrutinize the mental cultural sphere, has a peculiar consequence. He notes that between the social process and the truly cultural parts of this mental-cultural sphere with its various aspects and expressions in religion, art, and so on, a third element is interposed, a mental intermediary realm that is related far more vitally and distinctly to the shape and course of the social process than the truly *a potiori* cultural phenomena (the emergence of religions, systems of thought, art periods, and so on)—an intellectual cosmos, in fact, which supplies the social process with the technical means for its forms and structures and likewise appears to be one of the ground of culture phenomenology. More accurately expressed: he discovers that the mental-cultural process of the various historical organisms, viewed tentatively by him as a unity, is really in its essence, in its developmental phenomena, and in its relations to the social process no unity at all, but a duality, and that it carries within itself two entirely different spheres of human historical development.

What is revealed upon closer scrutiny is that in every great historical organism this "mental-cultural" process contains a threefold entity: first, purely mental and innermost, the development of a popular consciousness which proves to be the kernel of the purely mental process of growth and decline in the historical and cultural organisms once these are viewed from the mental-cultural angle. In all the great historic cycles within the range of his observation, including the Chinese, Hindu, Classical, and Occidental, the sociologist can observe that the development of consciousness proceeds typically toward the clarification of existence. Beginning with primitive stages when the forms, in which the world and one's own ego are seen, resemble those of the modern primitive and half-civilized peoples, he will watch consciousness in its development advance to deeper and deeper reflection about existence, and discard the totemistic and then the mystical notions, or at any rate, give them a reflectively determined, less naïve place in existence; he will watch it advance from a purely empirical attitude toward world and ego to a more or less scientific or, at least, an intellectual attitude—that is, determined in some way by intellectual abstractions. He will see how these abstractions are further developed, how at a certain stage every historical organism harbors some rationalized world view that can be still further elaborated and changed, a world view into which not only external experience, "the world," but also the personal ego, its emotions, its drives, and its immediate perceptions are woven by a process of systematized, intellectual reflection and given definite though varied forms.

The sociologist discovers that this process, occurring in all the historical organisms under his observation, is intimately bound up with a second and third process within the same unity. The second is an increasing mental domination over nature that presents, parallel to the intellectualization of world and ego, an intellectual structure of utilitarian science, experience, and wisdom, a process which, like the first, tends toward intellectual systematization. Moreover, it remains a self-contained process, retaining its identity through any number of changes in the various historical organisms.

Finally, the third mental process is none other than the actualization and concretion of this second intellectual cosmos; the objectification of this system of practical knowledge through the cultivation of an apparatus of tools and methods, principles of organization, and so on, which give concrete structure to existence.

At this point the whole mental sphere, projected in both the above-named senses and propelled from within by the development of rational consciousness, impinges upon the social process, influencing it through this technical apparatus. He now sees one distinct and self-contained rationalization process with only different aspects of expression pervading all the great historical organisms, codetermining their forms and its emanations affecting the inner existence as well as the observational and practical technique of the outer. This rationalization process has its own laws of development, necessities of growth, and conditions of stagnation. Manifestly, it is an essentially different entity from the emergence of religions, systems of thought, works of art, and cultures. It is a unique and vast sphere of development related to the social process quite differently from these. Once seen as a unity, it breaks up the previously assumed unity of the mental-cultural sphere into a "duality." This process of intellectualization and rationalization which pervades the historical organisms, the intellectual cosmos everywhere set up by this process, its unity which is reflected in its three expressions (inner intellectual enlightenment, bodies of intellectual knowledge, and intellec- tualized external apparatus), its operations, forms, and struc- tures—all these were on the whole not marked by previous historical and sociological thought as a vast and distinct sphere of historical events which should be separated conceptually both from the sphere of social process and from culture move- ment proper and investigated as a unity of functions and specific sequences.[6] I propose to call it the civilizational proc- ess and to demarcate sharply and fundamentally both the process and its sphere from social process and culture move- ment. The latter is also grounded in the social process of the great historical organisms but is related to it quite differently from the civilizational process. As we shall see, it is governed by entirely different laws of development, is of an entirely different nature, and has an entirely different place in the course of history. I propose, for the purposes of the culture- sociological approach—perhaps for the sociological approach

---

[6] Despite the many points in common between the above and the deductions of Max Weber in his essays on the sociology of religion, the latter derive from a somewhat different point of view which unfortunately does not permit of analysis here.

in general—to resolve the process of history so that the "corporeal" element in its development (that which we have named social process, the realm of originally natural impulse and will and their patterns) can be posited separately and considered, first, as being influenced by the civilizational process, man's sphere of rationalization. Then one can ask how the culture movement proper is related to both and to their interaction, whether it grows in some recognizable fashion out of the interplay of their forms and structures, whether and to what extent it proceeds independently of them, and how much it reacts upon both. I am proposing this kind of trichotomy because this is the way to attain a unified sociological view of the course of history and, especially (as I believe and intend to prove), a sociological analysis of its culture phenomenology.

III

THE civilizational process and culture movement are, as we have said, intrinsically different; they have divergent forms and laws of development and appear before us in the general course of history as mutually exclusive phenomenologies. The civilizational process with its various composite parts: its picture of world and ego, formed by the intellect (macrocosmos and microcosmos); its world of pragmatic knowledge; and its intellectually formed equipment for mastering existence may reach entirely different levels in the different historical organisms. It may variously express its world view, but in every historical organism it always builds, little by little, a cosmos of knowledge whose three indicated parts are merely aspects of the same thing and which, once launched in a certain direction, proceeds by a logic as strict as that of the inherent causal laws underlying the construction of a building. Whatever emerges is a whole, and its parts are not "created" but "discovered" (given the direction of the intellectual movement); they are already there before they are found, that is to say—from the point of view of development—preexistent. It is as if these parts were merely drawn into the realm of human consciousness, into the illumined sphere of being with which man surrounds himself. This applies to the entire world of practical knowledge in the natural sciences, to every separate "discovery" of natural science, to every theory of knowledge and epistemological insight. But it also applies to the entire technical apparatus: tools, machines, and methodical principles of work and organization. The propositions of Euclidean geometry are "present" prior to "discovery," else they would be undiscoverable; and the same is true of the Copernican formulas for planetary motion and Kant's a prioris to the extent that all these are "correctly" discovered and formulated—and likewise the steam engine, telephone, telegraph, ax, shovel, paper money, division of labor, and the whole body of technical means, methods, and principles concerned with the mastery of life and nature. Such are the "objects" of our pragmatic cosmos, those we already possess or shall acquire in the future; all of them are in essence there, that is, they are "preexistent" before we have had the chance to attract them into the conscious sphere and put them to use. The total civilizational process that actualizes this whole cosmos and supplies us with all its "objects," including the discoveries of a purely mental nature, merely discloses a world universally "prior" for all mankind, and renders it progressively accessible. In this world every part is valid for all mankind. This is proved—I shall soon touch upon apparent deviations—by the fact that the mental and physical concretions of this realm, whenever they are discovered in some historical organism, no matter where, and become a part of conscious life, spread as a matter of course throughout the world as if by natural movement. And they penetrate other historical organisms, to the extent that their social processes are sufficiently developed to receive them and their mental development high enough to "see" them—provided, of course, that intercommunication makes this penetration at all possible. The universality of technical discoveries is well known. But this universality is not restricted to the "technical" cosmos of civilization whose material and mental objects, whose methods and means, from the knowledge of working metals and the use of fire to modern ways of communication and production, have always spread with something akin to the speed of lightning, both in periods of universal communication or isolation. It holds good as well for the realm of intellect, although here the insights in mathematics, astronomy, the natural sciences, and so on, may spread at times more slowly, since their reception depends on the level of consciousness attained in the different historical organisms and since many of their practical products, as for instance chronology or accounting, may find no place in the social organization. But this does not prevent them from finally penetrating everywhere in the same measure. And the same universality, with certain modifications in the form and manner of expansion, soon to be discussed in further detail, holds good for the disclosure of new parts of the intellectually shaped view of world and ego, the intellectual results of enlightenment, the clarification of the partly inner aspect of the preexistent civilizational cosmos. The phenomenology of actualization and development of the civilizational cosmos, both in its practical and theoretical aspect, implies, when viewed as a unified historic picture, that the great historical organisms build entirely upon one another in the development of their civilizations and operate as if by agreement in the direction of ultimate unity—this despite wide divergence in their social and cultural development. Indeed, so viewed, the general course of history is really the process of elaborating the unified and universal civilizational cosmos, and mankind, as such, takes control in the halts, gaps, and breaks inherent in the destiny of the different historical organisms. The old West-Asiatic-Egyptian, Classical, Arabian, the modern Occidental, and (less strictly) the Chinese and Hindu cycles, no matter how acutely they deviate in their historic course, social development, and culture-movement, all are in this view only links, auxiliary factors in the continuous, logical elaboration of the civilizational cosmos which today is common to all mankind.

The technical parts of this civilizational cosmos first appear in their rational form in the organization of instruments and labor by the Egyptians and Babylonians as far back as 3000–4000 B.C. Having evolved in correlation with the historical cycles of India and China (the details of which are not known), this technique became not only the foundation of the whole civilized technical apparatus of the Classical and Arabian historical organisms, but through those of the Occident as well. The latter, taking the lead in technical invention since the fourteenth century, produced from the eighteenth century onward the modern apparatus of world civilization on the worldwide basis previously established.

In like fashion, the mental parts of this worldwide civilizational cosmos, mathematics, astronomy, and natural science, apparently had their intellectual inception in the enormous depths of the first and second historical organisms on the Euphrates and the Nile. They are then brought into sharper relief by the Classical, the Arabian, and the Chinese organisms, are taken over by the Occident during the period of expansion after the sixteenth century and carried through the famous "Era of Discovery" to the present universally prevalent conception of the world based on mathematics and the natural sciences, a conception which is valid for all mankind, and universally accepted.

The "realm of intellect" which, despite its present diverse forms, by its content is common civilizational possession of mankind, the intellectual notion of world and ego belonging to a single sphere, first seems to have received conscious impulse in the Brahmanic wisdom of the Hindu cycle. It then becomes a subject in the Classical and Arabic as well as the Chinese historical spheres, and finally, in the Occidental philosophy of the eighteenth century (Kant), it receives formal principles which seem to show the limitations of knowledge and at the same time bring together the different forms of enlightenment of the various historical spheres, and, insofar as they possess intellectual content, generalize them.

In this gradual emergence of the preexistent mental and material civilizational cosmos from the darkness into the light of man's collective consciousness, sketched here only in an amateurish and inadequate manner, it is of small moment—nay, it is no more than a "misfortune of a day"—if certain gained knowledge or insights get temporarily lost through historic contingencies, chiefly through the way history has of telescoping the series of historical organisms that become the carriers of enlightenment. Take, for example, the knowledge of the Copernican world view which, after its discovery during Greco-Roman antiquity, slumbered in the lap of history until its independent rediscovery by the Occident after the sixteenth century. It is likewise irrelevant to the nature of the whole process that in the projection of the "technical cosmos" certain technical means of civilization, "accidentally" discovered somewhere, perhaps remain at first unused until their rediscovery somewhere else, when they suddenly receive enormous significance and a universal, practical application. Thus, although the early Chinese discovery of the mechanical clock or the engine was not followed by social application, their rediscovery in the Occident ushered in the great technical revolution of modern times. These are not changes in the nature of development but the "jests" and curling arabesques that result from the lodgment of the process in the social and cultural movements.

And lastly, it is irrelevant to the essence of the civilizational process as a gradual emergence of a mental type of unity if the development of consciousness underlying it receives a severe setback in the early "history" of the various historical organisms and if somewhere it has to begin anew from a relatively primitive state. Note the development of the Classical consciousness, succeeding the West-Asiatic-Egyptian. (The migrating and invading Greeks were obviously barbaric compared to the Creto-Mycenaean offshoot of the West-Asiatic-Egyptian cycle which they met.) Note the development of the Arabian consciousness succeeding the Classical and that of the Occidental cycle succeeding both. This merely implies that where there is an influx of new peoples into the general civilizational cosmos of mankind, the "subjective" civilization or "civilized quality" of the new populations must always reascend the stages that have already been disclosed and traversed by others within the general and subjective civilizational cosmos. Here, by the way, the climbing and reaching for old subjective heights of civilization is always considerably facilitated by the fact that the most essential objective elements of civilization are taken over by each new historical organism and also those which are of supreme importance for the acceleration of the subjective process of civilization, the subjective intellectual enlightenment, and the conscious mastery of existence. When, for example, the Classical historical organism took over from the West-Asiatic and Egyptian not only the technical apparatus and the principles and forms of division of labor but also coined money, mathematics, and astronomy, it thereby took over the crucial elements of "objective" civilization which made possible directly a measurable intellectual mastery of existence and enormously facilitated the rationalistic domination of "inner" and "outer" things. They were certainly definite contributory factors in the rapid enlightenment and civilizational development of the "Greek barbarians" that lasted a few centuries after their incursion through the Doric migrations. These civilizational elements also influenced, in the matter of content, the remarkable early rational formulation of their view of world and ego. But this is only in passing. The same thing can be said, for example, of the transmission of the Classical money-accounting to the Occidental cycle after the migrations of the peoples, its effect in terms of development of consciousness and civilization upon this historical organism which had sunk back into a vast ignorance and expressed itself only in primitive social forms. We find a general money-accounting and, at the same time, the beginnings of "a calculating spirit" in the Greco-Roman historical organism—as is evident from the *leges barbarorum* —long before the essential importance of a constructed money-exchange economy came to light.

There is no doubt that "subjective civilization" is set back for centuries whenever there emerges a new historical organism, and whenever the new historical process shifts its center of gravity into a new geographical setting in which the historical organism must then grow and go through its social and cultural development. Subjectively, a type of antiquity must always recur, then a middle age, and a modern time. Consequently, the subjective civilizational process of all mankind presents a picture of constantly recurring darkness in certain of the "areas" where man is historically rooted, until gradually the earlier enlightenment reappears and is then surpassed. Unquestionably, however, the preservation of objective civilizational elements and subjective enlightenment in the other undisturbed historical "areas" creates the means whereby the losses of single parts can be speedily recovered and the general enlightenment reintroduced. This general enlightenment is the logically causal, though unevenly graded, disclosure of a new unity valid for all mankind, mankind's universal civilizational cosmos, objectively and subjectively preexistent.

Which aspect of the enlightenment process will predominate depends on the specific internal arrangement (I shall not as yet use a more specific or fundamental term) of the various great historical organisms, and (as is recently contended) perhaps also on the spiritual equipment of their populations, shortly to be discussed. The old West-Asiatic-Egyptian organism was led by its arrangement toward practice and technique. On the "theoretical" side it cultivated only the purely quantitative parts that were indispensable for the immediate mastery of existence (astronomy, time reckoning, accounting, and so on). On the other hand, the Classical organism, prevented, as it were, by its specific arrangement from "seeing" the technical parts of the civilizational cosmos, simply passed them by without special interest. (Except for the arch, no technical invention of Antiquity is worthy of mention.) Its field of attention was restricted to the intellectual and theoretical front, and hence it laid the foundations for mathematics, the natural sciences, philosophy, and all the other disciplines which we now call "sciences." At the same time, the Hindu historical organism with its remarkably appropriate arrangement, wrapped as it was in religious contemplation, chose for its single and indeed highly successful objective the philosophical illumination and penetration of the inmost cognition fields of world and ego, virtually ignoring everything else. Because of specific arrangement and specific means of expression, it is quite reasonable that every historical organism should clothe its insights, especially the most philosophical ones, in forms that do not always immediately reveal their universality and that impede their general expansion and application. This is particularly true when the insights, mixed with extracivilizational elements, appear in religious and metaphysical systems of thought, as illustrated by the "epistemological" inferences of the Brahmans. Further, it should be stressed that every historical organism has a repertory of ideas and concepts, consciously or unconsciously operative (which always contains a definite system of mathematics, that is, a definite structure of temporal and spatial ideas) and that the quality of these ideas and concepts can set quite various limits to enlightenment: without the idea of "function," which appeared first in the Occidental cycle, not only all higher mathematics but also the whole of modern Occidental knowledge could not have been built up. The same relation exists between the Euclidean idea of three-dimensional space and the whole knowledge of Antiquity, and between the Hindu idea that material being is mere "appearance," and all Hindu philosophy. But it was a distinct misapprehension to claim or, at least, to suggest the deduction that the "insights" (in our terminology, the disclosed parts of the intellectual civilizational cosmos) are therefore mere "symbols of the soul" of the various historical organisms, valid only for them, and that there existed, for example, an Occidental-Faustian, Arabian-Magian, or Classical-Appollonian mathematics whose truth and application were correspondingly limited to these organisms. The development of Euclidean geometry may have been a result of the "Appollonian soul" of Hellenism—we shall not dispute the fact here—and, at first, may have been expressed in purely Hellenic form. But its content of truth and knowledge is, in the human sense, eternal, that is, universally valid and necessary for all mankind. The same is true of the cognitive content of the Faustian infinitesimal calculus and all its consequences, or of the Kantian a prioris or of the Hindu opposition of "Appearance and Reality." It follows that whatever Kant in his test of the formal premises of knowledge excluded from the sphere of pure empirical knowledge and labeled metaphysics must once for all be excluded from the temples of universal "knowledge," from the temple of civilizational knowledge, and therewith from the enlightenment of the universal preexistent civilizational cosmos, its theory and its practice—not, however, from the temple of "truth" in general. For these metaphysically or religiously conditioned parts of the "mental realm of knowledge" we shall meet again in the realm of culture and culture movement. As will appear, they possess in this realm—no matter how slight their civilizational (universally valid and necessary) content—a wealth of cultural and, yes, spiritual truth which determines the content and essence of the cultural emanations. But of this later.

Let us now summarize: The phenomenology and apparent form of the civilizational process consist in the logically causal mode of development, the unevenly graded, accummulative clarification of something preexistent and latent in all mankind, and in the disclosure of this as universally valid and necessary. And the civilizational cosmos is an intellectually formed cosmos of universally valid and necessary things which cohere internally and, considered in their practical aspect, are equally and universally useful (that is, empirically true) for human ends, and considered in their theoretic aspect, are equally inevitable (that is, theoretically true), and in the illumination of world and ego, intuitively evident (that is, true a priori). This cosmos is the epitome of mankind's increasing enlightenment. Its disclosure proceeds by the laws of logical causality. At every step in the disclosure the concepts, true or untrue, are applicable. And its disclosed and illumined objects bear the stamp of universal validity and necessity, and spread throughout the trafficked world for the very reason that they are preexistent for all mankind.

BIBLIOGRAPHY

Auguste Comte

ORIGINAL WORKS:

Cours de philosophie positive. Ed. by E. Littré. 6 vols. 4th ed. Paris, Bachelier, 1877.

Discours sur l'esprit positif. Paris, Carilan-Goenry, 1844.

Système de politique positive. 4 vols. Paris, Mathias, 1851-1854.

TRANSLATED WORKS:

Positive Philosophy. Trans. by Harriet Martineau. 3 vols. London: George Bell and Sons, 1896.

The System of Positive Polity. Trans. by John Bridges *et al.* 4 vols. London: Longmans, Green and Co., 1875-77.

BOOKS ON COMTE:

Alengry, Franck. *La Sociologie chez Auguste Comte.* Paris, 1900.

Barnes, Harry Elmer (ed.). *An Introduction to the History of Sociology.* Chicago: The University of Chicago Press, 1948. *See* chap. iii, p. 81: "The Social and Political Philosophy of Auguste Comte: Positivist Utopia and the Religion of Humanity."

Bogardus, Emory S. *The Development of Social Thought.* New York: Longmans, Green and Co., 1955. *See* chap. xvi.

Caird, Edward. *The Social Philosophy and Religion of Comte.* Glasgow, 1885.

Chambliss, Rollin. *Social Thought.* New York: Dryden Press, 1954. *See* chap. xvi.

Chiappini, L. *Les Idées politiques d'Auguste Comte.* Paris, 1913.

Defourny, Maurice. *La Sociologie positiviste d'Auguste Comte.* Louvain, 1902.

Gruber, Herman. *Comte der Begründer des Positivismus.* Freiburg, 1889.

Hutton, H. D. *Comte's Theory of Man's Future.* London, 1877.

Lévy-Bruhl, Lucien. *The Philosophy of Auguste Comte.* New York, 1903.

Lewes, G. H. *Comte's Philosophy of the Sciences.* London, 1853.

Littré, Maximilien. *Auguste Comte et la philosophie positive.* Paris, 1863.

Marcuse, Herbert. *Reason and Revolution.* New York: Oxford University Press, 1941. Paperback edition Beacon Press, 1960. *See* p. 340: "The Positive Philosophy of Society: Auguste Comte." It forms a part of an excellent chapter on "The Foundations of Positivism and the Rise of Sociology," p. 323 (Beacon Press edition).

Roux, A. *La Pensee d'Auguste Comte.* Paris, 1920.

Timasheff, Nicholas S. *Sociological Theory.* New York: Doubleday and Co., 1955. *See* chap. ii.

Emile Durkheim

Note: The following is by no means a complete bibliography of Durkheim's works. I have emphasized for the reader the translated works, which for the most part were published in this country by The Free Press, Glencoe, Illinois. A separate list of Durkheim's books as they were published by The Free Press is given here.

An excellent bibliography of the writings of Emile Durkheim and his pupils can be found in the *Kölner Vierteljahrshefte für Soziologie,* Vol. VI, No. 3 (1927), pp. 278-83, compiled by E. Conze, "Zur Bibliographie der Durkheim-Schule."

PUBLICATIONS BY THE FREE PRESS, GLENCOE, ILLINOIS:

The Division of Labor in Society

Education and Sociology

The Elementary Forms of the Religious Life

Moral Education

Professional Ethics and Civic Morals

Rules of the Sociological Method

Sociology and Philosophy

Suicide: A Study in Sociology

THE FOLLOWING MONOGRAPHS APPEARED IN L'Année sociologique:

"La Prohibition de l'inceste et ses origines," Vol. I (1897).

"Définition des phénomènes religieux," Vol. II.

"Deux lois de l'évolution pénale," Vol. IV.

"Sur le totémisme," Vol. V.

"De quelques formes primitives de classification," Vol. VI (in collaboration with Mauss).

"Sur l'organisation matrimonale des sociétés australiennes," Vol. VIII.

ARTICLES PUBLISHED IN VARIOUS OTHER JOURNALS:

"Conférences sur la famille" in *Revue Philosophique* (1920).

"Introduction à la morale" in *Revue Philosophique* (1919).

"Introduction à la sociologie de la famille" in *Annales de la faculté des lettres de Bordeaux* (1888).

"La Notion du matérialisme économique" in *Revue Philosophique* (1898).

"La Sociologie en France" in *Revue Bleue* (1900).

"Sociologie et sciences sociales" (with P. Fauconnet) in *Revue Philosophique* (1903).

BOOKS AND ARTICLES ON DURKHEIM:

Alpert, Harry. *Emile Durkheim and His Sociology.* New York: Columbia University Press, 1939.

Becker, Howard, and Barnes, Harry Elmer. *Social Thought from Lore to Science.* Vol. II. Washington, D. C.: Harren Press, 1952. *See* pp. 829*ff.*

Benoit-Smullyan, Emile. "The Development of French Sociologism and Its Critics in France." Unpublished Ph.D. thesis. Cambridge, Mass.: Widener Library, Harvard University.

——. "The Sociologism of Emile Durkheim and His School" in *An Introduction to the History of Sociology.* Ed. by Harry Elmer Barnes. Chicago: University of Chicago Press, 1948. *See* pp. 499*ff.*

Davy, Georges. *Durkheim: Introduction et morceaux choisis.* Paris, 1911.

——. "Emile Durkheim: l'homme et l'oeuvre" in *Revue de métaphysique et de morale* (1919, 1920).

——. *Sociologues d'hier et d'aujourd'hui.* Paris, 1931.

"Durkheim-Simmel Commemorative Issue," *The American Journal of Sociology,* Vol. LXIII, no. 6 (May 1958).

Gehlke, Charles E. *Emile Durkheim's Contribution to Sociological Theory.* New York: Columbia University Press, 1915.

Halbwachs, Maurice. "La Doctrine d'Emile Durkheim" in *Revue Philosophique* (1918).

Marica, George. *Emile Durkheim: Soziologie und Soziologismus.* Berlin, 1932.

Marjolin, Robert. "French Sociology: Comte and Durkheim," *The American Journal of Sociology,* Vol. XLII, no. 5 (March 1937). Pp. 693-704.

Merton, Robert. "Durkheim's Division of Labor in Society," *The American Journal of Sociology,* Vol. LX (1934). Pp. 325-26.

Parsons, Talcott. *The Structure of Social Action.* New York: McGraw-Hill Book Co., 1937; Glencoe: The Free Press, 1949.

Note: Parsons has given a profound and excellent analysis of Durkheim in this book.

Seger, Imogen. *Durkheim and His Critics on the Sociology of Religion.* New York: Bureau of Applied Social Research, Columbia University, 1957. (Monograph series.)

Wolff, Kurt H. (ed.). *Emile Durkheim, 1858-1917, A Collection of Essays, with Translations and a Bibliography.* Columbus: Ohio State University Press, 1962.

Sigmund Freud

SELECTED WORKS:

Beyond the Pleasure Principle. Trans. by James Strachey. London: Hogarth Press, 1922; New York: Liveright, 1922. Paperback edition by Bantam Books, New York, 1959, with a special introduction by Gregory Zilboorg.

Civilization and Its Discontents. Trans. by J. T. Riviere. London: Hogarth Press, 1930; New York: Cape and Smith, 1930. Paperback edition by Doubleday Anchor, New York, 1958.

Collected Papers. Vols. I-V. London: Hogarth Press, 1956.

The Ego and the Id. Trans. by J. T. Riviere. London: Hogarth Press, 1927.

The Future of an Illusion. New York: Liveright, 1953. Paperback edition by Doubleday Anchor, New York, 1957.

Group Psychology and the Analysis of the Ego. London: Hogarth Press, 1922; New York: Liveright, 1940. Paperback edition by Bantam Books, New York, 1960, with a special introduction by Franz Alexander.

The Interpretation of Dreams. Trans. by A. A. Brill. London: Allen and Unwin, 1932; New York: The Macmillan Co., 1937. Also later edition by Basic Books, New York.

Moses and Monotheism. New York: Alfred A. Knopf, 1939. Paperback edition by Vintage Books, 1955.

The Origins and Development of Psychoanalysis. Clark University Lectures, *American Journal of Psychology* (1909). This became later *A General Introduction to Psychoanalysis.* New York: Liveright, 1924. Paperback edition by Permabooks, New York, 1953.

The Origins of Psychoanalysis. New York: Basic Books, 1954. Paperbook edition of Doubleday Anchor, New York, 1957.

The Problem of Anxiety. Trans. by H. A. Bunker. New York: Norton and Co., 1936.

The Psychopathology of Everyday Life. Trans. by A. A. Brill. New York: The Macmillan Co., 1914. Also in *The Basic Writings of Sigmund Freud.* Ed. by A. A. Brill. New York: Modern Library, 1938. Also in a pocketbook edition.

Studies in Hysteria (in collaboration with Joseph Breuer). Trans. by A. A. Brill. Paperback edition by Beacon Press, Boston, 1958.

Three Contributions to the Theory of Sex. Trans. by A. A. Brill. New York: Nervous and Mental Diseases Monograph, 1930. Dutton Paperback edition by E. P. Dutton & Co., 1962. Also in *The Basic Writings of Sigmund Freud.*

Totem and Taboo. English Text, London: Routledge, 1919; New York: New Republic, 1931. Also in *The Basic Writings of Sigmund Freud.* Paperback edition by Modern Library Paperback, New York, 1960. Both hard-cover and paperback edition trans. by A. A. Brill.

Wit and Its Relation to the Unconscious. Trans. by A. A. Brill. New York: Moffat, Yard, 1917. Also in *The Basic Writings of Sigmund Freud.*

BOOKS ON FREUD:

Arlow, Jacob. *The Legacy of Sigmund Freud.* New York: International Universities Press, 1956.

Binswanger, Ludwig. *Erinnerungen an Sigmund Freud.* Bern: A. Francke Verlag AG, 1956.

Freud and the Twentieth Century. Ed. by Benjamin Nelson. New York: Meridian Books, 1957.

Freud on Creativity and the Unconscious. Selected papers, ed. and intr. by Benjamin Nelson. New York: Harper Torchbooks, 1958.

Fromm, Erich. *Sigmund Freud's Mission.* New York: Harper and Bros., 1959.

Jones, Ernest. *The Life and Work of Sigmund Freud.* 3 vols. New York: Basic Books, 1955-57.

Marcuse, Ludwig. *Sigmund Freud: Sein Bild vom Menschen.* Hamburg: Rowolt, 1956.

Psychoanalysis and the Future. A Freud Centenary Memorial. New York: National Psychological Association for Psychoanalysis, 1957.

Rieff, Philip. *Freud: The Mind of The Moralist.* New York: Viking Press, 1959.

Sachs, Hanns. *Freud: Master and Friend.* Cambridge, Mass.: Harvard University Press, 1944.

Walker Puner, Helen. *Freud, His Life and His Mind.* New York: Dell Publishing Co., 1959.

Wittels, Fritz. *Freud and His Time.* New York: Liveright, 1931. Paperback edition by The Universal Library, New York, n.d.

———. *Sigmund Freud: His Personality, His Teaching and His School.* New York: Dodd, Mead and Co., 1924.

Zilboorg, Gregory. *Freud and Religion.* Westminster: Newman Paperback, 1958.

———. *Sigmund Freud.* New York: Scribner's, 1951. Paperback edition by Evergreen Books, Grove Press, New York, 1960.

Zweig, Stefan. *Mental Healers.* New York: Garden City Publishing Co., 1932.

Johann Gottfried Herder

Note: One can find an excellent bibliography of Herder's works and writings on Herder in Robert T. Clark, Jr., *Herder, His Life and Thought* (Berkeley: University of California Press, 1955), see p. 455.

SELECTED WORKS:

Düntzer, Heinrich, and Da Fonseca, Wollheim (eds.). *Herders Werke, nebst einer Biographie des Dichters.* Berlin: Hempel, 1869-79.

Koch, Willi A. (ed.). *Joh. Gottfried Herder, Mensch und Geschichte, sein werk im Grundriss.* Stuttgart: Alfred Kroner Verlag, 1957.

Leyen, Friedrich von der (ed.). *Johann Gottfried Herder: Ideen zur Philosophie der Geschichte der Menschheit.* Jena and Leipzig: E. Diederichs, 1904.

Naumann, E. (ed.). *Herders Werke. Auswahl in 8 Teilen.* Berlin: Bong, 1908.

Suphan, Bernhard, Redlich, Carl, and Steig, Reinhold (eds.). *Herders sämmtliche Werke.* 33 vols. Berlin: Weidmannsche Buchhandlung, 1877-1913.

TRANSLATED WORKS:

Outlines of a Philosophy of the History of Man. Trans. by T. Churchill. London: Johnson, 1800. 2nd ed., 1803.

God: Some Conversations. Trans. by Frederick H. Burkhardt. New York: Hafner Publishing Co., 1949. First published under the imprint New York: Veritas Press, 1940.

BOOKS ON HERDER:

Bäte, Ludwig. *Johann Gottfried Herder. Der weg-das werk-die Zeit.* Stuttgart: S. Hirzel, 1948.

Clark, Robert T., Jr., *Herder, His Life and Thought.* Berkeley: University of California Press, 1955.

Gillies, Alexander. *Herder.* Oxford: Basil Blackwell, 1945.

——. *Herder, der Mensch und sein Werk.* Trans. by Wilhelm Löw. Hamburg: Marion von Schröder Verlag, 1949.

McEachran, F. *The Life and Philosophy of Johann Gottfried Herder.* Oxford: Clarendon Press, 1929.

Nevinson, Henry. *A Sketch of Herder and His Times.* London: Chapman and Hall, 1884.

Rasch, Wolf Dietrich. *Herder, sein Leben und Werk im Umriss.* Halle: Niemeyer, 1938.

Wells, G. A. *Herder and After, A Study in the Development of Sociology.* The Hague: Mouton and Co., 1959.

Note: For the relationships of Herder's thought with the beginnings of sociology I recommend this book highly.

Karl Marx

Note: One of the most recent bibliographies on Marx appears in the *Kölner Zeitschrift für Soziologie und Sozialpsychologie,* Vol. X, no. 3 (1958) and was compiled by Hans-Joachim Lieber and Peter Ludz under the title "Zur Situation der Marxforschung."

SELECTED WORKS:

A Contribution to the Critique of Political Economy. Trans. by N. I. Stone. Chicago: Charles H. Kerr and Co., 1904.

Das Kapital. Trans. by S. Moore, E. Aveling, E. Untermann. 3 vols. Chicago: Charles H. Kerr and Co., 1906-09.

Grundrisse der Kritik der politischen Oekonomie. 2 vols. Moscow: Marx-Engels-Lenin Institut, 1939, 1941. Reissued in one volume in Berlin, 1953. This publication is the first version of *Das Kapital.*

Letters to Dr. Kugelmann. New York: International Publishers, 1934.

The Poverty of Philosophy. Trans. by H. Quelch. Chicago: Charles H. Kerr and Co., 1910.

Theorien über den Mehrwert. Ed. by Karl Kautsky. 3 vols. Stuttgart, 1905.

IN COOPERATION WITH FRIEDRICH ENGELS THE FOLLOWING WORKS:

Critique of the Gotha Program. New York: International Publishers, 1933.

The German Ideology. Ed. by R. Pascal. New York: International Publishers, 1933.

Germany: Revolution and Counter-Revolution. New York: International Publishers, 1933.

Marx & Engels, Basic Writings on Politics and Philosophy. Ed. by Lewis S. Feuer. New York: Doubleday Anchor, 1959.

Selected Works. 2 vols. Moscow: Marx-Engels Institute, 1935.

Books on Marx:

Hook, Sydney. *Marx and the Marxists,* New York, Anvil Books, 1955.

——. *From Hegel to Marx,* Ann Arbor, Ann Arbor Paperbacks, 1962.

Fromm, Erich. *Marx's Concept of Man,* New York, Frederick Ungar Publishing Co., 1961.

Mehring, Fritz. *Karl Marx,* Ann Arbor, Ann Arbor Paperbacks, 1962.

Rühle, Otto. *Karl Marx: His Life and Work,* London, George Allen & Unwin, 1929.

Tucker, Robert. *Philosophy and Myth in Karl Marx,* Cambridge, Cambridge University Press, 1961.

Wolfe, Bertram D. *Three Who Made a Revolution,* Boston, Beacon Press, 1955.

Henri, Comte de Saint-Simon

Note: There is an excellent bibliography on Saint-Simon in H. Gouhier, *La Jeunesse d'Auguste Comte* (Paris, 1936-41). *See* Appendices of Vols. II and III.

Selected works:

Catéchisme des industriels. 1823-24.

L'Industrie. 1816-18.

Introduction aux travaux scientifique du XIX siècle. 1807-1808.

Lettres d'un habitant de Genève. 1803.

Mémoire sur la science de l'homme. 1813.

Nouveau Christianisme. 1825.

Oeuvres complètes de Saint-Simon et Enfantin. Paris, 1865-76.

L'Organisateur. 1819-20.

De l'Organisation sociale. 1825.

La Politique. 1819.

Quelques opinions philosophiques. 1825.

De la Réorganisation de la Société Européenne. 1814.

Du Système industriel. 1821-22.

Translated work:

Selected Writings of Henri, Comte de Saint-Simon. Trans. by F. M. Markham. Oxford: Basil Blackwell, 1952.

Books on Saint-Simon:

D'Allemagne, H. R. *St. Simoniens.* Paris, 1930.

Durkheim, Emile. *Le Socialisme.* Ed. by Marcel Mauss. Paris, 1928.

An Exposition—The Doctrine of Saint-Simon. Trans. by Georg G. Iggers. Boston: Beacon Press, 1958.

Gouhier, H. *La Jeunesse d'Auguste Comte*. Vols. II-III. Paris, 1936-41.

Leroy, M. *Vie de Saint-Simon*. Paris, 1925.

Max Scheler

SELECTED WORKS:

Der Formalismus in der Ethik und die materielle Wertethik. 1913.

Philosophische Weltanschauung. Bern, 1954. Also translated under the title *Philosophical Perspectives*. Boston: Beacon Press, 1958.

Ressentiment. Translated by William W. Holdheim. Edited and introduced by Lewis A. Coser. Glencoe, Ill., The Free Press, 1960.

Die Stellung des Menschen im Kosmos. 1928. 5th ed. Munich, 1949.

Vom Ewigen im Menschen. 1921. 4th ed. Bern, 1954.

Wesen und Formen der Sympathie. 1922. Also translated under the title *Nature and Forms of Sympathy*.

Die Wissensformen und die Gesellschaft. Leipzig, 1926.

BOOKS ON SCHELER:

Becker, Howard, and Dahlke, Helmut Otto. "Max Scheler's Sociology of Knowledge," *Philosophy and Phenomenological Research*, Vol. II (March 1942), pp. 309-22.

Dahlke, H. O. "The Sociology of Knowledge" in H. E. Barnes, Howard Becker, and Frances Bennett Becker (eds.). *Contemporary Social Theory*. New York: Appleton-Century, 1940. Pp. 64-92.

Mandelbaum, Maurice. *The Problem of Historical Knowledge*. New York: Liveright, 1938. Pp. 147ff.

Georg Simmel

Note: For a most complete and excellent bibliography of Simmel's works in German and the available translations in English see *Georg Simmel, 1858-1918*, edited by Kurt H. Wolff and published by the Ohio University Press, 1959. "Bibliography of Simmel's Books in German and His Writings Which Are Available in English" by Kurt H. Wolff, pp. 377ff. In the same volume "Bibliography of Writings on Georg Simmel" by Kurt Gassen, pp. 357ff. Excellent.

In our bibliography we have emphasized the latest translations of the sociological works and articles of Simmel and also included a selected list of works on Simmel.

SELECTED WORKS:

Brücke und Tür. Essays des Philosophen zur Geschichte, Religion, Kunst und Gesellschaft. Im Verein mit Margarete Susman herausgegeben von Michael Landmann. Stuttgart: Koehler, 1957.

Grundfragen der Soziologie. Berlin and Leipzig, 1917, 1920.

Philosophie des Geldes. Leipzig, 1900. 6th ed. Berlin, 1958.

Soziologie. Untersuchungen über die Formen der Vergesellschaftung. Leipzig, 1908. 4th ed. Berlin, 1958.

TRANSLATED WORKS:

"A Chapter in the Philosophy of Value," *The American Journal of Sociology,* Vol. V, no. 5 (March 1900), pp. 577-603. No translator mentioned.

"A Contribution to the Sociology of Religion," *The American Journal of Sociology,* Vol. XI, no. 3 (November 1905), pp. 359-76. Reprinted in the same journal Vol. LX, Part II (May 1955), pp. 1-18. Trans. by W. W. Elwang.

"Fashion," *International Quarterly,* Vol. X, no. 1 (October 1904), pp. 130-55. This article was reprinted in *The American Journal of Sociology,* Vol. LXII, no. 6 (May 1957), pp. 541-58. Translator not mentioned.

"How Is Society Possible?" *The American Journal of Sociology,* Vol. XVI, no. 3 (November 1910), pp. 372-91.

"The Number of Members as Determining the Sociological Form of the Group," *The American Journal of Sociology,* Vol. VIII, no. 1 (July 1902), pp. 1-46; Vol. VIII, no. 2 (September 1902), pp. 158-96. Translator Albion W. Small.

"The Persistence of Social Groups," *The American Journal of Sociology,* Vol. III, no. 5 (March 1898), pp. 662-98; Vol. III, no. 6 (May 1898), pp. 829-36; Vol. IV, no. 1 (July 1898), pp. 35-50. Translator Albion W. Small.

"The Problem of Sociology," *Annals of the American Academy of Political and Social Science,* Vol. VI, no. 3 (November 1895), pp. 412-23.

"The Problem of Sociology," *The American Journal of Sociology,* Vol. XV, no. 3 (November 1909), pp. 289-320. Trans. by Albion W. Small.

"The Sociology of Conflict," *The American Journal of Sociology,* Vol. IX, no. 4 (January 1904), pp. 490-525; Vol. IX, no. 5 (March 1904), pp. 672-89; Vol. IX, no. 6 (May 1904), pp. 798-811. Translator Albion W. Small. The first part of "The Sociology of Conflict" was reprinted in this book.

"The Sociology of Secrecy and of Secret Societies," *The American Journal of Sociology*, Vol. XI, no. 4 (January 1906), pp. 441-98. Trans. by Albion W. Small.

"The Sociology of Sociability," *The American Journal of Sociology*, Vol. LV (November 1949), pp. 254-61. Trans. by Everett C. Hughes.

"Superiority and Subordination as Subject-Matter of Sociology," *The American Journal of Sociology*, Vol. II, no. 2 (September 1896), pp. 167-89; Vol. II, no. 3 (November 1896), pp. 392-415. Translator Albion W. Small.

IN THE FOLLOWING BOOKS ONE CAN FIND TRANSLATED ARTICLES (SOMETIMES REPRINTS) OF SIMMEL:

Park, Robert E., and Burgess, Ernest W. *Introduction to the Science of Sociology*. Chicago: University of Chicago Press, 1921. Besides some reprints one can find here the following new articles: "The Sociological Significance of the 'Stranger,'" pp. 322-27; "Sociology of the Senses," pp. 356-61; "Money and Freedom," pp. 552-53.

Wolff, Kurt H. *The Sociology of Georg Simmel*, Glencoe: The Free Press, 1950. This book contains numerous essays by Simmel, some of which were already published in *The American Journal of Sociology* or elsewhere. Professor Wolff has very ably translated and edited the various essays by Simmel. This book is one of the best anthologies on Simmel available. Excellent introduction.

——, and Bendix, Reinhard. *Conflict* and *The Web of Group-Affiliations*. Intr. by Everett C. Hughes. Glencoe: The Free Press, 1955.

——(ed.). *Georg Simmel, 1858-1918*. Columbus: Ohio University Press, 1959. Besides various essays on Simmel this book contains new translated material by Simmel.

OTHER REPRINTS, VERY OFTEN ABRIDGED, ONE CAN STILL FIND IN THE FOLLOWING TWO BOOKS:

Borgatta, Edgar F., and Meyer, Henry J. *Sociological Theory: Present-Day Sociology from the Past*. New York: Alfred A. Knopf, 1956.

Coser, Lewis A., and Rosenberg, Bernard. *Sociological Theory: A Book of Readings*. New York: The Macmillan Co., 1957.

BOOKS AND ARTICLES ON SIMMEL:

Abel, Theodore. "The Formal Sociology of Georg Simmel" in *Systematic Sociology in Germany: A Critical Analysis of Some Attempts to Establish Sociology as an Independent Science*. New York: Columbia University Press, 1929. Pp. 13-49.

Altmann, S. P. "Simmel Philosophy of Money" in *The American Journal of Sociology*, Vol. IX (1903), pp. 46-68.

Barnes, Harry Elmer, and Becker, Howard. *Social Thought from Lore to Science*. Vol. II. Washington: Harren Press, 1952. Pp. 889-90.

Bentley, Arthur F. "Simmel, Durkheim, and Ratzenhofer" in *The American Journal of Sociology*, Vol. XXXII (1926), pp. 250-56.

Bonner, Hubert. "Georg Simmel: Field Theory and Sociology" in *Sociology and Social Research*, Vol. XXXIII (1949), pp. 171-79.

"Durkheim-Simmel Commemorative Issue" *The American Journal of Sociology*, Vol. LXIII, no. 6 (May 1958).

Ekhart, Leonhard. "Georg Simmels philosophishe Begründung seiner Soziologie." Doctoral dissertation, University of Graz, 1957.

Freund, Ludwig. "Simmels unvermeidlicher Streit," *Politik und Ethik. Möglichkeiten und Grenzen ihrer Synthese*. Frankfurt am Main and Berlin: Metzner, 1955. Pp. 102-5*ff*.

Frischeisen-Köhler, Max. "Georg Simmel," *Kantstudien*, Vol. XXIV (1919), pp. 1-51. Also in book form—Berlin: Reuther und Reichard, 1919.

Gassen, Kurt, and Landmann, Michael (eds.). *Buch des Dankes an Georg Simmel. Briefe, Erinnerungen, Bibliographie*. Berlin: Duncker und Humblot, 1958.

Hawthorn, H. B. "A Test of Simmel on the Secret Society: the Doukhobors of British Columbia" in *The American Journal of Sociology*, Vol. LXII (1956), pp. 1-7.

Heberle, Rudolf. "The Sociology of Georg Simmel: The Forms of Social Interaction" in *An Introduction to the History of Sociology*. Ed. by Harry Elmer Barnes. Chicago: University of Chicago Press, 1948. Pp. 249-73.

Honigsheim, Paul. "Georg Simmel" in *Handwörterbuch der Sozialwissenschaften*, Vol. IV (1956), pp. 270-72.

Landmann, Michael. Einleitung zu George Simmels *Brücke und Tür: Essays des Philosophen zur Geschichte, Religion, Kunst und Gesellschaft*. Stuttgart: Koehler, 1957.

——. "Georg Simmel. Vorbereitung eines Archivs und einer Ausgabe" in *Zeitschrift für philosophische Forschung*, Sonderheft I (1949), pp. 204*ff*.

——. "Konflikt und Tragödie. Zur Philosophie Georg Simmels" in *Zeitschrift für philosophische Forschung*, Vol. VI (1951-52), pp. 115-33.

Levine, Donald N. "Simmel and Parsons: Two Approaches to the Study of Society." Unpublished Ph.D. dissertation, University of Chicago, 1957.

Masaryk, Thomas G. "Simmels Soziologie" in *Zeitschrift für Sozialwissenschaft*, Vol. XII (1909), pp. 600-607.

Newman, K. J. "Georg Simmel and Totalitarian Integration" in *The American Journal of Sociology*, Vol. LVI (1951), pp. 348-53.

Przywara, Erich. "Simmel-Husserl-Scheler," *In und Gegen, Stellungnahmen zur Zeit*. Nuremberg: Glock and Lutz, 1955. Pp. 33-54.

Rosenthal, Erich, and Oberlaender, Kurt. "Books, Papers, and Essays by Georg Simmel" in *The American Journal of Sociology*, Vol. LI (1945), pp. 238-47.

Spykman, Nicholas J. *The Social Theory of Georg Simmel*. Chicago: University of Chicago Press, 1925. Biography and Bibliography on pp. 277-92.

Tönnies, Ferdinand. "Simmel als Soziologe" in *Frankfurter Zeitung*, October 9, 1918.

Vannatta, Thomas A. "A Study in Polarities in the Writings of Georg Simmel." Unpublished Ph.D. dissertation, Ohio State University, 1948.

Vierkandt, Alfred. "Simmel" in *Encyclopaedia of the Social Sciences*, Vol. XIV (1934).

Weingartner, Rudolph H. "Experience and Culture: The Philosophy of Georg Simmel." Unpublished Ph.D. dissertation, Columbia University, 1959.

Werner Sombart

SELECTED WORKS:

Der Bourgeois. Trans. by M. Epstein under the title, *The Quintessence of Capitalism*. London, 1915.

Deutscher Sozialismus. Trans. by K. F. Geiser under the title, *A New Social Philosophy*. Princeton, 1937.

Die drei Nationalökonomien. Munich, 1930.

Die Juden und das Wirtschaftsleben. Trans. by Epstein under the title, *The Jews and Modern Capitalism*. London, 1913. Also by The Free Press, Glencoe, Ill.

Der moderne Kapitalismus (several editions). A condensed translation has been published in English under the title *A History of the Economic Institutions of Europe*. New York, 1933.

Der Proletarische Sozialismus. 1929.

BOOK ON SOMBART:

Plotnik, M. J. *Werner Sombart and His Type of Economics*. New York, 1937.

Georges Sorel

Note: One can find a complete bibliography of Sorel's writings in the *International Review for Social History*, entitled "Bibliographie Sorelienne" by Paul Delasalle, published by the International Institute for Social History, Leiden, 1939. Vol. IV, pp. 463-87.

SELECTED ORIGINAL WORKS:

L'ancienne et la nouvelle métaphysique. Paris, 1894.

Contribution a l'étude profane de la Bible. Paris, 1889.

De l'utilité du pragmatisme. Paris, 1921.

Décomposition du marxisme. Paris, 1908.

Etude sur Vico, le devenir social. Paris, 1896.

Les Illusions du progress. Paris, 1908.

Introduction a l'économie moderne. Paris, 1903.

Matériaux d'une théorie du Prolétariat. Paris, 1919.

Le Proces de Socrate. Paris, 1889.

Reflexions sur la violence. Paris, 1908. Trans. by T. E. Hulme and J. Roth. Ed. by Edward A. Shills. Glencoe: The Free Press, 1950.

BOOKS ON SOREL:

Andreu, Pierre. *Notre Maitre M. Sorel.* Paris, 1953.

Angel, Pierre. *Essais sur Georges Sorel.* Paris, 1936.

Ascoli, Max. *Georges Sorel.* Paris, 1921.

Barth, Hans. *Masse und Mythos, die Theorie der Gewalt: Georges Sorel.* Hamburg: Rowohlt, 1959.

Berth, Edouard. *Du "Capital" au "Reflexions" sur la violence.* Paris, 1932.

——. *Guerres des états ou guerres des classes.* Paris, 1924.

——. *Les Méfaits des intellectuels.* Paris, 1914.

Deroo, Jean. *Georges Sorel, le renversement du matérialisme historique.* Lille, 1939.

Freund, Michael. *Georges Sorel. Der revolutionäre Konservatismus.* Frankfurt am Main, 1932.

Humphrey, Richard Dale. *Georges Sorel, Prophet without Honor: A Study in Anti-Intellectualism.* Cambridge, Mass., Harvard University Press, 1951.

Lagardelle, Hubert. *Introduction aux oeuvres de Georges Sorel.* Paris, 1933.

Lewis, Wyndham. *The Art of Being Ruled.* London, 1926.

Pirou, Gaétan. *Georges Sorel.* Paris, 1927.

Variot, Jean. *Propos de Georges Sorel.* Paris, 1935.

Wanner, Jean. *Georges Sorel et la décadence. Essai sur l'idée de décadence dans la pensée de Georges Sorel.* Laussane, 1943.

Herbert Spencer

SELECTED WORKS:

An Autobiography. 2 vols. New York: Appleton and Co., 1904.

First Principles. New York: Appleton and Co., 1896.

Man Versus the State. New York, 1884.

Principles of Sociology. New York: Appleton and Co., 1876-96.

Social Statics. New York: Appleton and Co., 1896.

The Study of Sociology. New York Appleton and Co., 1873, 1901.

BOOKS ON SPENCER:

Barker, Ernest. *Political Thought in England from Herbert Spencer to the Present Day.* New York, 1915. *See* especially pp. 86-90.

Barnes, Harry Elmer. *An Introduction to the History of Sociology.* Chicago: University of Chicago Press, 1948. *See* especially pp. 110-37, chap. iv, "Herbert Spencer and the Evolutionary Defense of Individualism."

Duncan, David. *Life and Letters of Herbert Spencer.* 2 vols. New York, 1908.

Elliott, H. *Herbert Spencer.* New York, 1916.

Kardiner, Abram, and Preble, Edward. *They Studied Man.* New York: World Publishing Co., 1961. *See* pp. 37-55: "Herbert Spencer."

Macpherson, Hector. *Spencer and Spencerism.* New York, 1900.

Royce, Josiah. *Herbert Spencer: An Estimate and Review.* New York, 1904.

Rumney, Judah. *Herbert Spencer's Sociology.* London: Williams and Norgate, Ltd., 1934.

Gabriel Tarde

ORIGINAL WORKS:

La Criminalité comparée. Paris, 1886.

La Logique sociale. Paris, 1895.

Les Lois de l'imitation. Paris, 1890. 3rd ed., 1900.

Les Lois sociales. Paris, 1898.

L'Opposition universelle. Paris, 1897.

La Philosophie pénale. Paris, 1890.

TRANSLATED WORKS:

The Laws of Imitation. Trans. by Elsie C. Parsons. New York: Henry Holt and Co., 1903. *See* especially Giddings' introduction.

Penal Philosophy. Trans. by R. Howell. Boston: Little, Brown and Co., 1912.

Social Laws. Trans. by H. G. Warren. New York: The Macmillan Co., 1899.

BOOKS ON TARDE:

Davis, Michael M., Jr. *Gabriel Tarde.* New York, 1906.
——. *Psychological Interpretations of Society.* New York: Columbia University Press, 1909. Mr. Davis' book, *Gabriel Tarde* (1906), was incorporated in this book.

Ross, E. A. *Social Psychology.* New York, 1908.
    Note: example of an adaptation of Tarde's sociological theories.

Small, A. W. *See* his review of Tarde's *Social Laws* in *The American Journal of Sociology,* Vol. IV (1899) pp. 395-400.

Tosti, G. "The Sociological Theories of Gabriel Tarde" in *Political Science Quarterly* (1897), pp. 490-511.

Wilson, Margaret S. "Pioneers in Criminology: I-Gabriel Tarde," *The Journal of Criminal Law, Criminology and Police Science,* Vol. XLV (June 1954), pp. 3-11.

Ferdinand Tönnies

Note: One can find the most comprehensive list of Tönnies' writings in *Reine und angewandte Soziologie, eine Festgabe für Ferdinand Tönnies, zu seinem achtzigsten Geburtstage* (Leipzig, 1936). It was compiled by Else Brenke and entitled "Verzeichnis der Schriften von Ferdinand Tönnies aus den Jahren 1875 bis 1935."

SELECTED ORIGINAL WORKS:

"Eigentum," "Moderne Familie," "Gemeinschaft und Gesellschaft," "Stände und Klassen," articles in *Handwörterbuch der Soziologie.* Stuttgart, 1931.

Einführung in die Soziologie. Stuttgart, 1931.

"Einteilung der Soziologie" in *Zeitschrift für die gesamte Staatswissenschaft,* Vol. LXXIX (1925). Also published in *Atti del V. congresso internazionale di filosofia.* Napoli, 1925.

"Entwicklung der Soziologie in Deutschland im 19. Jahrhundert" in *Entwicklung der Deutschen Volkswirtschaftslehre im 19. Jahrhundert.* Festgabe für Gustav Schmoller, 1908.

Fortschritt und soziale Entwicklung, geschichtsphilosophische An-sichten. Karlsruhe, 1926.

Gemeinschaft und Gesellschaft. 8 vols. Leipzig, 1887, 1935.

Marx, Leben und Lehre. Berlin, 1921.

"Mein Verhältnis zur Soziologie" in R. Thurnwald (ed.). *Soziol-ogie von Heute: Ein Symposium der Zeitschrift für Völker-psychologie und Soziologie.* Leipzig, 1932.

Soziologische Studien und Kritiken. Vol. I, Jena, 1925; Vol. II, Jena, 1926; Vol. III, Jena, 1929.

"Das Wesen der Soziologie" in *Neue Zeit und Streitfragen,* Vol. IV (1907).

"Zweck und Mittel im Sozialen Leben" in *Hauptprobleme der So-ziologie, erinnerungsgabe für Max Weber.* München und Leipzig, 1923.

SELECTED TRANSLATED WORKS:

Community and Society, Gemeinschaft und Gesellschaft. Trans. and ed. by Charles P. Loomis. East Lansing, Mich.: State University Press, 1957.

"Estates and Classes (Stände und Klassen)." Trans. by R. Bendix in *Class, Status, and Power: A Reader in Social Stratification.* Glencoe: The Free Press, 1953.

Fundamental Concepts of Sociology: Gemeinschaft und Gesell-schaft. Trans. and supplemented by Charles P. Loomis. New York, 1940.

"Gemeinschaft (Community) and Gesellschaft (Society)" in *Readings in Sociology.* Ed. by A. M. Lee. New York: Barnes and Noble, 1951. P. 81.

"Philosophical Terminology" in *Mind, A Quarterly Review of Psy-chology and Philosophy,* New Series, Vol. VIII (1889); Vol. IX (1900).

"The Present Problems of Social Structure" in *The American Jour-nal of Sociology,* Vol. X (1905), pp. 569ff.

BOOKS ON TÖNNIES:

Baltzer, A. *Ferdinand Tönnies: Gemeinschaft und Gesellschaft.* Berlin, 1890.

Freyer, Hans. "Ferdinand Tönnies und seine Stellung in der deutschen Soziologie," *Weltwirtschaftliches Archiv,* Vol. XLIV (1936).

Heberle, Rudolf. "Ferdinand Tönnies," *Internationales Handwör-terbuch des Gewerkschaftswesens.* Berlin, 1932.

———. "The Sociology of Ferdinand Tönnies," *American Sociological Review,* Vol. II, no. 1 (February 1937).

——. "The Sociological System of Ferdinand Tönnies: 'Community' and 'Society'" in *An Introduction to the History of Sociology.* Ed. by Harry Elmer Barnes. Chicago: University of Chicago Press, 1948. Chap. x.

Jahn, Georg. *Ferdinand Tönnies.* Leipzig, 1935.

Jurkat, E. "Die Soziologie von Ferdinand Tönnies" in *Geistige Arbeit* (November 1936).

Kölner Vierteljahrshefte für Soziologie, Vol. V, Heft ½ (1925). Contains several articles dedicated to Tönnies at the occasion of his seventieth birthday *(Zum 70 Geburtstage von Ferdinand Tönnies).*

Leemans, V. *Ferdinand Tönnies en de Duitsche Sociologie.* Brugge, 1932 (in Dutch). Also translated into French, *Ferdinand Tönnies et la sociologie contemporaine en Allemagne.* Paris, 1933.

Leif, J. *La Sociologie de Tönnies.* Paris, 1946.

Rosenbaum, Eduard. "Ferdinand Tönnies' Werk" in *Schmollers Jahrbuch,* Vol. XXXVIII (1914).

Stoltenberg, H. L. *Wegweiser durch F. Tönnies "Gemeinschaft und Gesellschaft."* Berlin, 1919.

Salomon, Albert. "In Memoriam Ferdinand Tönnies (1855-1936)" in *Social Research,* Vol. III (1936).

Wirth, Louis. "The Sociology of Ferdinand Tönnies" in *The American Journal of Sociology,* Vol. XXXII, no. 3 (November 1926), pp. 412*ff.*

Ernst Troeltsch

SELECTED WORKS:

Christian Thought, Its History and Application. New York: Meridian Books, 1957.

The Social Teachings of the Christian Churches. (Part of his collected works.) Original German ed., 1911. Also published in London: Allen and Unwin, 1931; New York: The Macmillan Co., 1931; and New York: Harper Torchbooks, 1960.

Edward Tylor

SELECTED WORKS:

Anahuac. 1861.

Anthropology. 1881. Reprinted in paperback edition, 1960.

Primitive Culture. Vols. I, II. First ed. 1871. Reprinted in Harper Torchbooks, New York, 1958.

Researches into the Early History of Mankind and the Development of Civilization. 1865.

Alfred Weber

Note: Most of the work of Alfred Weber is not translated into English. In this bibliography I have listed some of his more better known works.

SELECTED WORKS:

Abschied von bisherigen Geschichte. 1946.

Der Dritte oder der vierte Mensch. Vom Sinn des geschichtlichen Daseins. München, 1953.

Einführung in die Soziologie. München: Piper, 1955.

Ideen zur Staats- und Kultursoziologie. Karlsruhe, 1927.

Kulturgeschichte als Kultursoziologie. Leiden, 1935. Also in a new edition published by Piper, München, 1960.

"Kultursoziologie" in *Handwörterbuch der Soziologie.* Stuttgart, 1931.

"Kultursoziologische Versuche" in *Archiv für Sozialwissenschaft,* Vol. LV (1926).

"Principielles zur Kultursoziologie" in *Archiv für Sozialwissenschaft und Sozialpolitik,* Vol. XLVIII (1920-21).

Prinzipien der Geschichts- und Kultursoziologie. München, 1951.

"Der soziologische Kulturbegriff" in *Verhandlungen des 2. deutschen Soziologentages.* Tübingen, 1915.

Das Tragische und die Geschichte. Hamburg, 1943.

Über den Standort der Industrien. First ed., 1909; 2nd ed., 1922. Also in English translation by Carl Joachim Friedrich under the title, *Theory of the Location of Industries.* Chicago, 1926.

"Was ist der Mensch?" in *Neue Rudschau* (September 1938).

BOOKS ON WEBER:

Lederer, Emil. "Aufgaben einer Kultursoziologie" in *Hauptprobleme der Soziologie: Erinnerungsgabe für Max Weber.* München, 1923.

Neumann, Sigmund. "Alfred Weber's Conception of Historicocultural Sociology" in *An Introduction to the History of Sociology.* Ed. by Harry Elmer Barnes. Chicago: University of Chicago Press, 1948. Pp. 353-61.

Salomon, Albert. "The Place of Alfred Weber's Kultursoziologie in Social Thought" in *Social Research,* Vol. III (November 1936). Pp. 494-500.

Max Weber

SELECTED WORKS:

Ancient Judaism. Glencoe: The Free Press, 1952. *Note:* The volumes on the religions of China, India and Ancient Judaism were published as a set by The Free Press.

The City. Glencoe. The Free Press, 1958.

From Max Weber: Essays in Sociology. Trans. and ed. by Hans H. Gerth and C. Wright Mills. New York: Oxford University Press, 1946. In paperback edition by Galaxy Books, New York, 1958.

General Economic History. Trans. by F. H. Knight. London: George Allen and Unwin, 1927. Glencoe: The Free Press, 1950.

Gesammelte Aufsätze zur Religionssoziologie. 3 vols. Tübingen: J. C. B. Mohr (P. Siebeck), 1920-21.

Gesamelte Aufsätze zur Sozial- und Wirtschaftsgeschichte. Tübingen: J. C. B. Mohr (P. Siebeck), 1924.

Gesammelte Aufsätze zur Soziologie und Sozialpolitik. Tübingen: J. C. B. Mohr (P. Siebeck), 1924.

Gesammelte Aufsätze zur Wissenschaftslehre. Tübingen: J. C. B. Mohr (P. Siebeck), 1922.

Gesammelte politische Schriften. Münich: Drei Masken Verlag, 1921.

Max Weber on Law in Economy and Society. Cambridge, Mass.: Harvard University Press, 1954.

The Methodology of the Social Sciences. Glencoe: The Free Press, 1949.

The Protestant Ethic and the Spirit of Capitalism. Trans. by Talcott Parsons. London: George Allen and Unwin, 1930; New York: Charles Scribner's Sons, 1958 (in paperback edition).

Rational and Social Foundations of Music. Carbondale: The Southern Illinois Press, 1958.

Rechtssoziologie. Herausgegeben und eingeleitet von Johannes Winckelmann. Neuwied: Herman Luchterhand Verlag, 1960.

The Religion of China: Confucianism and Taoism. Glencoe: The Free Press, 1951.

The Religion of India: The Sociology of Hinduism and Buddhism. Glencoe: The Free Press, 1958.

"The Social Causes of the Decay of Ancient Civilization" in *Journal of General Education,* Vol. V (1950), pp. 75-88.

The Theory of Social and Economic Organization. New York: Oxford University Press, 1947. Out of print.

"The Three Types of Legitimate Rule" in *Berkeley Publications in Society and Institutions,* Vol. IV (1958), pp. 1-11.

Wirtschaft und Gesellschaft. 2 vols. Tübingen: J. C. B. Mohr (P. Siebeck), 1925.

BOOKS ON WEBER:

Bendix, Reinhard. *Max Weber, An Intellectual Portrait.* New York: Doubleday and Co., 1960.

Bibliography 463

Bennion, L. L. *Max Weber's Methodology*. Dissertation, University of Strasbourg. Paris: Les Presses Modernes, 1933.

Halbwachs, Maurice. "Max Weber, un homme, une oeuvre" in *Annales d'histoire economique et sociale*, Vol. I (January 1929), pp. 81-88.

——. "Les Origines puritaines du capitalisme moderne" in *Revue d'histoire et philosophie religieuse*, Vol. V (1925), pp. 132-34.

Jaspers, Karl. *Max Weber: Deutsches Wesen im politischen Denken, im Forschen und Philosophieren*. Oldenburg: G. Stalling, 1932. Reprinted by Piper after the Second World War. München: Piper and Co., 1946. *Note:* I recommend this little book by Jaspers very highly.

Parsons, Talcott. "H. M. Roberston on Max Weber and His School" in *Journal of Political Economy*, Vol. XLIII (1935), pp. 688-96.

——. "Max Weber's Sociological Analysis of Capitalism and Modern Institutions" in *An Introduction to the History of Sociology*. Ed. by Harry Elmer Barnes. Chicago: University of Chicago Press, 1948. Pp. 287-308.

Robertson, Hector M. *Aspects of the Rise of Economic Individualism: A Criticism of Max Weber and His School*. Cambridge, England: University Press, 1933.

Salomon, Albert. "Max Weber's Methodology" in *Social Research*, Vol. XI (1934), pp. 147-68.

——. "Max Weber's Political Ideas," *Social Research*, Vol. II (1935), pp. 368-84.

——. "Max Weber's Sociology," *Social Research*, Vol. II (1935), pp. 60-73.

Schelting, Alexander von. "Die logische Theorie der historischen Kulturwissenschaften von Max Weber und im besonderen sein Begriff des Idealtypus" in *Archiv für Sozialwissenschaft und Sozialpolitik*.

——. *Max Weber's Wissenschaftslehre*. Tübingen: J. B. C. Mohr, 1934.

Troeltsch, Ernst, "Max Weber" in his *Deutscher Geist und Westeuropa*. Tübingen: J. C. B. Mohr, 1925.

Weber, Alfred. "Max Weber" in *Einführung in die Soziologie*. München: Piper, 1955. Pp. 162-70.

Weber, Marianne. *Max Weber: ein Lebensbild*. Tübingen: J. C. B. Mohr, 1926.

Note: For a complete bibliography see Marianne Weber's book on her husband.